SAMS
Teach
Yourself

Microsoft®
Visual C#® 2005

in 24 Hours

COMPLETE STARTER KIT

James Foxall

SAMS   800 East 96th Street, Indianapolis, Indiana, 46240 USA

Sams Teach Yourself Microsoft® Visual C#® 2005 in 24 Hours, Complete Starter Kit

International Standard Book Number: 0-672-32740-6

Library of Congress Catalog Card Number: 2006922044

Printed in the United States of America

First Printing: May 2006

09   08   07   4   3

Trademarks

All terms mentioned in this book that are known to be trademarks or service marks have been appropriately capitalized. Sams Publishing cannot attest to the accuracy of this information. Use of a term in this book should not be regarded as affecting the validity of any trademark or service mark.

Warning and Disclaimer

Every effort has been made to make this book as complete and as accurate as possible, but no warranty or fitness is implied. The information provided is on an "as is" basis. The author and the publisher shall have neither liability nor responsibility to any person or entity with respect to any loss or damages arising from the information contained in this book or from the use of the CD or programs accompanying it.

Bulk Sales

Sams Publishing offers excellent discounts on this book when ordered in quantity for bulk purchases or special sales. For more information, please contact

U.S. Corporate and Government Sales

1-800-382-3419

corpsales@pearsontechgroup.com

For sales outside of the U.S., please contact

International Sales

international@pearsoned.com

Publisher
Paul Boger

Acquisitions Editor
Neil Rowe

Development Editor
Mark Renfrow

Managing Editor
Charlotte Clapp

Project Editor
Andy Beaster

Indexer
Larry Sweazy

Proofreader
Linda Seifert

Technical Editor
John Couture

Publishing Coordinator
Cindy Teeters

Interior Designer
Gary Adair

Cover Designer
Alan Clements

Page Layout
Juli Cook

Contents at a Glance

Table of Contents

About the Author

James Foxall is Vice President of Tigerpaw Software, Inc., (www.tigerpawsoftware.com)—a Bellevue, Nebraska, Microsoft Certified Partner specializing in commercial database applications. James manages Tigerpaw CRM+, an award-winning CRM product designed to automate contact management, marketing, service and repair, proposal generation, and inventory control and purchasing. James's experience in creating certified Office-compatible software has made him an authority on application interface and behavior standards of applications for the Microsoft Windows and Microsoft Office environments.

James has personally written more than 300,000 lines of commercial production Visual C# code both in single programmer and multiple programmer environments. He's the author of numerous books, including *Practical Standards for Microsoft Visual C#* and *MCSD in a Nutshell: The Visual C# Exams*, and he has written articles for *Access-Office-VBA Advisor* and *Visual C# Programmer's Journal*. James has a Bachelor's degree in Management of Information Systems (MIS), is a Microsoft Certified Solution Developer, and an international speaker on Microsoft Visual C#. When not programming or writing about programming, he enjoys spending time with his family, playing guitar, listening to Pink Floyd, and playing computer games. You can reach James at www.jamesfoxall.com/forums.

Dedication

This book is dedicated to Sensei William Hill, for teaching me far more about life than I realized at the time.

Acknowledgments

I would like to thank Neil, Mark, Andrew, John, and everyone else who worked on this book for their dedication and patience.

We Want to Hear from You!

As the reader of this book, *you* are our most important critic and commentator. We value your opinion and want to know what we're doing right, what we could do better, what areas you'd like to see us publish in, and any other words of wisdom you're willing to pass our way.

As an associate publisher for Sams Publishing, I welcome your comments. You can email or write me directly to let me know what you did or didn't like about this book—as well as what we can do to make our books better.

Please note that I cannot help you with technical problems related to the topic of this book. We do have a User Services group, however, where I will forward specific technical questions related to the book.

When you write, please be sure to include this book's title and author as well as your name, email address, and phone number. I will carefully review your comments and share them with the author and editors who worked on the book.

Email: feedback@samspublishing.com

Mail: Paul Boger
            Publisher
            Sams Publishing
            800 East 96th Street
            Indianapolis, IN 46240 USA

For more information about this book or another Sams Publishing title, visit our website at www.samspublishing.com. Type the ISBN (excluding hyphens) or the title of a book in the Search field to find the page you're looking for.

Introduction

With Microsoft's introduction of the .NET platform, a new, exciting programming language was born. Visual C# is now the language of choice for developing on the .NET platform, and Microsoft has even written a majority of the .NET Framework using Visual C#. Visual C# is a modern object-oriented language designed and developed from the ground up with a best-of-breed mentality, implementing and expanding on the best features and functions found in other languages. Visual C# 2005 combines the power and flexibility of C++ with some of the simplicity of Visual Basic.

Audience and Organization

This book is targeted toward those who have little or no programming experience or who might be picking up Visual C# as a second language. The book has been structured and written with a purpose: to get you productive as quickly as possible. I've used my experiences from writing large commercial applications to create a book that I hope cuts through the fluff and teaches you *what you need to know*. All too often, authors fall into the trap of focusing on the technology rather than on the practical application of the technology. I've worked hard to keep this book focused on teaching you practical skills that you can apply immediately toward a development project. Feel free to post your suggestions or success stories at www.jamesfoxall.com/forums.

This book is divided into five parts, each of which focuses on a different aspect of developing applications with Visual C# 2005. These parts generally follow the flow of tasks you'll perform as you begin creating your own programs using Visual C# 2005. I recommend that you read them in the order in which they appear.

- ▶ Part I, "The Visual C# 2005 Environment," teaches you about the Visual C# environment, including how to navigate and access Visual C#'s numerous tools. In addition, you'll learn some key development concepts such as objects, collections, and events.

- ▶ Part II, "Building a User Interface," shows you how to build attractive and functional user interfaces. In this part, you'll learn about forms and controls—the user interface elements such as text boxes and list boxes.

- ▶ Part III, "Making Things Happen—Programming," teaches you the nuts and bolts of Visual C# 2005 programming—and there's a lot to learn. You'll discover how to create methods, as well as how to store data, perform loops, and make decisions in code.

After you've learned the core programming skills, you'll move into object-oriented programming and debugging applications.

▶ Part IV, "Working with Data," introduces you to working with text files and programming databases and shows you how to automate external applications such as Word and Excel. In addition, this part teaches you how to manipulate a user's file system and the Windows Registry.

▶ Part V, "Deploying Solutions and Beyond," shows you how to distribute an application that you've created to an end user's computer. In Hour 24, "The 10,000 Foot View," you'll learn about Microsoft's .NET initiative from a higher, less-technical level.

Many readers of previous editions have taken the time to give me input on how to make this book better. Overwhelmingly, I was asked to have examples in new chapters build upon the examples in previous chapters. In this book, I have done that as much as possible. Now, instead of learning concepts in isolated bits, you'll be building a feature-rich Picture Viewer program throughout the course of this book. You'll begin by building the basic application, and, as you progress through the chapters, you'll add menus and toolbars to the program, build an Options dialog box, modify the program to use the Windows Registry and a text file, and even build a setup program to distribute the application to other users. I hope you find this approach beneficial in that it allows you to learn the material in the context of building a real program.

Conventions Used in This Book

This book uses several conventions to help you prioritize and reference the information it contains:

▶ *Tips* highlight information that can make your Visual C# programming more effective.

▶ *Cautions* focus your attention on problems or side effects that can occur in specific situations.

▶ *Notes* provide useful sidebar information that you can read immediately or circle back to without losing the flow of the topic at hand.

▶ *New Terms* are set off in italic when they are first defined.

In addition, this book uses various typefaces to help you distinguish code from regular English. Code is presented in a monospace font. Placeholders—words or characters used temporarily to represent the real words or characters you would type in code—are typeset in *italic monospace*. If you are asked to type or enter text, that text will appear in **bold**.

Onward and Upward!

This is an exciting time to be learning how to program, and it's my sincerest wish that when you finish this book, you feel capable of creating, debugging, and deploying modest Visual C# programs using many of Visual C#'s tools. Although you won't be an expert, you'll be surprised at how much you've learned. And I hope this book will help you determine your future direction as you proceed down the road to Visual C# mastery.

PART I

The Visual C# Environment

HOUR 1

Jumping In with Both Feet: A Visual C# 2005 Programming Tour

What You'll Learn in This Hour:

▶ Building a simple (yet functional) Visual C# application
▶ Letting a user browse a hard drive
▶ Displaying a picture from a file on disk
▶ Getting familiar with some programming lingo
▶ Learning about the Visual Studio .NET IDE

Learning a new programming language can be intimidating. If you've never programmed before, the act of typing seemingly cryptic text to produce sleek and powerful applications probably seems like a black art, and you might wonder how you'll ever learn everything you need to know. The answer is, of course, one step at a time. The first step to learning a language is the same as that of any other activity: building confidence. Programming is part art and part science. Although it might seem like magic, it's more akin to illusion; after you know how things work, a lot of the mysticism goes away, freeing you to focus on the mechanics necessary to produce the desired result.

In this hour, you'll complete a quick tour that takes you step-by-step through creating a complete, albeit small, Visual C# 2005 program. Most introductory programming books start out with the reader creating a simple Hello World program. I've yet to see a Hello World program that's the least bit helpful (they usually do nothing more than print `hello world` to the screen—oh, fun). So, instead, you'll create a picture viewer application that lets you view Windows bitmaps and icons on your computer. You'll learn how to let a user browse for a file and how to display a selected picture file on the screen. Both of these skills will come in handy in the real-world applications that you'll create.

Producing large, commercial solutions is accomplished by way of a series of small steps. After you've finished creating the project in this hour, you'll have a feel for the overall development process and will have taken the first step toward becoming an accomplished programmer. In fact, you will be building upon this Picture Viewer program in subsequent chapters. By the time you complete this book, you will have built a robust application, complete with sizable screens, an intuitive interface, and professional error handling.

By the end of this hour, you'll realize just how much fun it is to program using Visual C# 2005.

Starting Visual C# 2005

Before you begin creating programs in Visual C# 2005, you should be familiar with the following terms:

▶ *Distributable component*   The final, compiled version of a project. Components can be distributed to other people and other computers, and they don't require the Visual C# 2005 development environment (the tools you use to create a .NET program) to run (although they do require the .NET runtime, which I'll discuss in Hour 23, "Deploying A Visual C# .NET Application"). Distributable components are often called *programs*. In Hour 23, you'll learn how to distribute the Picture Viewer program that you're about to build to other computers.

▶ *Project*   A collection of files that can be compiled to create a distributable component (program). There are many types of projects, and complex applications might consist of multiple projects, such as a Windows application project, and support dynamic link library (DLL) projects.

▶ *Solution*   A collection of projects and files that make up an application or component.

Visual C# 2005 is part of a larger entity known as the *.NET Framework*. The .NET Framework encompasses all the .NET technology, including Visual Studio .NET (the suite of development tools) and the Common Language Runtime (CLR), which is the set of files that make up the core of all .NET applications. You'll learn about these items in more detail as you progress through this book. For now, realize that Visual C# 2005 is one of many languages that exist within the .NET family. Many other languages, such as Visual Basic, are also .NET languages, make use of the common language runtime, and are developed within Visual Studio .NET.

Visual Studio .NET is a complete development environment, and it's called the IDE (short for *integrated development environment*). The IDE is the design framework in which you build applications; every tool you'll need to create your Visual C# 2005 projects is accessed from within the Visual C# IDE. Again, Visual Studio .NET supports development using many different languages—Visual C# 2005 being one of the most popular. The environment itself is not Visual C# 2005, but the language you'll be using within Visual Studio .NET *is* Visual C# 2005. To work with Visual C# 2005 projects, you first start the Visual Studio .NET IDE.

Start Visual Studio .NET now by choosing Microsoft Visual C# 2005 Express Edition on your Start/Programs menu. If you are running the full retail version of .NET, your shortcut may have a different name. In this case, locate the shortcut on your Start menu and click it once to start the Visual Studio .NET IDE.

Creating a New Project

When you first start Visual Studio .NET, you're shown the Start Page tab within the IDE. You can open projects created previously or create new projects from this Start page (see Figure 1.1). For this quick tour, you're going to create a new Windows application, so open the File menu and click New Project to display the New Project dialog box shown in Figure 1.2.

If your Start page doesn't look like the one in Figure 1.1, chances are that you've changed the default settings. In Hour 2, "Navigating Visual C# 2005," I'll show you how to change them back.

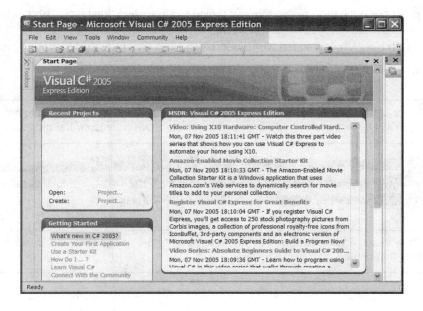

FIGURE 1.1
You can open existing projects or create new projects from the Visual Studio Start page.

FIGURE 1.2
The New Project
dialog box
enables you to
create many
types of .NET
projects.

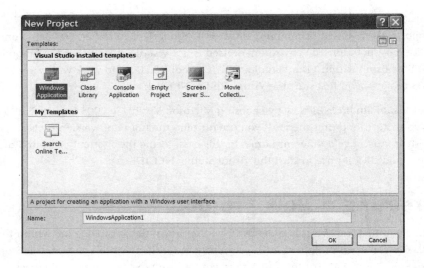

The New Project dialog box is used to specify the type of Visual C# project to create. (You can create many types of projects with Visual C#, as well as with the other supported languages of the .NET Framework.) Create a new Windows application by following these steps:

1. Make sure that the Windows Application icon is selected (if it's not, click it once to select it).

2. At the bottom of the New Project dialog box is a Name text box. This is where, oddly enough, you specify the name of the project you're creating. Enter **Picture Viewer** in the Name text box.

3. Click OK to create the project.

Did you Know?

Always set the Name text box to something meaningful before creating a project, or you'll have more work to do later if you want to move or rename the project.

When Visual C# creates a new Windows application project, it adds one form (the empty gray window) for you to begin building the *interface*—the graphical windows that you interact with, for your application (see Figure 1.3).

By the Way

Within Visual Studio .NET, *form* is the term given to the design-time view of windows that can be displayed to a user.

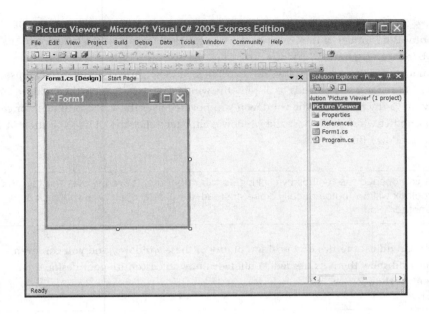

FIGURE 1.3
New Windows
applications
start with a
blank form; the
fun is just
beginning!

Your Visual Studio .NET environment might look different from that shown in the figures of this hour due to the edition of Visual Studio .NET you're using, whether you've already played with Visual Studio .NET, and other factors such as the resolution of your monitor. All the elements discussed in this hour exist in all editions of Visual Studio .NET, however. (If a window shown in a figure isn't displayed in your IDE, use the View menu to display it.)

By the Way

To create a program that can be run on another computer, you start by creating a project and then compiling the project into a component such as an *executable* (a program a user can run) or a *DLL* (a component that can be used by other programs and components). The compilation process is discussed in detail in Hour 23. The important thing to note at this time is that when you hear someone refer to *creating* or *writing a program*, just as you're creating the Picture Viewer program now, they're referring to the completion of all steps up to and including compiling the project to a distributable file.

Understanding the Visual Studio .NET Environment

The first time you run Visual Studio .NET, you'll notice that the IDE contains a number of windows, such as the Solutions Explorer window on the right, which is used to view and the files that make up a project. In addition to these windows, the IDE contains a number of tabs, such as the vertical Toolbox tab on the left edge of the IDE (refer to Figure 1.3). Try this now: Click the Toolbox tab to display the Toolbox window (clicking a tab displays an associated window). You can hover the mouse over a tab for a few seconds to display the window as well. To hide the window, simply move the mouse off the window if you hovered over the tab to display it, or click on another window. To close the window completely, click the Close (X) button in the window's title bar.

> If you opened the toolbox by clicking its tab rather than hovering over the tab, the toolbox will not automatically close. Instead, it will stay open until you click on another window.

You can adjust the size and position of any of these windows, and you can even hide and show them as needed. You'll learn how to customize your design environment in Hour 2.

> Unless specifically instructed to do so, don't double-click *anything* in the Visual Studio .NET design environment. Double-clicking most objects produces an entirely different result than single-clicking does. If you mistakenly double-click an object on a form (discussed shortly), a code window is displayed. At the top of the code window is a set of tabs: one for the form design and one for the code. Click the tab for the form design to hide the code window and return to the form.

The Properties window at the right side of the design environment is perhaps the most important window in the IDE, and it's the one you'll use most often. If your computer display resolution is set to 800×600, you can probably see only a few properties at this time. This makes it difficult to view and set properties as you create projects. All the screen shots in this book are taken at 800×600 due to size constraints, but you should run at a higher resolution if you can. I highly recommend that you develop applications with Visual C# 2005 at a screen resolution of 1024×768 or higher because it offers plenty of work space. Keep in mind, however, that end users might be running at a lower resolution than you are using for development. If you need to change your display settings, right-click your desktop and select Properties.

Changing the Characteristics of Objects

Almost everything you work with in Visual C# is an object. Forms, for instance, are objects, as are all the items you can put on a form to build an interface such as list boxes and buttons. There are *many* types of objects, and objects are classified by type.

For example, a form is a Form object, whereas items you can place on a form are called Control objects, or controls. (Hour 3, "Understanding Objects and Collections," discusses objects in detail.) Some objects don't have a physical appearance but exist only in code, and you'll learn about these kinds of objects in later hours.

Every object has a distinct set of attributes known as properties (regardless of whether the object has a physical appearance). You have certain properties about you, such as your height and hair color. Visual C# objects have properties as well, such as Height and BackColor. Properties define the characteristics of an object. When you create a new object, the first thing you need to do is set its properties so that the object appears and behaves the way you want. To display the properties of an object, click the object in its designer (the main work area in the IDE).

First, make sure your Properties Window is displayed by opening the View menu and choosing Properties Window. Next, click anywhere in the default form now (its title bar says Form1) and check to see whether its properties are displayed in the Properties window. You'll know because the drop-down list box at the top of the properties window will contain the form's name: Form1 System.Windows.Forms.Form. Form1 is the name of the object, while System.Windows.Forms.Form is the type of object.

Naming Objects

The property you should always set first for any new object is the Name property. Scroll toward the top of the properties list until you see the "(Name)" property (see Figure 1.4). If the Name property isn't one of the first properties listed, your Properties Window is set to show properties categorically instead of alphabetically. You can show the list alphabetically by clicking the Alphabetical button that appears just above the properties grid.

I recommend that you keep the Properties window set to show properties in alphabetical order; doing so makes it easier to find properties that I refer to in the text. Note, the Name property always stays toward the top of the list and is referred to as (Name). If you're wondering why it has parentheses around it, that's because the parentheses force the property to the top of the list, since symbols come before letters in an alphabetical sort.

When saving a project, you choose a name and a location for the project and its files. When you first create an object, Visual C# gives the object a unique, generic name based on the object's type. Although these names are functional, they simply aren't descriptive enough for practical use. For instance, Visual C# named your form Form1, but it's common to have dozens of forms in a project, and it would be extremely difficult to manage such a project if all forms were distinguishable only by a number (Form2, Form3, and so forth).

FIGURE 1.4
The Name property is the first property you should change when you add a new object to your project.

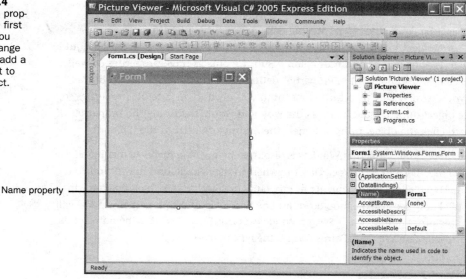

Name property ————

What you're actually working with is a *form class*, or *template*, that will be used to create and show forms at runtime. For the purpose of this quick tour, I simply refer to it as a form. See Hour 5, "Building Forms—The Basics," for more information.

To better manage your forms, give each one a descriptive name. Visual C# gives you the chance to name new forms as they're created in a project. Visual C# created this default form for you, so you didn't get a chance to name it. It's important to not only change the name of the form but also to change the filename of the form. Change the programmable name and the filename and the same time by following these steps:

1. Click the Name property and change the text from Form1 to **frmViewer**. Notice that this does not change the filename of the form as it's displayed in the Solution Explorer window.

2. Right-click Form1.cs in the Solution Explorer window (the window above the Properties window).

3. Choose Rename from the context menu that appears.

4. Change the text from Form1.vb to **frmViewer.cs**.

I use the frm prefix here to denote that the file is a form class. Prefixes are optional, but I find they really help you keep things organized.

The Name property of the form is actually changed for you automatically when you rename the file. I had you explicitly change the Name property because it's something you're going to be doing a lot—for all sorts of objects.

Setting the Text Property of the Form

Notice that the text that appears in the form's title bar says Form1. This is because Visual C# sets the form's title bar to the name of the form *when it's first created* but doesn't change it when you change the name of the form. The text in the title bar is determined by the value of the Text property of the form. Change the text now by following these steps:

1. Click the form once more so that its properties appear in the Properties window.

2. Use the scrollbar in the Properties window to locate the Text property.

3. Change the text to **Picture Viewer**. Press the Enter key or click on a different property. You'll see the text in the title bar of the form change.

Saving a Project

The changes you've made so far exist only in memory; if you were to turn off your computer at this time (don't do this), you would lose all of your work up to this point. Get into the habit of frequently saving your work (committing the changes to disk).

Click the Save All button on the toolbar (the picture of a stack of diskettes) now to save your work. Visual C# then displays the Save Project dialog box shown in Figure 1.5. Notice that the Name property is already filled in because you named the project when you created it. The Location text box is where you specify the location in which to save the project. Visual C# creates a subfolder in this location using the value in the Name text box (in this case, Picture Viewer). You can use the default location, or change it to suit your purposes. Don't worry about the Solution Name text box or the check box for Create directory for solution at this time, just be sure to leave the checkbox checked as it appears in Figure 1.5. Click Save to save the project.

FIGURE 1.5
When saving a project, choose a name and a location for the project and its files.

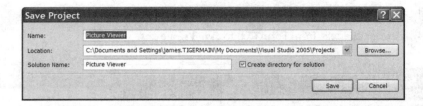

Giving the Form an Icon

Everyone who has used Windows is familiar with icons—the little pictures that represent programs. Icons most commonly appear in the Start menu next to the name of their respective programs. In Visual C# 2005, you not only have control over the icon of your program file, you can also give every form in your program a unique icon if you want to.

> The following instructions assume that you have access to the source files for the examples in this book. They are available at www.samspublishing.com. You can also get these files, as well as discuss this book, at my website at http://www.jamesfoxall.com/books.htm. When you unzip the samples, a folder will be created for each hour, and within each hour's folder will be subfolders for the sample projects. You'll find the icon in the folder Hour 1\Picture Viewer.
>
> You don't have to use the icon I've provided for this example; you can use any icon of your choice. If you don't have an icon available (or you want to be a rebel), you can skip this section without affecting the outcome of the example.

To give the form an icon, follow these steps:

1. In the Properties window, click the Icon property to select it.

2. When you click the Icon property, a small button with three dots appears to the right of the property. Click this button.

3. Use the Open dialog box that appears to locate the PictureViewer.ico file or another icon file of your choice. When you've found the icon, double-click it, or click it once to select it and then click Open.

After you've selected the icon, it appears in the Icon property along with the word "Icon." A small version of the icon appears in the upper-left corner of the form as well. Whenever this form is minimized, this is the icon displayed on the Windows taskbar.

Changing the Size of the Form

Next, you're going to change the Width and Height properties of the form. The Width and Height values are shown collectively under the Size property; Width appears to the left of the comma, Height to the right. You can change the Width or Height property by changing the corresponding number in the Size property. Both values are represented in pixels (that is, a form that has a Size property of 200,350 is 200 pixels wide by 350 pixels tall). To display and adjust the Width and Height properties separately, click the small plus sign (+) next to the Size property (see Figure 1.6).

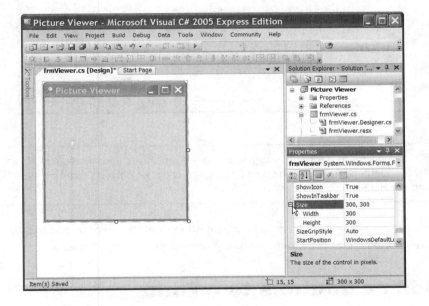

FIGURE 1.6
Some properties can be expanded to show more specific properties.

A *pixel* is a unit of measurement for computer displays; it's the smallest visible "dot" on the screen. The resolution of a display is always given in pixels, such as 800×600 or 1024×768. When you increase or decrease a property by one pixel, you're making the smallest possible visible change to the property.

By the Way

Change the Width property to **400** and the Height to **325** by typing in the corresponding box next to a property name. To commit a property change, press Tab or Enter, or click a different property or window. Your screen should now look like the one in Figure 1.7.

FIGURE 1.7
Changes
made in the
Properties
window are
reflected as
soon as they're
committed.

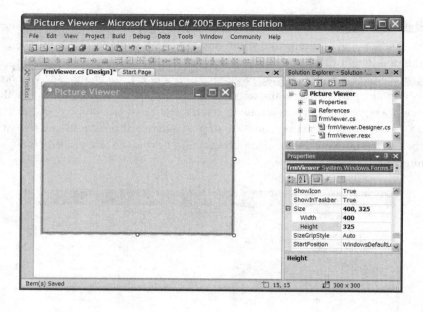

> **By the Way**
>
> You can also size a form by dragging its border, which you'll learn about in Hour 2. This property can also be changed by program code, which you'll learn how to write in Hour 5.

Save the project now by choosing File, Save All from the menu or by clicking the Save All button on the toolbar—it has a picture of stacked diskettes on it.

Adding Controls to a Form

Now that you've set the initial properties of your form, it's time to create a user interface by adding objects to the form. Objects that can be placed on a form are called *controls*. Some controls have a visible interface with which a user can interact, whereas others are always invisible to the user. You'll use controls of both types in this example. On the left side of the screen is a vertical tab titled Toolbox. Click the Toolbox tab now to display the Toolbox window and click the plus sign next to Common Controls to see the most commonly used controls (see Figure 1.8). The toolbox contains all the controls available in the project, such as labels and text boxes.

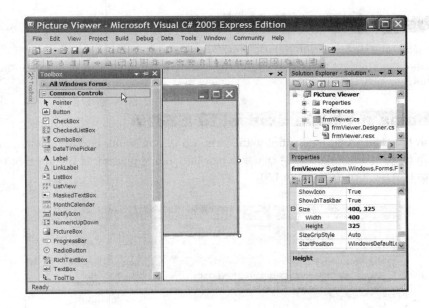

FIGURE 1.8
The toolbox is used to select controls to build a user interface.

There are four ways to add a control to a form, and Hour 5 explains them in detail. In this hour, you will use the technique of double-clicking a tool in the toolbox and copying and pasting a control.

Did you Know?

The toolbox will close as soon as you've added a control to a form and when the pointer is no longer over the toolbox. To make the toolbox stay visible, you would click the little picture of a pushpin located in the toolbox's title bar.

See Hour 2 for more information on customizing the design environment.

By the Way

I don't want you to add them yet, but your Picture Viewer interface will consist of the following controls:

▶ *Two Button controls*   The standard buttons that you're used to clicking in pretty much every Windows program you've ever run

▶ *A PictureBox control*   A control used to display images to a user

▶ *An OpenFileDialog control*   A hidden control that exposes the Windows Open File dialog box functionality

Designing an Interface

It's generally best to design the user interface of a form and then add the code behind the interface to make the form functional. You'll build your interface in the following sections.

Adding a Visible Control to a Form

Start by adding a Button control to the form. Do this by double-clicking the Button item in the toolbox. Visual C# creates a new button and places it in the upper-left corner of the form (see Figure 1.9).

FIGURE 1.9
When you double-click a control in the toolbox, the control is added to the upper-left corner of the form.

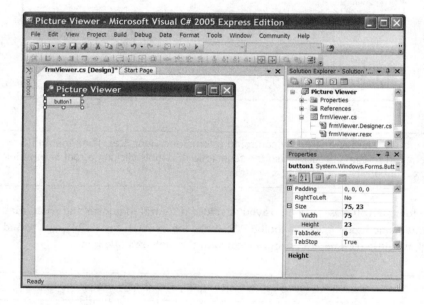

Using the Properties window, set the button's properties as follows. Remember, when you view the properties alphabetically, the Name property is listed first, so don't go looking for it down in the list or you'll be looking awhile.

Property	Value
Name	**btnSelectPicture**
Location	**301,10** (Note: 301 is the x coordinate; 10 is the y coordinate.)
Size	**85,23**
Text	**Select Picture**

You're now going to create a button that the user can click to close the Picture Viewer program. Although you could add another new button to the form by double-clicking the Button control on the toolbox again, this time you'll add a button to the form by creating a copy of the button you've already defined. This allows you to easily create a button that maintains the size and other style attributes of the original button when the copy was made.

To do this, right-click the button and choose Copy from its shortcut menu. Next, right-click anywhere on the form and choose Paste from the form's shortcut menu (you could have also used the keyboard shortcuts Ctrl+C to copy and Ctrl+V to paste). The new button appears centered on the form, and it's selected by default. Notice that it retained almost all of the properties of the original button, but the name has been reset. Change the properties of the new button as follows:

Property	Value
Name	**btnQuit**
Location	**301,40**
Text	**Quit**

The last visible control you need to add to the form is a PictureBox control. A PictureBox has many capabilities, but its primary purpose is to show pictures, which is precisely what you'll use it for in this example. Add a new PictureBox control to the form by double-clicking the PictureBox item in the toolbox and set its properties as follows:

Property	Value
Name	**picShowPicture**
BorderStyle	**FixedSingle**
Location	**8,8**
Size	**282,275**

After you've made these property changes, your form will look like the one in Figure 1.10. Click the Save All button on the toolbar to save your work.

Adding an Invisible Control to a Form

All the controls that you've used so far sit on a form and have a physical appearance when the application is run. Not all controls have a physical appearance, however. Such controls, referred to as *nonvisual controls* (or *invisible-at-runtime controls*), aren't designed for direct user interactivity. Instead, they're designed to give you, the programmer, functionality beyond the standard features of Visual C# 2005.

FIGURE 1.10
An application's interface doesn't have to be complex to be useful.

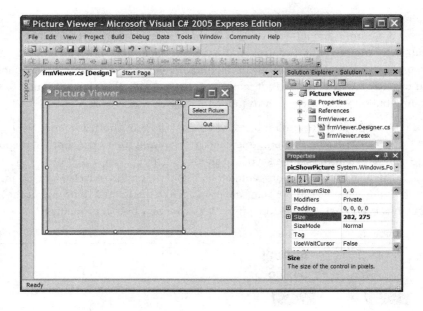

To enable the user to select a picture to display, you need to give them the ability to locate a file on their hard drive. You might have noticed that whenever you choose to open a file from within any Windows application, the dialog box displayed is almost always the same. It doesn't make sense to force every developer to write the code necessary to perform standard file operations, so Microsoft has exposed the functionality via a control that you can use in your projects. This control is called the OpenFileDialog control, and it will save you dozens and dozens of hours that would otherwise be necessary to duplicate this common functionality.

By the Way

> Other controls in addition to the OpenFileDialog control give you file functionality. For example, the SaveFileDialog control provides features for allowing the user to specify a filename and path for saving a file.

Display the toolbox now and scroll down using the down arrow in the lower part of the toolbox until you can see the OpenFileDialog control (it's in the Dialogs category), and then double-click it to add it to your form. Note that the control isn't placed on the form, but rather it appears in a special area below the form (see Figure 1.11). This happens because the OpenFileDialog control has no form interface to display to a user. It does have an interface (a dialog box) that you can display as necessary, but it has nothing to display directly on a form.

Select the OpenFileDialog control and change its properties as follows:

Property	Value
Name	**ofdSelectPicture**
Filename	*<delete existing text and make empty>*
Filter	Windows Bitmaps|*.BMP|JPEG Files|*.JPG
Title	**Select Picture**

The Filter property is used to limit (Filter) the types of files that will be displayed in the Open File dialog box. The format for a filter is *description|filter*. The text that appears before the first pipe symbol is the descriptive text of the file type, whereas the text after the pipe symbol is the pattern to use to filter files. You can specify more than one filter type by separating each description|filter value by another pipe symbol. Text entered into the Title property appears in the title bar of the Open File dialog box.

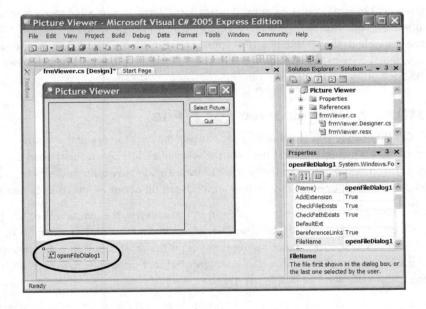

FIGURE 1.11
Controls that have no interface appear below the form designer.

The graphical interface for your Picture Viewer program is now finished. If you pinned the toolbox open, click the pushpin in the title bar of the toolbox now to close it.

Writing the Code Behind an Interface

You have to write code for the program to be capable of performing actions and responding to user interaction. Visual C# 2005 is an *event-driven* language, which means that code is executed in response to events. These events might come from users, such as a user clicking a button, or from Windows itself (see Hour 4, "Understanding Events," for a complete explanation of events). Currently, your application looks nice, but it won't do a darn thing (sort of like me on Saturday mornings—before kids). The user can click the Select Picture button until they can file for disability with carpel tunnel syndrome, but nothing will happen because you haven't told the program what to do when the user clicks the button. You can see this for yourself now by pressing F5 to run the project. Feel free to click the buttons, but they don't do anything. When you're finished, close the window you created to return to Design mode.

You're going to write code to accomplish two tasks. First, you're going to write code that lets the user browse their hard drives to locate and select a picture file and then display the file in the picture box (this sounds a lot harder than it is). Second, you're going to add code to the Quit button that shuts down the program when the user clicks the button.

Letting a User Browse for a File

The first bit of code you're going to write enables the user to browse their hard drives, select a picture file, and then see the selected picture in the PictureBox control. This code executes when the user clicks the Select Picture button; therefore, it's added to the Click event of that button (you'll learn all about events in later hours).

When you double-click a control on a form in Design view, the default event for that control is displayed in a code window. The default event for a Button control is its Click event, which makes sense because clicking is the most common action a user performs with a button. Double-click the Select Picture button now to access its Click event in the code window (see Figure 1.12).

When you access an event, Visual C# builds an *event handler* (the code highlighted in the rectangle in Figure 1.12), which is essentially a template procedure in which you add the code that executes when the event occurs. The cursor is already placed within the code procedure, so all you have to do is add code. By the time you're finished with this book, you'll be madly clicking away as you write your own code to make your applications do exactly what you want them to do—well, most of the time. For now, just enter the code as I present it here.

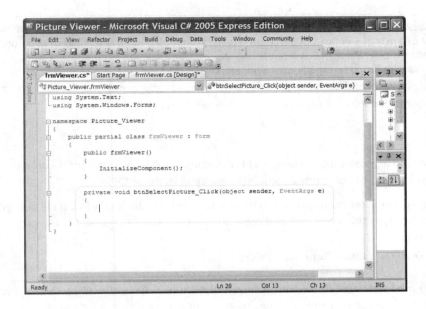

FIGURE 1.12
You'll write all code in a window such as this.

It's important that you get in the habit of commenting your code, so the first statement you're going to enter is a comment. Beginning a statement with two forward slashes designates the statement as a comment; the compiler won't do anything with the statement, so you can enter whatever text you want after the two forward slashes. Type the following statement exactly as it appears and press the Enter key at the end of the line:

```
// Show the open file dialog box.
```

The next statement you'll enter triggers a method of the OpenFileDialog control that you added to the form. You'll learn all about methods in Hour 3. For now, think of a method as a mechanism to make a control do something. The ShowDialog() method tells the control to show its Open dialog box and let the user select a file. The ShowDialog() method returns a value that indicates its success or failure, which you'll then compare to a predefined result (DialogResult.OK). Don't worry too much about what's happening here; you'll be learning the details of all this in later hours, and the sole purpose of this hour is to get your feet wet. In a nutshell, the ShowDialog() method is invoked to let a user browse for a file. If the user selects a file, more code is executed. Of course, there's a lot more to using the OpenFileDialog control than I present in this basic example, but this simple statement gets the job done. Enter the following two code statements, pressing Enter at the end of each line:

> Capitalization is important. Visual C# is a *case-sensitive language*, which means ShowDialog() is not the same as Showdialog(). If you get the case of even one letter wrong, Visual C# will not recognize the word and you're code won't work, so *always* enter code exactly as it appears in this book!

```
if (ofdSelectPicture.ShowDialog() == DialogResult.OK)

{
```

The opening brace (the { character) is necessary for this if statement because it denotes that this if construct will be made up of multiple lines.

Time for another comment. Your cursor is currently on the line below the { that you entered. Type this statement and remember to press Enter at the end of the code line.

```
// Load the picture into the picture box.
```

This next statement, is the line of code that actually displays the picture in the picture box. (If you're itching to know more about graphics, take a look at Hour 18, "Working with Graphics.")

Enter the following statement:

```
picShowPicture.Image = Image.FromFile(ofdSelectPicture.FileName);
```

In addition to displaying the selected picture, your program is also going to display the path and filename of the picture in the title bar. When you first created the form, you changed the Text property of the form using the Properties window. To create dynamic applications, properties need to be constantly adjusted at runtime, and this is done using code. Insert the following two statements (press Enter at the end of each line):

```
// Show the name of the file in the form's caption.
this.Text = string.Concat("Picture Viewer(" + ofdSelectPicture.FileName + ")");
```

The last statement you need to enter is a closing brace (a } character). Whenever you have an opening brace, you have to have a closing brace. This is how Visual C# groups multiple statements of code. Enter this statement now:

```
}
```

After you've entered all the code, your editor should look like that shown in Figure 1.13.

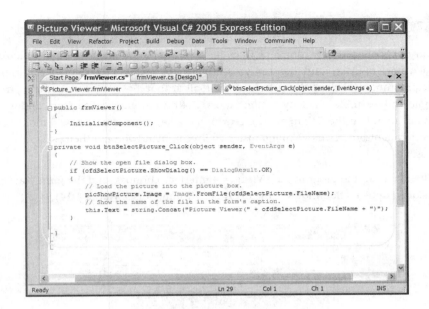

FIGURE 1.13
Make sure that
your code exact-
ly matches the
visible code
shown here.

Terminating a Program Using Code

The last bit of code you'll write terminates the application when the user clicks the Quit button. To do this, you'll need to access the Click event handler of the btnQuit button. At the top of the code window are two tabs. The current tab has the text frmViewer.cs*. This is the tab containing the code window for the form with the file-name frmViewer.cs. Next to this is a tab that contains the text frmViewer.cs [Design]*. Click this tab now to switch from Code view to the form designer. If you receive an error when you click the tab, the code you entered contains an error, and you need to edit it to make it the same as shown in Figure 1.13. After the form designer appears, double-click the Quit button to access its Click event.

Enter the following code in the Quit button's Click event handler, press Enter at the end of each statement:

```
// Close the window and exit the application

this.Close();
```

The this.Close(); statement closes the current form. When the last loaded form in a program is closed, the application shuts itself down—completely. As you build more robust applications, you'll probably want to execute all kinds of clean-up routines before terminating an application, but for this example, closing the form is all you need to do.

Running a Project

Your application is now complete. Click the Save All button on the toolbar (it looks like a stack of disks), and then run your program by pressing F5. You can also run the program by clicking the button on the toolbar that looks like a right-facing triangle and resembles the Play button on a VCR (this button is called Start, and it can also be found on the Debug menu). Learning the keyboard shortcuts will make your development process move along faster, so I recommend you use them whenever possible.

When you run the program, the Visual C# interface changes, and the form you've designed appears floating over the design environment (see Figure 1.14).

FIGURE 1.14
When in Run mode, your program executes the same as it would for an end user.

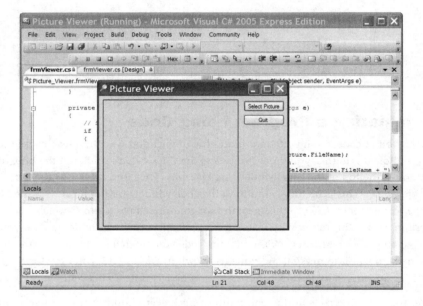

You are now running your program as though it were a standalone application running on another user's machine; what you see is exactly what users would see if they ran the program (without the Visual Studio .NET design environment in the background, of course). Click the Select Picture button to display the Select Picture dialog box (see Figure 1.15). Use the dialog box to locate a picture file. When you've found a file, double-click it, or click once to select it and then click Open. The selected picture is then displayed in the picture box, as shown in Figure 1.16.

When you click the Select Picture button, the default path shown depends on the last active path in Windows, so it will be different for you than shown in Figure 1.15.

FIGURE 1.15
The OpenFileDialog control handles all the details of browsing for files. Cool, huh?

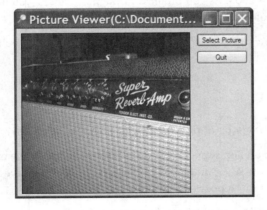

FIGURE 1.16
Visual C# makes it easy to display pictures with very little work.

If you want to select and display a picture from your digital camera, chances are the format is JPEG, so you'll need to select this from the Files of type drop-down. Also, if your image is very large, you'll see only the upper-left corner of the image (what fits in the picture box) . In later hours, I'll show you how you can scale the image to fit the picture box, and even resize the form to show a larger picture in its entirety.

By the Way

Summary

When you're finished playing with the program, click the Quit button to return to Design view.

That's it! You've just created a bona fide Visual C# program. You've used the toolbox to build an interface with which users can interact with your program, and you've written code in strategic event handlers to empower your program to do things. These are the basics of application development in Visual C#. Even the most complicated programs are built using this fundamental approach; you build the interface and add code to make the application do things. Of course, writing code to do things *exactly* the way you want things done is where the process can get complicated, but you're on your way.

If you take a close look at the organization of the hours in this book, you'll see that I start out by teaching you the Visual C# (Visual Studio .NET) environment. I then move on to building an interface, and later I teach you all about writing code. This organization is deliberate. You might be a little anxious to jump in and start writing serious code, but writing code is only part of the equation—don't forget the word *Visual* in Visual C# 2005. As you progress through the hours, you'll be building a solid foundation of development skills.

Soon, you'll pay no attention to the man behind the curtain—you'll be that man (or woman)!

Q&A

Q. *Can I show pictures of file types other than BMP and JPG?*

A. Yes. The PictureBox supports the display of images with the extensions BMP, JPG, ICO, EMF, WMF, and GIF. The PictureBox can even save images to a file using any of the supported file types.

Q. *Is it possible to show pictures in other controls?*

A. The PictureBox is *the* control to use when you are just displaying images. However, many other controls allow you to display pictures as part of the control. For instance, you can display an image on a button control by setting the button's Image property to a valid picture.

Workshop

The Workshop is designed to help you anticipate possible questions, review what you've learned, and get you thinking about how to put your knowledge into practice.

Quiz

1. What type of Visual C# project creates a standard Windows program?

2. What window is used to change the attributes (location, size, and so on) of a form or control in the IDE?

3. How do you access the default event (code) of a control?

4. What property of a picture box do you set to display an image?

5. What is the default event for a button control?

Answers

1. Windows Application

2. Properties Window

3. Double-click the control in the designer

4. The Image property

5. The Click event

Exercises

1. Change your Picture Viewer program so that the user can also locate and select GIF files. (Hint: Change the Filter property of the OpenFileDialog control.)

2. Create a new project and put two buttons on it. Place them in the bottom-right corner of the form.

HOUR 2

Navigating Visual C# 2005

The key to expanding your knowledge of Visual C# is to become as comfortable as possible—as quickly as possible—with the Visual C# design environment. Just as a carpenter doesn't think much about hammering a nail into a piece of wood, performing actions such as saving projects, creating new forms, and setting object properties should become second nature to you. The more comfortable you are with Visual C#'s tools, the more you can focus your energies on what you're creating with the tools.

In this hour, you'll learn how to customize your design environment by moving, docking, floating, hiding, and showing design windows, as well as how to customize menus and toolbars. You'll even create a new toolbar from scratch. After you've gotten acquainted with the environment, I'll teach you about projects and the files that they're made of (taking you beyond what was briefly discussed in Hour 1, "Jumping In with Both Feet: A Visual C# 2005 Programming Tour"), and I'll introduce you to the design windows with which you'll work most frequently. Finally, I'll show you how to get help when you're stuck.

Using the Visual C# 2005 Start Page

By default, the Visual C# 2005 Start Page shown in Figure 2.1 is the first thing you see when you start Visual C# (if Visual C# isn't running, start it now). The Visual C# 2005 Start Page is a gateway for performing tasks with Visual C#. From this page, you can open previously edited projects, create new projects, and get help.

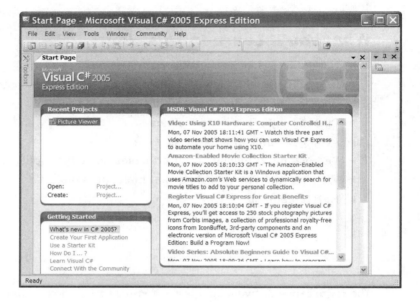

Creating New Projects

The Start Page consists of three category boxes. The Recent Projects category in the upper-left corner is used to work with projects. To create new projects, click the Create: Project... link in the Recent Projects category. This opens the New Project dialog box shown in Figure 2.2. The Templates list varies from machine to machine, depending on which products of the Visual Studio .NET family are installed. Of course, we're interested only in the Visual C# Project types in this book.

By the Way

You can create many types of projects with Visual C#, but this book focuses mostly on creating Windows applications, the most common of the project types and the primary application type of the Express edition of Visual C# .NET. You will learn about some of the other project types as well, but when you're told to create a new project, make sure that the Windows Application icon is selected unless you're told otherwise.

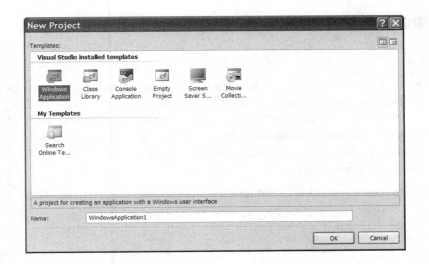

FIGURE 2.2
Use the New Project dialog box to create Visual C# projects from scratch.

When you create a new project, be sure to enter a name for it in the Name text box before clicking OK or double-clicking a Templates icon. This ensures that the project is created with the proper path and filenames, eliminating work you would otherwise have to do to change these values later. After you specify a name, you can create the new project either by double-clicking the icon that represents the Template type of project you want to create or by clicking the template icon once to select it and then clicking OK. After you've performed either of these actions, the New Project dialog box closes and a new project of the selected type is created.

When you first create a project, the project files are virtual—they haven't been saved to the hard drive. When you click Save or Save All for the first time, you are prompted to specify a path in which to save the project. The name you give your project is used as its folder name by default, but the path chosen depends on the last project you created. If you're on a team of developers, you might choose to locate your projects on a shared drive so that others can access the source files.

> You can create a new project at any time (not just when starting Visual C#) by choosing File, New Project from the menu. When you create or open a new project, the current project is closed. Visual C# asks whether you want to save any changes to the current project before it closes it, however.

After you enter a project name and click OK, Visual C# creates the project. Again, nothing is saved to the hard drive until you click Save or Save All on the toolbar (or use the menu equivalent).

Opening an Existing Project

Over time, you'll open existing projects more often than you create new ones. There are essentially two ways to open projects from the Visual Studio Start Page:

▶ If it's a project you've recently opened, the project name appears in the Recent Projects category toward the upper-left corner of the Start Page (as Picture Viewer does in Figure 2.1). Because the name displayed for the project is the one given when it was created, it's important to give your projects descriptive names. Clicking a project name opens the project. I'd venture to guess that you'll use this technique 95% of the time.

▶ To open a project for the first time (such as when opening sample projects), click the Open Project... link on the Visual Studio 2005 Start Page. This displays a standard dialog box that you can use to locate and select a project file.

As with creating new projects, you can open an existing project at any time, not just when starting Visual C#, by selecting File, Open. Remember that opening a project causes the current project to be closed. Again, if you've made changes to the current project, you'll get a chance to save them before the project is closed.

Navigating and Customizing the Visual C# Environment

Visual C# lets you customize many of its interface elements, such as windows and toolbars, enabling you to be more efficient in the work that you do. Create a new Windows application now by opening the File menu and clicking New Project. This project illustrates manipulating the design environment. Name this project **Environment Tutorial** and click OK to create the project. (This exercise won't create anything reusable, but it will help you learn how to navigate the design environment.) Your screen should look like the one shown in Figure 2.3.

Your screen might not look exactly like that shown in Figure 2.3, but it'll be close. By the time you've finished this hour, you'll be able to change the appearance of the design environment to match this figure—or to any configuration you prefer.

Working with Design Windows

Design windows, such as the Properties window and Solution Explorer shown in Figure 2.3 provide functionality for building complex applications. Just as your desk isn't organized exactly like that of your coworkers, your design environment doesn't have to be the same as anyone else's either.

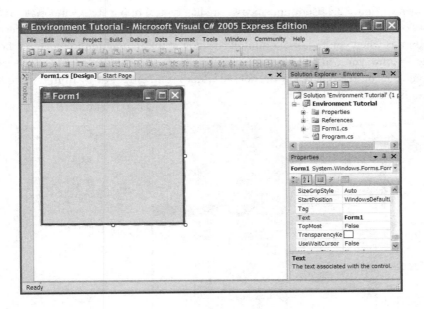

FIGURE 2.3
This is pretty much how the integrated development environment (IDE) appears when you first install Visual C#.

A design window can be placed into one of four primary states:

▶ *Closed*   The window is not visible.

▶ *Floating*   The window appears floating over the IDE.

▶ *Docked*   The window appears attached to an edge of the IDE.

▶ *Automatically hidden*   The window is docked, but it hides itself when not in use.

Showing and Hiding Design Windows

When a design window is closed, it doesn't appear anywhere. There is a difference between being closed and being automatically hidden, as you'll learn shortly. To display a closed or hidden window, choose the corresponding menu item from the View menu. For example, if the Properties window isn't displayed in your design environment, you can display it by choosing View, Properties Window from the menu (or by pressing its keyboard shortcut—Ctrl+W,P). Whenever you need a design window and can't find it, use the View menu to display it. To close a design window, click its Close button (the button on the right side of the title bar with the X on it), just as you would to close an ordinary window.

Floating Design Windows

Floating design windows are visible windows that float over the workspace, as shown in Figure 2.4. Floating windows are like typical application windows in that you can drag them around and place them anywhere you please, even on other monitors when you're using a multiple-display setup. In addition to moving a floating window, you can also change its size by dragging a border. To make a window float, click on the title bar of the docked window and drag it away from the edge that is currently docked.

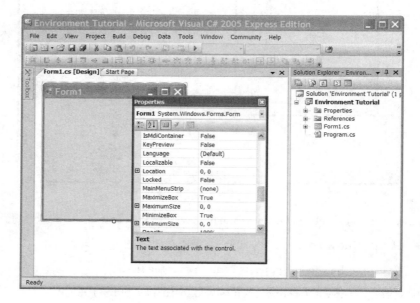

Docking Design Windows

Visible windows appear docked by default. A *docked* window appears attached to the side, top, or bottom of the work area or to some other window. The Properties window in Figure 2.3, for example, is docked to the right side of the design environment (contrast this to where it's floating in Figure 2.4). To make a floating window become a docked window, drag the title bar of the window toward the edge of the design environment to which you want to dock the window. As you drag the window, guide diamonds appear on the screen (see Figure 2.5). If you move the mouse over one of the icons that appear as part of the guide diamond, Visual C# will show a blue rectangle where the window will appear if you release the mouse button. This is a quick and easy way to dock window. You can also drag the window to an edge and get the same blue rectangle. This rectangle will "stick" in a docked position.

If you release the mouse while the rectangle appears this way, the window will be docked. Although difficult to explain, this is very easy to do.

> You can size a docked window by dragging its edge opposite the side that's docked. If two windows are docked to the same edge, dragging the border between them enlarges one while shrinking the other.

To try this, you'll need to float a window that's already docked. To float a window, you "tear" the window away from the docked edge by dragging the title bar of the docked window away from the edge to which it's docked. Note that this technique won't work if a window is set to Auto Hide (which is explained next). Try docking and floating windows now by following these steps:

1. Ensure that the Properties window is currently displayed (if it's not, show it by choosing Properties Window from the View menu). Make sure that the Properties window isn't set to Auto Hide by right-clicking its title bar and deselecting Auto Hide from the shortcut menu (if it's selected).

2. Drag the title bar of the Properties window away from the docked edge (drag it to the left). When the window is away from the docked edge, release the mouse button. The Properties window should now float.

3. Dock the window once more by dragging the title bar of the window toward the right edge of the design environment. When the Guide Diamond appears, mouse over the bottom icon (see Figure 2.5). You'll see a blue rectangle appear where the Properties window will be docked. Release the mouse button to dock the window.

> If you don't want a floating window to dock, regardless of where you drag it to, right-click the title bar of the window and choose Floating from the context menu. To allow the window to be docked again, right-click the title bar and choose Dockable.

Auto Hiding Design Windows

Visual C# windows have the capability to auto hide themselves when you're not using them. Although you might find this a bit disconcerting at first, after you get the hang of things, this is a productive way to work; your workspace is freed up, yet design windows are available by simply moving the mouse. Windows that are set to Auto Hide are always docked; you can't set a floating window to Auto Hide. When a window auto hides, it appears as a vertical tab on the edge to which it's docked— much like minimized applications are placed in the Windows taskbar.

FIGURE 2.5
The Guide
Diamond icons
make it easy to
dock a window.

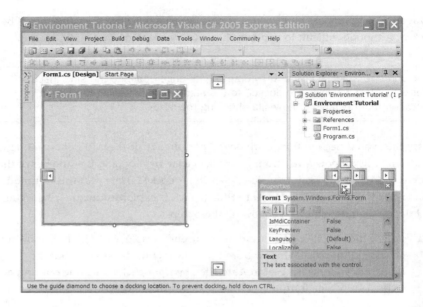

Look at the left edge of the design environment. Notice the vertical tab titled
Toolbox. This tab represents an auto-hidden window. To display an auto-hidden
window, move the pointer over the tab representing the window. When you move
the pointer over a tab, Visual C# displays the design window so that you can use its
features. When you move the pointer away from the window, the window automatically hides itself—hence the name. To make any window hide itself automatically,
right-click its title bar and select Auto Hide from its shortcut menu. You can also
click the little picture of a pushpin appearing in the title bar next to the Close button to toggle the window's Auto Hide state.

Using the techniques discussed so far, you can tailor the appearance of your design
environment in all sorts of ways. There is no one best configuration. You'll find that
different configurations work better for different projects and in different stages of
development. Sometimes when I'm designing the interface of a form, for example, I
want the toolbox to stay visible but out of my way, so I tend to make it float, or I
turn off its Auto Hide property and leave it docked to the left edge of the design
environment. However, after the majority of the interface elements have been added
to a form, I want to focus on code. Then I dock the toolbox and make it Auto Hide
itself; it's there when I need it, but it's out of the way when I don't. Don't be afraid
to experiment with your design windows, and don't hesitate to modify them to suit
your changing needs.

Working with Toolbars

Toolbars are the mainstay for performing functions quickly in almost every Windows program (you'll probably want to add them to your own programs at some point, and in Hour 9, "Adding Menus and Toolbars to Forms," you'll learn how). Every toolbar has a corresponding menu item, and buttons on toolbars are essentially shortcuts to their corresponding menu items. To maximize your efficiency when developing with Visual C# 2005, you should become familiar with the available toolbars. As your skills improve, you can customize existing toolbars and even create your own toolbars to more closely fit the way you work.

Showing and Hiding Toolbars

Visual C# includes a number of built-in toolbars you can use when creating projects. One toolbar is visible in most of the figures shown so far in this hour: the Standard toolbar. You'll probably want this toolbar displayed all the time.

The toolbars you'll use most often as a new Visual C# developer are the Standard, Text Editor, and Debug toolbars, and each of these is discussed in this hour. You can also create your own custom toolbars to contain any functions you think necessary.

To show or hide a toolbar, open the View menu and click Toolbars to display a list of available toolbars. Toolbars that are currently visible have a check mark displayed next to them (see Figure 2.6). Click a toolbar name to toggle its visible state.

> **Did you Know?**
>
> You can also right-click any visible toolbar to quickly access the list of available toolbars.

Docking and Resizing Toolbars

Just as you can dock and undock Visual C#'s design windows, you can dock and undock the toolbars. Unlike the design windows, however, Visual C#'s toolbars don't have a title bar that you can click and drag when they're in a docked state. Instead, each docked toolbar has a *drag handle* (a vertical stack of dots along its left edge). To float (undock) a toolbar, click and drag the grab handle away from the docked edge. When a toolbar is floating, it has a title bar, which you can drag to an edge to dock the toolbar. This is the same technique you use to dock design windows.

> **Did you Know?**
>
> A shortcut for docking a floating toolbar, or any other floating window, is to double-click its title bar.

FIGURE 2.6
Hide or show
toolbars to
make your work-
space more effi-
cient.

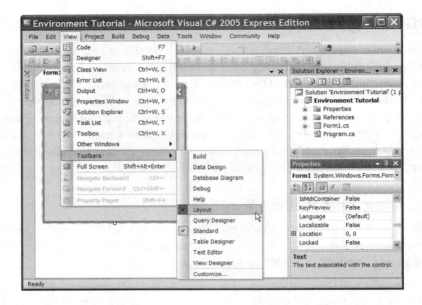

Although you can't change the size of a docked toolbar, you can resize a floating toolbar (a floating toolbar behaves like any other normal window). To resize a floating toolbar, move the pointer over the edge you want to stretch and then click and drag to the border to change the size of the toolbar.

Adding Controls to a Form Using the Toolbox

The IDE offers some fantastic tools for building a graphical user interface (GUI) for your applications. Most GUIs consist of one or more forms (Windows) with various elements on the forms, such as text boxes and list boxes. The toolbox is used to place controls onto a form. Figure 2.7 shows the default toolbox you see when you first open or create a Visual C# project. These controls are discussed in detail in Hour 7, "Working with Traditional Controls," and Hour 8, "Using Advanced Controls."

You can add a control to a form in one of four ways:

▶ In the toolbox, click the tool representing the control that you want to place on a form, and then click and drag on the form where you want the control placed; you're essentially drawing the border of the control. The location at which you start dragging is used for one corner of the control, and the point at which you release the mouse button and stop dragging becomes the lower-right corner.

FIGURE 2.7
The standard toolbox contains many useful controls you can use to build robust interfaces.

▶ Double-click the desired control type in the toolbox. When you double-click a control in the toolbox, a new control of the selected type is placed in the upper-left corner of the form if the form is selected. If a control is selected when you do this, the new control will appear slightly to the right and down from the selected control. The control's height and width are set to the default height and width of the selected control type. If the control is a runtime only control, like the Open File Dialog control you used in Hour 1, it will appear below the form.

▶ Drag a control from the toolbox and drop it on a form. If you hover over the form for a second, the toolbox disappears, and you can drop the control on the form anywhere you want.

▶ Right-click an existing control and choose Copy, then right-click the form and choose Paste to create a duplicate of the control.

If you prefer to draw controls on your forms by clicking and dragging, I strongly suggest that you dock the toolbox to the right or bottom edge of the design environment or float it. The toolbar tends to interfere with drawing controls when it's docked to the left edge because it covers part of the form.

Did you Know?

The first item in each category in the toolbox, titled Pointer, isn't actually a control. When the pointer item is selected, the design environment is placed in a select mode rather than in a mode to create a new control. With the pointer item selected, you can click a control on the form to display all its properties in the Properties window.

Setting Object Properties Using the Properties Window

When developing the interface of a project, you'll spend a lot of time viewing and setting object properties using the Properties window (see Figure 2.8). The Properties window contains four items:

▶ An object drop-down list

▶ A list of properties

▶ A set of tool buttons used to change the appearance of the properties grid

▶ A section showing a description of the selected property

FIGURE 2.8
Use the
Properties win-
dow to view and
change proper-
ties of forms
and controls.

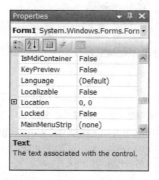

Selecting an Object and Viewing Its Properties

The drop-down list at the top of the Properties window contains the name of the form with which you're currently working and all the objects on the form (the form's controls). To view the properties of a control, select it from the drop-down list or find it on the form and click it. Remember that you must have the pointer item selected in the toolbox to click an object to select it.

Viewing and Changing Properties

The first two buttons in the Properties window (Categorized and Alphabetic) enable you to select the format in which you view properties. When you select the Alphabetic but-tonthe selected object's properties appear in the Properties window in alphabetical order. When you click the Categorized button, all the selected object's properties are list-ed by category. The Appearance category, for example, contains properties such as BackColor and BorderStyle. When working with properties, select the view you're most comfortable with and feel free to switch back and forth between the views.

The Properties pane of the Properties window is used to view and set the properties of a selected object. You can set a property in one of the following ways:

► Type in a value.

► Select a value from a drop-down list.

► Click a Build button for property-specific options.

Many properties can be changed by more than one of these methods. For example, color properties supply a drop-down list of colors, but you can enter a numeric color value as well.

To better understand how changing properties works, follow these steps:

1. Add a new text box to the form now by double-clicking the TextBox tool in the toolbox. You're now going to change a few properties of the new text box.

2. Select the (Name) property in the Properties window by clicking it. (If your properties are alphabetic, it will be at the top of the list, not with the N's.) Type in a name for the text box—call it **txtComments**.

3. Click the BorderStyle property and try to type in the word **Big**. You can't; the BorderStyle property only supports selecting values from a list, though you can type a value that exists in the list. When you select the BorderStyle property, a drop-down arrow appears in the value column. Click this arrow now to display a list of the values that the BorderStyle property accepts. Select FixedSingle and notice how the appearance of the text box changes. To make the text box appear three-dimensional again, open the drop-down list and select Fixed3D.

If you are running your display using the Windows XP Theme, controls won't take on a 3D appearance—they'll appear flat with a light blue border. I'm a big fan of this newer interface, and all the figures in this book were captured running with the Windows XP Theme enabled.

4. Select the BackColor property, type the word **guitar**, and press the Tab key to commit your entry. Visual C# displays a message telling you the property value isn't valid. This happens because although you can type in text, you're restricted to entering specific values. In the case of BackColor, the value must be a named color or a number that forms an RGB value (Red, Green, Blue). For example, to change the BackColor to blue, you could use the value 0,0,255 (0 reg, 0 green, and full blue). Clear out the text and then click the

drop-down arrow of the BackColor property and select a color from the drop-down list. (Selecting colors using the color palette is discussed later in this hour, and detailed information on using colors is provided in Hour 18, "Working with Graphics").

5. Select the Font property. Notice that a Build button appears (a small button with three dots on it). When you click the Build button, a dialog box specific to the property you've selected appears. In this instance, a dialog box that enables you to manipulate the font of the text box appears (see Figure 2.9). Different properties display different dialog boxes when you click their Build buttons. Feel free to change the font and then close the window.

6. Scroll down to the Size property and notice that it has a plus sign next to it. This indicates that the property has one or more subproperties. Click the plus sign to expand the property, and you'll see that Size is composed of Width and Height.

By simply clicking a property in the Properties window, you can easily tell the type of input the property requires.

FIGURE 2.9
The Font dialog box allows you to change the appearance of text in a control.

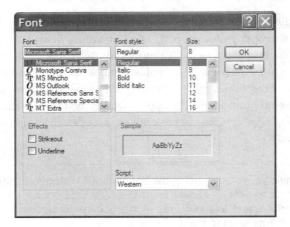

Working with Color Properties

Properties that deal with colors are unique in the way in which they accept values, yet all color-related properties behave the same way. In Visual C# 2005, colors are expressed as a set of three numbers, each number having a value from 0 to 255. A given set of numbers represents the red, green, and blue (RGB) components of a color, respectively. The value 0,255,0, for example, represents pure green, whereas the value 0,0,0 represents black and 255,255,255 represents white. In some cases, colors have also been given specific names that you can use. (See Hour 18 for more information on the specifics of working with color.)

A color rectangle is displayed for each color property in the Properties window; this color is the selected color for the property. Text is displayed next to the colored rectangle. This text is either the name of a color or a set of RGB values that define the color. Clicking in a color property causes a drop-down arrow to appear, but the drop-down you get by clicking the arrow isn't a typical drop-down list. Figure 2.10 shows what the drop-down list for a color property looks like.

FIGURE 2.10
The color drop-down list enables you to select from three sets of colors.

The color drop-down list is composed of three tabs: Custom, Web, and System. Most color properties use a system color by default. Hour 5, "Building Forms—The Basics," goes into great detail on system colors. I only want to mention here that system colors vary from computer to computer; they're determined by the user when he right-clicks the desktop and chooses Properties from the desktop's shortcut menu. Use a system color when you want a color to be one of the user's selected system colors. When a color property is set to a system color, the name of the system color appears in the property sheet.

The Custom tab, shown in Figure 2.11, is used to specify a specific color, regardless of the user's system color settings; changes to system colors have no effect on the property. The most common colors appear on the palette of the Custom tab, but you can specify any color you want.

> The colors visible in the various palettes are limited by the number of colors that can be produced by your video card. If your video card doesn't support enough colors, some will appear *dithered*, which means they will appear as dots of colors rather than as a true, solid color. Keep this in mind as you develop your applications: What looks good on your computer might turn to mush if a user's display isn't as capable.

By the Way

FIGURE 2.11
The Custom tab of the color drop-down list lets you specify any color imaginable.

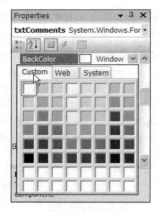

The bottom two rows in the Custom color palette are used to mix your own colors. To assign a color to an empty color slot, right-click a slot in one of the two rows to access the Define Color dialog box (see Figure 2.12). Use the controls on the Define Color dialog box to create the color you want, and then click Add Color to add the color to the color palette in the slot you selected. In addition, the custom color is automatically assigned to the current property.

FIGURE 2.12
The Define Color dialog box enables you to create your own colors.

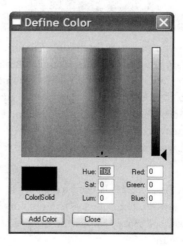

The Web tab is used in web applications to pick from a list of browser-safe colors. You can, however, use these colors even if you're not creating a web application.

Viewing Property Descriptions

It's not always immediately apparent just exactly what a property is or does—especially for new users of Visual C#. The Description section at the bottom of the Properties window shows a simple description of the selected property. To view a description, click a property or value area of a property. For a more complete description of a property, click it once to select it and then press F1 to display Help about the property.

You can hide or show the Description section of the Properties window at any time by right-clicking anywhere within the Properties window (other than in the value column or on the title bar) to display the Properties window shortcut menu and choosing Description. Each time you do this, you toggle the Description section between visible and hidden. To change the size of the Description box, click and drag the border between it and the Properties pane.

Managing Projects

Before you can effectively create an interface and write code, you need to understand what makes up a Visual C# 2005 project and how to add and remove various components within your own projects. In this section, you'll learn about the Solution Explorer window and how it's used to manage project files. You'll also learn specifics about projects and project files, including how to change a project's properties.

Managing Project Files with the Solution Explorer

As you develop projects, they'll become more and more complex, often containing many objects such as forms and modules (grouped sets of code). Each object is defined by one or more files on your hard drive. In addition, you can build complex solutions composed of more than one project. The Solution Explorer window shown in Figure 2.13 is *the* tool for managing all the files in a simple or complex solution. Using the Solution Explorer, you can add, rename, and remove project files, as well as select objects to view their properties. If the Solution Explorer window isn't visible on your screen, show it now by choosing View, Solution Explorer from the menu.

To better understand the Solution Explorer window, follow these steps:

1. Locate the Picture Viewer program you created in the Quick Tour by choosing Open Project on the File menu.

2. Open the Picture Viewer project. The file you need to select is located in the Picture Viewer folder that Visual C# created when the project was constructed. The file has the extension .sln (for Visual C# Solution). If you're asked whether you want to save the current project, choose No.

FIGURE 2.13
Use the
Solution
Explorer window
to manage all
the files that
make up a
project.

FIGURE 2.13
Use the
Solution
Explorer window
to manage all
the files that
make up a
project.

3. Select the Picture Viewer project item in the Solution Explorer. When you do, a button becomes visible toward the top of the window. This button has a picture of pieces of paper and has the ToolTip Show All Files (see Figure 2.14). Click this button and the Solution Explorer displays all files in the project.

Your Solution Explorer should now look like the one in Figure 2.14. Be sure to widen the Solution Explorer window so that you can read all the text it contains.

FIGURE 2.14
Notice that the
form you
defined appears
as two files in
the Solution
Explorer.

You can view any object listed within the Solution Explorer using the object's default viewer by double-clicking the object. Each object has a default viewer but might actually have more than one viewer. For instance, a form has a Form Design view as well as a Code view. By default, double-clicking a form in the Solution Explorer displays the form in Form Design view, where you can manipulate the form's interface.

You've already learned one way to access the code behind a form: double-click an object to access its default event handler. You'll frequently need to get to the code of a form without adding a new event handler. One way to do this is to use the Solution Explorer. When a form is selected in the Solution Explorer, buttons are visible at the top of the Solution Explorer window that can be used to display the code editor or the form designer, respectively.

You'll use the Solution Explorer window so often that you'll probably want to dock it to an edge and set it to Auto Hide, or perhaps keep it visible all the time. The Solution Explorer window is one of the easiest to get the hang of in Visual C#; navigating the Solution Explorer window will be second nature to you before you know it.

Working with Solutions

A project is what you create with Visual C#. Often, the words *project* and *program* are used interchangeably, and this isn't much of a problem if you understand the important distinctions. A *project* is the set of source files that make up a program or component, whereas a *program* is the binary file that you build by compiling source files into something such as a Windows executable file (.exe). Projects always consist of a main project file and can be made up of any number of other files, such as form files, module files, or class module files. The main project file stores information about the project—all the files that make up the project, for example—as well as properties that define aspects of a project, such as the parameters to use when the project is compiled into a program.

What, then, is a solution? As your abilities grow and your applications increase in complexity, you'll find that you have to build multiple projects that work harmoniously to accomplish your goals. For instance, you might build a custom user control such as a custom data grid that you use within other projects you design, or you might isolate the business rules of a complex application into separate components to run on isolated servers. All the projects used to accomplish those goals are collectively called a *solution*. Therefore, a *solution* (at its most basic level) is really nothing more than a grouping of projects. By default, when you save a project, Visual C# creates a solution for the project. When you open the solution file, as you did in this example, all projects in the solution get loaded. If the solution contains only one project, then opening the solution is pretty much the same as opening that single project.

> You should group projects into a single solution only when the projects relate to one another. If you're working on a number of projects, but each of them is autonomous, work with each project in a separate solution.

Understanding Project Components

As I stated earlier, a project always consists of a main project file, and it might consist of one or more secondary files, such as files that make up forms or code modules. As you create and save objects within your project, one or more corresponding files are created and saved on your hard drive. Each file that's created for a Visual C# 2005 source object has the extension .cs, denoting that it defines a Visual C# object. Make sure that you save your objects with understandable names, or things will get confusing as the size of your project grows.

All files that make up a project are text files. Some objects need to store binary information, such as a picture for a form's BackgroundImage property. Binary data is stored in an XML file (which is still a text file). Suppose that you had a form with an icon on it. You'd have a text file defining the form (its size, the controls on it, and the code behind it), and an associated resource filewith the same name as the form file but with the extension .resx. This secondary file would be in XML format and would contain all the binary data needed to create the form.

> If you want to see what the source file of a form file looks like, use Notepad to open one on your computer. Don't save any changes to the file, however, or it might never work again (</insert evil laugh here/>).

The following is a list of some of the components you might use in your projects:

▶ *Class modules*   Class modules are a special type of module that enables you to create object-oriented applications. Throughout the course of this book, you're learning how to program using an object-oriented language, but you're mostly learning how to use objects supplied by Visual C#. In Hour 16, "Designing Objects Using Classes," you'll learn how to use class modules to create your own objects.

▶ *Forms*   Forms are the visual windows that make up the interface of your application. Forms are defined using a special type of class module.

▶ *User controls*   User controls (formerly ActiveX controls, which themselves are formerly OLE controls) are controls that can be used on the forms of other projects. For example, you could create a user control with a calendar interface for a contact manager. Creating user controls requires the skill of an experienced programmer, so I won't be covering them in this book.

Setting Project Properties

Visual Basic projects have properties, just as other objects such as controls do. Projects have many properties, many of them relating to advanced functionality not covered in this book. You need to be aware, of how to access project properties, however, and how to change some of the more commonly used properties.

To access the properties for a project, right-click the project name (Picture Viewer) in the Solution Explorer window and choose Properties from the shortcut menu. You could also double-click the project name in the Solutions Explorer to accomplish the same goal. Do one of these actions now.

The properties for a project are presented as a set of vertical tabs (see Figure 2.15).

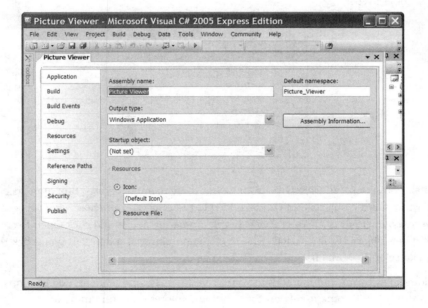

FIGURE 2.15
The Project Properties are used to tailor the project as a whole.

As you work through the hours in this book, I'll refer to the Project Properties dialog box as necessary, explaining pages and items in context with other material. Feel free to take a look at your Picture Viewer properties, but don't change any at this time. You can close the project properties by clicking the small X in the upper-right corner of the tab section in the IDE. You can also just click a different tab.

Adding and Removing Project Files

When you first start Visual C# 2005 and create a new Windows Application project, Visual C# creates the project with a single form. You're not limited to having one form in a project, however; you can create new forms or add existing forms to your project at will (feeling powerful yet?). You can also create and add class modules as well as other types of objects.

You can add a new or existing object to your project in one of three ways:

▶ Choose the appropriate menu item from the Project menu.

▶ Click the small drop-down arrow that's part of the Add New Item button on the Standard toolbar, and then choose the object type from the drop-down list that displays (see Figure 2.16).

▶ Right-click the project name in the Solution Explorer window and then choose Add from the shortcut menu to access a submenu from which you can select object types.

FIGURE 2.16
This tool button drop-down is one of three ways to add objects to a project.

When you select Add *ObjectType* from any of these menus, a dialog box appears, showing you the objects that can be added to the project. Your chosen item type is selected by default (see Figure 2.17). Simply name the object and click Open to create a new object of the selected type. To create an object of a different type, click the type to select it, name it, and then click Open.

Adding new forms and modules to your project is easy, and you can add as many as you want. You'll come to rely on the Solution Explorer more and more to manage all the objects in the project as the project becomes more complex.

Although it won't happen as often as adding project files, you might sometimes need to remove an object from a project. Removing objects from your project is even easier than adding them. To remove an object, right-click the object in the Solution Explorer window and select Delete. This not only removes the object from the project, it also deletes the source file from the disk.

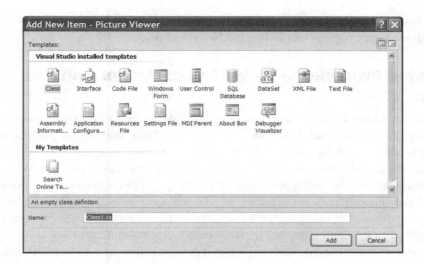

FIGURE 2.17
Regardless of the menu option you select, you can add any type of object you want using this dialog box.

A Quick-and-Dirty Programming Primer

Programming is complicated. Everything is so interrelated that it's difficult, if not impossible, to isolate each programming concept and then present the material in a linear fashion. Instead, while learning one subject, you often have to touch on elements of another subject before you've had a chance to learn about the secondary topic. I've made every effort to avoid such forward references, but there are some concepts with which you'll need to be at least slightly familiar with before proceeding. You'll learn the guts of each of these topics in their respective lessons, but you'll need to have at least heard of them before digging any deeper into this book.

Storing Values in Variables

A *variable* is an element in code that holds a value. You might create a variable that holds the name of a user or the perhaps the user's age, for example. Each variable (storage entity) must be created before it can be used. The process of creating a variable is known as *declaring a variable*. In addition, each variable is declared to hold data of a specific type, such as text (called a *string*) for a person's name or a number for a person's age. An example of a variable declaration is

```
string strFirstName;
```

This statement creates a variable called `strFirstName`. This variable is of type String, which means it can hold any text that you choose to put into it. The contents of a variable can be changed as often as desired.

The key primer point to remember: Variables are storage locations that must be declared before use and that hold a specific type of data.

Using Procedures to Write Functional Units of Code

When you write Visual C# code, you place the code in a *procedure*. A procedure is a group of code statements that perform a specific function. You can call a procedure from code in another procedure. For example, you might create one procedure that totals the items on an order and another procedure that calculates the tax on the entire sale. There are two types of procedures: procedures that don't return values and procedures that do return values. In addition, some procedures allow data to be passed to them. For example, the tax calculation procedure mentioned previously might allow a calling statement to pass a monetary total into the procedure and then use that total to calculate tax. When a procedure accepts data from the calling code, the data is called a *parameter*. Procedures don't have to accept parameters.

A procedure that doesn't return a value is declared using the keyword void, and looks like this:

```
public void MyProcedure()
{
    // The procedure's code goes here.
}
```

Notice the beginning and ending braces—all Visual C# procedures use them to surround the code of the procedure.

A procedure that returns a value is declared with a return data type specified before the procedure name, which denotes the type of data returned by the procedure:

```
public string AuthorName()
{
    return "James";
}
```

Notice the word string. This is a data type. In this example, the function returns text (the name "James"), which is a string.

If a procedure accepts a parameter, it is enclosed in the parentheses, like this:

```
public string AuthorName(string BookName)
{
    // procedure code goes here
}
```

MessageBox.Show()

You're almost certainly familiar with the Windows message box—it's the little dialog box used to display text to a user (see Figure 2.18). Visual C# 2005 provides a way to display such messages using a single line of code: the MessageBox.Show() statement. The following is a MessageBox.Show() statement in its most basic form:

```
MessageBox.Show("Text to display goes here");
```

FIGURE 2.18
Visual C# makes it easy to display simple message boxes like this.

You'll use message boxes throughout this book, and you'll learn about them in detail in Hour 17, "Interacting with Users."

Getting Help

Although Visual C# was designed to be as intuitive as possible, you'll find that you occasionally need assistance in performing a task. In all honesty, Visual C# isn't very intuitive—with all the power and flexibility come complexity. It doesn't matter how much you know, Visual C# is so complex and contains so many features that you'll have to use Help at times. This is particularly true when writing Visual C# code; you won't always remember the command you need or the syntax of a command. Fortunately, Visual C# includes a comprehensive Help feature.

To access Help from within the design environment, press F1. Generally, when you press F1, Visual C# shows you a Help topic directly related to what you're doing. This is known as *context-sensitive help*, and when it works, it works well. For example, you can display help for any Visual C# syntax or keyword (functions, objects, methods, properties, and so on) when writing Visual C# code by typing the word into the code editor, positioning the cursor anywhere within the word (including before the first letter or after the last), and pressing F1. You can also get to Help from the Help menu on the menu bar.

If your project is in Run mode, Visual C#'s Help won't be displayed when you press F1. Instead, the Help for your application will appear—if you've created Help.

By the Way

Summary

In this hour, you learned how to use the Visual C# Start Page—your gateway to Visual C# 2005. You learned how to create new projects and how to open existing projects. The Visual C# environment is your workspace, toolbox, and so much more. You learned how to navigate this environment, including how to work with design windows (hide, show, dock, and float).

Visual C# has many different design windows, and in this hour, you began learning about some of them in detail. You learned how to get and set properties using the Properties window, how to manage projects using the Solution Explorer, and how to add controls to a form using the toolbox. You'll use these skills often, so it's important to get familiar with them right away. Finally, you learned how to access Visual C#'s Help feature, which I guarantee you'll find important as you learn to use Visual C#.

Visual C# 2005 is a vast and powerful development tool—far more powerful than any version that's come before it. Don't expect to become an expert overnight; that's simply impossible. However, by learning the tools and techniques presented in this hour, you've begun your journey. Remember, you'll use most of what you learned in this hour each time you use Visual C#. Get proficient with these basics, and you'll be building useful programs in no time!

Q&A

Q. *How can I easily get more information about a property when the Description section of the Properties window just doesn't cut it?*

A. Click the property in question to select it, and then press F1—context-sensitive help applies to properties in the Properties window, as well.

Q. *I find that I need to see a lot of design windows at one time, but I can't find that "magic" layout. Any suggestions?*

A. Run at a higher resolution. Personally, I won't develop in less than 1024×768. As a matter of fact, all my development machines have two displays, both running at 1152×864. You'll find that any investment you make in having more screen real estate will pay you big dividends.

Workshop

The Workshop is designed to help you anticipate possible questions, review what you've learned, and get you thinking about how to put your knowledge into practice.

Quiz

1. Unless instructed otherwise, you're to create what type of project when building examples in this book?

2. To make a docked design window appear when you hover over its tab and disappear when you move the mouse away from it, you change what setting of the window?

3. What design window do you use to add controls to a form?

4. What design window is used to change the attributes of an object?

5. To modify the properties of a project, you must select the project in what design window?

6. Which Help feature adjusts the links it displays to match what you are doing?

Answers

1. Windows Application

2. Its Auto-Hide settings

3. The toolbox

4. The Properties window

5. The Solutions Explorer window

6. Dynamic Help

Exercises

1. Use the Custom Color dialog box to create a color of your choice and then assign the color to the BackColor property of a form.

2. Move the toolbox to the right side of the IDE and dock it there. Make it Auto Hide. When you're finished, move it back.

HOUR 3

Understanding Objects and Collections

What You'll Learn in This Hour:

▶ Understanding objects
▶ Getting and setting properties
▶ Triggering methods
▶ Understanding method dynamism
▶ Writing object-based code
▶ Understanding collections
▶ Using the Object Browser

In Hour 1, "Jumping In with Both Feet: A Visual C# 2005 Programming Tour," you were introduced to programming in Visual C# by building a Picture Viewer project. You then spent Hour 2, "Navigating Visual C# 2005," digging into the integrated development environment (IDE) and learning skills critical to your success with Visual C#. In this hour, you're going to start learning about an important programming concept, namely *objects*.

The term *object* as it relates to programming might have been new to you prior to this book. The more you work with Visual C#, the more you'll hear about objects. Visual C# 2005 is a true object-oriented language. This hour isn't going to discuss object-oriented programming in any detail—object-oriented programming is a complex subject and well beyond the scope of this book. Instead, you'll learn about objects in a more general sense.

Everything you use in Visual C# is an object, so understanding this material is critical to your success with Visual C#. For example, forms are objects, as are the controls you place on a form; pretty much every element of a Visual C# project is an object and belongs to a collection of objects. All objects have attributes (called *properties*), most have methods, and many have events. Whether creating simple applications or building large-scale enterprise solutions, you must understand what an object is and how it works to be successful. In this hour, you'll learn what makes an object an object, and you'll also learn about collections.

> If you've listened to the programming press at all, you've probably heard the term object oriented, and perhaps words such as polymorphism, encapsulation, and inheritance. In truth, these object-oriented features of Visual C# are exciting, but they're far beyond Hour 3 (or Hour 24, for that matter). You'll learn a little about object-oriented programming in this book, but if you're really interested in taking your programming skills to the next level, you should buy a book dedicated to the subject after you've completed this book.

Understanding Objects

Object-oriented programming has been a technical buzzword for quite some time. Almost everywhere you look—the Web, publications, books—you read about objects. What exactly is an object? Strictly speaking, an *object* is a programming structure that encapsulates data and functionality as a single unit and for which the only public access is through the programming structure's interfaces (properties, methods, and events). In reality, the answer to this question can be somewhat ambiguous because there are so many types of objects—and the number grows almost daily. All objects share specific characteristics, however, such as properties and methods.

The most commonly used objects in Visual C# are the form object and the control object. Earlier hours introduced you to working with forms and controls and even showed you how to set form and control properties. In your Picture Viewer project from Hour 1, for example, you added a picture box and two buttons to a form. Both the PictureBox and the Button controls are *control objects*, but each is a specific type of control object. Another, less-technical example uses pets. Dogs and cats are definitely different entities (objects), but they both fit into the category of Pet objects. Similarly, text boxes and buttons are each a unique type of object, but they're both considered a control object. This small distinction is important.

Understanding Properties

All objects have attributes used to specify and return the state of the object. These attributes are properties, and you've already used some of them in previous hours using the Properties window. Indeed, every object exposes a specific set of properties, but not every object exposes the same set of properties. To illustrate this point, I'll continue with the hypothetical Pet object. Suppose that you have an object, and the object is a dog. This Dog object has certain properties common to all dogs. These properties include attributes such as the dog's name, the color of its hair, and even the number of legs it has. All dogs have these same properties; however, different dogs have different values for these properties. Figure 3.1 illustrates such a Dog object and its properties.

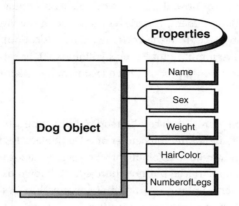

FIGURE 3.1
Properties are the attributes that describe an object.

Getting and Setting Properties

You've already seen how to read and change properties using the Properties window. The Properties window is available only at design time, however, and is used only for manipulating the properties of forms and controls. Most getting and changing of properties you'll perform will be done with Visual C# code, not by using the Properties window. When referencing properties in code, you specify the name of the object first, followed by a period (.), and then the property name as in the following syntax:

```
{ObjectName}.{Property}
```

If you had a Dog object named Bruno, for example, you would reference Bruno's hair color this way:

```
Bruno.HairColor
```

This line of code would return whatever value was contained in the HairColor property of the Dog object Bruno. To set a property to some value, you use an equal sign (=). To change the Dog object Bruno's Weight property, for example, you'd use a line of code such as the following:

```
Bruno.Weight = 90;
```

The following line of code places the value of the Weight property of the Dog object called Bruno into a temporary variable. This statement retrieves the value of the

Weight property because the `Weight` property is referenced on the right side of the equal sign.

```
fltWeight = Bruno.Weight;
```

Variables are discussed in detail in Hour 11, "Using Constants, Data Types, Variables, and Arrays." For now, think of a variable as a storage location. When the processor executes this statement, it retrieves the value in the Weight property of the Dog object Bruno and places it in the variable (storage location) titled `fltWeightVariable`. Assuming that Bruno's Weight is 90, as set in the previous example, the computer would process the code statement like this:

```
fltWeight = 90;
```

Just as in real life, some properties can be read but not changed. Suppose that you have a Sex property to designate the gender of a Dog object. It's impossible for you to change a dog from a male to a female or vice versa (at least I think it is). Because the Sex property can be retrieved but not changed, it's known as a *read-only* property. You'll often encounter properties that can be set in Design view but become read-only when the program is running.

One example of a read-only property is the Height property of the combo box control. Although you can view the value of the Height property in the Properties window, you can't change the value—no matter how hard you try. If you attempt to change the Height property using Visual C# code, Visual C# simply changes the value back to the default—eerie gremlins.

By the Way

> The best way to determine which properties of an object are read-only is to consult the online help for the object in question.

Working with an Object and Its Properties

Now that you know what properties are and how they can be viewed and changed, you're going to experiment with properties by modifying the Picture Viewer project you built in Hour 1. Recall from Hour 1 how you learned to set the Height and Width properties of a form using the Properties window. Here, you're going to change the same properties using Visual C# code.

You're going to add two buttons to your Picture viewer. One button will enlarge the form when clicked, whereas the other will shrink the form. This is a simple example, but it illustrates well how to change object properties in Visual C# code.

Start by opening your Picture Viewer project from Hour 1 (you can open the project or the solution file). If you download the code samples from my site, I provide a Picture Viewer project for you to start with.

When the project first runs, the form has the Height and Width you specified in the Properties window. You're going to add buttons to the form that a user can click to enlarge or shrink the form at runtime by following these steps:

1. Double-click frmViewer.cs in the Solutions Explorer window to display the form designer.

2. Add a new button to the form by double-clicking the Button tool in the toolbox. Set the new button's properties as follows:

Property	Set To
Name	**btnEnlarge**
Location	**342, 261**
Size	**21, 23**
Text	^ (Note, this is Shift+6)

3. Now for the Shrink button. Again, double-click the Button tool in the toolbox to create a new button on the form. Set this new button's properties as follows:

Property	Set To
Name	**btnShrink**
Location	**365,261**
Size	**21, 23**
Text	**v**

Your form should now look like the one in shown in Figure 3.2.

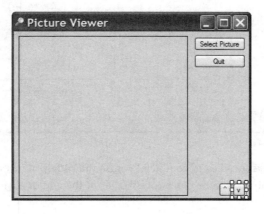

FIGURE 3.2
Each button is an object, as is the form the buttons sit on.

To complete the project, you need to add the small amount of Visual C# code necessary to modify the form's Height and Width properties when the user clicks a button.

4. Access the code for the Enlarge button now by double-clicking the button with the caption ^. Type the following statement exactly as you see it here. Do not press the Enter key or add a space after you've entered this text.

```
this.Width
```

When you type the period, or *dot*, as it's called, a small drop-down list like the one shown in Figure 3.3 appears. Visual C# is smart enough to realize that this represents the current form (more on this in a moment), and to aid you in writing code for the object, it gives you a drop-down list containing all the properties and methods of the form. This feature is called *IntelliSense*. When an IntelliSense drop-down box appears, you can use the up and down arrow keys to navigate the list and press Tab to select the highlighted list item. This prevents you from misspelling a member name thereby reducing compile errors. Because Visual C# is fully object-oriented, you'll come to rely on IntelliSense drop-down lists in a big way; I think I'd rather dig ditches than program without them.

FIGURE 3.3
IntelliSense drop-down lists (also called *auto-completion drop-down lists*) make coding dramatically easier.

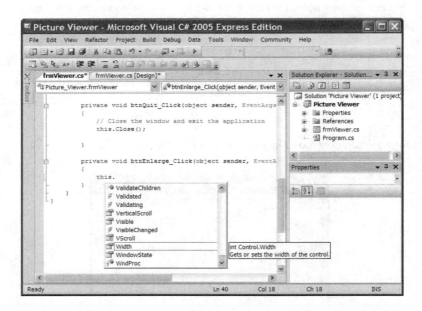

5. Use the Backspace key to completely erase the code you just entered and enter the following code in its place (press Enter at the end of each line):

```
this.Width = this.Width + 20;
this.Height = this.Height + 20;
```

Notice that all Visual C# statements end with a semicolon. This semicolon is required, and it lets the Visual C# compiler know that it has reached the end of a statement.

Remember from before that the word this refers to the object to which the code belongs (in this case, the form). this is a *reserved* word; it's a word that you can't use to name objects or variables because Visual C# has a specific meaning for it. When writing code within a form module, as you're doing here, always use the reserved word this rather than the name of the form. this is much shorter than using the full name of the current form, and it makes the code more portable (you can copy and paste the code into another form module and not have to change the form name to make the code work). Also, should you change the name of the form at any time in the future, you won't have to change references to the old name.

The code you've entered does nothing more than set the Width and Height properties of the form to whatever the current value of the Width and Height properties happens to be, plus 20 pixels.

6. Redisplay the form designer by selecting the tab named frmViewer.cs [Design] at the top of the designer window. Then double-click the button with the caption v to access its Click event and add the following code:

```
this.Width = this.Width - 20;
this.Height = this.Height - 20;
```

This code is similar to the code in the btnEnlarge_Click event, except that it reduces the Width and Height properties of the form by 20 pixels. Your screen should now look like Figure 3.4.

As you create projects, it's a good idea to save frequently. Save your project now by clicking the Save All button on the toolbar.

Once again, display the form designer by clicking the tab frmViewer.cs [Design]. Your Properties Example project is now ready to be run! Press F5 to put the project in Run mode. Before continuing, click the Select Picture button and choose a picture from your hard drive.

FIGURE 3.4
The code you've
entered should
look exactly like
this.

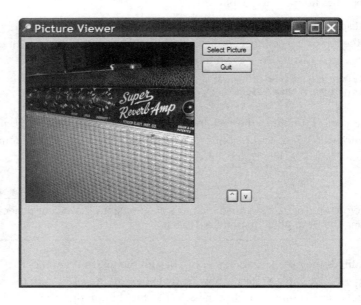

```
private void btnQuit_Click(object sender, EventArgs e)
{
    // Close the window and exit the application
    this.Close();

}

private void btnEnlarge_Click(object sender, EventArgs e)
{
    this.Width = this.Width + 20;
    this.Height = this.Height + 20;
}

private void btnShrink_Click(object sender, EventArgs e)
{
    this.Width = this.Width - 20;
    this.Height = this.Height - 20;
}
```

Next, click the ^ button a few times and notice how the form gets bigger. The form
will grow bigger (see Figure 3.5).

FIGURE 3.5
What you see is
what you get—
the form you
created should
look just as you
designed it.

Next, click the v button to make the form smaller. When you've clicked enough to satisfy your curiosity (or until you get bored), end the running program and return to Design mode by clicking the Stop Debugging button on the toolbar.

Did you notice how the buttons and the image on the form didn't resize as the form's size was changed? In Hour 6, "Building Forms—Advanced Techniques," you'll learn how to make your forms resize their contents.

Understanding Methods

In addition to properties, most objects have *methods*. Methods are actions the object can perform, in contrast to attributes that describe the object. To understand this distinction, think about the Pet object example. A Dog object has a certain set of actions that it can perform. These actions, called methods in Visual C#, include barking, tail wagging, and chewing carpet (don't ask). Figure 3.6 illustrates the Dog object and its methods.

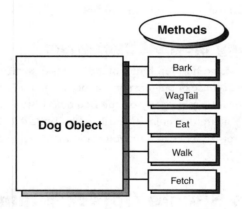

FIGURE 3.6
Invoking a method causes the object to perform an action.

Triggering Methods

Think of methods as functions—which is exactly what they are. When you invoke a method, code is executed. You can pass data to a method, and methods can return values. However, a method is neither required to accept *parameters* (data passed to it by the calling code) nor to return a value; many methods simply perform an action in code. Invoking (triggering) a method is similar to referencing the value of a property: You first reference the object's name, and then a dot, and then the method name as shown next:

```
{ObjectName}.{Method}
```

For example, to make the hypothetical Dog object Bruno bark using Visual C# code, you would use this line of code:

```
Bruno.Bark();
```

Methods calls in Visual C# must always have parentheses. Sometimes they'll be empty, but at other times they'll contain data to pass to the method.

Methods are generally used to perform an action using an object, such as saving or deleting a record in a database. Properties, on the other hand, are used to get and set attributes of the object. One way to tell in code whether a statement is a property reference or method call is that a method call will have a set of parentheses after it, as in `frmAlbum.ShowDialog();`.

Invoking methods is simple; the real skill lies in knowing what methods an object supports and when to use a particular method.

Understanding Method Dynamism

Properties and methods go hand in hand, and at times a particular method might become unavailable because of one or more property values. For example, if you were to set the NumberofLegs property on the Dog object Bruno equal to zero, the `Walk()` and `Fetch()` methods would obviously be inapplicable. If you were to set the NumberofLegs property back to four, you could then trigger the `Walk()` or `Fetch()` method again.

Building a Simple Object Example Project

The only way to really grasp what objects are and how they work is to use them.

Every project you've built so far uses objects, but you're now going to create a sample project that specifically illustrates using objects. If you're new to programming with objects, you'll probably find this a bit confusing. However, I'll walk you through step-by-step, explaining each section in detail.

You're going to modify your Picture Viewer project to include a button that, when clicked, draws a colored border around the picture.

In Hour 18, "Working with Graphics," you'll learn all about the drawing functionality within Visual C#.

Creating the Interface for the Drawing Project

Continuing on with the Picture Viewer project you've been using in this chapter, add a new button to the form and set its properties as shown in the following table:

Property	Value
Name	**btnDrawBorder**
Location	**301, 69**
Size	**85, 23**
Text	**Draw Border**

Writing the Object-Based Code

You're now going to add code to the Click event of the button. I'm going to explain each statement, and at the end of the steps, I'll show the complete code listing.

1. Double-click the Draw Border button to access its Click event.

2. Enter the first line of code as follows (remember to press Enter at the end of each statement):

```
Graphics objGraphics = null;
```

Here you've just created a variable that will hold an instance of an object. Objects don't materialize out of thin air; they have to be created. When a form is loaded into memory, it loads all its controls (that is, creates the control objects), but not all objects are created automatically like this. The process of creating an instance of an object is called *instantiation*. When you load a form, you instantiate the form object, which in turn instantiates its control objects. You could load a second instance of the form, which in turn would instantiate a new instance of the form and new instances of all controls. You would then have two forms in memory, and two of each used control.

To instantiate an object in code, you create a variable that holds a reference to an instantiated object. You then manipulate the variable as an object. The variable declaration statement you wrote in step 2 creates a new variable called objGraphics, which holds a reference to an object of type Graphics (the type comes first, then the variable name). You learn more about variables in Hour 18.

Next, enter the second line of code exactly as shown here:

```
objGraphics = this.CreateGraphics();
```

CreateGraphics() is a method of the form (remember, the keyword this is shorthand for referencing the current form). Under the hood, the CreateGraphics() method is pretty complicated, and I discuss it in detail in Hour 18. For now, understand that the method CreateGraphics() instantiates a new object that represents the client area of the current form. The client area is the gray area within the borders and title bar of a form. Anything drawn onto the objGraphics() object will appear on the form. What you've done is set the variable objGraphics() to point to an object that was returned by the CreateGraphics() method. Notice how values returned by a property or method don't have to be traditional values such as numbers or text; they could also be objects.

Enter the third line of code as shown next:

```
objGraphics.Clear(SystemColors.Control);
```

This statement clears the background of the form using whatever color the user has selected as the Windows Control color, which Windows uses to paint forms.

How does this happen? After declaring the objGraphics object, you used the CreateGraphics() method of the form to instantiate a new graphics object in the variable objGraphics(). With the code statement you just entered, you're calling the Clear() method of the objGraphics() object. The Clear() method is a method of all Graphics objects used to clear the graphic surface. The Clear() method accepts a single parameter: the color you want used to clear the surface.

The value you're passing to the parameter might seem a bit odd. Remember that "dots" are a way of separating objects from their properties and methods (properties, methods, and events are often called object *members*). Knowing this, you can discern that SystemColors is an object because it appears before any of the dots. Object references can and do go pretty deep, and you'll use many dots throughout your code. The key points to remember are

- ▶ Text that appears to the left of a dot is always an object (or namespace).

- ▶ Text that appears to the right of a dot is a property reference or method call. If the text is followed by a set of parentheses (), it's a method call. If not, it's most likely a property.

- ▶ Methods can return objects, just as properties can. The only surefire ways to know whether the text between two dots is a property or method is to look at the icon of the member in the IntelliSense drop-down or to consult the documentation of the object.

The final text in this statement is the word `Control`. Because `Control` isn't followed by a dot, you know that it's not an object; therefore, it must be a property or method. Because you expect this string of object references to return a color value to be used to clear the graphic object, you know that `Control` in this instance must be a property or a method that returns a value (because you need the return value to set the `Clear()` method). A quick check of the documentation would tell you that `Control` is indeed a property, but you don't even need to do that because there are no parenthesis at the end of `Control`, so it *can't* be a method and therefore has to be a property. The value of `Control` always equates to the color designated on the user's computer for the face of forms and buttons. By default, this is a light gray (often fondly referred to as *battleship gray*), but users can change this value on their computers. By using this property to specify a color rather than supplying the actual value for gray, you're assured that no matter the color scheme used on a computer, the code will clear the form to the proper system color. System colors are explained in Hour 18.

Enter the following statement. Note: Press Enter after each line. Remember, Visual C# uses a semicolon to denote the end of a statement, so it will consider all three lines as being one code statement.

```
objGraphics.DrawRectangle(Pens.Blue,
        picShowPicture.Left - 1, picShowPicture.Top - 1,
        picShowPicture.Width + 1, picShowPicture.Height + 1);
```

This statement draws a blue rectangle around the picture on the form. Within this statement is a single method call and five property references. Can you tell what's what? Immediately following `objGraphics` (and a dot) is `DrawRectangle`. Because no equal sign is present, you can deduce that this is a method call. As with the `Clear()` method, the parentheses after `DrawRectangle` are used to enclose values passed to the method.

The `DrawRectangle()` method accepts the following parameters in the order in which they appear here:

▶ A pen

▶ X value of the upper-left corner

▶ Y value of the upper-left corner

▶ Width of the rectangle

▶ Height of the rectangle

The `DrawRectangle()` method draws a prefect rectangle using the X, Y, Width, and Height values passed to it. The attributes of the line (color, width, and so on) are determined by the pen specified in the Pen parameter. I'm not going to go into detail on pens here (see Hour 18). Looking at the dots once more, notice that you're passing the Blue property of the Pens object. Blue is an object property that returns a predefined Pen object that has a width of 1 pixel and the color blue.

For the next two parameters, you're passing property values. Specifically, you're passing the top and left values for the picture, less one. If you passed the exact left and top values, the rectangle would be drawn on the form at exactly the top and left properties of the PictureBox, and you wouldn't see them because controls by default overlap any drawing performed on the form.

The last two property references are for the Height and Width of the PictureBox. Again, we adjust the values by one to ensure that the rectangle is drawn outside the borders of the PictureBox.

Finally, you have to clean up after yourself by entering the following code statement:

```
objGraphics.Dispose();
```

Objects often use other objects and resources. The underlying mechanics of an object can be truly mind boggling and are almost impossible to discuss in an entry-level programming book. The net effect, however, is that you must explicitly destroy most objects when you're finished with them. If you don't destroy an object, it might persist in memory, and it might hold references to other objects or resources that exist in memory. This means that you can create a *memory leak* within your application that slowly (or rather quickly) munches system memory and resources. This is one of the cardinal no-no's of Windows programming, yet the nature of using resources and the fact you're responsible for telling your objects to clean up after themselves makes this easy to do. If your application causes memory leaks, your users won't call for a plumber, but they might reach for a monkey wrench....

Objects that must explicitly be told to clean up after themselves usually provide a Dispose() method. When you're finished with such an object, call Dispose() on the object to make sure that it frees any resources it might be holding.

For your convenience, here are all the lines of code:

```
Graphics objGraphics = null;
objGraphics = this.CreateGraphics();
objGraphics.Clear(SystemColors.Control);
objGraphics.DrawRectangle(Pens.Blue,
     picShowPicture.Left - 1, picShowPicture.Top - 1,
     picShowPicture.Width + 1, picShowPicture.Height + 1);
objGraphics.Dispose();
```

Click Save All on the toolbar to save your work before continuing.

Testing Your Object Example Project

Now the easy part: Run the project by pressing F5 or by clicking the Start button on the toolbar. Your form looks pretty much like it did at design time. Clicking the button causes a blue rectangle to be drawn around the PictureBox (see Figure 3.7).

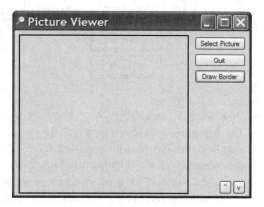

FIGURE 3.7
Simple lines and complex drawings are accomplished using objects.

Stop the project now by clicking Stop Debugging on the Visual C# toolbar. What I hope you've gained from building this example is not necessarily that you can now draw a rectangle (which is cool), but rather an understanding of how objects are used in programming. As with learning almost anything, repetition aids in understanding. That said, you'll be working with objects *a lot* throughout this book.

Understanding Collections

A *collection* is just what its name implies: a collection of objects. Collections make it easy to work with large numbers of similar objects by enabling you to create code that performs iterative processing on items within the collection. *Iterative processing* is an operation that uses a loop to perform actions on multiple objects, rather than writing the operative code for each object. In addition to containing an indexed set of objects, collections also have properties and might have methods. Figure 3.8 illustrates the structure of a collection.

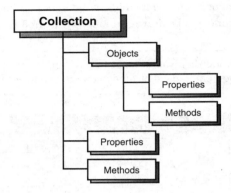

Continuing with the Dog/Pet object metaphor, think about what an Animals collection might look like. The Animals collection might contain one or more Pet objects, or it might be empty (contain no objects). All collections have a Count property that returns the total count of objects contained within the collection. Collections might also have methods, such as a Delete() method used to remove objects from the collection and an Add() method used to add a new object to the collection.

To better understand collections, you're going to create a small Visual C# project that cycles through the Controls collection of a form and tells you the value of the Name property of every control on the form. To create your sample project, follow these steps:

1. Start Visual C# now (if it's not already loaded) and create a new Windows Application project titled **Collections Example**.

2. Rename the form from Form1.vs to **frmCollectionsExample.cs** using the Solution Explorer. If prompted to update all code references to use the new name, select Yes. Next, set the form's Text property to **Collections Example** (you will need to click the form once to display its properties).

3. Add a new button to the form by double-clicking the Button tool in the toolbox. Set the button's properties as follows:

Property	Value
Name	**btnShowNames**
Location	**88,112**
Size	**120,23**
Text	**Show Control Names**

4. Next, add some text box and button controls to the form. As you add the controls to the form, be sure to give each control a unique name. Feel free to use any name you want, but you can't use spaces in a control name. You might want to drag the controls to different locations on the form so that they don't overlap.

5. When you're finished adding controls to your form, double-click the Show Control Names button to add code to its Click event. Enter the following code:

```
for (int intIndex = 0; intIndex < this.Controls.Count; intIndex++)
   {
      MessageBox.Show("Control #" + intIndex.ToString() +
            " has the name " + this.Controls[intIndex].Name);
   }
```

Every form has a Controls collection, which might not contain any controls. Even if no controls are on the form, the form still has a Controls collection.

By the Way

The first statement (the one that begins with `for`) accomplishes a few tasks. First, it initializes the variable intIndex to 0, and then tests the variable. It also starts a loop executing the statement block (loops are discussed in Hour 14, "Looping for Efficiency"), incrementing intIndex by one until intIndex equals the number of controls on the form, less one. The reason that intIndex must always be less than the Count property is that when referencing items in a collection, the first item is always item zero—collections are zero-based. Thus, the first item is in location zero, the second item is in location one, and so forth. If you tried to reference an item of a collection in the location of the value of the Count property, an error would occur because you would be referencing an index that is one higher than the actual locations within the collection.

The MessageBox.Show() method (discussed in detail in Hour 17, "Interacting with Users") is a class available in the .NET Framework that is used to display a simple dialog box with text. The text that you are providing, which the `MessageBox.Show()` method will display, is a concatenation of multiple strings of text. (*Concatenation* is the process of adding strings together; it is discussed in Hour 12, "Performing Arithmetic, String Manipulation, and Date/Time Adjustments.")

Run the project by pressing F5 or by clicking Start on the toolbar. Ignore the additional controls that you placed on the form and click the Show Control Names button. Your program then displays a message box similar to the one shown in Figure 3.9 for each control on your form (because of the loop). When the program is finished displaying the names of the controls, choose Stop Debugging from the Debug menu to stop the program and then save the project.

FIGURE 3.9
The Controls
collection
enables you to
get to each and
every control on
a form.

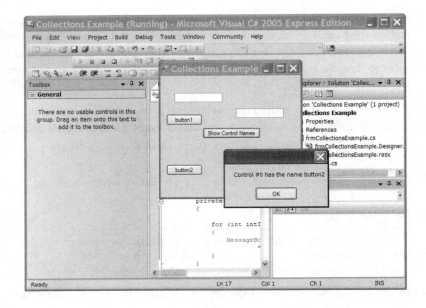

Because everything in Visual C# 2005 is an object, you can expect to use numerous collections as you create your programs. Collections are powerful, and the quicker you become comfortable using them, the more productive you'll be.

Using the Object Browser

Visual C# 2005 includes a useful tool that enables you to easily view members (properties, methods, and events) of all the objects in a project: the Object Browser (see Figure 3.10). This is useful when dealing with objects that aren't well documented because it enables you to see all the members an object supports. To view the Object Browser, choose View, Other Windows, Object Browser from the menu.

The Browse drop-down list in the upper-left corner of the Object Browser is used to determine the *browsing scope*. You can choose My Solution to view only the objects referenced in the active solution, or you can choose All Components to view all possible objects. You can customize the object set by clicking the drop-down arrow next to the Object Browser Settings button to the far right of the Browse drop-down list. I don't recommend changing the custom object setting until you have some experience using Visual C# objects as well as experience using the Object Browser.

The top-level nodes (each item in the tree is referred to as a node) in the Objects tree are libraries. *Libraries* are usually DLL or EXE files on your computer that contain one or more objects. To view the objects within a library, simply expand the library node. As you select objects within a library, the list to the right of the Objects tree shows information regarding the members of the selected object (refer to Figure 3.10). For even more detailed information, click a member in the list on the right, and the Object Browser shows information about the member in the area below the two lists.

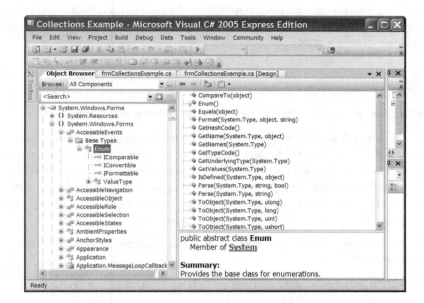

FIGURE 3.10
The Object Browser enables you to view all properties and methods of an object.

Summary

In this hour, you learned a lot about objects. You learned how objects have properties, which are attributes that describe the object. Some properties can be set at design time using the Properties window, and most can also be set at runtime in Visual C# code. You learned that referencing a property on the left side of the equal sign has the effect of changing a property, whereas referencing a property on the right side of the equal sign retrieves a property's value.

In addition to properties, you learned that objects have executable functions, called *methods*. Like properties, methods are referenced by using a dot at the end of an object reference. An object might contain many methods and properties, and some properties can even be objects themselves. You learned how to "follow the dots" to interpret a lengthy object reference.

Objects are often used as a group, called a *collection*. You learned that a collection often contains properties and methods, and that collections let you easily iterate through a set of like objects. Finally, you learned that the Object Browser can be used to explore all the members of an object in a project.

The knowledge you've gained in this hour is fundamental to understanding programming with Visual C# because objects and collections are the basis on which applications are built. After you have a strong grasp of objects and collections—and you will have by the time you've completed all the hours in this book—you'll be well on your way to fully understanding the complexities of creating robust applications using Visual C# 2005.

Q&A

Q. *Is there an easy way to get help about an object's member?*

A. Absolutely. Visual C#'s context-sensitive Help extends to code as well as to visual objects. To get help on a member, write a code statement that includes the member (it doesn't have to be a complete statement), position the cursor within the member text, and press F1. For instance, to get help on the int data type, you could type **int**, position the cursor within the word int, and press F1.

Q. *Are there any other types of object members besides properties and methods?*

A. Yes. An event is actually a member of an object, although it's not always thought of that way. Although not all objects support events, most objects do support properties and methods.

Workshop

The Workshop is designed to help you anticipate possible questions, review what you've learned, and get you thinking about how to put your knowledge into practice.

Quiz

1. True or False: Visual C# .NET is a true object-oriented language.

2. An attribute that defines the state of an object is called a _____.

3. To change the value of a property, the property must be referenced on which side of an equal sign?

4. What is the term for when a new object is created from a template?

5. An external function of an object (one that is available to code using an object) is called a _____.

6. True or False: A property of an object can be another object.

7. A group of like objects is called a _____.

8. What tool is used to explore the members of an object?

Answers

1. True

2. Property

3. The left side

4. Instantiation

5. Method

6. True

7. Collection

8. The Object Browser

Exercises

1. Create a new project and add two text boxes and a button to the form. Write code that, when a button is clicked, places the text in the first text box into the second text box. Hint: Use the Text property of the text box controls.

2. Modify the collections example in this hour to print the height of all controls, rather than the name.

HOUR 4

Understanding Events

What You'll Learn in This Hour:

▶ Understanding event-driven programming
▶ Triggering events
▶ Avoiding recursive events
▶ Accessing an object's events
▶ Working with event parameters
▶ Creating event handlers
▶ Keeping event names current

It's easy to produce an attractive interface for an application using Visual C# 2005's integrated design tools. You can create beautiful forms that have buttons to click, text boxes in which to type information, picture boxes that display pictures, and many other creative and attractive elements with which users can interact. However, that's just the start of producing a Visual C# program. In addition to designing an interface, you have to empower your program to perform actions in response both to how a user interacts with the program and how Windows interacts with the program. This is accomplished by using *events*. In Hour 3, "Understanding Objects and Collections," you learned about objects and their members—notably, properties and methods. In this hour, you'll learn about object events and event-driven programming, and you'll learn how to use events to make your applications responsive.

Understanding Event-Driven Programming

With traditional programming languages (often referred to as *procedural languages*), the program itself fully dictates what code is executed as well as when it's executed. When you start such a program, the first line of code in the program executes, and the code continues to execute in a completely predetermined path. The execution of code might branch and loop on occasion, but the execution path is wholly determined by the program. This often means that such a program is restricted in how it can respond to the user. For example, the program might expect text to be entered into controls on the screen in a predetermined order. This is unlike a Windows application in which a user can interact with different parts of the interface—often in any order the user chooses.

Visual C# 2005 incorporates an event-driven programming model. Event-driven applications aren't bound by the constraints of procedural programs. Instead of the top-down approach of procedural languages, event-driven programs have logical sections of code placed within events. There's no predetermined order in which events occur; the user often has complete control over what code is executed in an event-driven program by interactively triggering specific events, such as by clicking a button. An event, along with the code it contains, is called an *event procedure*.

Triggering Events

In Hour 3, you learned that a method is simply a function of an object. Events, in a sense, are really a special kind of method used by an object to signal state changes that might be useful to clients (code using the object). In fact, the Visual C# 2005 documentation refers to events as *methods* quite frequently (something that will no doubt cause confusion in new programmers). Events are methods that can be called in special ways—usually by the user interacting with something on a form or by Windows itself—rather than being called from a statement in your code.

There are many types of events and many ways to trigger those events. You've already seen how a user can trigger the event of a button by clicking it. User interaction isn't the only thing that can trigger an event; an event can be triggered in one of the following four ways:

▶ Users can trigger events by interacting with your program. Clicking a button, for example, triggers the Click event of the button.

▶ Objects can trigger their own events as needed. The Timer control, for example, can trigger its Timer event at regular intervals.

▶ The operating system (whichever version of Windows the user is running) can trigger events.

▶ You can trigger events by calling them much like you would invoke a method using Visual C# code.

Events Triggered Through User Interaction

The most common way an event is triggered is by a user interacting with a program. Every form, and almost every control you can place on a form, has a set of events specific to its object type. The Button control, for example, has a number of events, including the Click event that you've already used in previous hours. When the user clicks a button, the button's Click event is triggered and then the code within the Click event executes.

The Textbox control enables users to enter information using the keyboard, and it also has a set of events. The Textbox control has some of the same types of events as the Button control, such as a Click event, but the Textbox control also has events not supported by the Button control, such as the MultilineChanged event. The MultilineChanged event occurs when the Multiline property of the text box changes. Because a user can't enter text into a Button control, it doesn't have a Multiline property and therefore no MultilineChanged event. Every object that supports events supports a unique set of events.

Each type of event has its own behavior, and it's important to understand the events you work with. The TextChanged event, for example, exhibits a behavior that might not be intuitive to a new developer because the event fires each time the contents of the text box change. Consider what would happen if you were to type the following sentence into an empty text box in a project you created:

```
Visual C# 2005 is very cool!
```

Although it's easy to think that the TextChanged event fires only when you commit your entry, such as by leaving the text box or pressing Enter, this isn't how it works. Instead, the TextChanged event would be triggered 28 times—once for each character typed—because each time you enter a new character, the contents of the text box is changed. Again, it's important to learn the nuances and the exact behavior of the events you're using. If you use events without fully understanding how they work, your program might exhibit unusual (which usually means undesirable) results.

Triggering events (which are just a type of procedure) using Visual C# code is discussed in detail in Hour 10, "Creating and Calling Methods."

By the Way

Events Triggered by an Object

Sometimes an object triggers its own events. The most common example of this is the Timer control's Tick event. The Timer control is a non-visual control like the common dialog control; it doesn't appear on a form when the program is running, it appears at design time in the space reserved for non-visual controls. The Timer control's sole purpose is to trigger its `Tick` event at an interval specified in its Interval property.

By setting the Timer control's Interval property, you control the interval (in milliseconds) at which the `Timer` event executes. After firing its `Timer` event, a Timer control resets itself and fires its `Timer` event again when the interval has passed. This occurs until the interval is changed, the Timer control is disabled, or the Timer control's form is unloaded. A common use of timers is to create a clock on a form. You can display the time in a label and update it at regular intervals by placing the code to display the current time in the `Timer` event. You'll create a project with a Timer control in Hour 8, "Using Advanced Controls."

Events Triggered by the Operating System

The third way an event can be triggered is by Windows itself. Often, you might not even realize these events exist. For example, when a form is fully or partially obstructed by another window, the program needs to know when the offending window is resized or moved so that it can repaint the area of the window that's hidden. Windows and Visual C# work together in this respect. When the obstructing window is moved or resized, Windows tells Visual C# to repaint the form, which Visual C# does. This also causes Visual C# to raise the form's `Paint` event. You can place code into the `Paint` event to create a custom display for the form, such as drawing shapes on the form using a Graphics object. By doing so, your custom drawing code executes every time the form repaints itself.

Avoiding Recursive Events

You must ensure that you never create code where an event can endlessly trigger itself. An event that continuously triggers itself is called a *recursive* event. To illustrate a situation that causes a recursive event, think of the Textbox control's `TextChanged` event discussed earlier. The `TextChanged` event fires every time the text within the text box changes. Placing code into the `TextChanged` event that alters the text within the text box causes the Change event to be fired again, which could result in an endless loop. Recursive events terminate when Windows returns a `StackOverflow` exception (see Figure 4.1), indicating that Windows no longer has the resources to follow the recursion.

Recursive behavior can occur with more than one event in the loop. For example, if Event A triggers Event B, which in turn triggers Event A, you can have infinite looping of the two events. Recursive behavior can take place among a sequence of many events, not just one or two.

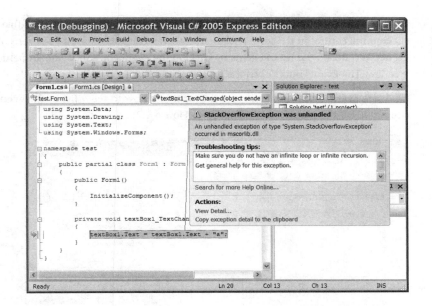

FIGURE 4.1
When you receive a StackOverflow exception, you should look for a recursive event as the culprit.

> Uses for recursive procedures actually exist, such as when writing complex math functions. For instance, recursive events are often used to compute factorials. However, when you purposely create a recursive event, you must ensure that the recursion isn't infinite.

By the Way

Accessing an Object's Events

Accessing an object's events is simple, and if you've been following the examples in this book, you've already accessed a number of objects' default events. To access an object's events, you double-click the object in Form Design view.

You're now going to create a project to get a feel for working with events. Start Visual C# 2005, create a new Windows Application project titled **View Events**, and then follow these steps:

1. Right click Form1.cs in the Solution Explorer, choose Rename, and then change the name of the form to **frmViewEvents.cs**. Again, choose Yes if prompted to update any code references.

2. Click the form once to display its properties and then change the Text property to **View Events Example**.

3. Use the toolbox to add a picture box to the form. Change the name of the picture box to **picTest**.

You already know that you can access the default event for a control by double-clicking the control in the form designer. However, controls often have dozens of events. You access the list of events by clicking the Events button in the Properties Window. The Events button has the image of a lightning bolt on it.

4. Click the Events button in the Properties window now to see a list of the events supported by the picture box control (see Figure 4.2).

FIGURE 4.2
The events supported by a control are accessed using the Properties Window.

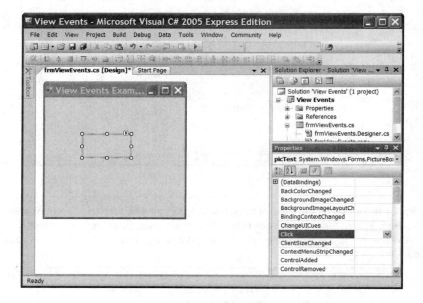

5. Scroll down in the list and locate MouseDown, and double-click it. This will bring up the code editor, ready for you to enter code in the MouseDown event (see Figure 4.3)

Currently, you're viewing the MouseDown event for the picTest object. The cursor is placed within the MouseDown event procedure, ready for you to enter code. The code statement above the cursor is the event declaration. An *event declaration* is a statement that defines the structure of an event. Notice that this event declaration contains the name of the object, an underscore character (_), and then the event name. Following the event name is a set of parentheses. The items within the parentheses are called *parameters*, which are the topic of the next section. This is the standard declaration structure for an event procedure.

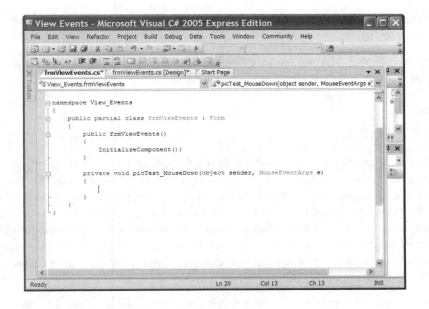

FIGURE 4.3
Visual C# cre-
ates an empty
event procedure
the first time
you select an
object's event.

When you double-click an event in the Events list, Visual C# creates a new event
procedure for that event. The full event declaration and event structure is shown
here:

```
private void picTest_MouseDown(object sender, MouseEventArgs e)
{
}
```

> The open and closed braces denote the beginning and ending of the procedure;
> all code for the procedure needs to be placed between these two braces.

**By the
Way**

Working with Event Parameters

As mentioned previously, the items within the parentheses of an event declaration
are called *parameters*. An event parameter is a variable that's created and assigned a
value by Visual C#. These parameter variables are used to get, and sometimes set,
relevant information within the event. This data may be text, a number, an object—
almost anything. Multiple parameters within an event procedure are always separated by commas. As you can see, the MouseDown event has two parameters. When
the event procedure is triggered, Visual C# automatically creates the parameter variables and assigns them values for use in this single execution of the event procedure; the next time the event procedure occurs, the values in the parameters are

reset. You use the values in the parameters to make decisions or perform operations in your code.

The MouseDown event of a form has the following parameters:

```
object sender
```

and

```
MouseEventArgs e
```

The first piece of text in a parameter indicates the type of data the parameter contains, and the second piece of text is the name of the variable containing the data. The first parameter, sender, holds a generic object. Object parameters can be any type of object supported by Visual C#. It's not critical that you understand data types right now, just be aware that different parameter variables contain different types of information. Some contain text, others contain numbers, and still others (many others) contain objects. In the case of the sender parameter, *it will always hold a reference to the control causing the event.*

The e parameter of the MouseDown event, on the other hand, is where the real action is. The e parameter also holds an object, but in this case the object is of type MouseEventArgs. This object has properties that relate to the MouseDown event. To see them, type in the following code, but don't press anything after entering the dot (period):

```
e.
```

When you press the period, you'll get a drop-down list showing you the members (properties and methods) of the e object (see Figure 4.4). Using the e object, you can determine a number of things about the occurrence of the MouseDown event. I've listed some of the more interesting items in Table 4.1.

TABLE 4.1   Commonly Used Members of MouseEventArgs

Property	Description
Clicks	Returns the number of times the user clicked the mouse button
Button	Returns the button that was clicked (left, middle, right)
X	Returns the horizontal coordinate at which the pointer was located when the user clicked
Y	Returns the vertical coordinate at which the pointer was located when the user clicked

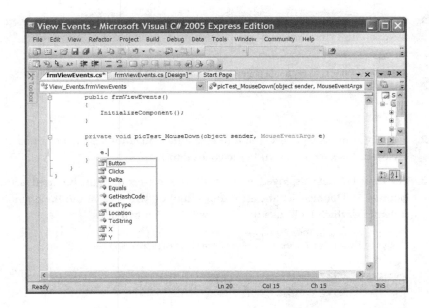

FIGURE 4.4
IntelliSense
drop-down lists
alleviate the
need for memo-
rizing the make
up of hundreds
of objects.

Each time the event occurs, the parameters are initialized by Visual C# so that they always reflect the current occurrence of the event.

By the Way

Each event has parameters specific to it. For instance, the `TextChanged` event returns parameters that are different from the `MouseDown` event. As you work with events—and you'll work with a *lot* of events—you'll quickly become familiar with the parameters of each event type. You'll learn how to create parameters for your own functions and procedures in Hour 10.

Deleting an Event Handler

Deleting an event handler involves more than just deleting the event procedure. When you add a new event handler to a class, Visual C# automatically creates the event procedure for you and positions you to enter code within the event. However, Visual C# does a little bit more "under the hood" to hook the event procedure to the control. It does this by creating a code statement in the hidden code of the class. Ordinarily, you don't have to worry about this statement. However, when you delete an event procedure, Visual C# doesn't automatically delete the hidden code state-ment, and your code won't compile. The easiest way to correct this is simply to run the project; when Visual C# encounters the error, it will show you the offending statement, which you can delete. Try this now:

1. Delete the entire MouseDown procedure code shown here. (You have to delete the open and close braces of the procedure, as well as any code between them.)

```
private void picTest_MouseDown(object sender, MouseEventArgs e)
{
    e.
}
```

2. Press F5 to run the project. You'll receive a message that a build error has occurred. Click No to return to the code editor.

3. The Error List gets displayed, with details of the error that just occurred (see Figure 4.5). Double-click the error and Visual C# will take you to the offending statement, which looks like this (I show it here on two lines):

```
this.picTest.MouseDown += new
    System.Windows.Forms.MouseEventHandler(this.picTest_MouseDown);
```

FIGURE 4.5
Visual C#
shows you com-
pile errors
(errors in your
code) in the
Error List win-
dow.

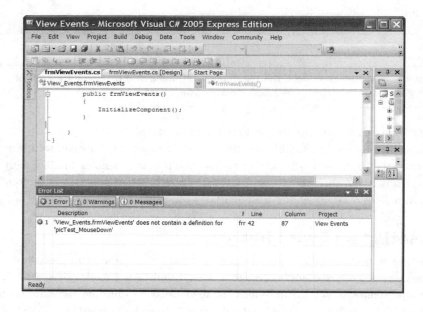

4. Notice the procedure drop-down list in the upper-left corner says InitializeComponent(). This is an event of the form (you can see the form name in the object dropdown list to the left). You do not want to change anything in this procedure unless you know *exactly* what you're doing! In this case, we want to delete a code reference to an event procedure that no longer exists, so delete this entire statement. Now your code will compile and run.

Whenever you delete an event procedure, you'll have to delete the corresponding statement that links the procedure to its object before the code will run.

Now that you've learned the process of deleting an event handler, here's the quickest and easiest way: View the object in design view and click the Events button on the Properties window to view the object's events. Then, highlight the event name in the Properties window and press the Delete key. This will leave event code that will remain in the class until you delete it, but it will no longer be used.

Building an Event Example Project

You're now going to learn how to use the MouseMove event by modifying the Picture Viewer project of Hour 3. You're going to make it so that, as a user moves the mouse over a picture, the X and Y coordinates of the cursor are displayed on the form. You'll be using the e parameter to get the coordinate of the mouse pointer.

Creating the User Interface

Start with a copy of the Picture Viewer project that you completed in Hour 3. If you don't have this project, you can download it from my website.

You'll need two label controls on the form; one for the X value and one for the Y value. Label controls are used to display static text; users can't type text into a label. Follow these steps:

1. Double-click frmViewer.cs in the Solution Explorer to display the form in the designer.

2. Add a label control to the form by double-clicking the Label tool in the toolbox. Set its properties as follows:

Property	Value
Name	**lblX**
Location	**300, 110**
Text	**X:**

3. Use the toolbox to add one more Label control to the form. Set its properties as follows:

Property	Value
Name	**lblY**
Location	**300, 125**
Text	**Y:**

Your form should now look like the one in Figure 4.6. It's a good idea to save frequently, so save your project now by clicking the Save All button on the toolbar.

FIGURE 4.6
Label controls
display static
text to the user.

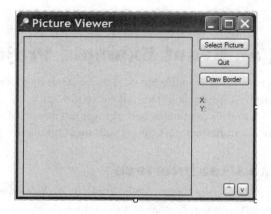

Creating Event Handlers

The interface for this example is complete—now on to the fun part. You're now going to create the event procedures that empower the program to do something. The first event that we're interested in is the MouseMove event. Follow these steps to create the code:

1. Click the picture box on the form to select it, and then click the Event button in the Properties Window (the button with the lightning bolt) to view a list of the events supported by the picture box.

2. Scroll down and locate MouseMove, and then double-click it to create the new MouseMove event (see Figure 4.7).

3. Enter the following code into the MouseMove event procedure:

```
lblX.Text = "X: " + e.X.ToString();
lblY.Text = "Y: " + e.Y.ToString();
```

This code is fairly simple, and may already make sense to you. If it's still not clear, it will be soon. Consider the first line (called a *statement*). lblX.Text is on the left of the = sign, so Text is a property of the label, and we're going to be setting it to some value. The text **"X: "** is a literal value that we're placing in the Text property of the label control. The reason you include this literal is that when you set the Text property, you completely overwrite the current value of the property. So, even though you entered X: as the property in the properties window, you need to include it when setting the property as well. To make this useful, we also have to include the actual value for X, which is stored in the X property of the e object. Again, we're *concatenating* the literal value of **"X: "** with the value stored in e.X; the + sign concatenates two strings. Notice that we use the ToString() method of the X property. This is necessary because Visual C# will only concatenate text (strings), but the X and Y properties hold numbers. The ToString() method converts the number to a string.

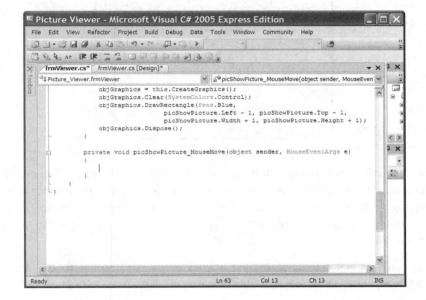

FIGURE 4.7
Each time you select a new event, Visual C# creates an empty event procedure —if one hasn't been created previously for the control.

The second statement does the same thing, only with the Y value.

The nice thing about objects is that you don't have to commit every detail about them to memory. For example, you don't need to memorize the return values for each type of button (who wants to remember e.X, e.Y, or e.Button anyway?). Just remember that the e parameter contains information about the event. When you type e and press the period, the IntelliSense drop-down list appears and shows you the members of e. Don't feel overwhelmed by all the object references you'll encounter throughout this book. Simply accept that you can't memorize them all, nor do you need to; you'll learn the ones that are important, and you'll use Help when you're stuck. Also, after you know the parent object in a situation (such as the e object in this example), it's easy for you to determine the objects and members that belong to it by using the IntelliSense drop-down lists.

Click Save All in the toolbar now to save your work (you wouldn't want to lose it!). Next, press F5 to run the project now and move the mouse over the picture box. You'll see the coordinates of the pointer (as it relates to the picture box) displayed in the two label controls you created (see Figure 4.8).

FIGURE 4.8
The MouseMove event makes it easy to track the pointer over a control.

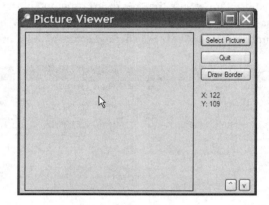

Now, move the mouse pointer off the picture box. Notice that the labels display the last coordinate that the pointer moved over on the picture box. The MouseMove event fires only when the mouse is moved over the control the event is attached to: the picture box in this example. Well, we can't leave those numbers just dangling there can we?

The PictureBox just so happens to have another event we can use to fix this: the MouseLeave event. Oddly enough, the MouseLeave event fires when the mouse leaves the space of the control (yeah, something that's actually intuitive!). Follow these steps to clear the coordinates when the cursor leaves the picture box:

1. Stop the project if it's still running by closing the Picture Viewer form.

2. Click the frmViewer.cs [Design] tab to return to the form designer.

3. Click the picture box (if it's not already selected) to view its events. Locate MouseLeave in the list of events and double-click it to create a new event procedure.

4. Enter the following code into the MouseLeave event:

```
lblX.Text = "";
lblY.Text = "";
```

Press F5 to run the project again and move the mouse over the picture box and then off it. Notice that the coordinates go away. Move the pointer over the picture box again, and they reappear—perfect! Go ahead and stop the running project now.

There's only one thing left to do. Did you notice that when you first start the project, the labels have "X:" and "Y:" in them? Wouldn't it be better to not display this text until the user mouses over the picture box? You could set the Text properties of these labels to empty using the Properties window. However, if you do this, you won't see the labels on the form in the designer and may place other controls over the top of them. A better solution is to initialize their values when the form first loads. You're going to do just that by following these steps:

1. Click the frmViewer.cs [Design] once more to return to the form designer.

2. Click the form to select it and view its events.

3. In the event list for the picture box, locate the Load event and double-click it to create a new event handler. The Load event executes automatically when the form first loads—the perfect place to initialize the label controls.

4. Enter the following two code statements:

```
lblX.Text = "";
lblY.Text = "";
```

That's it—you're finished! Go ahead and Press F5 to run the project and give it a test drive. When the form first loads, the coordinate labels should be empty (this makes them appear invisible). When you mouse over the picture box, the coordinates are displayed, and when you leave the confines of the picture box, the coordinates are hidden once again. A little bit of code and the right event selection can go a long way.

Summary

In this hour, you learned about event-driven programming, including what events are, how to trigger events, and how to avoid recursive events. In addition, you learned how to access an object's events and how to work with parameters. Much of the code you write will execute in response to an event of some kind, and you'll often write code for multiple events of one control. By understanding how events work, including being aware of the available events and their parameters, you'll be able to create complex Visual C# programs that react to a multitude of user and system input.

Q&A

Q. *Is it possible to create custom events for an object?*

A. Yes, you can create custom events for your own objects (you'll learn about such objects in Hour 16, "Designing Objects Using Classes"), and you can also create them for existing objects. Creating custom events, however, is beyond the scope of this book.

Q. *Is it possible for objects that don't have an interface to support events?*

A. Yes. To use the events of such an object, however, the object variable must be dimensioned a special way or the events aren't available. This gets a little tricky and is beyond the scope of this book.

Workshop

The Workshop is designed to help you anticipate possible questions, review what you've learned, and get you thinking about how to put your knowledge into practice.

Quiz

1. Name three things that can cause events to occur.

2. True or False: All objects support the same set of events.

3. What is the default event type for a button?

4. Writing code in an event that causes that same event to be triggered, setting off a chain reaction with the event triggered again and again is called what?

5. What is the easiest way to access a control's default event handler?

6. All control events pass a reference to the control causing the event. What is the name of the parameter that holds this reference?

Answers

1. User input, system input, and other code

2. False

3. Click

4. Recursion

5. Double-click the control in the form designer

6. Sender

Exercises

1. Use the knowledge you've gained so far to create a new project with a form that is gray at design time but that appears blue when the form displays.

2. Create a project with a form and a text box. Add code to the `TextChange` event to cause a recursion when the user types in text. Hint: Concatenate a character to the end of the user's text using a statement such as

   ```
   txtMyTextBox.Text = txtMyTextBox.Text + "a";
   ```

   The + sign tells Visual C# to add the letter a to the end of the existing text box contents. Notice how you eventually get a Stack Over-Flow error—not a good thing!

PART II

Building a User Interface

HOUR 5

Building Forms—The Basics

What You'll Learn in This Hour:

▶ Changing the name of a form
▶ Changing the appearance of a form
▶ Displaying text on a form's title bar
▶ Adding an image to a form's background
▶ Giving a form an icon
▶ Preventing a form from appearing in the taskbar
▶ Specifying the initial display position of a form
▶ Displaying a form in a normal, maximized, or minimized state
▶ Changing the mouse pointer
▶ Showing and hiding forms

With few exceptions, forms are the cornerstones of every Windows application interface. Forms are essentially windows, and the two terms are often used interchangeably. More accurately, *window* refers to what's seen by the user and what the user interacts with, whereas *form* refers to what you see when you design. Forms enable users to view and enter information in a program (such as the form you built in your Picture Viewer program in Hour 1, "Jumping In with Both Feet: A Visual C# 2005 Programming Tour"). Such information may be text, pictures, graphs—almost anything that can be viewed on the screen. Understanding how to design forms correctly enables you to begin creating solid interface foundations for your programs.

Think of a form as a canvas on which you build your program's interface. On this canvas, you can print text, draw shapes, and place controls with which users can interact. The wonderful thing about Visual C# forms is that they behave like a dynamic canvas; not only can you adjust the appearance of a form by manipulating what's on it, you can also manipulate specific properties of the form itself.

In previous hours, you manipulated a few basic properties of a form.

The capability to tailor your forms goes far beyond these basic property manipulations, as you'll see.

There's so much to cover about Windows forms that I've broken the material into two hours. In this hour, you'll learn the basics of forms—adding them to a project, manipulating their properties, and showing and hiding them using Visual C# code. Although you've done some of these things in previous hours, here you'll learn the nuts and bolts of the tasks you've performed. In the next hour, you'll learn more advanced form techniques.

Changing the Name of a Form

The first thing you should do when you create a new object is give it a descriptive name, so that's the first thing I'll talk about in this hour. Start by opening the Picture Viewer project you completed in Hour 4, "Understanding Events." If you don't have this project, you can download it from my website.

Your Picture Viewer currently has some useful functionality, but it's not very flexible. In this hour, you'll start building an Options dialog box for the program. Add a new form for the dialog box by following these steps:

1. Choose Project, Add Windows Form from the menu to display the Add New Item dialog box.

2. In the Name text box, enter **frmOptions.cs**. This will be the name of your form as well as the name of the file that defines the form on the hard drive.

3. Click the Add button (or double-click the Windows Form icon) to close the Add New Item dialog box and add the form to your project (see Figure 5.1).

You can change the name of a form using the (Name) property in the Properties window at any time, and doing so changes the name property of the form, (but not the name of the file on the hard disk). Whenever possible, give your forms solid names when you first create them.

I'm a big fan of using three character naming prefixes, such as **frm** for form. I find it makes complicated code much more readable when objects have prefixes. I discuss naming conventions in Hour 11, "Using Constants, Data Types, Variables, and Arrays."

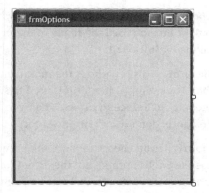

FIGURE 5.1
Each new form
starts off as a
blank canvas.

Changing the Appearance of a Form

The Properties window can actually show two different sets of properties for a form. Right now, it's probably showing the file properties of the form (the properties that describe the physical file(s) on the hard drive as shown in Figure 5.2). If so, click the form in the designer once again to view its development properties. Clicking the form itself will show the form's development properties, while clicking the name of the form in the Solution Explorer will show you the physical file properties for the form. This is why I usually tell you to click the form before setting its properties.

Take a moment to browse the form's properties in the Properties window. In this hour, I'll show you how to use the more common properties of the form to tailor its appearance.

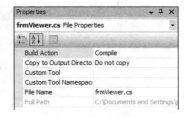

FIGURE 5.2
File properties
can be useful,
but they don't
allow you to do
much with the
form.

Displaying Text on a Form's Title Bar

You should always set the text in a form's title bar to something meaningful. (Note: Not all forms have title bars, as you'll see later in this hour.) The text displayed in the title bar is the value placed in the form's Text property. Generally, the text should be one of the following:

▶ **The name of the program**   This is most appropriate when the form is the program's main or only form. You used the name of the program for your main form when you defined it in Hour 1.

▶ **The purpose of the form**   This is perhaps the most common type of text displayed in a title bar. For example, if a form is used to select a printer, consider setting the Text property to **Select Printer**. When you take this approach, use active voice (for instance, don't use **Printer Select**).

▶ **The name of the form**   If you choose to place the name of the form into the form's title bar, use the English name, not the actual form name. For instance, if you've used a naming convention and named a form frmLogin, use the text **Login** or **Login User**.

Change the Text property of your form to **Picture Viewer Options**. Your form should now look like the one in Figure 5.3.

FIGURE 5.3
Use common sense when setting title bar text.

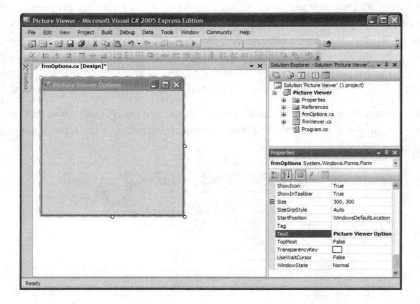

As with most other form properties, you can change the Text property at any time using Visual C# code.

Changing a Form's Background Color

Although most forms appear with a gray background (this is part of the standard 3D color scheme in Windows), you can change a form's background to any color you want. To change a form's background color, you change its BackColor property. The BackColor property is a unique property in that you can specify a named color or an RGB value in the format red, green, blue.

By default, the BackColor property is set to the color named Control. This color is a system color and might not be gray. When Windows is first installed, it's configured to a default color scheme. In the default scheme for all Windows versions other than XP, the color for forms and other objects is the familiar battleship gray. For XP installations, this color is a light tan (although it still looks gray on most monitors). As a Windows user, however, you're free to change any system color you want. For instance, some people with color blindness prefer to change their system colors to colors that have more contrast than the defaults so that objects are more clearly distinguishable. When you assign a system color to a form or control, the appearance of the object adjusts itself to the current user's system color scheme. This doesn't just occur when a form is first displayed; changes to the system color scheme are immediately propagated to all objects that use the affected colors.

> Try to use system colors whenever possible, to make your application behave as closely as possible to what the user expects and to avoid problems such as using colors that are indistinguishable from one another to someone who is color blind!

By the Way

Change the background color of your form to blue now by deleting the word *Control* in the BackColor property in the Properties window. In its place enter **0,0,255** and press Enter or Tab to commit your entry. When you commit the entry, the RGB value changes to the word *Blue*. If Visual C# has a named color that matches your RBG values, it automatically switches to the name for you.

Your form should now be blue because you entered an RGB value in which you specified no red, no green, and maximum blue (color values range from 0 to 255). In reality, you'll probably rarely enter RGB values. Instead, you'll select colors from color palettes. To view color palettes from which you can select a color for the BackColor property, click the drop-down arrow in the BackColor property in the Properties window (see Figure 5.4).

> System colors are discussed in detail in Hour 18, "Working with Graphics."

By the Way

FIGURE 5.4
All color proper-
ties have
palettes from
which you can
choose a color.

When the drop-down list appears, the color blue is selected on the Web tab. Again, this happens because when you enter the RGB value **0,0,255**, Visual C# looks for a named color composed of the same values and finds blue. The color palettes were explained in Hour 2, "Navigating Visual C# 2005," so I'm not going to go into detail about them here. For now, select the System tab to see a list of the available system colors and choose Control from the list to change the BackColor property of your form back to the default Windows color.

Adding an Image to a Form's Background

In addition to changing the color of a form's background, you can place a picture on it. To add a picture to a form, set the form's BackgroundImage property. When you add an image to a form, the image is painted on the form's background. All the controls that you place on the form appear on top of the picture.

Add an image to your form now by following these steps:

1. Click on the form to select it.

2. Change the Size property of the form to **400,300**.

3. Click the BackgroundImage property in the Properties window.

4. Click the Build button that appears next to the property (the small button with three dots).

5. The Select Resource dialog box appears (see Figure 5.5). Click the Local Resource option button.

6. Click Import and locate the file Options.bmp, which you can get from down-loading the example files from my website.

7. You are returned to the Select Resource dialog box. Click OK to load the picture. The selected image then is displayed on the form's background (see Figure 5.6).

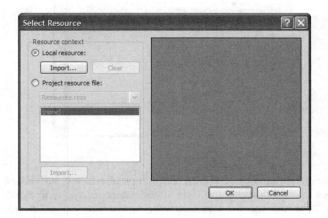

FIGURE 5.5
Images on your
hard drive are
considered local
resources.

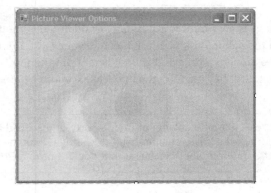

FIGURE 5.6
A form can dis-
play a picture,
just like a pic-
ture box.

If the image you select is smaller than the form, Visual C# displays additional copies of the picture, creating a tiled effect. The image you selected was specifically made to be the same size as the form, so you don't have to worry about this.

Notice that to the left of the BackgroundImage property in the Properties window is a small box containing a plus sign. This indicates that there are related properties, or *sub-properties*, of the BackgroundImage property. Click the plus sign now to expand the list of subproperties (see Figure 5.7). In the case of the BackgroundImage property, Visual C# shows you a number of properties related to the image assigned to the property, such as its dimensions and image format. Note that these subproperties are read-only (with the exception of the Tag property); not all subproperties are read-only.

FIGURE 5.7
The subproper-
ties show you
details about
the image.

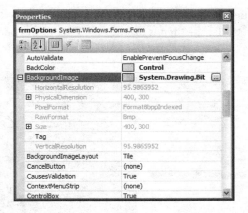

Adding a background image to a form can add pizzazz to a program, but it can also confuse users by making the form unnecessarily busy. Try to avoid adding images just because you can. Use discretion and add an image to a form only when the image adds value to the interface.

Removing an image from a form is just as easy as adding the image in the first place. To remove the picture that you just added to your form, right-click the BackgroundImage property name and choose Reset from the shortcut menu that appears. Feel free to try this, but load the image once again before continuing.

By the Way

You must right-click the Name column of the property or the Build button in the value column, but not the Value column itself. If you right-click the value of the property, you get a different shortcut menu that doesn't have a Reset option.

Giving a Form an Icon

The icon assigned to a form appears in the left side of the form's title bar, in the taskbar when the form is minimized, and in the iconic list of tasks when you press Alt+Tab to switch to another application, as well as other places. The icon often represents the application; therefore, you should assign an icon to any form that a user can minimize. If you don't assign an icon to a form, Visual C# supplies a default icon to represent the form when it's minimized. This default icon is generic, unattractive, and doesn't really represent anything—you should avoid it.

In the past, it was recommended that every form have a unique icon that represented the form's purpose. This proved difficult to accomplish in large applications containing dozens or even hundreds of forms. Instead, it's usually just best to set the Icon property of all your forms to the icon that best represents your application.

You assign an icon to a form in much the same way that you assign an image to the BackgroundImage property. Add an icon to your form now by clicking the form's Icon property in the Properties window, clicking the Build button that appears, and selecting an icon file from your hard drive (use the same icon you used in Hour 1). After you've selected the icon, it appears in the form's title bar to the left.

Adding Minimize, Maximize, and Control Box Buttons to a Form

Take a look at the title bar of the Picture Viewer Options form that you've created and notice that it has three buttons on it (see Figure 5.8).

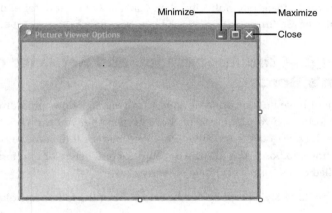

FIGURE 5.8
You control which, if any, of these buttons are displayed.

The three buttons in the form's title bar are

▶ Minimize

▶ Maximize

▶ Close

Also note that the form's icon acts as a button as well, but only while running the application, not in design mode. If the user clicks the icon, a drop-down menu appears with some basic options.

The Minimize and Maximize buttons make it easy for a user to quickly hide a form or make it fill the entire display, respectively. You've probably used these buttons on applications you work with. You'll be happy to know that you don't have to write code to implement this—it's handled automatically by Windows. All you have to do is decide whether you want a Maximize or Minimize button on a form. In the case of this Options form, the contents won't be resizable, so there's no need for a Maximize button. Also, you're going to want the user to close the form when they're finished with it, so there's no need for a Minimize button either. Remove these buttons now by setting the following properties of the form:

Property	Value
MinimizeBox	**False**
MaximizeBox	**False**

If you don't want the user to be able to close the form with the Close button (the button with the X in it in the upper-right corner of the form), you would set the ControlBox property to False. Be aware, however, that the minimize and maximize buttons are hidden automatically when `ControlBox` is set to false. If you want a Minimize or Maximize button, you have to set `ControlBox = True`.

Changing the Appearance and Behavior of a Form's Border

You might have noticed while working with other Windows programs that the borders of forms can vary. Some forms have borders that you can click and drag to change the size of the form, some have fixed borders that can't be changed, and still others have no borders at all. The appearance and behavior of a form's border is controlled by its FormBorderStyle property.

The FormBorderStyle property can be set to one of the following values:

- ▶ None
- ▶ FixedSingle
- ▶ Fixed3D
- ▶ FixedDialog
- ▶ Sizable
- ▶ FixedToolWindow
- ▶ SizableToolWindow

Run your project now by pressing F5, and move the mouse pointer over one of the borders of your main Picture Viewer form. This form has a sizable border, which means that you can resize the form by dragging the border. Move the pointer over an edge of the form and notice how the pointer changes from a large arrow to a line with arrows pointing on either side, indicating the direction you can stretch the border. When you move the pointer over a corner, you get a diagonal cursor that indicates that you can stretch both of the sides that meet at the corner. Clicking and dragging the border changes the size of the form.

Stop the project now by choosing Debug, Stop Debugging from the menu (or click the Close button on the form) and change the frmOptions form's FormBorderStyle property to **None** (you'll need to double-click frmOptions.cs in the Solution Explorer to display the form in the form designer again). Notice that the title bar disappears as well (see Figure 5.9). Of course, when the title bar is gone, there's no visible title bar text, no control box, and no Minimize or Maximize buttons. In addition, there's no way to move or resize the form. It's rarely appropriate to specify None for a form's BorderStyle, but if you need to do so (a splash screen comes to mind), Visual C# 2005 makes it possible.

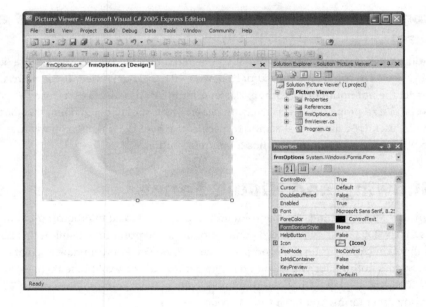

FIGURE 5.9
A form with no border also has no title bar.

Next, change the frmOptions form's FormBorderStyle property to FixedToolWindow. This setting causes the title bar of the form to appear smaller than normal and the text to display in a smaller font (see Figure 5.10). In addition, the only thing displayed on the title bar besides the text is a Close button. Visual C#'s various design windows, such as the Properties window and the toolbox, are good examples of tool windows.

FIGURE 5.10
A tool window is
a special win-
dow whose title
bar takes up
the minimum
space possible.

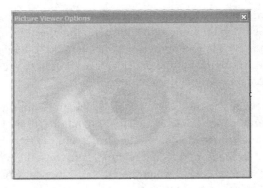

The FormBorderStyle is a good example of how changing a single property can greatly affect the look and behavior of an object.

Controlling the Minimum and Maximum Size of a Form

Ordinarily, if a form can be resized, it can be maximized to fill the user's entire display. The form can be minimized right down to the taskbar as well. If you want to restrict the minimum or maximum size of a form, set the `MinimumSize` or `MaximumSize` properties, respectively. In general, you should avoid doing this, but it can be useful. Be aware that setting a specific `MinimumSize` doesn't stop the user from minimizing the form, if it has a minimize button.

Showing and Hiding Forms

Part III, "Making Things Happen—Programming," is devoted to programming in Visual C# 2005, and I've avoided going into much programming detail in this hour so that you can focus on the concepts at hand. However, knowing how to create forms does nothing for you if you don't have a way to show and hide them. Visual C# 2005 can display a single form automatically only when a program starts. To display other forms, you have to write code.

Showing Forms

In Visual C# 2005, everything is an object, and objects are based on classes (see Hour 16, "Designing Objects Using Classes," for information on creating classes). Because the definition of a form is a class, you have to create a new Form object using the class as a template. In Hour 3, I discussed objects and object variables and these principles apply to creating forms.

As discussed in Hour 3, the process of creating an object from a class (template) is called instantiation. The syntax you'll use most often to instantiate a form is the following:

```
{ formclassname } {objectvariable} = new {formclassname()};
```

The parts of this declaration are as follows:

▶ *formclassname*   The name of the class that defines the form.

▶ *objectvariable*   The name for the form that you will use in code.

▶ *The keyword new*   Indicates that you want to instantiate a new object for the variable.

Last, you specify the name of the class used to derive the object—your form class. If you have a form class named frmLoginDialog, for example, you could create a new Form object using the following code:

```
frmLoginDialog frmLogin = new frmLoginDialog();
```

Thereafter, for as long as the object variable remains in scope (scope is discussed in Hour 11, "Using Constants, Data Types, Variables, and Arrays"), you can manipulate the Form object using the variable. For instance, to display the form, you call the Show() method of the form or set the Visible property of the form to true using code such as this:

```
frmLogin.Show();
```

or

```
frmLogin.Visible = true;
```

Follow these steps to enable the Picture Viewer project to show the Options form:

1. Display the main form by double-clicking frmViewer.cs in the Solution Explorer.

2. Add a new button to the frmViewer form by double-clicking the Button item on the toolbox. Set the button's properties as follows:

Property	Value
Name	**btnOptions**
Location	**301,156**
Size	**85, 23**
Text	**Options**

3. Double-click the button to access its Click event and enter the following code:

```
frmOptions frmOptionsDialog = new frmOptions();
frmOptionsDialog.Show();
```

The first statement creates a new object variable called frmOptionsDialog and instantiates an instance of the frmOptions form. The second statement uses the object variable (now holding a reference to a Form object) to display the form. Press F5 to run the project, and click the Options button. (If the button doesn't appear on the form, you might have accidentally added it to the wrong form.) When you click the button, a new instance of the second form is created and displayed. Move this form and click the button again. Each time you click the button, a new form is created. Stop the project now and click Save All on the toolbar.

Understanding Form Modality

You can present two types of forms to the user: modal and modeless forms. A *non-modal window* is one that doesn't cause other windows to be disabled (when you used Show( ) to display the Options form, you displayed it as a modeless form, which is why you were able to click over to the main Picture Viewer form while the Options form remained displayed). Another example of a modeless window is the Find and Replace window in Word (and in Visual C# 2005, as well). When the Find and Replace window is visible, the user can still access other Windows.

On the other hand, when a form is displayed as a modal form, all other forms in the same application become disabled until the modal form is closed; the other forms won't accept any keyboard or mouse input. The user is forced to deal with only the modal form. After the modal form is closed, the user is free to work with other visible forms within the program. If the form was displayed by another modal form, that form retains the focus until closed, and so on. Modal forms are most often used to create dialog boxes in which the user works with a specific set of data and controls before moving on. The Print dialog box of Microsoft Word, for example, is a modal dialog box. When the Print dialog box is displayed, you can't work with the document on the main Word window until the Print dialog box is closed. Most secondary windows in any given program are modal windows.

By the Way

You can display one modal form from another modal form, but you cannot display a modeless form from a modal form.

The modality of a form is determined by how you *show* the form rather than by how you *create* the form (both modal and nonmodal forms are created the same way).

You already learned that to show a form as a modeless window, you use the Show() method of the form. To show a form as a modal form, you call the form's ShowDialog() method instead. Display the form in the designer and then double-click the Options button to access its Click event. Next, change the code in your button's Click event to read:

```
frmOptions frmOptionsDialog = new frmOptions();

frmOptionsDialog.ShowDialog();
```

When your code looks like this, press F5 to run the project. Click the Options button to display your Options form. Drag the form away from the main form just a bit, and then try to click the main Picture Viewer form or some control on it; you can't. Close the modal form now by clicking the Close button in the title bar. Now, the main Picture Viewer form is enabled again, and you can click the Options button once more (or any other button of your choosing). When you're finished testing this, stop the running project.

You can test to see whether a form has been shown modally by testing the form's Modal property in code.

Specifying the Initial Display Position of a Form

The location on the display (monitor) where a form first appears isn't random, but rather it is controlled by the form's StartPosition property. The StartPosition property can be set to one of the values in Table 5.1.

TABLE 5.1 Values for the StartPosition Property

Value	Description
Manual	The value of the Location property at design time determines where the form first appears.
CenterScreen	The form appears centered in the display.
WindowsDefaultLocation	The form appears in the Windows default location, which is toward the upper left of the display.
WindowsDefaultBounds	The form appears in the Windows default location with its bounds (size) set to the Windows default bounds.
CenterParent	The form is centered within the bounds of its parent form (the initial form that displayed the form in question).

> It's generally best to set the StartPosition property of all your forms to
> CenterParent unless you have a specific reason to do otherwise. For the
> first form that appears in your project, you might consider using the
> WindowsDefaultLocation (but I generally prefer CenterScreen).

To see how this property affects a form, try this:

1. Press F5 to run the project.

2. Move the Picture Viewer form and click the Options button. Notice where the
   Options form appears.

3. Close the Options form.

4. Move the Picture Viewer form to the upper-right corner and click the Options
   button again.

Did you notice that the Options form always appears in the same location, regard-
less of where the Picture Viewer form is placed when the Options button is clicked?
I'm not fond of this behavior. Stop the running project now and change the
StartPosition of the Options form to CenterParent now. Next, repeat the previous
steps, and you'll see that the Options form always appears centered over the Picture
Viewer form, regardless of where that form is positioned.

Displaying a Form in a Normal, Maximized, or Minimized State

Using the Size and Location properties of a form in conjunction with the
StartPosition property enables you to display forms at any location and at any size.
You can also force a form to appear minimized or maximized. Whether a form is
maximized, minimized, or shown normally is known as the form's *state* and it's
determined by the WindowState property of the form.

Click the frmOptions.cs [Design] tab to view the form designer. Look at your form's
WindowState property now in the Properties window. New forms have their
WindowState property set to Normal by default. When you run the project, as you
have several times, the form displays in the same size as it appears in the form
designer and at the location specified by the form's Location property. Now change
the WindowState property to Minimized. Nothing happens in the Form Design view,
but run your project by pressing F5 and then click the Options button. At first, you
might think the form didn't get displayed, but it did. It just appeared minimized to
the taskbar.

Stop the project and change the WindowState property to Maximized. Again, nothing happens in the Form Design view. Press F5 to run the project and then click the Options button. This time, the Options form fills the screen. Notice too how the image is tiled to fill the form, as explained when you added the image to the form (see Figure 5.11).

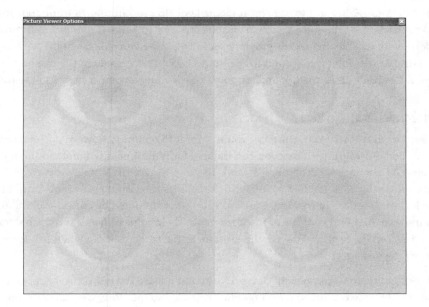

Picture Viewer Options

FIGURE 5.11
Images placed on a form are tiled if the BackgroundImageLayout property of the form is set to Tiled.

When a form is maximized, it fills the entire screen regardless of the current screen resolution being used in Windows.

By the Way

Stop the project and change the WindowState property back to **Normal**. You'll rarely set a form's WindowState property to Minimize at design time (though you might specify Maximize), but you'll probably encounter situations in which you need to change (or determine) the WindowState at runtime. As with most properties, you can accomplish this using code. For example, the following statement would minimize the Options form (but it would have to appear in the form's class):

```
frmOptionsDialog.WindowState = FormWindowState.Minimized;
```

You don't have to remember the names of the values when entering code; you'll get an IntelliSense drop-down list when you type the equal sign.

Stop the project now and save your work.

Preventing a Form from Appearing in the Taskbar

Being able to display an icon for a minimized form is nice, but sometimes it's necessary to prevent a form from even appearing in the taskbar. If your application has a number of tool windows that float over a main window, such as the Solutions Explorer and Toolbox in Visual C# 2005 for example, it's unlikely that you'd want any but your main form to appear in the taskbar. To prevent a form from appearing in the taskbar, set the form's ShowInTaskbar property to False. If the user minimizes a form with its ShowInTaskbar property set to False, she can still get to the window by pressing Alt+Tab even though the program can't be accessed via the taskbar; Visual C# won't allow the application to become completely inaccessible to the user.

Unloading Forms

After a form has served its purpose, you'll want it to go away. However, *go away* can mean one of two things. First, you can make a form disappear without closing it or freeing its resources (this is called *hiding*). To do so, you set its Visible property to false or use the Hide method of the form. This hides the visual part of the form, but the form still resides in memory and can still be manipulated by code. In addition, all the variables and controls of the form retain their values when a form is hidden, so if the form is displayed again, the form looks the same as it did when its Visible property was set to False.

The second method completely closes a form and release the resources it consumes. You should close a form when it's no longer needed so that Windows can reclaim all resources used by the form. To do so, you invoke the Close method of the form like this:

```
this.Close();
```

In Hour 3 you learned how this is used to reference the current Form object. Because this represents the current Form object, you can manipulate properties and call methods of the current form using this. (this.Visible = false;, and so forth).

The Close() method tells Visual C# not to simply hide the form but to destroy it—*completely*.

Follow these steps to create a button to close the Options form:

1. Select the frmOptions.cs [Design] tab to display the form designer for the Options form (if it isn't displayed already).

2. Add a new button to the form and set its properties as follows:

Property	Value
Name	**btnOK**
Location	**305,12**
Text	**OK**

3. Next, double-click the OK button in the designer to access its Click event and then enter the following statement:

```
this.Close();
```

4. Finally, run the project by pressing F5. Click the Options button to display the Options form and then click OK to close the Options form. Again, the form isn't just hidden; the form is completely unloaded from memory and no longer exists.

If you simply wanted to hide a form, but not unload it from memory, you would call the Hide() method of the form or set the form's Visible property to False. This would preserve the state of the form for the time you choose to show it again (by setting it's Visible property to True or by using a method to display the form).

By the Way

Summary

In this hour, you learned the basics of creating forms. You learned how to add them to your project, set basic appearance properties, and show and hide them using Visual C# code. In the next hour, you'll learn more advanced functionality for working with forms. After you've mastered the material in this hour and in the next hour, you'll be ready to dig into Visual C#'s controls—that's where the fun of building an interface *really* begins!

Q&A

Q. *How many form properties should I define at design time as opposed to runtime?*

A. You should set all properties that you can at design time. First, it'll be easier to work with the form because you can see exactly what the user will see. Also, debugging is easier because there's less code.

Q. *Should I let the user minimize and maximize all forms?*

A. Probably not. First, there's no point in letting a form be maximized if the form isn't set up to adjust its controls accordingly. About forms, print dialog boxes, and spell check windows are examples of forms that should not be resizable.

Workshop

The Workshop is designed to help you anticipate possible questions, review what you've learned, and get you thinking about how to put your knowledge into practice.

Quiz

1. True or False: The text displayed in the form's title bar is determined by the value in the TitleBarText property.

2. The named color Control is what kind of color?

3. Name three places where a form's icon is displayed.

4. A window with a smaller than normal title bar is called a what?

5. For a Minimize or Maximize button to be visible on a form, what other element must be visible?

6. What, in general, is the best value to use for the StartPosition property of a form?

7. To maximize, minimize, or restore a form in code, you set what property?

8. What property do you set to make a hidden form appear?

Answers

1. False. The text displayed in the form's title bar is determined by the value in the form's Text property.

2. A system color.

3. In the title bar, on the task bar, and when the user presses Alt+Tab.

4. Tool window.

5. The ControlBox property of the form must be set to True.

6. CenterScreen for the main form and CenterParent for all other forms.

7. The form's WindowState property.

8. Set the form's Visible property to True.

Exercises

1. Create a Windows Application project with a single form that has two buttons on it. One button, when clicked, should move the form to the left by two pixels. The other should move the form to the right by two pixels. Hint: Use the X and Y subproperties of the Location property.

2. Create a Windows Application with three forms. Give the startup form two buttons. Make the other two forms tool windows, and make one button display the first tool window and the other button display the second tool window.

HOUR 6

Building Forms—Advanced Techniques

What You'll Learn in This Hour:

▶ Adding controls to a form
▶ Positioning, aligning, sizing, spacing, and anchoring controls
▶ Creating intelligent tab orders
▶ Adjusting the z-order of controls
▶ Creating transparent forms
▶ Creating forms that always float over other forms
▶ Creating Multiple Document Interfaces

A form is just a canvas, and although you can tailor a form by setting its properties, you'll need to add controls to it to make it functional. In the previous hour, you learned how to add forms to a project, set basic form properties, and show and hide forms. In this hour, you'll learn all about adding controls to a form, including arranging and aligning controls to create an attractive and functional interface. You'll also learn how to create advanced multiple document interfaces (MDIs) as used in applications such as Photoshop. After you complete the material in this hour, you'll be ready to learn the details about the various controls available in Visual C#.

Working with Controls

Controls are the objects that you place on a form for users to interact with. If you've followed the examples in the previous hours, you've already added controls to a form. However, you'll be adding a lot of controls to forms, and it's important for you to understand all aspects of the process. After you learn about forms in this hour, the next two hours will teach you the ins and outs of the powerful controls provided by Visual C#.

Adding Controls to a Form

All the controls that you can add to a form can be found in the toolbox. The toolbox appears as a docked window on the left side of the design environment by default. This location is useful when you're only occasionally adding controls to forms. However, when doing serious form-design work, I find it best to dock the toolbox to the right edge of the design environment, where it doesn't overlap so much (if any) of the form I'm working with.

> Remember that before you can undock a toolbar to move it to a new location, you must make sure that it isn't set to Auto Hide.

There are category headings in the toolbox that you can expand and collapse. For most of your design, you'll use the controls in the Common Controls category. As your skills progress, however, you might find yourself using more complex and highly specialized controls found in the other categories.

You can add a control to a form in four ways, and you're now going to use three primary methods (you've already used the forth, which is to paste a copy of a control onto a form). Open the Picture Viewer project you created in the previous hour (or open the starting project provided at my website) and double-click frmOptions.cs in the Solution Explorer window to view the Options form in the designer.

Adding a Control by Double-Clicking It in the Toolbox

The easiest way to add a control to a form is to double-click the control in the toolbox. Try this now: Display the toolbox and double-click the TextBox tool. Visual C# creates a new text box in the upper-left corner of the form (you'll have to move the mouse away from the toolbox to close the toolbox and see the new control). When you double-click a control in the toolbox (excluding controls that are invisible at runtime), Visual C# creates the new control on top of the control that currently has the focus, with the default size for the type of control you're adding. If no other controls are on the form, the new control is placed in the upper-left corner as you've seen here. After the control is added to the form, you're free to move and size the text box as you please. A text box cannot be resized unless its Multiline property is set to True. Set it to True now.

Adding a Control by Dragging from the Toolbox

If you want a little more authority over where a new control is placed, you can drag a control to the form. Try this now: Display the toolbox, click the Button control, and drag it to the form. When the cursor is roughly where you want the button created, release the mouse button.

Adding a Control by Drawing It

The last and most precise method of placing a control on a form is to draw the control on a form. Follow these steps:

1. Display the toolbox and click the ListBox tool *once* to select it.

2. Move the pointer to where you want the upper-left corner of the list box to appear and then click and hold the mouse button.

3. Drag the pointer to where you want the bottom-right corner of the list box to be and release the button.

The list box is created with its dimensions set to the rectangle you drew on the form. This is by far the most precise method of adding controls to a form.

If you prefer to draw controls on your forms by clicking and dragging, I *strongly* suggest that you float the toolbox or dock it to the right or bottom edge of the design environment. The toolbox interferes with drawing controls when it's docked to the left edge and set to Auto Hide because it obscures a good bit of the underlying form.

Did you Know?

It's important to note that the first item in each tool category is titled Pointer. Pointer isn't actually a control. When the pointer item is selected, the design environment is placed in Select mode rather than in a mode to create a new control. With the pointer chosen, you can select a control and view its properties simply by clicking it in the designer. This is the default behavior of the development environment.

Manipulating Controls

Getting controls on a form is the easy part. Arranging them so that they create an intuitive and attractive interface is the challenge. Interface possibilities are nearly endless, so I can't tell you how to design any given interface here (though I strongly suggest you create forms that closely match the appearance and behavior of similar commercial applications). I can, however, show you the techniques to move, size, and arrange controls so that they appear the way *you* want them to. By mastering these techniques, you'll be much more efficient at building interfaces, freeing your time for writing the code that makes things happen.

Using the Grid (Size and Snap)

You may have noticed as you worked with controls so far in this book that controls seem to "snap" to an invisible grid. You're not crazy—they actually do. When you draw or move a control on a form in a project with grids enabled (which they are by default in Visual C# 2005), the coordinates of the control automatically snap to the nearest grid coordinate. This offers some precision when adjusting the size and location of controls. In practical use, I often find the grid to be only slightly helpful because the size or location I want often doesn't fit neatly with the grid locations. You can, however, control the granularity and even the visibility of the grid, and I suggest you do both.

Grid settings are global to Visual C# 2005—you don't set them for each individual project or form. To display the grid settings on your computer, choose Tools, Options from the menu to display the Options form. Next, select the checkbox named Show all settings, and then click Windows Form Designer in the tree on the left to view the designer settings (see Figure 6.1).

FIGURE 6.1
Grid settings
are global to
Visual C# 2005.

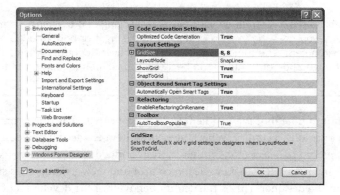

The settings we're interested in here are

▶ GridSize   This determines the granularity of the grid in pixels both horizontally and vertically. A smaller grid size means that you have finer control over control size and placement.

▶ ShowGrid This determines whether grid dots are displayed on forms in the designer.

▶ SnapToGrid This determines whether the grid is used. If this setting is false, the grid size setting is ignored, and nothing is snapped to the grid.

▶ LayoutMode Determines whether the designer snaps a control you are moving to the grid or aligns it with other controls.

Right now, you're not using the grid for drawing controls, but you are using snap lines when moving controls because your LayoutMode is set to SnapLines. I'll talk about this in more detail later in this section. Right now, I want to show you how grids work, so change your LayoutMode setting to SnapToGrid.

You're now going to assign a higher level of granularity to the grid (the space between the grid points will be smaller). I find that this helps with design because edges aren't so easily snapped to unwanted places.

To adjust the granularity of the grid, you change the GridSize setting. Setting the Width or Height of the grid to a smaller number creates a more precise grid, which allows for finer control over sizing and placement, whereas using larger values creates a much coarser grid and offers less control. With a larger grid, you'll find that edges snap to grid points much easier and at larger increments, making it impossible to fine-tune the size or position of a control. Follow these steps:

1. Change the GridSize property to **4,4**.

2. Change the ShowGrid property to **True**.

3. Click OK to save your changes and return to the form designer. Notice that grid dots now appear (see Figure 6.2). Note: There is a bug in the initial release that prevents the grid from appearing. If you can't see the grid, close down Visual C# and then restart it—the grid will then appear. Microsoft has acknowledged this problem, but they have not committed to changing the behavior.

Try dragging the controls on your form or dragging their edges to size them (leave the OK button alone). Notice that you have more control over the placement with the finer grid. Try changing the GridSize to a set of higher numbers, such as **25,25** and see what happens. When you're finished experimenting, change the GridSize values back to **4,4**. If you have a list box on your form, you might notice that the list box won't resize perfectly to match the grid. This is because the list box always retains a height that allows full rows of data to be displayed. It will go close the grid, but might not align perfectly with it.

FIGURE 6.2
Grids don't have
to be visible to
be active.

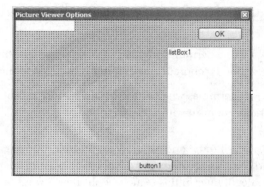

An unfortunate side effect of a smaller grid is that the grid can become distracting. Again, you'll decide what you like best, but I generally turn the grids off on my forms. In fact, I prefer the new Snap to Lines feature discussed next.

> The ShowGrid property determines *only* whether the grid is drawn, not whether it's active; whether a grid is active is determined by the form's SnapToGrid property.

Using Snap Lines

A new and useful feature is the Snap to Lines layout feature. Tell Visual C# to use Snap to Lines now by following these steps:

1. Choose Tools, Options from the menu to display the Options dialog box.

2. Click Windows Forms Designer to display the layout settings.

3. Change the LayoutMode property to **SnapToLines**.

4. Turn off the grid by setting the ShowGrid property to **False**.

5. Click OK to save your settings. You may need to close the form designer and then double-click the form in the Solution Explorer to redisplay the form with the grid.

Snap lines is a feature designed to help you create better interfaces faster by "snapping" control edges to imaginary lines along the edges of other controls. The easiest way to understand this is to try it.

Follow these steps:

1. Drag your controls so that they are roughly in the position of Figure 6.3.

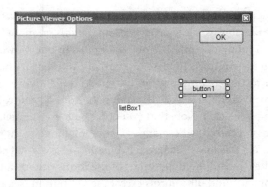

FIGURE 6.3
Start from this layout.

2. Click the ListBox to select it.

3. Click on the white square that appears on the right edge of the control and drag it to the right. As the edge nears vertical alignment with the button above it, a snap line will appear, and the edge will "snap" to the line (see Figure 6.4). If you don't see this behavior, restart Visual C# and reload the project.

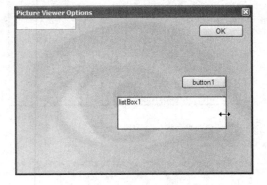

FIGURE 6.4
Snap lines makes it easy to align the edges of controls.

You're free to continue dragging the edge, and as you do so Visual C# creates more snap lines as you near vertical alignment with other controls. Controls also support horizontal snap lines, and all snap lines work when dragging a control as well. This may seem like a small feature to you now, but trust me when I say this is a great addition to Visual C# and will save you many tedious hours over time.

Selecting a Group of Controls

As your skills increase, you'll find your forms becoming increasingly complex. Some forms might contain dozens, or even hundreds, of controls. Visual C# has a set of features that make it easy to align groups of controls.

By default, clicking a control on a form selects it while *simultaneously* deselecting any controls that were previously selected. To perform actions on more than one control, you need to select a group of controls. You can do this in one of two ways, the first of which is to *lasso* the controls. To lasso a group of controls, you first click and drag the mouse pointer anywhere on the form. As you drag the mouse, a rectangle is drawn on the form. When you release the mouse button, all controls intersected by the rectangle become selected. Note that you don't have to completely surround a control with the lasso (also called a *marquee*), you only have to intersect part of the control to select it. Try this now: Click somewhere in the lower-left corner of the form and drag the pointer toward the upper-right of the form without releasing the button. Intersect or surround all controls *except* the OK button (see Figure 6.5). When the rectangle has surrounded or intersected all the controls, release the button, and the controls will be selected (see Figure 6.6).

FIGURE 6.5
Click and drag to create a selection rectangle.

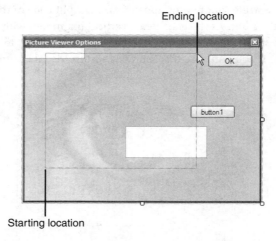

FIGURE 6.6
All selected controls appear with a dotted border and sizing handles (rectangles).

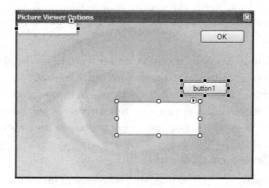

When a control is selected, it has a dotted border and a number of sizing handles (squares located in the dotted border at the corners and midpoints of the control). Pay careful attention to the sizing handles. The control with the white sizing handles is the active control in the selected group. When you use Visual C#'s tools to work on a group of selected controls (such as the alignment and formatting tools), the values of the active control are used. For example, if you were to align the left side of the selected controls shown in Figure 6.6, each of the controls would have its Left property value set to that of the active control (the control with the white handles). When you use the lasso technique to select a group of controls, you really don't have much influence over which control Visual C# makes the active control. Deselect all the controls now by clicking anywhere on the form (don't click on a control.

> Not all sizing handles are movable at all times. For example, Visual C# won't allow you to change the height of the text box until you set the Multiline property of a text box to **True**, so only the sizing handles at the left and right edges are the only ones available when the control is selected.

By the Way

The second technique for selecting multiple controls is to use the Shift or Ctrl key while clicking controls (either can be used to the same effect). This method is much like selecting multiple files in Explorer. Follow these steps:

1. Click the bottom control (the list box) to select it. (When only one control is selected, it's considered the active control.)

2. Next, hold down the Shift key and click the text box in the upper-left corner; the list box and text box are now selected. The list box is the active control because it is the first control you clicked on when selecting this group. Again, when more than one control is selected, the active control has its sizing handles set to white so that you can identify it.

3. Finally, with the Shift key still pressed, click the button control (not the OK button) to add it to the group of selected controls. All the controls should now be selected, and the list box should be the active control.

> Clicking a selected control while holding down the Shift key deselects the control.

By the Way

You can combine the two selection techniques when needed. For instance, you could first lasso all controls to select them. If you happened to select a control that you don't want in the group, simply hold down the Shift key and click that control to deselect it.

Did you
Know?

If you must click the same control twice, such as to deselect and then reselect it, do so s-l-o-w-l-y. If you click too fast, Visual C# interprets your actions as a double-click and creates a new event handler for the control.

Aligning Controls

Visual C# includes a number of formatting tools you can use to design attractive interfaces. Most of these are accessed using the Layout toolbar. Display the Layout toolbar now by right-clicking a toolbar at the top of Visual C# and choose Layout from the shortcut menu that appears (if it appears checked, then it is already visible). The Layout toolbar includes options for aligning controls horizontally and vertically to the controls' edges or centers (see Figure 6.7).

FIGURE 6.7
The Layout toolbar makes it quick and easy to align controls.

Slowly move your pointer over the buttons on this toolbar to read their Tooltips—move from left to right. Notice that with this toolbar you can

▶ Align the left edge, middle, or right edge of selected controls.

▶ Align the top edge, middle, or bottom edge of selected controls.

▶ Make the selected controls the same width, height, or both.

▶ Make horizontal or vertical spacing between the selected controls nice and even.

▶ Move layering of the selected controls backward or forward.

▶ Set a Tab Order for the controls.

The first item simply aligns the selected controls to the grid—not much fun there. However, the remainder of the buttons are very useful. Remember that Visual C# uses the active control as its baseline when performing alignment. This is important. Click the Align Tops button now and notice that the selected controls are now aligned with the active control (see Figure 6.8).

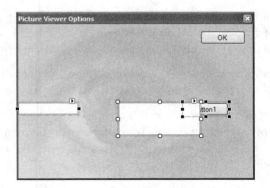

FIGURE 6.8
The selected
control is used
as the baseline
when aligning
groups of
selected con-
trols.

Making Controls the Same Size

In addition to aligning controls, you can also make all selected controls the same size—height, width, or both. To do this, use the Make Same Size button on the toolbar. Make all your controls the same size now by clicking the Make the Same Size button. This makes the selected controls the same size as the list box (rather large). Now try this: In the Properties window, enter **75,25** in the Size property and press Tab to commit the entry. Notice that your change affects all the selected controls. Having the Properties window affect all selected controls like this makes it easy to quickly modify a number of controls that need to share property values, and I talk about this in a little more detail shortly.

Evenly Spacing a Group of Controls

As many a salesman has said, "…and that's not all!" You can also make the spacing between controls uniform using the Layout toolbar. Try this now: Click the Make Horizontal Spacing Equal button on the toolbar. All the controls are now evenly spaced. Next, click the Decrease Horizontal Spacing button on the toolbar a few times and notice how the spacing between the controls decreases slightly with each click. You can also increase the horizontal or vertical spacing or completely remove spacing from between controls using buttons on the Layout toolbar. Save your project now by clicking the Save All button on the toolbar.

Setting Property Values for a Group of Controls

The following is a technique that many experienced Visual C# developers seem to overlook: You can change a property value in the Properties window when multiple controls are selected. This causes the corresponding property to change for all selected controls.

Make sure that all three controls are still selected and then display the Properties window (if it's not already displayed). When a group of controls is selected, the Properties window appears with some modifications (see Figure 6.9):

▶ No Name property is shown. This occurs because you're not allowed to have two controls with the same name, so Visual C# won't let you even try.

▶ Only properties shared by all controls are displayed. Because you have selected controls of different types, only a small subset of common properties are available. If you selected controls all of the same type, you'd see more properties available.

▶ For properties where the values of the selected controls differ (such as the Location property in this example), the value is left empty in the Properties window.

Entering a value in a property changes the corresponding property for *all* selected controls. To see how this works, change the BackColor property to a shade of yellow, and you'll see that all controls have their BackColor set to yellow.

FIGURE 6.9
You can view the property values of many controls at once, with some caveats.

You're not going to actually use the three controls you've been experimenting with so far in this chapter, so press the Delete key on your keyboard now to delete all the selected controls.

Anchoring and Autosizing Controls

Some of my favorite additions to the new forms engine in Visual C# 2005 are the capability to anchor controls to one or more edges of a form and the capability for controls to size themselves appropriately when the user sizes a form. In the past, you had to use a (usually cumbersome) third-party component or resort to writing code in the form Resize event to get this behavior, but it's an intrinsic capability of Visual C# 2005's form engine.

The default behavior of all new controls is that controls are docked to the top and left edges of their containers. What if you want a control to always appear in the upper-right corner or lower-left corner of a form? You're now going to learn how to anchor controls so that they adapt accordingly when the form is resized.

Follow theses steps:

1. Double-click the form frmViewer.cs in the Solutions Explorer window. This is the form you'll be modifying.

2. Press F5 to run the project.

3. Drag the lower-right corner of the form to make the form bigger. Notice that the controls don't follow the edge of the form (see Figure 6.10).

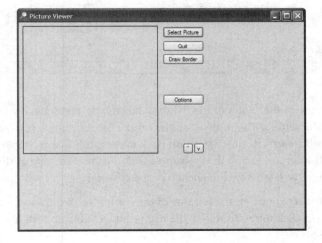

FIGURE 6.10
By default, controls are anchored to the top-left corner of the form.

4. Stop the running project now by choosing Debug, Stop Debugging from the menu.

5. Click the Select Picture button to select it and, more importantly, deselect the form.

6. Hold down the Shift key and click on the following additional buttons: Quit, Draw Border, Options, ^, and v.

7. Next, click the Anchor property in the Properties window, and then click the drop-down arrow that appears. You'll see a drop-down box that's unique to the Anchor property (see Figure 6.11).

FIGURE 6.11
You use this
unique drop-
down box to set
the Anchor
property of a
control.

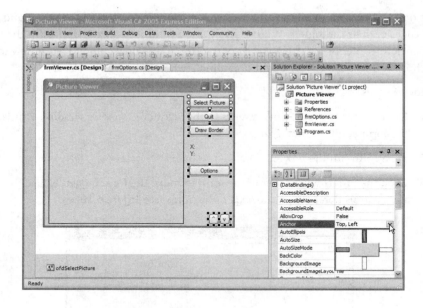

The gray square in the center of the the drop-down box represents the control whose property you're setting. The thin rectangles on the top, bottom, left, and right represent the possible edges to which you can dock the control; if a rectangle is filled in, the edge of the control facing that rectangle is docked to that edge of the form. Follow these steps to see how the Anchor property works:

1. Click the rectangle on the left side of the control so that it's no longer filled in, and then click the rectangle to the right of the control so that it is filled in (see Figure 6.12).

2. Click any other property to close the drop-down box. The Anchor property should now read Top, Right.

3. Press F5 to run the project, and then drag an edge of the form to make it larger.

Pretty interesting, huh? What Visual C# has done is anchored the right edge of the buttons to the right edge of the form (see Figure 6.13). Really, anchoring means keeping an edge of the control a constant, relative distance from an edge of the form, and it's an *unbelievably powerful* tool for building interfaces.

Notice that the picture box and the coordinate labels still retain their original locations when the form is resized. No problem—you can address that with the Anchor property as well. Start by changing the anchoring of the X and Y labels by following these steps:

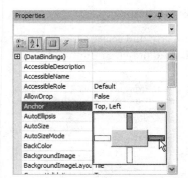

FIGURE 6.12
This setting anchors the controls to the top and right edges of the form.

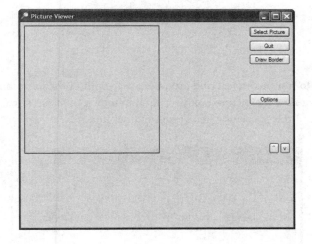

FIGURE 6.13
Anchoring is a powerful feature for creating adaptable forms.

1. Stop the running project and then click the X label on the form designer to select it.

2. Hold down the Shift key and click the Y label to select it.

3. Set the Anchor property the same as you did for the buttons—deselect the left side and select the right side (refer to Figure 6.12).

4. Click any other property to close the Anchor drop-down box.

Now the picture box is a bit a different thebeast from the other controls in that you want the top and left anchored the way they are now, but you want the right and bottom edge to grow and shrink with the form. This is actually easy to accomplish. Follow these steps:

1. Click the picture box to select it.

2. Open the Anchor property and select all four anchor points (all four rectangles should be filled with solid gray (see Figure 6.14).

FIGURE 6.14
This setting will anchor the control relative to all four sides of the form.

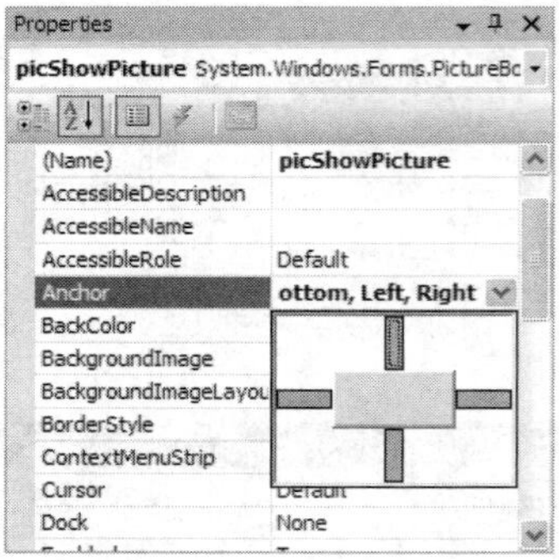

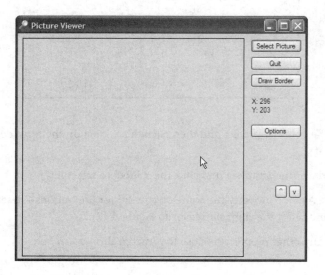

Now press F5 to run the project and drag the lower-right of the form to make it bigger. Notice that now the picture box sizes itself to match the form size (see Figure 6.15). You'll find this is useful when viewing larger images.

FIGURE 6.15
Proper use of the Anchor property allows you to build flexible forms.

Now that you know how to use the Anchor property, you can make forms that users can resize with no code. One caveat: Depending on its Anchor setting, a control might disappear if the form is shrunk quite small.

Creating a Tab Order

Tab order is something often (emphasis on *often*) overlooked by even seasoned Visual C# programmers. You're probably familiar with tab order as a user, although you might not realize it. When you press Tab while on a form, the focus moves from the current control to the next control in the tab order. This enables easy keyboard navigation on forms. The tab order for controls on a form is determined by the TabIndex properties of the controls. The control with the TabIndex value of 0 is the first control that receives the focus when the form first displays. When you press Tab, the control with the TabIndex of 1 receives the focus, and so on. When you add a control to a form, Visual C# assigns the next available TabIndex value to the new control (it will be last in the tab order). Each control has a unique TabIndex value, and TabIndex values are always used in ascending order.

If the tab order isn't set correctly for a form, pressing Tab causes the focus to jump from control to control in no apparent order. This is a great way to frustrate a user. In the past, the only way to change the tab order for controls on a form was to manually change the TabIndex values using the Properties window. For instance, to make a control the first control in the tab order, you would change its TabIndex property to 0; Visual C# would then bump the values of all other controls accordingly. This was often a painful process—believe me. Although it can be handy to set a TabIndex property manually, such as when you want to insert a control into an existing tab sequence, there is a much better way to set the tab order of forms.

Press F5 to run the project now (if its not already running) and notice that the Select Picture button has the focus (it's highlighted by a blue rectangle). If you press Enter now, the button would be "clicked" because it has the focus. Now, press Tab, and the Quit button has the focus. This is because you added the Quit button to the form right after you added the Select picture button. Press Tab once more. Did you expect the Draw Border button to get the focus? So would a user. Instead, the ^ button receives the focus because it was the next control you added to the form. You're about to fix that, so stop the project now by closing the form.

You're now going to set the tab order of the form via the visual method of .NET:

1. The last button on the Layout toolbar is the Tab Order button. Click it now and notice how Visual C# superimposes a set of numbers over the controls (see Figure 6.16). The number on a control indicates its TabIndex property value. Now it's easy to see that the tab order is incorrect.

2. Click the Select Picture button. The background of the number changes from blue to white to show that you selected the control. Had this control had a TabIndex value other than 0, it would have been changed to 0 when you clicked it.

3. Click the Quit button to designate it as the next button on the tab order.

4. Currently, the Draw Border button is fifth in the tab order. Click it now and the number changes to 2.

5. Click the remaining controls in the following order: X label, Y label, Options button, ^ button, and v button.

6. When you click the last button, all numbers change back to a blue background; the tab order is now set. Click the Tab Order button once more on the Layout toolbar to take the designer out of Tab Order mode.

7. Press F5 to run the project once again and you'll see that pressing Tab now moves the focus logically.

FIGURE 6.16
The numbers over each control indicate the control's TabIndex.

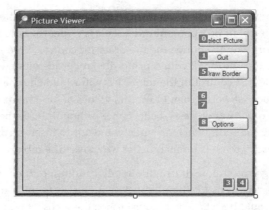

You can programmatically move the focus via the tab order by calling the SelectNextControl() method of a control or a form.

To remove a control from the tab sequence, set its TabStop property to False. When a control's TabStop property is set to False, users can still select the control with the mouse, but they can't enter the control using the Tab key. You should still set the TabIndex property to a logical value so that if the control receives the focus (such as by being clicked), pressing Tab moves the focus to the next logical control.

Layering Controls (Z-Order)

Tab order and visual alignment are key elements for effectively placing controls on forms. However, these two elements address control placement in only two dimensions—the *x,y* axis. Although it's rare that you'll need to do so, at times, you might need to have controls overlap. Whenever two controls overlap, whichever control is added to the form most recently appears on top of the other. You can control the ordering of controls using the Bring to Front or Send to Back buttons found on the right side of the Layout toolbar.

You can move a control forward or backward using code by invoking the
`BringToFront` or `SendToBack()` methods of the control.

Did you Know?

Creating Topmost Nonmodal Windows

As you're probably aware, when you click a window it usually comes to the fore-ground, and all other windows are shown behind it (unless it's a modal window). At times, you might want a window to stay on top of other windows, regardless of whether it's the current window (that is, it has the focus). An example of this is the Find window in Visual C# and other applications such as Word. Regardless of which window has the focus, the Find form always appears floating over all other win-dows. Such a window is created by setting the form's `TopMost` property to True. Not exactly rocket science, but that's the point: A simple property change or method call is often all it takes to accomplish what might otherwise seem to be a difficult task.

Creating Transparent Forms

A new property of forms that I think is very cool is the `Opacity` property. This prop-erty controls the opaqueness of the form as well as all controls on the form. The default Opacity value of 100% means that the form and its controls are completely opaque (solid), whereas a value of 0% creates a completely transparent form (no real point in that). A value of 50% then, creates a form that's between solid and invisible as shown in Figure 6.17. Microsoft Outlook 2003 and newer makes good use of opacity in its alerts that pop up to tell you when you've received an email. The Opacity of these alerts is cycled from 0 to 100, left at 100 for a short time, and then cycled back down to 0 as it disappears. You can do this in your program using a simple loop as discussed in Hour 14, "Looping for Efficiency."

FIGURE 6.17
Ghost forms!

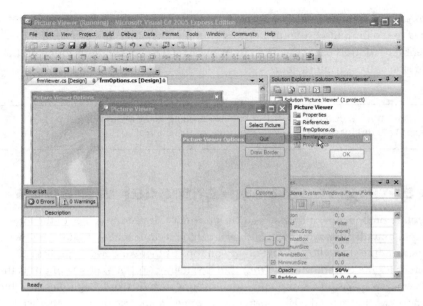

Creating Scrollable Forms

A *scrollable form* is one that can display scrollbars when its contents are larger than the physical size of the form. Earlier versions of the Visual C# form engine lacked the capability to create scrollable forms. It seems odd that this has never been possible before, and I'm personally happy to see this feature added. Not only is this a great feature, it's also trivial to implement in your own applications.

The scrolling behavior of a form is determined by the following three properties:

Property	Description
AutoScroll	This property determines whether scrollbars will ever appear on a form.
AutoScrollMinSize	The minimum size of the scroll region (area). If the size of the form is adjusted so that the client area of the form (the area of the form not counting borders and title bar) is smaller than the AutoScrollMinSize, scrollbars will appear.
AutoScrollMargin	This property determines the margin given around controls during scrolling. This essentially determines how far past the edge of the outermost controls you can scroll.

Press F5 to run your project now and size the form smaller than it is by dragging the lower-right corner toward the upper-left. Notice that, although the controls adjust themselves the best they can, some controls disappear from view completely as the form gets smaller. The only way you can access these controls is to make the form bigger again—unless you make this form a scrollable form.

Follow these steps:

1. If the project is still running, stop it now.

2. Set the AutoScroll property of the frmViewer.cs form to True.

3. Press F5 to run the project.

4. Drag the lower-right corner of the form toward the upper-left to make the form smaller. Notice that as you do so, a scrollbar appears on the form (see Figure 6.18). You can use the scrollbar to scroll the contents of the form and access controls that would otherwise be unavailable.

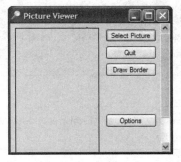

FIGURE 6.18
Without scroll-bars, it's possible to have controls that can't be seen.

Stop the project now and save your work.

Creating MDI Forms

All the projects you've created so far have been single document interface (SDI) projects. In SDI programs, every form in the application is a peer of all other forms; no intrinsic hierarchy exists between forms. Visual C# also lets you create multiple document interface (MDI) programs. An MDI program contains one parent window (also called a *container*) and one or more child windows. A classic example of an MDI program is Adobe Photoshop. When you run Photoshop, a single parent window appears. Within this parent window, you can open any number of documents, each appearing in its own child window. In an MDI program, all child windows share the same toolbar and menu bar, which appears on the parent window.

One restriction of child windows is that they can exist only within the confines of the parent window. Figure 6.19 shows an example of Photoshop running with a number of child document windows open.

FIGURE 6.19
Le Collage! MDI applications consist of a single parent window and one or more child windows.

> MDI applications can have any number of normal windows (dialog boxes, for example) in addition to child windows.

You're now going to create a simple MDI project. Follow these steps to create the project:

1. Choose File, New Project from the menu to display the New Project dialog box (note how this is a modal form).

2. Enter the name **MDI Example** and click OK to create the project.

3. Right-click Form1.cs in the Solutions Explorer window and choose Rename from the shortcut menu. Change the name of the form to **fclsMDIParent.cs**. Next, change the form's Text property to **MDI Parent,** and change its IsMdiContainer property to **True**. (If you don't set the IsMdiContainer property to True, this example won't work.)

    The first thing you'll notice is that Visual C# changed the client area to a dark gray and gave it a sunken appearance. This is the standard appearance for MDI parent windows, and all visible child windows appear in this area.

4. Create a new form by choosing Project, Add Windows Form from the menu. Name the form **fclsChild1.cs** and change its Text property to **Child 1**.

5. Add a third form to the project in the same way. Name it **fclsChild2.cs** and set its Text property to **Child 2**.

6. Click Save All on the toolbar.

7. Double-click fclsMDIParent.cs in the Solution Explorer to show the parent window in the designer.

8. Next, double-click the form to access its default event—the Load event. Enter the following code:

```
fclsChild1 objChild = new fclsChild1();
objChild.MdiParent = this;
objChild.Show();
```

By now, you should know what the first and last statements do: The first statement instantiates a new object whose type is fclsChild1. The last statement shows the form nonmodally. What we're interested in here is the second statement. It sets the MdiParent property of the form to the current form (this always references the current object), which is an MDI parent form because its IsMdiContainer property is set to True. When the new form is displayed, it's shown as an MDI child.

Press F5 to run the project now and notice how the child form appears on the client area of the parent form. If you size the parent form so that one or more child windows can't fully be displayed, scrollbars appear (see Figure 6.20). If you were to remove the statement that set the MdiParent property, the form would simply appear floating over the parent form (because it wouldn't be a child) and therefore wouldn't be bound by the confines of the parent.

Stop the project by choosing Debug, Stop Debugging from the menu and follow these steps:

1. Display the Solution Explorer, and double-click the fclsChild1 form to display it in the designer.

2. Add a button to the form and set the button's properties as follows:

Property	Value
Name	**btnShowChild2**
Location	**105,100**
Size	**85,23**
Text	**Show Child 2**

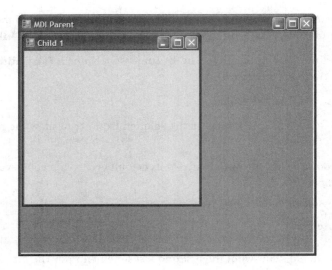

3. Double-click the button to access its Click event, and then add the following
code:

```
fclsChild2 objChild = new fclsChild2();
objChild.MdiParent = this.MdiParent;
objChild.Show();
```

This code shows the second child form. Note that differences exist between this
code and the code you entered earlier. You can't set the second child's
MdiParent property to this because this refers to the current form
(fclsChild1, which is not an MDI container). However, you know that
this.MDIParent references the parent form of a child because this is precisely
the property you set to make the form a child in the first place. Therefore, you
can simply pass the parent of the first child to the second child, and they'll
both be children of the same form.

Any form can be a child form (except, of course, an MDI parent form). To make a
form a child form, set its MDIParent property to a form that's defined as an MDI
container.

4. Press F5 to run the project now. You'll see the button on the child form, so go
ahead and click it (if you don't see the button, you might have mistakenly
added it to the second child form). When you click the button, the second
child form appears. Notice how this is also bound by the constraints of the
parent form (see Figure 6.21).

The MDI parent form has an `ActiveMdiChild` property, which you can use to get a reference to the currently active child window.

Did you Know?

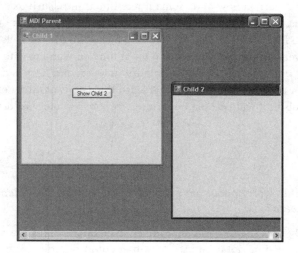

FIGURE 6.21
Child forms are peers with one another.

To make the parent form larger when the project is first run, you would set the `Size.Height` and `Size.Width` properties of the form either at design time or at runtime in the Load event of the form.

By the Way

One thing to keep in mind about forms is that you can create as many instances of a form as you want. Managing multiple instances of the same form gets tricky, however, and is beyond the scope of this book.

If MDI forms still confuse you, don't worry. Most of the applications you'll write as a new Visual C# programmer will be SDI programs. As you become more familiar with creating Visual C# projects in general, start experimenting with MDI projects. Remember, you don't have to make a program an MDI program simply because you can; make an MDI program if the requirements of the project dictate that you do so.

Summary

Understanding forms is critical because forms are the dynamic canvases on which you build your user interface. If you don't know how to work with forms, your entire application will suffer. Many things about working with forms go beyond simply setting properties, especially as you begin to think about the end user. As your experience grows, you'll get into the groove of form design, and things will become second nature to you.

In this hour, you learned how to do some interesting things, such as creating transparent forms, as well as some high-end techniques, such as building an MDI application. You also learned how to create scrolling forms (an interface element that shouldn't be overlooked), and you spent a lot of time on working with controls on forms, which is important because the primary function of a form is as a place to host controls. In the next two hours, you'll learn the details of many of Visual C#'s powerful controls that will become important weapons in your vast development arsenal.

Q&A

Q. *Do I need to worry about the anchoring and scrolling capabilities of every form I create?*

A. Absolutely not. The majority of forms in most applications are dialog boxes. A dialog box is a modal form used to gather data from the user. A dialog box is usually of a fixed size, which means that its border style is set to a style that can't be sized. With a fixed-size form, you don't need to worry about anchoring or scrolling.

Q. *How do I know whether a project is a candidate for an MDI interface?*

A. If the program will open many instances of the same type of form, it's a candidate for an MDI interface. For example, if you're creating an image-editing program and the intent is to enable the user to open many images at once, MDI makes sense. Also, if you'll have many forms that will share a common toolbar and menu, you might want to consider MDI.

Workshop

The Workshop is designed to help you anticipate possible questions, review what you've learned, and get you thinking about how to put your knowledge into practice.

Quiz

1. True or False: The first control selected in a series is always made the active control.

2. How many methods are there to add a control to a form from the toolbox?

3. If you double-click a tool in the toolbox, where on the form is it placed?

4. Which property fixes an edge of a control to an edge of a form?

5. What do you change to hide the grid on a form?

6. Which toolbar contains the functions for spacing and aligning controls?

7. Which property do you set to make a form an MDI parent?

Answers

1. True.

2. There are four primary methods: double-click a tool in the toolbox, drag a tool from the toolbox, clicking a tool in the toolbox and then drawing it on a form, and copying and pasting a control.

3. The control is placed over the currently selected control, or in the upper-left corner if no control is selected.

4. The Anchor property.

5. The ShowGrid property found on the Options dialog box.

6. The Layout toolbar.

7. You set the IsMdiContainer property to True to make a form an MDI parent.

Exercises

1. Create a new Windows Application and add a button to the middle of the form. Experiment with different values for the button's Anchor property, running the project in between property changes.

2. Modify the MDI Example project in this hour so that the first child that appears is fclsChild2, which in turns shows fclsChild1.

HOUR 7

Working with Traditional Controls

What You'll Learn in This Hour:

▶ Displaying static text with the Label control
▶ Allowing users to enter text using a text box
▶ Creating password fields
▶ Working with buttons
▶ Using panels, group boxes, check boxes, and option buttons
▶ Displaying lists with list boxes and combo boxes

The previous two hours described how to work with forms in considerable detail. Forms are the foundation of a user interface but are pretty much useless by themselves. To create a functional interface, you need to use *controls*. Controls are the various widgets and doo-dads on a form with which users interact. Dozens of different types of controls exist, from the simple Label control used to display static text to the more complicated Tree View control used to present trees of data like those found in Explorer. In this hour, I'll introduce you to the most common (and simple) controls, which I call *traditional* controls. In Hour 8, "Using Advanced Controls," you'll learn about the more advanced controls that you can use to create professional-level interfaces.

Displaying Static Text with the Label Control

Label controls are used to display static text to the user. By *static*, I mean that the user can't change the text directly (but you can change the text with code). Label controls are one of the most commonly used controls, and, fortunately, they're also one of the easiest.

Labels are most often used to provide descriptive text for other controls, such as text boxes. Labels are also great for providing status-type information to a user, as well as for providing general instructions on a form.

You're going to build on the Picture Viewer project from Hour 6, "Building Forms—Advanced Techniques," for most of this hour. Although you'll be adding the controls to the interface, you won't be making them functional until you progress into the chapters on writing code.

Start by following these steps:

1. Open the Picture Viewer you worked on in Hour 6.

2. Double-click frmOptions.cs in the Solution Explorer window to display the Options form in the designer.

3. Add a new Label control to the form by double-clicking the Label item in the toolbox. The primary property of the Label control is the Text property, which determines the text displayed to the user. When a Label control is first added to a form, the Text property is set to the name of the control—this isn't very useful. Set the properties of the new Label control as follows:

Property	Value
Name	**lblUserName**
Location	**40,41**
Text	**User Name:**

Notice how the label resized automatically to fit your text. This is a new feature to Visual C# 2005. To create a multiline label, you would click in the Text property to display a drop-down arrow and then click the arrow to access a text entry box. You could then enter text and separate the lines by pressing Enter. In most cases, it's best to place label text on a single line, but it's nice to have the option.

Another interesting aspect of the label control is that a label can have an associated hot-key. A hotkey appears as an underlined character in the label's text, as in First Name:. When the user presses the Alt key in conjunction with the hot-key (Alt+F in this example), the focus is moved to the next control in the tab order *after* the label. To assign a hot-key to a label, you preface the hot-key in the label's Text property with an ampersand (&). For example, to create the F hot-key for the First Name label, you would enter the following into the Text property of the label: **&First Name:**.

Allowing Users to Enter Text Using a Text Box

A Label control is usually the best control for displaying text that a user can't change. However, when you need to enable users to enter or edit text, the text box is the tool for the job. If you've ever typed information on a form, you've almost certainly used a text box. Add a new text box to your form now by double-clicking the TextBox item in the toolbox. Set the text box's properties as follows:

Property	Value
Name	**txtUserName**
Location	**105,38**
Size	**139,20**

In previous versions of Visual C#, a new text box's Text property was always set to its default name. This required that you manually change the Text property for every new text box you added to a form. Fortunately, Microsoft changed this behavior, and you don't have to muck with the Text property unless you want to. Your form should now look like Figure 7.1.

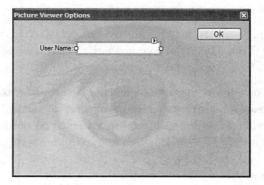

Although you'll leave the Text property of a text box empty 99% of the time, certain aspects of the text box are easier to understand when a text box contains text. For now, set the text box's Text property to **This is sample text**. Remember to press Enter or Tab to commit your property change.

Specifying Text Alignment

Both the Text Box and the Label control have a TextAlign property (as do many other controls). The TextAlign property determines the alignment of the text within the control—much like the justification setting in a word processor. You can select from Left, Center, and Right.

Follow these steps to see how the `TextAlign` property works:

1. Change the `TextAlign` property of the text box to Right, and see how the text becomes right-aligned within the text box.

2. Next, change `TextAlign` to Center to see what center alignment looks like. As you can see, this property is pretty straightforward.

3. Finally, change the `TextAlign` property back to Left before continuing.

Creating a Multiline Text Box

Hour 6, I talked about the sizing handles of a selected control. I mentioned how handles that can be sized are filled with white. If a corner or edge can't be resized, then no handle will appear at that corner or edge. Notice how only the left and right edges of the text box have white sizing handles. This means that you can adjust only the left and right edges of the control (you can alter only the width, not the height). This is because the text box is defined as a single-line text box, meaning that it will display only one line of text. What would be the point of a really tall text box that showed only a single line of text?

To allow a text box to display multiple lines of text, set its `Multiline` property to True. Set the `Multiline` property of your text box to **True** now, and notice how all the sizing handles for adjusting the height become visible.

Change the `Text` property of the text box to **This is sample text. A multiline text box will wrap its contents as necessary.** Press Enter or Tab to commit the property change. Notice how the text box displays only part of what you entered because the control simply isn't big enough to show all the text (see Figure 7.2). Change the `Size` property to **139,52**, and you'll then see the entire contents of the text box (see Figure 7.3).

There will be times when you won't want a user to be able to interact with a control. For example, you might implement a security model in an application, and if the user doesn't have the necessary privileges, you might not want the user to be able to alter data. The `Enabled` property, which almost every control has, determines whether the user can interact with the control. Change the `Enabled` property of the text box to **False** now, press F5 to run the project, and click Options to show the Options form. Although no noticeable change occurred in the control in Design view, there's a big change to the control at runtime: The text appears in gray rather than black, and the text box won't accept the focus or allow you to change the text (see Figure 7.4).

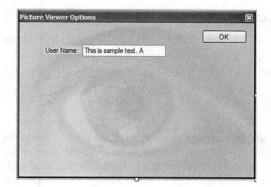

FIGURE 7.2
A text box might contain more text than it can display.

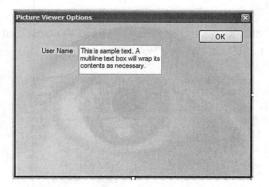

FIGURE 7.3
A multiline text box can be sized as large as necessary.

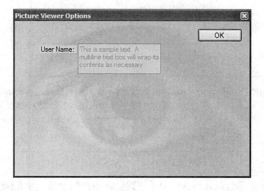

FIGURE 7.4
You can't interact with a text box whose Enabled property is set to False.

Stop the project now by choosing Debug, Stop Debugging from the menu, and then change the control's Enabled property back to **true**.

Adding Scrollbars

Even though you can size a multiline text box, there still will be times when the contents of the control are more than can be displayed. If you believe that this is a possibility for a text box you're adding to a form, give the text box scrollbars by changing the ScrollBars property from None to Vertical, Horizontal, or Both.

By the Way

> For a text box to display scrollbars, its Multiline property *must* be set to True. Also, if you set the ScrollBars property to both, the horizontal scrollbar won't appear unless you also set the WordWrap property to False. If you set WordWrap equal to True, text will always wrap to fit the control, so there will never be any text off to the right of the text box, and no need for a horizontal scroll bar.

Change the ScrollBars property of your text box to **Vertical** and notice how scrollbars appear in the text box (see Figure 7.5).

FIGURE 7.5
If a text box might contain a lot of text, give it a scrollbar.

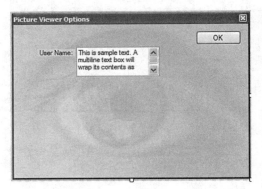

By the Way

> If you set a text box's AcceptReturn property to True, the user can press Enter to create a new line in the text box. When the AcceptTabs property is set to True, the user can press Tab within the control to create columns (rather than moving the focus to the next control).

Limiting the Number of Characters a User Can Enter

You can limit the number of characters a user can type into a text box by using the MaxLength property. All new text boxes are given the default value of 32767 for MaxLength, but you can change this as needed. To see how this works, follow these steps:

1. Change the text box's properties as follows:

Property	Value
Text	(make empty)
MaxLength	**10**
Multiline	**False**
ScrollBars	**None**

2. Press F5 to run the project.

3. Click the Options button to display the Options form.

4. Enter the following text into the new text box: **So you run and you run**. Be sure to try and enter more than 10 characters of text—you can't. All that you're allowed to enter is **So you run** (10 characters). The text box allows only 10 characters, whether that's via entry using the keyboard or a Paste operation. The MaxLength property is most often used when the text box's content is to be written to a database, in which field sizes are usually restricted. (Using a database is discussed in Hour 21, "Working with a Database.")

5. Stop the project now and change the MaxLength property of the text box to **0**, which effectively means there is no maximum defined.

Now would be a good time to save your work.

Creating Password Fields

You've probably used a password field: a text box that displays an asterisk for each character entered. Any text box can be made a password field by assigning a character to its PasswordChar property. Select the PasswordChar property of the text box now and enter an asterisk (*) for the property value. Run the project once more and display the Options form. Next, enter text into the text box. Now an asterisk is displayed for each character you enter (see Figure 7.6). Although the user doesn't see the actual text contained in the text box, referencing the Text property in code always returns the True text.

> A text box displays password characters only if its Multiline property is set to False.

By the Way

Stop the project by choosing Debug, Stop Debugging from the menu. Delete the asterisk from the PasswordChar field and then save the project by clicking Save All on the toolbar.

FIGURE 7.6
A password field displays its password character for all entered text.

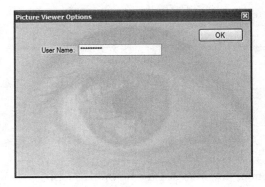

Understanding the Text Box's Common Events

You'll rarely use the label's events, but you'll probably use text box events quite a bit. The text box supports many different events; Table 7.1 lists the events you're most likely to use regularly.

TABLE 7.1   Commonly Used Events of the Text Box Control

Event	Description
TextChanged	Occurs every time the user presses a key. Use this event to deal with specific keypresses (such as capturing specific keys) or when you need to perform an action whenever the contents changes.
Click	Occurs when the user clicks the text box. Use this event to capture clicks when you don't care about the coordinates of the mouse pointer.
MouseDown	Occurs when the user first presses down a mouse button over the text box. This event is often used in conjunction with the MouseUp event.
MouseUp	Occurs when the user releases a mouse button over the text box. Use MouseDown and MouseUp when you need more functionality than provided by the Click event.
MouseMove	Occurs when the user moves the mouse over the text box. Use this event to perform actions based on the movement of the cursor.
KeyDown	Occurs when a key is pressed while the control has the focus.
KeyUp	Occurs when a key is released while the control has the focus.
KeyPress	Occurs when a key is pressed while the control has the focus. Occurs between the KeyDown and the KeyUp events.

Creating Buttons

Every dialog box that Windows displays has at least one button on it. Buttons enable a user to invoke a function with a click of the mouse.

You already have an OK button on the form. Typically, an OK button accepts the user's values and closes the form. Later in the coding section you'll make your OK button do just that. When you have an OK button, it's also a good idea to create a Cancel button, which unloads the form but doesn't save the user's values.

Add a new button to the form by double-clicking the Button item in the toolbox. Set the button's properties as follows:

Property	Value
Name	**btnCancel**
Location	**304,38**
Text	**Cancel**

There's no point in having a button that doesn't do anything, so double-click the button now to access its Click event, and then add the following statement:

```
this.Close();
```

Recall from Hour 5, "Building Forms—The Basics," that this statement closes the current form. Right now, the Cancel button does the same thing as the OK button, but you'll change that soon.

> You can programmatically trigger a button's Click event, just as though a user clicked it, by calling the button's PerformClick method.

 Did you Know?

Accept and Cancel Buttons

When creating dialog boxes, it's common to assign one button as the default button (called the Accept button). If a form has an Accept button, that button's Click event is fired when the user presses Enter, regardless of which control has the focus. This is great for dialog boxes in which the user enters some text and presses Enter to commit the data and close the form.

Follow these steps to designate the OK button as the Accept button:

1. Double-click frmOptions.cs in the Solution Explorer Window to show the form in the designer once more.

2. Click the form to display its properties in the Properties window.

3. Click the `AcceptButton` property of the form in the Properties window, and a drop-down arrow appears. Click the arrow and choose the button btnOK from the list. Notice that the button now has a blue border on the form, indicating that it is the default button for the form (see Figure 7.7).

FIGURE 7.7
Only one button
can be defined
as a form's
Accept button.

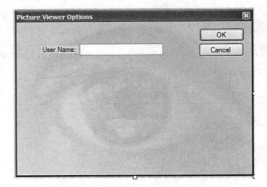

4. Press F5 to run the project and then click Options to display the Options form.

5. Click in the text box to make sure that it has the focus and then press Enter; the form closes. Again, pressing Enter on a form that has a designated Accept button causes that button's `Click` event to fire the same as if the user clicked it with the mouse, regardless of which control has the focus. Actually, there is one exception to this. If the control with the focus is a multiline text box with its AcceptsReturns property set to True, pressing Enter will create a new line in the text box and won't cause the Accept button's click even to fire.

Generally, when you create an Accept button for a form, you should also create a Cancel button. A Cancel button fires its `Click` event when the user presses the Esc key (as opposed to the Enter key), regardless of which control has the focus. Generally, you place code in a Cancel button to shut down the form without committing any changes made by the user. Make your Cancel button an official Cancel button by following these steps:

1. Stop the running project.

2. Change the form's `CancelButton` property to **btnCancel**.

Use the following hints when deciding what buttons to assign as the Accept and Cancel buttons of a form:

▶ If a form has an OK or Close button, chances are good that button should be assigned as the AcceptButton.

▶ If a form has both an OK and a Cancel button, assign the OK button as the AcceptButton and the Cancel button as the CancelButton (yeah, this is pretty obvious, but it's often overlooked).

▶ If a form has a single Close or OK button, assign it to both the `AcceptButton` and `CancelButton` properties of the form.

▶ If the form has a Cancel button, assign it to the `CancelButton` property of the form.

Presenting Yes/No Options Using Check Boxes

A check box is used to display True/False and Yes/No values on a form, and you've probably run into many of them as you've worked with different Windows applications. Clicking the check box control toggles it between checked and unchecked (True/false, yes/no, and so on).

Add a new check box to the Options form now and set its properties as follows:

Property	Value
Name	**chkPromptOnExit**
Location	**105,79**
Text	**Prompt to confirm on exit**

The `CheckState` property of the check box determines whether the check box is checked. Try changing the value of this property and watch the effect on the form. Notice that you can set the check box's `CheckState` to Indeterminate, which shows a big square in the control. You won't often need to use this, but it's good to know the feature is available. Be sure to set the CheckState to Unchecked before continuing.

Your form should now look like Figure 7.8.

FIGURE 7.8
Use the check box to indicate a True/false or yes/no state.

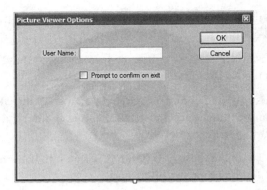

Creating Containers and Groups of Option Buttons

In this section, you'll learn how to create containers for groups of controls using panels and group boxes. You'll also learn how to use the Option Button control in conjunction with these container controls to present multiple choices to a user.

Using Panels and Group Boxes

Controls can be placed on a form because the form is a *container* object—an object that can host controls. A form isn't the only type of container, however. Some controls act as containers as well, and a container can host one or more other containers. The Panel and Group Box controls are both container controls that serve a similar purpose, yet each is more suited to a particular application.

For the most part, the Panel control is a slimmed-down version of the Group Box control, so I won't discuss the Panel in depth. If you need a basic container control without the additional features offered by the Group Box control (such as a border and caption), use the Panel control. The primary exception to this is that the panel offers scrolling capabilities just like those found on forms, which group boxes do not support.

The Group Box is a container control with properties that let you create a border, called a *frame*, and caption. Add a new group box to your form now by double-clicking the GroupBox item in the toolbox (you'll find it in the Containers control category). When you create a new group box, it has a border by default, and its caption is set to the name of the control.

Try clicking in the center of the group box and dragging it around like you would another type of control: You can't. Think of the group box like a mini form—you can't click and drag a form to move it around. Clicking and dragging on a group box would allow you to lasso any controls placed on the group box—the same behavior you experience on a form. To drag a group box, click and drag the little image with the four arrows on it (see Figure 7.9).

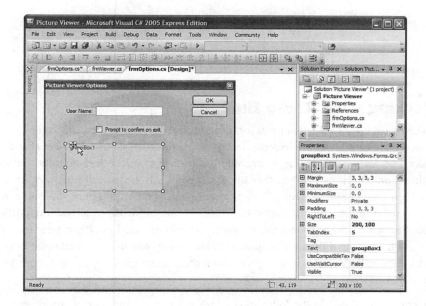

FIGURE 7.9
Click and drag this box to move a group box.

Set the properties of the group box as follows:

Property	Value
Name	**grpDefaultBackcolor**
Location	**105,112**
Size	**200,72**
Text	**Default Picture Background Color**

Your group box should now look like the one in Figure 7.10.

The Group Box is a fairly straightforward control. Other than defining a border and displaying a caption, the purpose of a group box is to provide a container for other controls. The next section, "Working with Radio Buttons," demonstrates the benefits of using a group box as a container.

FIGURE 7.10
A group box
acts like a form
within a form.

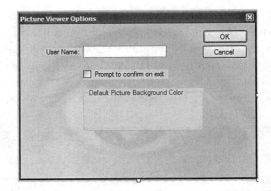

Working with Radio Buttons

Check boxes are excellent controls for displaying True/false and yes/no values. However, check boxes work independently of one another; if you have five check boxes on a form, each one of them could be checked or unchecked—in any combination. Radio buttons, on the other hand, are mutually exclusive to the container on which they're placed. This means that only one radio button per container can be selected at a time. Selecting one radio button automatically deselects any other radio buttons on the same container. Radio buttons are used to offer a selection of items to a user when the user is allowed to select only one item. To better see how mutual exclusivity works, you're going to create a small group of radio buttons for your Options form.

You can perform any of the following actions to place a control on a group box:

▶ Draw the control directly on the group box.

▶ Drop the control on the group box.

▶ Add the control to the form, cut the control from the form, select the group box, and paste the control on the group box.

You're going to use the second method: dropping a new control directly on the group box. Follow these steps:

1. Click the RadioButton item in the toolbox and drag it to the group box.

2. Release the mouse when you're over the group box.

3. Move the radio button around by clicking and dragging it. Don't drag the radio button off of the container, or it will be moved to the new container or form over which it is placed when you release the mouse.

Set the properties of the radio button as follows:

Property	Value
Name	**optBackgroundDefault**
Checked	**True**
Location	**6,19**
Text	**Default Gray**

Note that the Location property is always in reference to the container object. If the control is on a form, it's relative to the upper-left corner of the form. If the control is on a group box, the location is relative to the upper-left corner of the group box, etc. You're now going to copy this radio button and paste a copy of the control on the group box:

1. Right-click the radio button and choose Copy from its context menu.

2. Click the group box to select it.

3. Right-click the group box, and choose Paste from its context menu to create a new radio button. Set the properties of the radio button as follows:

Property	Value
Name	**optBackgroundWhite**
Checked	**False**
Location	**6,42**
Text	**White**

You might notice that both radio buttons appear selected in the designer. At run-time, only one of them will appear selected.

Now that you have your two radio buttons (see Figure 7.11), run the project by pressing F5.

Click the Options button to display your Options form and take a look at the radio buttons. The first radio button is selected, so click the second radio button (White) and notice how the first radio button becomes deselected automatically (its Checked property is set to False). Two radio buttons are sufficient to demonstrate mutual exclusivity, but be aware that you could add as many radio buttons to the group box as you want to and the behavior would be the same.

The important thing to remember is that mutual exclusivity is shared only by radio buttons *placed on the same container*. To create radio buttons that behave independently of one another, you would need to create a second set on another container.

You could easily create a new group box (or panel for that matter) and place the second set of radio buttons on the new container. The two sets of radio buttons would behave independently of one another, but mutual exclusivity would still exist among the buttons within each set.

FIGURE 7.11
Radio buttons
restrict a user
to selecting a
single item.

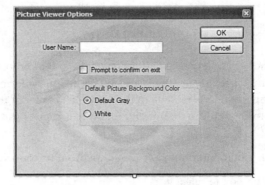

Stop the running project and save your work.

Displaying a List with the List Box

A list box is used to present a list of items to a user. You can add items to, and remove items from, the list at any time with very little Visual C# code. In addition, you can set up a list box so that a user can select only a single item or multiple items. When a list box contains more items than it can show due to the size of the control, scrollbars are automatically displayed.

By the
Way

> The cousin of the list box is the combo box, which looks like a text box with a down-arrow button at its right side. Clicking a combo box's button causes the control to display a drop-down list box. Working with the list of a combo box is pretty much identical to working with a list box, so I'll discuss the details of list manipulation in this section and then discuss the features specific to the combo box in the next section.

You're not going to be adding a list box or combo box to your Picture Viewer project at this time, so follow these steps to create a new project:

1. Create a new Windows Application project titled **Lists**.

2. Right-click Form1.cs in the Solution Explorer, choose Rename, and then change the name of the default form to **fclsLists.cs** and set its Text property to **Lists Example**.

3. Add a new List Box control to the form by double-clicking the ListBox item in the toolbox and then set the properties of the list box as follows:

Property	Value
Name	**lstPinkFloydAlbums**
Location	**64,21**
Size	**160,121**

Every item contained in a list box is a member of the list box's *Items* collection. Working with items, including adding and removing items, is performed using the Items collection. You'll most often manipulate the Items collection using code (which I'll show you a little later in this hour), but you can also work with the collection at design time by using the Properties window.

Manipulating Items at Design Time

The Items collection is available as a property of the list box. Locate the `Items` property in the Properties window and click it to select it. The familiar button with three dots appears, indicating that you can do advanced things with this property. Click the button now to show the String Collection Editor. To add items to the collection, simply enter the items into the text box—one item to a line.

Enter the following items:

- ▶ **Atom Heart Mother**
- ▶ **A Saucerful of Secrets**
- ▶ **Wish You Were Here**
- ▶ **Animals**
- ▶ **Echoes**
- ▶ **Meddle**

When you're finished, your screen should look like that shown in Figure 7.12. Click OK to commit your entries and close the window. Notice that the list box contains the items that you entered.

Manipulating Items at Runtime

In Hour 3, "Understanding Objects and Collections," you learned about objects, properties, methods, and collections. All this knowledge comes into play when manipulating lists at runtime. The `Items` property of a list box (and a combo box, for that matter) is an object property that returns a collection (collections in many ways are like objects—they have properties and methods). To manipulate list items, you manipulate the Items collection.

FIGURE 7.12
Use this dialog box to manipulate an Items collection at design time.

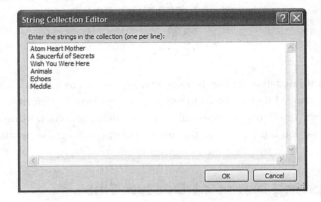

A list can contain duplicate values, as you'll see in this example. Because of this, Visual C# 2005 needs a mechanism other than an item's text to treat each item in a list as unique. This is done by assigning each item in an Items collection a unique index. The first item in the list has an index of 0, the second an index of 1, and so on. The index is the ordinal position of an item relative to the first item in the Items collection—*not* the first item visible in the list.

Adding Items to a List

New items are added to the Items collection using the Add() method of the Items collection. You're now going to create a button that adds an album to the list. Add a new button to the form and set its properties as follows:

Property	Value
Name	**btnAddItem**
Location	**95,148**
Size	**96,23**
Text	**Add an Item**

Double-click the button to access its Click event and add the following code:

```
lstPinkFloydAlbums.Items.Add("Dark Side of the Moon");
```

Notice that the Add() method accepts a string argument—the text to add to the list.

By the
Way

Unlike items added at design time, items added through code aren't preserved when the program ends.

Press F5 to run the project now and click the button. When you do, the new album is added to the bottom of the list. Clicking the button a second time adds another item to the list with the same album name. The list box doesn't care whether the item already exists in the list; each call to the Add() method of the Items collection adds a new item to the list.

The Add() method of the Items collection can be called as a function, in which case it returns the index (ordinal position of the newly added item in the underlying collection), as in the following:

```
int intIndex;

intIndex = lstPinkFloydAlbums.Items.Add("Dark Side of the Moon");
```

Knowing the index of an item can be useful, as you will see.

Stop the running project and save your work before continuing.

Did you
Know?

To add an item to an Items collection at a specific location in the list, use the Insert() method. The Insert() method accepts an index in addition to text. For example, to add an item at the top of the list you could use a statement such as lstPinkFloydAlbums.Items.Insert(0,"Dark Side of the Moon");. Remember, the first item in the list has an index of 0.

Removing Items from a List

Removing an individual item from a list is as easy as adding an item and requires only a single method call: a call to the Remove() method of the Items collection. The Remove method accepts a string, which is the text of the item to remove. You're now going to create a button that removes an item from the list.

Display the form designer now and create a new button on the form. Set the button's properties as follows:

Property	Value
Name	**btnRemoveItem**
Location	**95,177**
Size	**96,23**
Text	**Remove an Item**

Double-click the new button to access its Click event and enter the following statement:

```
lstPinkFloydAlbums.Items.Remove("Dark Side of the Moon");
```

The Remove() method tells Visual C# to search the Items collection, starting at the first item (index = 0), and to remove the first item found that matches the specified text. Remember, you can have multiple items with the same text. The Remove() method removes only the first occurrence. After the text is found and removed, Visual C# stops looking.

Press F5 to run the project again. Click the Add an Item button a few times to add *Dark Side of the Moon* to the list (see Figure 7.13). Next, click the Remove an Item button and notice how Visual C# finds and removes one instance of the specified album.

FIGURE 7.13
The list box can contain duplicate entries, but each entry is a unique item in the Items collection.

 To remove an item at a specific index, use the RemoveAt() method. For example, to remove the first item in the list, you would use the following statement: lstPinkFloydAlbums.Items.RemoveAt(0);.

Stop the running project and save your work.

Clearing a List

To completely clear the contents of a list box, use the Clear() method. You're now going to add a button to the form that, when clicked, clears the list. Add a new button to the form and set the button's properties as follows:

Property	Value
Name	**btnClearList**
Location	**95,206**
Size	**96,23**
Text	**Clear List**

Double-click the new button to access its `Click` event and enter the following statement:

```
lstPinkFloydAlbums.Items.Clear();
```

Press F5 to run the project, and then click the Clear List button. The `Clear()` method doesn't care whether an item was added at design time or runtime; `Clear()` always removes all items from the list. Stop the project and again save your work.

Remember that the `Add()`, `Insert()`, `Remove()`, `RemoveAt()`, and `Clear()` methods are all methods of the Items collection, not of the list box itself. If you forget that these are members of the Items collection, you might be confused when you don't find them when you enter a period after typing a list box's name in code.

Retrieving Information About the Selected Item in a List

Two properties provide information about the selected item: `SelectedItem` and `SelectedIndex`. It's important to note that these are properties of the list box itself, not of the Items collection of a list box. The `SelectedItem` method returns the text of the currently selected item. If no item is selected, the method returns an empty string. It is sometimes desirable to know the index of the selected item. This is obtained using the `SelectedIndex` property of the list box. As you know, the first item in a list has the index of 0. If no item is selected, `SelectedIndex` returns –1, which is never a valid index for an item.

You're now going to add a button to the form that, when clicked, displays the selected item's text and index in a message box. Add a new button to the form and set its properties as follows:

Property	Value
Name	**btnShowItem**
Location	**95,235**
Size	**96,23**
Text	**Show Selected**

Double-click the new button to access its `Click` event and enter the following statement (be sure to press Enter at the end of the first line):

```
MessageBox.Show("You selected " + lstPinkFloydAlbums.SelectedItem +

    " which has an index of " + lstPinkFloydAlbums.SelectedIndex);
```

`MessageBox.Show()` is a Visual C# function used to show a message to the user. You'll learn about `MessageBox.Show()` in detail in Hour 17, "Interacting with Users."

Press F5 to run the project and click the Show Selected button. Notice that because nothing is selected, the message box doesn't read quite right, and it says that the selected index is -1 (which indicates nothing is selected). Click an item in the list to select it, and then click Show Selected again. This time, you'll see the text of the selected item and its index in the message box. Stop the running project and save your work.

> You can set up a list box to allow multiple items to be selected at once. To do this, you change the `SelectionMode` property of the list box to MultiSimple (clicking an item toggles its selected state) or MultiExtended (you have to hold down Ctrl or Shift to select multiple items). To determine which items are selected in a multiselection list box, use the list box's SelectedItems collection.

Sorting a List

List boxes and combo boxes have a `Sorted` property. This property is set to False when a control is first created. Changing this property value to True causes Visual C# to sort the contents of the list alphabetically. When the contents of a list are sorted, the index of each item in the Items collection is changed; therefore, you can't use an index value obtained prior to setting Sorted to True.

`Sorted` is a property, not a method. Realize that you don't have to call Sorted to sort the contents of a list; Visual C# enforces a sort order as long as the `Sorted` property is set to True. This means that all items added using the Add() method or the Insert() method are automatically inserted into the proper sorted location, in contrast to being inserted at the end of the list or in a specific location.

Creating Drop-Down Lists Using the Combo Box

List boxes are great, but they have two shortcomings. First, they take up quite a bit of space. Second, users can't enter their own values; they have to select from the items in the list. If you need to conserve space, or if you want to enable a user to enter a value that might not exist in the list, use the Combo Box control.

Combo boxes have an Items collection that behaves *exactly* like that of the List Box control (refer to the previous section for information on manipulating lists). Here I'll show you the basics of how a combo box works.

First, change the Size of the form to **300,330** to make room for the combo box. Next, add a new combo box to the form by double-clicking the ComboBox item in the toolbox. Set the combo box's properties as follows:

Property	Value
Name	**cboColors**
Location	**64,264**
Size	**160,21**

The first thing you should note is that the combo box has a Text property, whereas the list box doesn't. This works the same as the Text property of a text box. When the user selects an item from the drop-down list, the value of the selected item is placed in the Text property of the combo box. The default behavior of a combo box is to allow the user to enter any text in the text box portion of the control—even if the text doesn't exist in the list. I'll show you how to change this behavior shortly.

Select the Items property of the combo box in the Properties window and click the button that appears. Add the following items to the String Collection Editor and click OK to commit your entries:

- ▶ **Black**
- ▶ **Blue**
- ▶ **Gold**
- ▶ **Green**
- ▶ **Red**
- ▶ **Yellow**

Press F5 to run the project. Click the arrow at the right side of the combo box, and a drop-down list appears (see Figure 7.14).

Next, try typing in the text **Magenta**. Visual C# lets you do this. Indeed, you can type any text that you want. This may be the behavior you want, but more often you'll want to restrict a user to entering only values that appear in the list. To do this, you change the DropDownStyle property of the combo box. Close the form to stop the running project and change the `DropDownStyle` property of the combo box to **DropDownList**. Press F5 to run the project again and try to type text into the combo box. You can't. However, if you enter a character that's the start of a list item, Visual C# selects the closest matching entry.

FIGURE 7.14
Combo boxes
conserve space.

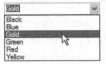

When set as a `DropDownList`, a combo box won't allow any text entry, and therefore, the user is limited to selecting items from the list. As a matter of fact, clicking in the "text box" portion of the combo box opens the list the same as though you clicked the drop-down arrow.

Stop the running project now and save your work. As you can see, the combo box and list box offer similar functionality, and in fact, the coding of their lists is identical. Each one of these controls serves a slightly different purpose, however. Which one is better? That depends entirely on the situation. As you use professional applications, pay attention to their interfaces; you'll start to get a feel for which control is appropriate in a given situation.

Summary

In this hour, you learned how to present text to a user. You learned that the Label control is perfect for displaying static text (text the user can't change) and that the text box is the control to use for displaying editable text. You can now create text boxes that contain many lines of text, and you know how to add scrollbars when the text is greater than what can be displayed in the control.

I don't think I've ever seen a form without at least one button on it, and you've now learned how to add buttons to your forms. For the most part, working with buttons is a simple matter of adding one to a form, setting its Name and Text properties, and adding some code to its `Click` event—all of which you now know how to do.

Check boxes and radio buttons are used to present True/false and mutually exclusive options, respectively. In this hour, you learned how to use each of these controls and how to use group boxes to logically group sets of related controls.

Finally, you learned how to use list boxes and combo boxes to present lists of items to a user. You now know how to add items to a list at design time as well as runtime, and you know how to sort items. The List Box and Combo Box are powerful controls, and I encourage you to dig deeper into the functionality they possess.

Without controls, users would have nothing to interact with on your forms. In this hour, you learned how to use the standard controls to begin building functional interfaces. The controls discussed in this hour have been around since the early days of Visual C#, and in fact, behave much like they did years ago. Keep in mind that I only scratched the surface of each of these controls and that most do far more than I've hinted at here. Mastering these controls will be easy for you because you'll be using them a lot. Also, as you progress through this book, you will add code that "hooks up" the controls you placed on your Options form.

Q&A

Q. *Can I place radio buttons directly on a form?*

A. Yes. The form is a container, so all radio buttons placed on a form are mutually exclusive to one another. If you wanted to add a second set of mutually exclusive buttons, they'd have to be placed on a container control. In general, I think it's best to place radio buttons in a group box rather than on a form because the group box provides a border and a caption for the radio buttons and makes it much easier to move around the set of radio buttons when you're designing the form (you simply move the group box).

Q. *I've seen what appear to be list boxes that have a check box next to each item in the list. Is this possible?*

A. Yes. In Visual C# 2005, this is accomplished using an entirely different control: the checked list box.

Workshop

Quiz

1. Which control would you use to display text that the user can't edit?

2. What common property is shared by the Label control and text box and whose value determines what the user sees in the control?

3. What property must be set to True before you can adjust the height of a text box control?

4. What is the default event of a Button control?

5. A button whose Click event is triggered when the user presses Enter while another control has the focus is called an _____?

6. Which control would you use to display a yes/no value to a user?

7. How would you create two distinct sets of mutually exclusive option buttons?

8. To manipulate items in a list, you use what collection?

9. What method adds an item to a list in a specific location?

Answers

1. A label control.

2. The Text property.

3. The MultiLine property to True.

4. The Click event.

5. Accept button.

6. You would use the check box.

7. Place the buttons on two different container controls.

8. The Items collection.

9. The Insert() method.

Exercises

1. Use the skills you learned in the previous hours to set the tab order for your Lists form. Make the Add an Item button the first control to get the focus, and the list box the last to get the focus.

2. Create a form with two list boxes. Add a number of items to one list box at design time using the Properties window. Create a button that, when clicked, removes the selected item in the first list and adds it to the second list.

HOUR 8

Using Advanced Controls

What You'll Learn in This Hour:

- ▶ Creating timers
- ▶ Creating tabbed dialog boxes
- ▶ Storing pictures in an Image List control
- ▶ Building enhanced lists using the List View control
- ▶ Creating hierarchical lists with the Tree View control

The standard controls presented in Hour 7, "Working with Traditional Controls," enable you to build many types of functional forms. However, to create truly robust and interactive applications, you must use the more advanced controls. As a Windows user, you've encountered many of these controls, such as the Tab control, which presents data on tabs, and the Tree View control, which displays hierarchical lists such as the one in Explorer. In this hour, you'll learn about these advanced controls and learn how to use them to make professional interfaces like those you're accustomed to seeing in commercial products.

> In many of the examples in this hour, I show how to add items to collections at design time. Keep in mind that everything you can do at design time can also be accomplished using Visual C# code.

By the Way

Creating Timers

All the controls you used in Hour 7 had in common the fact that the user can interact with them. Not all controls have this capability—or restriction—depending on how you look at it. Some controls are designed for use only by the developer. One such control is the Open File Dialog control you used in your Picture Viewer application in Hour 1, "Jumping In with Both Feet: A Visual C# 2005 Programming Tour." Another control that's invisible at runtime is the Timer control. The Timer control's sole purpose is to trigger an event at a specified interval of time.

Follow these steps to build a timer example project.

1. Create a new Windows Application titled **Timer Example**.

2. Right-click Form1.cs in the Solution Explorer, choose Rename, and then change the name of the default form to **fclsTimerExample.cs**.

3. Set the form's Text property to **Timer Example**.

4. Add a new Timer control to your form by double-clicking the Timer item in the toolbox (it's located in the Components toolbox category).

The Timer control is invisible at runtime, so it's added to the gray area at the bottom of the screen rather than placed on the form (see Figure 8.1).

FIGURE 8.1
Invisible-at-runtime controls are shown at the bottom of the designer, not on a form.

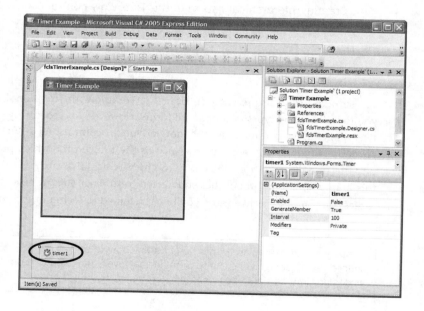

Set the properties of the Timer control as follows:

Property	Value
Name	**tmrClock**
Enabled	**True**
Interval	**1000**

You probably noticed that there are very few properties for the Timer control compared to the other controls you've worked with. The most important property of the Timer control is the `Interval` property. The `Interval` property determines how often the Timer control fires its `Tick` event (where you'll be placing code to do something when the designated time elapses). The `Interval` property is specified in milliseconds, so a setting of 1,000 is equal to 1 second, which is exactly what you set the `Interval` to for this example. As with many controls, the best way to understand how the Timer control works is to use it. You are now going to create a simple clock using the Timer control and a Label control. The way the clock works is that the Timer control fires its `Tick` event once every second (because you've set the `Interval` property to 1,000 milliseconds). Within the `Tick` event, you update the label's `Text` property to the current system time.

Add a new label to the form and set its properties as follows:

Property	Value
Name	**lblClock**
AutoSize	**False**
BorderStyle	**FixedSingle**
Location	**96,120**
Size	**100,23**
Text	(make blank)
TextAlign	**MiddleCenter**

The `AutoSize` property of the label determines whether the label automatically adjusts its size when its `Text` property changes. Because we're aligning the text to the middle of the control, we don't want it to autosize.

Next, double-click the Timer control to access its `Tick` event. When a timer is first enabled, it starts counting (in milliseconds) from 0. When the amount of milliseconds specified in the `Interval` property passes, the `Tick` event fires, and the timer starts counting from 0 once again. This cycle continues until the timer is disabled (its `Enabled` property is set to False). Because you've set the `Enabled` property of the timer to True at design time, it starts counting as soon as the form on which it's placed is loaded. Enter the following statement in the `Tick` event:

```
lblClock.Text = DateTime.Now.ToLongTimeString();
```

The .NET Framework provides date/time functionality in the System namespace. The Now property of the `DateTime` class returns the current time. Using the `ToLongTimeString` method returns the time as a string with a format of hh:mm:ss. This code causes the Text property of the label to show the current time of day, updated once a second. Press F5 to run the project now, and you'll see the Label control acting as a clock, updating the time once every second (see Figure 8.2).

FIGURE 8.2
Timers make it
easy to execute
code at speci-
fied intervals.

Stop the running project now and save your work.

Timers are powerful, but you must take care not to overuse them. For a timer to work, Windows must be aware of the timer and must constantly compare the current internal clock to the interval of the timer. It does all this so that it can notify the timer at the appropriate time to execute its Tick event. In other words, timers take system resources. This isn't a problem for an application that uses a few timers, but I wouldn't overload an application with a dozen timers unless I had no other choice (and there's almost always another choice).

Creating Tabbed Dialog Boxes

Windows 95 was the first version of Windows to introduce a tabbed interface. Since then, tabs have been widely adopted as a primary interface element. Tabs provide two major benefits: a logical grouping of controls and a reduction of required screen space. Although tabs might look complicated, they are actually easy to build and use.

You're going to add a set of tabs to your Options dialog box in your Picture Viewer program. In this case, the tabs will be overkill because you won't have much on them, but the point is to learn how they work, so follow these steps:

1. Start by opening the Picture Viewer project you completed in Hour 7.

2. Double-click frmOptions.cs in the Solution Explorer to display it in the designer.

3. Next, add a new Tab control to your form by double-clicking the TabControl item in the Toolbox (it's located in the Containers toolbox category). The Tab control defaults to having two tabs, which happens to be what you need for this example. Set the Tab control's properties as follows:

Property	Value
Name	**tabOptions**
Location	**2,2**
Size	**202,94**

4. The tabs that appear on a Tab control are determined by the control's TabPages collection. Click the TabPages property of the Tab control in the Properties window and then click the small button that appears. Visual C# shows the TabPage Collection Editor. As you can see, your Tab control has two tabs by default (see Figure 8.3).

FIGURE 8.3
Use the TabPage Collection Editor to define tabs.

5. Each tab in the collection is referred to as a *page*. Visual C# names each new page TabPage*X*, where *x* is a unique number. Although you technically don't have to change the name of a page, it's easier to work with a Tab control if you give each tab a meaningful name, such as pgeGeneralPage, pgePreferencesPage, and so forth. TabPage1 is selected by default, and its properties appear to the right. Change the Name of the tab to **pgeGeneral** and set its Text property (which is what actually appears on the tab) to **General** (you might want to view the properties alphabetically to make this easier).

6. Click TabPage2 in the list on the left to select it; then change its Name property to **pgeAppearance** and set its Text property to **Appearance**.

7. Click OK to save your changes.

Your Tab control now has two properly defined tabs (pages) (see Figure 8.4).

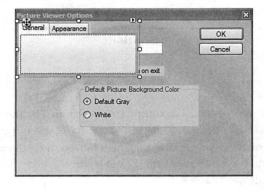

A quick way to add or remove a tab is to use the shortcuts provided in the
description pane at the bottom of the Properties window. If the shortcuts aren't
visible, you can show them by right-clicking somewhere in the properties window
and choosing Commands from the shortcut menu.

Each page on a Tab control acts as a container, much like a Panel or Group Box
control. This is why you can't drag the Tab control by clicking in the middle of it. To
drag a container control, you have to click and drag the small image with the four
arrows that appears over the General tab (refer to Figure 8.4). Follow these steps to
move the options controls you created in Hour 7 to your new tabs:

1. Click the group box grpDefaultBackcolor to select it; then right-click it and
choose Cut.

2. Click the Tab control once to select it.

3. Now that the Tab control is selected, click the Appearance page to switch to
the second page of the Tab control and then click the center of the
Appearance page.

4. Right-click in the center of the Appearance page and choose Paste.

5. Click the General tab to return to the first page of the Tab control.

6. Get the Tab control out of the way now by dragging the move image (the little
square with the directional arrows). Drag the tabs to the bottom of the form.

7. Click the User Name Label control to select it; then hold down the Shift key and click the User Name text box and the Prompt to confirm on exit check box.

8. Press Ctrl+X to cut the selected controls from the form.

9. Click the Tab control once to select it.

10. Right-click in the center of the General tab and choose Paste.

11. Set the Tab control's Location property to **12,12** and its Size property to **287,145**.

12. Click and drag the controls on the Appearance tab so they appear roughly centered on the tab (see Figure 8.5).

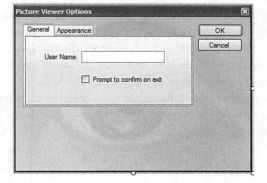

FIGURE 8.5
Tabs make it easy to group related controls.

To wrap up the Tab control, click the Appearance tab now to switch to the Appearance page and then move the group box to the middle of the page (by dragging and dropping it). When you're satisfied with its location, click the General tab again to switch to the first page.

By understanding two simple programming elements, you'll be able to do 99% of what you need to with the Tab control. The first element is that you'll need to know which tab is selected at runtime. The SelectedIndex property of the control (not the TabIndex property) sets and returns the index of the currently selected tab: 0 for the first tab, 1 for the second, and so forth. The second thing to know is how to tell when the user switches tabs. The Tab control has a SelectedIndexChanged event, which fires whenever the selected tab is changed. In this event, you can check the value of SelectedIndex to determine the tab that's been selected by the user.

Perhaps the trickiest issue with the Tab control is that each tab page has its own set of events. If you double-click the tabs themselves, you'll get a set of global events for the Tab control (this is where you'll find the `SelectedIndexChanged` event). If you double-click a page on the tabs, you'll get a unique set of events for that page; each page has its own set of events.

Feel free to run your project now and check out how your tabs work. When you're finished, be sure to save your project.

Storing Pictures in an Image List

Many of the controls I discuss in this hour have the capability to attach pictures to different types of items. The Tree View control, which is used in Explorer for navigating folders, for example, displays images next to each folder node. Not all of these pictures are the same; the control uses specific pictures to denote information about each node. It would have been possible for Microsoft to make each control store its images internally, but that would be highly inefficient because it wouldn't allow controls to share the same pictures—you'd have to store the pictures in each control that needed them. This would also cause a maintenance headache. For example, say that you had 10 Tree View controls and each displays a folder image for folder nodes. Now, it's time to update your application and you want to update the folder image to something a bit nicer. If the image were stored in each Tree View control, you'd have to update all 10 of them (and risk missing one). Instead, Microsoft created a control dedicated to storing pictures and serving them to other controls: the Image List. When you put images in an Image List control, it's easy to share them among other types of controls.

You're *not* going to use the Picture Viewer for this section, so follow these steps to create a new project:

1. Create a new Windows Application named **Lists and Trees**.

2. Right-click Form1.cs in the Solution Explorer, choose Rename, and change the name of the form to **fclsListsAndTrees.cs**. Also, set its `Text` property to **Lists and Trees** (you'll need to click the form once to access its design properties).

3. Next, add a new Image List control to the form by double-clicking the ImageList item in the toolbox (it's located in the Components toolbox category). As with the Timer control, the Image List is an invisible-at-runtime control, so it appears below the form, not on it. Change the name of the Image List to **imgMyImages**.

4. The sole purpose of an Image List control is to store pictures and make them available to other controls. The pictures are stored in the Images collection of the control. Click the `Images` property of the Image List control in the

Properties window and then click the small button that appears (the button with the three dots, called a Build button). Visual C# displays the Image Collection Editor. Notice that this editor is similar to other editors you've used in this hour.

5. Click Add to display the Open dialog box and use this dialog box to locate and select a 16×16 pixel icon. If you don't have a 16×16 pixel icon, you can create a BMP using Microsoft Paint, or download samples I've provided at http://www.samspublishing.com/ or http://www.jamesfoxall.com/books.htm. After you've added an image, click OK to close the Image Collection Editor.

Take a look at the `ImageSize` property of the Image control. It should be 16,16. If it isn't, the bitmap you selected isn't 16×16 pixels; this property is set to the dimensions of the first picture added to the Image List.

You can't always rely on the background of where a picture will be displayed to be white—or any other color for that matter. Because of this, the Image List control has a `TransparentColor` property. By default, the `TransparentColor` property is set to Transparent. Because we used an icon file here, and icon files maintain their own transparency information, we are going to leave this property alone. If we were using a BMP file, or some other format that doesn't retain transparency information, we would want to use this property to designate a color in the bitmap that would appear transparent when used with another control.

That's all there is to adding images to an Image List control. The power of the Image List lies not in properties or methods of the control itself, but in its capability to be linked to other controls so that they can access the pictures the Image List stores.

Building Enhanced Lists Using the List View

The List View control is a lot like a list box on steroids—without all the aggression. The List View can be used to create simple lists, multicolumn grids, and icon trays. The right pane in Windows Explorer is a List View. The primary display options available for Explorer's List View are Large Icon, List, Details, Small Icon, and Tiles (though Explorer refers to them by slightly different names). These correspond to the display options available for a List View by way of its `View` property. (You might not know it, but you can change the appearance of the List View in Explorer by right-clicking it and using the View submenu of the shortcut menu that appears.) You're now going to create a List View with a few items on it and experiment with the different views—including showing a picture for the items.

I can only scratch the surface of this great control here. After you've learned the basics in this hour, I highly recommend that you spend some time with the List View control, the help text, and whatever additional material you can find. I use the List View all the time, and it's a powerful tool to have in your arsenal—displaying lists is *very* common.

Add a List View control to your form now by double-clicking the ListView item in the toolbox. Set the properties of the List View as follows:

Property	Value
Name	**lvwMyListView**
Location	**8,8**
Size	**275,97**
SmallImageList	**imgMyImages**
View	**Details**

As you can see, you can attach an Image List to a control via the Properties window (and with code as well, of course). Not all controls support the Image List, but those that do make it as simple as setting a property to link to an Image List control. The List View actually allows linking to two Image Lists: one for large images (32×32 pixels) and one for small images (16×16 pixels). In this example, you're going to use only small pictures. If you wanted to use the large format, you could hook up a second Image List containing larger images to the List View control's LargeImageList property.

Creating Columns

When you changed the View property to Details, an empty header was placed at the top of the control. The contents of this header are determined by the columns defined in the Columns collection.

Follow these steps to create columns in your List View:

1. Select the Columns property on the Properties window and click the small Build button that appears. Visual C# then displays the ColumnHeader Collection Editor window.

2. Click Add to create a new header and change its Text property to **Name** and its Width property to **120**.

3. Click Add once more to create a second column and change its Text property to **State**. I haven't had you change the names of the columns in this example

because you're not going to be referencing them by name. In a production project, you should give every control you place on a form a descriptive name.

4. Click OK to save your column settings and close the window.

Your List View should now have two named columns (see Figure 8.6).

Adding List Items

Complete the following steps to add two items to the List View:

1. Click the Items property in the Properties window and then click the small button that appears, which displays the ListViewItem Collection Editor dialog box.

2. Click Add to create a new item, and change the item's Text property to **James Foxall**.

3. Next, open the drop-down list for the ImageKey property. Notice how the list contains the picture in the linked Image List control (see Figure 8.7). Select the image.

   The Text property of an item determines the text displayed for the item in the List View. If the View property is set to Details and multiple columns have been defined, the value of the Text property appears in the first column. Subsequent column values are determined by the SubItems collection.

4. Click the SubItems property (it's located in the Data category of the ListViewItem's properties but is only visible if you are view by category, not alphabetically) and then click the small button that appears, which displays the ListViewSubItem Collection Editor.

5. Click Add to create a new subitem and change its text to **Nebraska**.

FIGURE 8.7
Pictures from a
linked Image
List are readily
available to the
control.

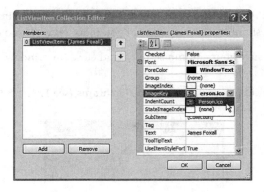

FIGURE 8.7
Pictures from a
linked Image
List are readily
available to the
control.

6. Click OK to return to the ListViewItem Collection Editor.

7. Click the Add button to create another item. This time, change the Text property to your name and use the techniques you just learned to add a subitem. Go ahead and give it an image just as you did for my name. For the Text property of the subitem, enter your state of residence.

8. When you're finished, click OK to close the ListViewItem Collection Editor. Your List View should now contain two list items (see Figure 8.8).

FIGURE 8.8
List Views offer
much more
functionality
than a standard
list box.

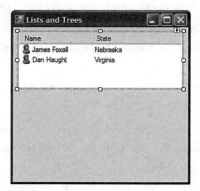

9. Next, experiment with the View property of the List View control to see how the various settings affect the appearance of the control. The Large Icons setting doesn't display an icon because you didn't link an Image List control to the LargeImageList property of the List View. Be sure to set the View property back to **Details** before continuing.

10. Press F5 to run the project and try selecting your name by clicking your state. You can't. The default behavior of the List View is to consider only the clicking of the first column as selecting an item.

11. Stop the project and change the `FullRowSelect` property of the List View to **True**; then run the project once more.

12. Click your state again and this time your name becomes selected (actually, the entire row becomes selected). Personally, I prefer to set up all my List Views with `FullRowSelect` set to True, but this is just a personal preference. Stop the project now and save your work.

Manipulating a List View Using Code

You've just learned the basics of working with a List View control. Even though you performed all the steps in Design view for this example, you'll probably manipulate your list items using code because you won't necessarily know ahead of time what to display in the list. Next, I'll show you how to work with the List View in code.

Adding List Items Using Code

Adding an item using Visual C# code is simple—if the item you're adding is simple. To add an item to your List View, you use the `Add()` method of the Items collection, like this:

```
lvwMyListView.Items.Add("Monty Sothmann");
```

If the item is to have a picture, you can specify the index of the picture as a second parameter, like this:

```
lvwMyListView.Items.Add("Jason Goss",0);
```

If the item has subitems, things get more complicated. The `Add()` method enables you to specify only the text and image index. To access the additional properties of a list item, you need to get a reference to the item in code. Remember that new items have only one subitem by default; you have to create additional items. The `Add()` method of the Items collection returns a reference to the newly added item. Knowing this, you can create a new variable to hold a reference to the item, create the item, and manipulate anything you choose to about the item using the variable (see Hour 11, "Using Constants, Data Types, Variables, and Arrays," for information about using variables). The following code creates a new item and appends a subitem to its SubItems collection:

```
ListViewItem objListItem;
objListItem = lvwMyListView.Items.Add("Mike Saklar", 0);
objListItem.SubItems.Add("Nebraska");
```

Determining the Selected Item in Code

The List View control has a collection that contains a reference to each selected item in the control: the SelectedItems collection. If the MultiSelect property of the List View is set to True (as it is by default), the user can select multiple items by holding down the Ctrl or Shift key when clicking items. This is why the List View supports a SelectedItems collection rather than a SelectedItem property. To gather information about a selected item, you refer to it by its index. For example, to display the text of the first selected item (or the only selected item if just one is selected) you could use code like this:

```
if (lvwMyListView.SelectedItems.Count > 0)
MessageBox.Show(lvwMyListView.SelectedItems[0].Text);
```

The reason you check the Count property of the SelectedItems collection is that if no items are selected, a runtime error would occur if you attempt to reference element 0 in the SelectedItems collection.

Removing List Items Using Code

To remove a list item, use the Remove() method of the Items collection. The Remove() method accepts and expects a reference to a list item. To remove the currently selected item, for example, you could use a statement such as

```
lvwMyListView.Items.Remove(lvwMyListView.SelectedItems[0]);
```

Again, you'd want to make sure that an item is actually selected before using this statement.

Removing All List Items

If you're filling a List View using code, you'll probably want to clear the contents of the List View first. That way, if the code to fill the List View is called a second time, you won't end up with duplicate entries. To clear the contents of a List View, use the Clear() method of the Items collection, like this:

```
lvwMyListView.Items.Clear();
```

The List View control is an amazingly versatile tool. As a matter of fact, I rarely use the standard List Box control; I prefer to use the List View because of its added functionality, such as displaying an image for an item. I've barely scratched the surface here, but you now know enough to begin using this powerful tool in your own development.

Creating Hierarchical Lists with the Tree View

The Tree View control is used to present hierarchical data. Perhaps the most commonly used Tree View control is found in Explorer, where you can use the Tree View to navigate the folders and drives on your computer. The Tree View is perfect for displaying hierarchical data, such as a departmental display of employees. In this section, I'll teach you the basics of the Tree View control so that you can use this powerful interface element in your applications.

The Tree View's items are contained in a Nodes collection, much like items in a List View are stored in an Items collection. To add items to the tree, you append them to the Nodes collection. As you can probably see by now, after you understand the basics of objects and collections, you can apply that knowledge to almost everything in Visual C#. For instance, the skills you learned in working with the Items collection of the List View control are similar to the skills needed for working with the Nodes collection of the Tree View control. In fact, these concepts are similar to working with list boxes and combo boxes.

Add a Tree View control to your form now by double-clicking the TreeView item in the toolbox. Set the Tree View control's properties as follows:

Property	Value
Name	**tvwLanguages**
ImageList	**imgMyImages**
Location	**8,128**
Size	**275,97**

> When you change the name of a control, you might be prompted with a Refactoring Warning dialog box. If so, click OK to continue.

By the Way

Adding Nodes to a Tree View

Working with nodes at design time is similar to working with a List View's Items collection. So, I'll show you how to work with nodes in code. To add a node you call the Add() method of the Nodes collection (which you'll do in this example). Add a new button to your form and set its properties as follows:

Property	Value
Name	**btnAddNode**
Location	**8,235**
Size	**75,23**
Text	**Add Node**

Double-click the button to access its Click event and enter the following code:

```
tvwLanguages.Nodes.Add("James");
tvwLanguages.Nodes.Add("Visual C#");
```

Press F5 to run the project, and then click the button. Two nodes appear in the tree, one for each Add() method call (see Figure 8.9).

FIGURE 8.9
Nodes are the items that appear in a tree.

Notice how both nodes appear at the same level in the hierarchy; neither node is a parent or child of the other. If all your nodes will be at the same level in the hierarchy, consider using a List View control instead because what you're creating is simply a list.

Stop the project and return to the button's Click event. Any given node can be both a parent to other nodes and a child of a single node (the parent node of any given node can be referenced via the Parent property of a node). For this to work, each node has its own Nodes collection. This can be confusing, but if you realize that children nodes belong to the parent node, it starts to make sense.

You're now going to create a new button that adds the same two nodes as before but makes the second node a child of the first. Return to the Design view of the form and then create a new button and set its properties as shown:

Property	Value
Name	**btnCreateChild**
Location	**96,235**
Size	**80,23**
Text	**Create Child**

Double-click the new button to access its `Click` event and add the following code:

```
TreeNode objNode;

objNode = tvwLanguages.Nodes.Add("Monte Sothman");

objNode.Nodes.Add("Visual C#");
```

This code is similar to what you created in the List View example. The `Add()`
method of the Nodes collection returns a reference to the newly created node. Thus,
this code creates a variable of type `TreeNode` (variables are discussed in detail in
Hour 11), creates a new node whose reference is placed in the variable, and then
adds a new node to the Nodes collection of the first node. To see the effect this has,
press F5 to run the project and click the Create Child button. You'll see a single item
in the list, with a plus sign to the left of it. This plus sign indicates that child nodes
exist. Click the plus sign, and the node is expanded to show its children (see Figure
8.10).

FIGURE 8.10
You can create
as deep a hier-
archy as you
need using the
Tree View con-
trol.

This example is a simple one—a single parent node having a single child node.
However, the principles used here are the same as those used to build complex trees
with dozens or hundreds of nodes.

Removing Nodes

To remove a node, you call the `Remove()` method of the Nodes collection. The
`Remove()` method accepts and expects a valid node, so you must know which node
to remove. Again, the Nodes collection works much like the Items collection in the
List View control, so the same ideas apply. For example, the currently selected node
is returned in the `SelectedNode` property of the Tree View control. So, to remove the
currently selected node you could use this statement:

```
tvwLanguages.Nodes.Remove(tvwLanguages.SelectedNode);
```

If this statement were called when no node is selected, an error would occur. In Hour
11, you'll learn all about data types and equalities, but here's a preview: If an object
variable doesn't reference an object, it's equivalent to the Visual C# keyword
`Nothing`. Knowing this, you could validate whether an item is selected with a little
bit of logic using code like the following. (Note that unlike with the List View control, only one node can be selected at a time in a Tree View control.)

```
if (!(tvwLanguages.SelectedNode == null))
tvwLanguages.Nodes.Remove(tvwLanguages.SelectedNode);
```

| Removing a parent node causes all its children to be removed as well. |

Clearing All Nodes

To clear all nodes in a Tree View, invoke the `Clear()` method of the Nodes collection, like this:

```
tvwLanguages.Nodes.Clear();
```

As with the List View, I've only scratched the surface of the Tree View. Spend some
time becoming familiar with the basics of the Tree View, as I've shown here, and
then dig a bit deeper to discover the not-so-obvious power and flexibility of this control.

Summary

Visual C# includes a number of controls that go beyond the standard functionality
of the traditional controls discussed in Hour 7. In this hour, I discussed the most
commonly used advanced controls. You learned how to use the Timer control to trigger events at predetermined intervals. You also learned how to use the Tab control to
create the tabbed dialog boxes with which you're so familiar.

Also in this hour, you learned how to add pictures to an Image List control so that other controls can use them. The Image List makes it easy to share pictures among many controls, making it a useful tool. Finally, I taught you the basics of the List View and Tree View controls—two controls you can use to build high-end interfaces that present structured data. The more time you spend with all these controls, the better you'll become at creating great interfaces.

Q&A

Q. *What if I need a lot of timers, but I'm concerned about system resources?*

A. When possible, use a single timer for multiple duties. This is easy when two events occur at the same interval—why bother creating a second timer? When two events occur at different intervals, you can use some decision skills along with static variables (discussed in Hour 11) to share Timer events.

Q. *What else can I do with an Image List control?*

A. You can assign a unique picture to a node in a Tree View control when the node is selected. You can also display an image in the tab of a tab page in a Tab control. There are many uses, and as you learn more about advanced controls, you'll see additional opportunities for using images from an Image List.

Workshop

Quiz

1. What unit of time is applied to the Interval property of the Timer control?

2. What collection is used to add new tabs to a Tab control?

3. What property returns the index of the currently selected tab?

4. True or False: You should use different Image List controls for storing images of different sizes.

5. To see columns in a List View control, the View property must be set to what?

6. The additional columns of data that can be attached to an item in a List View are stored in what collection?

7. What property of what object would you use to determine how many items are in a List View?

8. Each item in a Tree View control is called what?

9. How do you make a node the child of another node?

Answers

1. Milliseconds

2. The TabPages collection

3. The `SelectedIndex` property

4. True

5. Details

6. The SubItems collection

7. You check the `Count` property of the Items collection.

8. A node

9. Add it to the Nodes collection of the parent node

Exercises

1. Add a second Image List control to your project with the List View. Place an icon (32×32 pixels) in this Image List and link the Image List to the `LargeImageList` property of the List View control. Change the `View` property to Large Icons. Does the icon appear next to a list item? If not, is there a property of an item you can set so that it does?

2. Create a new project and add a List View, a button, and a text box to the default form. Create a new item in the List View using the text entered into the text box when the button is clicked.

HOUR 9

Adding Menus and Toolbars to Forms

What You'll Learn in This Hour:

▶ Adding, moving, and deleting menu items
▶ Creating checked menu items
▶ Programming menus
▶ Implementing context menus
▶ Assigning shortcut keys
▶ Creating toolbar items
▶ Defining toggle buttons and separators
▶ Creating a status bar

The use of a graphical user interface (GUI) for interacting with and navigating programs is one of the greatest features of Windows. Despite this, a number of Windows users still rely primarily on the keyboard, preferring to use a mouse only when absolutely necessary. Data-entry people in particular never take their hands off the keyboard. Many software companies receive support calls from angry customers because a commonly used function is accessible only by using a mouse. Menus are the easiest way to navigate your program for a user who relies on the keyboard, and Visual C# 2005 makes it easier than ever to create menus for your applications. In this hour, you'll learn how to build, manipulate, and program menus on a form. In addition, I'll teach you how to use the Toolbar control to create attractive and functional toolbars. Finally, you'll learn how to finish off a form with a status bar.

Building Menus

When I said that Visual C# 2005 makes building menus easier than ever, I wasn't kidding. Building menus is now an immediately gratifying process. I can't stress enough how important it is to have good menus, and now that it's so easy to do, there's no excuse for not putting menus in an application.

Did you Know?

When running an application for the first time, users often scan the menus before opening a manual. (Most users never open the manual!) When you provide comprehensive menus, you make your program easier to learn and use.

Creating Top-Level Menu Items

Adding menus to a form is accomplished by way of a control: the Main Menu control. The Menu Strip control is a bit odd in that it's the only control I know of (besides the context menu control discussed later in this hour) that sits at the bottom of the form in the space reserved for controls without an interface (like a Timer control), yet actually has a visible interface on the form.

Follow these steps to get started:

1. You're going to be using the Picture Viewer project that you worked on in Hour 8, "Using Advanced Controls," so open that project now.

2. Double-click frmViewer.cs in the Solution Explorer to display the main picture viewer form in design view.

3. You're going to need room at the top of the form, so change the `Size.Height` property of the form to **375**.

4. Change the PictureBox's `Location` to **8,52** and its `Size` to **282,279**.

5. Next, select *all* of the controls on the form *except the picture box* by Shift-clicking them or lassoing them. Make sure to get the X and Y labels! When they're all selected, click and drag the Select Picture button until its top aligns with the picture box (when you drag, all controls should move with the Select Picture button). Your form should now look like Figure 9.1.

6. Add a new Menu Strip control to your form by double-clicking the MenuStrip item in the toolbox and change its name to **mnuMainMenu**. As you can see, the control is added to the pane at the bottom of the Form Designer. Take a look at the top of the form—you'll see the text Type Here (see Figure 9.2).

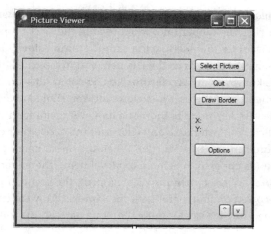

FIGURE 9.1
You'll need space for menus and tool-bars at the top of your form.

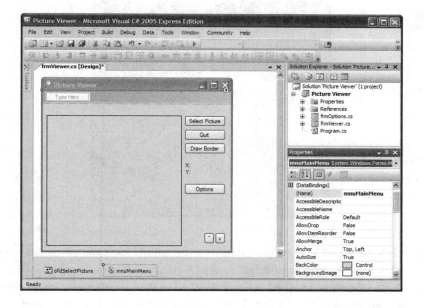

FIGURE 9.2
A menu has no items when first added to a form.

7. Click this text *Type Here* and type **&File** and press Enter. As you begin typing, Visual C# displays two new boxes that say Type Here (see Figure 9.3).

Notice the Properties window (if it's not visible, press F4 to show it). The text you just entered creates a new menu item. Each menu item is an object, and therefore, the item has properties. By default, Visual C# gives the menu the name FileToolStripMenuItem. It's a long name, but it gets the job done.

You might be wondering why I had you enter the ampersand (**&**) in front of the word **File**. Take a look at your menu now, and you'll see that Visual C#

doesn't display the ampersand; instead, it displays the text with the F under-lined, as in File. The ampersand, when used in the Text property of a menu item, tells Visual C# to underline the character immediately following it. For top-level menu items, such as the File item you just created, this underlined character is known as an **accelerator key**. Pressing Alt + an accelerator key opens the menu as if the user had clicked it. You should avoid assigning the same accelerator key to more than one top-level menu item on a form. To avoid conflicts, you can make any character the accelerator character, not just the first character(i.e. F&ile for File). When the menu item appears on a drop-down menu (as opposed to being a top-level item), the underlined character is called a *hotkey*. When a menu is visible (open), the user can press a hotkey to trigger the corresponding menu item the same as if it were clicked. Again, don't use the same hotkey for more than one item on the same menu.

FIGURE 9.3
Creating a menu item automatically prepares the control for more items.

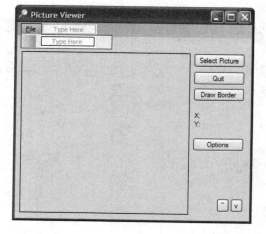

8. Click the Type Here text that appears to the immediate right of the File item, enter **&Tools,** and press Enter. Visual C# gives you two more Type Here items—the same as when you entered the File item. Adding new menu items is a matter of clicking a Type Here box and entering the text for an item.

If you click a Type Here box *below* an existing menu item, you'll add a new item to the same menu as the item above the box. If you click the Type Here box to the right of a menu item, you'll create a submenu using the menu to the left of the box as the entry point for the submenu. As you've already seen, clicking the Type Here box along the top of the menu bar creates a top-level menu.

Creating Menu Items for a Top-Level Menu

You can create as many top-level menus as you have room for on a form. For the Picture Viewer, the File and Tools menus are adequate. Now, you need to create the menu items that a user can select for these top-level menus. Follow these steps to create the menu items:

1. Click once more on the File item to display a Type Here box *below* it. Click this Type Here box, enter **&Open Picture...**, and then press Enter.

2. Change the name of the new item to **mnuOpenPicture** (you'll need to click it to give it the focus before you can change its properties in the Properties Window).

3. Click the Type Here box below the Open Picture item you created, type **&Quit**, and then press Enter. Change the name of the new item to **mnuQuit**. Now is a good time to save your work, so click Save All on the toolbar.

4. Click the Tools menu to select it. This displays a Type Here box to the right and below the Tools item. Click the Type Here box *below* the Tools menu, type **&Draw Border**, and then press Enter. Change the name of the new item to **mnuDrawBorder**.

5. Now, this can be tricky. Hover the pointer over the Type Here box below the Draw Border item. A small drop arrow appears. Click this arrow and select Separator (see Figure 9.4). This drop-down is used to specify what type of item you want on the menu. You can create a combo box or text box or, as in this case, a separator to isolate groups of unrelated menu items.

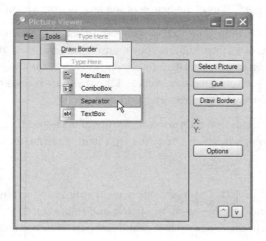

FIGURE 9.4
You can create text boxes, combo boxes, and separators in addition to regular menu items.

6. After choosing Separator, a line appears under Draw Border, and a new Type Here box appears. Click this box to select it, enter the text **&Options...**, and then press Enter to create the menu item. Change the name of this new item to **mnuOptions**.

7. Finally, click the picture box or some other control to stop editing the menu.

Moving and Deleting Menu Items

Deleting and moving menu items are even easier than adding new items. To delete a menu item, right-click it and choose Delete from the context menu that appears (or simply click it to select it and press Delete). To move an item, drag it from its current location and drop it in the location in which you want it placed. Unfortunately, items can only be moved within the same menu.

Creating Checked Menu Items

A menu item that isn't used to open a submenu can display a check mark next to its text. Check marks are used to create menu items that have state—the item is either selected or it isn't. You're now going to create a checked menu item. Remember from Hour 8 the check box you created for the Options form? It was used to specify whether the user should be prompted before the Picture Viewer closes. You're now going to create a menu item for this as well. Follow these steps:

1. Click the File menu to open it up.

2. Click the Type Here box below the Quit menu item, enter **Confirm on Exit**, and press Enter. Change the Name of the new item to **mnuConfirmOnExit**.

3. Right-click on Confirm on Exit and choose Checked from the shortcut menu that appears (see Figure 9.5). If your menu is different than the one in Figure 9.5, click a different menu item and then right-click the Confirm on Exit item once more. You could have also clicked the menu item once and changed its Checked property in the Properties window.

4. Next, click and drag the Confirm on Exit item and drop it on the Quit menu item. This moves the item above the Quit item. Your menu now looks like Figure 9.6.

Press F5 to run the project. The menu appears on your form, just as you designed it (see Figure 9.7). Click the File menu to open it and then click Quit; nothing happens. In fact, the checked state of your menu item doesn't even change if you click that item. In the next section, I'll show you how to add code to menu items to make them actually do something (as well as change their checked state).

FIGURE 9.5
Menu items can be used to indicate state.

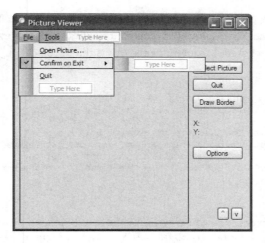

FIGURE 9.6
You have complete control over the structure of your menus.

Stop the project now and save your work.

Programming Menus

Every menu item is a unique object—you could actually edit each item by clicking an item once to select it and then changing the item's properties in the Properties window. Although individual menu items aren't controls per se, adding code behind them is similar to adding code behind a control. You're now going to add code to menu items you created.

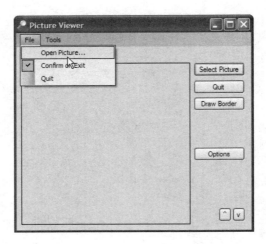

Follow these steps to create the code for the menus:

1. Click the File menu now to open it.

2. Double-click the Open Picture menu item. Just as when you double-click a control, Visual C# displays the code editor with the default event for the menu item you've clicked. For menu items, this is the `Click` event.

3. Enter the following code:

    ```
    // Show the open file dialog box.
    if (ofdSelectPicture.ShowDialog() == DialogResult.OK)
    {
        // Load the picture into the picture box.
        picShowPicture.Image = Image.FromFile(ofdSelectPicture.FileName);
        // Show the name of the file in the form's caption.
        this.Text = string.Concat("Picture Viewer(" + ofdSelectPicture.FileName
    + ")");
    }
    ```

    This is the exact code you entered for the Select Picture button you created in Hour 1, "Jumping In with Both Feet: A Visual C# 2005 Programming Tour," so I won't discuss it here.

4. Click the frmViewer.cs [Design] tab in the form designer to switch back to the form designer for the Picture Viewer form.

5. Double-click the Confirm on Exit menu item to access its `Click` event. Enter the following code statement:

    ```
    mnuConfirmOnExit.Checked = !(mnuConfirmOnExit.Checked);
    ```

When the item Confirm on Exit is clicked, this code sets the item's checked state to the opposite of the item's current checked state. The ! operator is used to perform a negation of a Boolean (true or false) value. Don't worry; I discuss this in detail in Hour 12, "Performing Arithmetic, String Manipulation, and Date/Time Adjustments." For now, realize that if the current value of the Checked property is True, ! returns False. If Checked is currently False, ! returns True. Therefore, the checked value toggles between True and False each time the menu item is clicked.

6. Double-click frmViewer.cs in the Solution Explorer window to switch back to the Form Designer for the Picture Viewer form again.

7. Double-click the Quit menu item to access its Click event and enter the following code:

```
this.Close();
```

Again, recall from Hour 1 that this statement simply closes the form, which has the effect of closing the application because it's the only form that's loaded.

8. Return to the form viewer yet again, click Tools to display the Tools menu, and then double-click the Draw Border menu item to access its Click event. Enter the following code:

```
Graphics objGraphics = null;
objGraphics = this.CreateGraphics();
objGraphics.Clear(SystemColors.Control);
objGraphics.DrawRectangle(Pens.Blue,
picShowPicture.Left - 1, picShowPicture.Top - 1,
      picShowPicture.Width + 1, picShowPicture.Height + 1);
objGraphics.Dispose();
```

This code is also directly from Hour 1, so refer to that chapter for the specifics on how this code works.

9. Return to the Form Designer, double-click the Options menu item, and enter the following two code statements in its Click event:

```
frmOptions frmOptionsDialog = new frmOptions();
frmOptionsDialog.ShowDialog();
```

You have just added all the code necessary for your menu to function. Follow these steps to test your work:

1. Press F5 to run the project. Open the File menu by pressing Alt+F (remember, the F is the accelerator key).

   2. Next, click the Confirm on Exit button. The menu closes, so click File again to open it and notice that the item is no longer checked. Clicking it again would check it.

   3. Click all the menu items except Quit to make sure that they work as expected. When you're finished, choose Quit from the File menu to close the running project.

If you selected Confirm on Exit, you might have noticed that you weren't asked whether you really wanted to quit. That's because the quit code hasn't been written to consider the checked state of the Ask Before Closing button. You'll be hooking up this item, as well as all of the options, in Hour 11, "Using Constants, Data Types, Variables, and Arrays."

> When designing your menus, look at some of the many popular Windows applications available and consider the similarities and differences between their menus and yours. Although your application might be unique and therefore have different menus than other applications, there are probably similarities as well (such as Cut, Copy, Paste, Open, etc.). When possible, make menu items in your application follow the same structure and design as similar items in the popular programs. This will shorten the learning curve of your application, reduce user frustration, and save you time.

Implementing Context Menus

Context menus (also called shortcut menus) are the pop-up menus that appear when you right-click an object on a form. Context menus get their name from the fact that they display context-sensitive choices—menu items that relate directly to the object that's right-clicked. Most Visual C# controls have a default context menu (also called a *shortcut menu*), but you can assign custom context menus if you want. Creating context menus is much like creating regular menus. Context menus, however, are created using a different control: the Context Menu Strip control.

Follow these steps to implement a custom context menu in your project:

   1. Display the frmViewer.cs form in the Form Designer.

   2. Add a new context menu strip to the form by double-clicking the Context Menu Strip item in the toolbox. Like the MainMenucontrol, the Context Menu Strip control is placed in the pane below the Form Designer. Change its name to **mnuPictureContext**.

3. When the Context Menu Strip control is selected, a context menu appears toward the top for editing. Click the Type Here box, enter the text **Draw Border** (see Figure 9.8), and press Enter to create the menu item. You've just created a context menu with a single menu item.

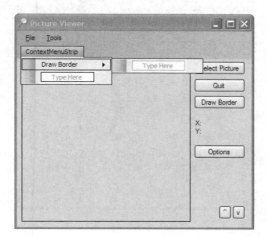

FIGURE 9.8
Context menus are edited much like regular menus.

4. Double-click the new menu item to access its Click event and enter the following code:

```
Graphics objGraphics = null;
objGraphics = this.CreateGraphics();
objGraphics.Clear(SystemColors.Control);
objGraphics.DrawRectangle(Pens.Blue,
picShowPicture.Left - 1, picShowPicture.Top - 1,
      picShowPicture.Width + 1, picShowPicture.Height + 1);
objGraphics.Dispose();
```

Yes, this is the exact same code you entered for the Draw Border menu item *and* the Draw Border button. It seems sort of redundant to enter the same code in three places doesn't it? In Hour 10, "Creating and Calling Methods," I'll show you how to share code so that you don't have to enter it in multiple places!

5. Double-click frmViewer.cs in the Solution Explorer to return to the designer for the Picture Viewer form.

6. Linking a control to a context menu is accomplished by setting a property. Click the picture box on the form now to select it, and then change the ContextMenuStrip property of the text box to **mnuPictureContext**; the context menu is now linked to the picture box.

7. Press F5 to run the project and right-click the picture box. You'll see the context menu shown in Figure 9.9. Go ahead and choose Draw Border, and the border will be drawn.

FIGURE 9.9
Context menus
make handy
shortcuts.

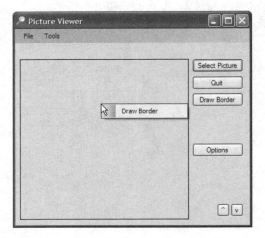

8. Stop the project and save your work.

Assigning Shortcut Keys to Menu Items

If you've spent any time learning a Microsoft application, you've most likely learned some keyboard shortcuts. For example, pressing Alt+P in any application that prints has the same effect as opening the File menu and choosing Print.

Add shortcuts to your menus now by following these steps:

1. Click the File menu at the top of the form to open it and then click Open Picture to select it.

2. In the Properties window, click the ShortcutKeys property and then click the down arrow that appears. This drop-down allows you to define a shortcut key for the selected menu item (see Figure 9.10).

3. Click Ctrl and then select **O** (for Open) from the key drop-down menu; then click another property to close the drop-down.

4. Press F5 to run the project once more. Next, press Ctrl+O, and the application behaves just as though you opened the File menu and clicked the Open Picture item.

FIGURE 9.10
A shortcut key
is assigned
using the
ShortcutKeys
property of a
menu item.

Although it isn't always possible, try to assign logical shortcut key combinations. The meaning of F6 is hardly intuitive, for example. But, when assigning modifiers such as Ctrl with another character, you have some flexibility. For instance, the key combination of Ctrl+Q might be a more intuitive shortcut key for Quit than Ctrl+T. Again, if the menu item is the same or similar to a menu item in a commercial application, use the same shortcut key as the commercial application.

Did you Know?

Stop the running project and save your work before continuing.

Using the Toolbar Control

Generally, when a program has a menu (as most programs should), it should also have a toolbar. Toolbars (called *toolstrips* in Visual C# 2005 for some reason) are one of the easiest ways for a user to access program functions. Unlike menu items, toolbar items are always visible and therefore immediately available. In addition, toolbar items have ToolTips, which enable a user to discover a tool button's purpose simply by hovering the pointer over the button.

Toolbar items are really shortcuts for menu items; every item on a toolbar should have a corresponding menu item. Remember that some users prefer to use the keyboard, in which case they need to have keyboard access to functions via menus.

The actual items you place on a toolbar depend on the features supported by the application. However, the mechanics of creating toolbars and toolbar items are the same regardless of the buttons you choose to use. Toolbars are created using the ToolStrip control.

Follow these steps to add a toolbar to the main form in your Picture Viewer project:

1. Display the frmViewer.cs form in the Form Designer (if it's not already).

2. Add a new ToolStrip control to your form now by double-clicking the Toolstrip item in the toolbox. A new toolbar is then added to the top of your form. Change the name of the toolbar to **tbrMainToolbar**. Your form should now look like Figure 9.11.

3. Notice that the toolbar appears above your menu. Anyone who has used a Windows application knows that toolbars belong *below* menus. Right-click the toolbar and choose Bring To Front from its shortcut menu. That causes the toolbar to move below the menu.

FIGURE 9.11
New toolbars default to the top of the form and have no buttons.

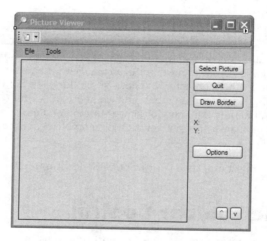

Adding Toolbar Buttons Using the Buttons Collection

Like many other controls you've already learned about, the ToolStrip control supports a special collection: the Items collection. The Items collection contains the buttons that appear on the toolbar. Click the Items property in the Properties window, and then click the small Build button that appears; the Items Collection Editor displays. The list of members shows the toolbar itself, but no buttons because new toolbars have no buttons.

You are going to be adding three images to your toolbar: One for Open, one for Draw Border, and one for Options. You can download these images from my website at www.jamesfoxall.com/books.htm.

Take a moment to open the drop-down list in the upper-left corner (see Figure 9.12). This list contains the types of items that can be added to a toolbar.

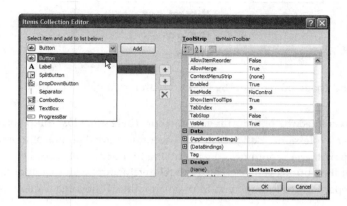

FIGURE 9.12
Toolbars may contain a number of different types of items.

For this example, you will be creating buttons and separators. Feel free to experiment with the different item types in another project. Follow these steps:

1. With Button selected in the drop-down list, click Add to create a new button. Set its properties as follows:

Property	Value
Name	**tbbOpenPicture**
Text	**Open Picture**
TooltipText	**Open Picture**

2. Click the Image property for the button and then click the Build button that appears. Click Import; then browse and select the Open image. If you don't see the image when you browse, you may have your browse filter set to not show icons, so open Files of Type on the Open dialog box and choose All.

3. Click OK to save the image in the button.

4. Click Add to create a new button and set its properties as follows:

Property	Value
Name	**tbbDrawBorder**
Text	**Draw Border**
ToolTipText	**Draw Border**

5. Set the Image property of the Draw Border button to a valid bitmap file.

6. Click Add again to create the final button. Set its properties as follows:

Property	Value
Name	**tbbOptions**
Text	**Options**
ToolTipText	**Options**

7. Set the Image property of the Options button to a valid bitmap file.

You've now created the buttons for your toolbar. There's one last thing you should do, however. Professional designers always separate related groups of tool buttons using a **separator**. A separator is a vertical line that appears between two buttons. All three of the buttons you've created are relatively unrelated, so you're now going to create separators to isolate them from one another. Follow these steps:

1. Choose Separator from the drop-down list and click Add. The separator is added to the bottom of the list. Click the up arrow that appears to the right of the list *twice* to move the separator up between the Open button and the Draw Border button.

2. Click Add again to create another separator and click the up arrow once this time to move the separator between the Draw Border button and the Options button.

3. Click OK to save your toolbar definition. Your screen should now look like Figure 9.13.

FIGURE 9.13
Your toolbar is now ready for some code to make it work.

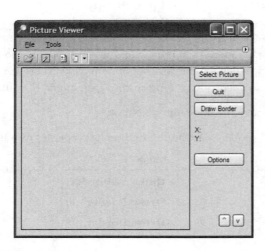

> You can add buttons to the ToolStrip control dynamically like you added menu items by using the default button that appears on the ToolStrip. I chose to have you use the Items Collection Editor instead, though, so that you could see there are often multiple ways to attack a problem.

By the Way

Programming Toolbars

Programming toolbars is pretty much the same as programming menus. As you will see, Microsoft has chosen to standardize things whenever possible. For example, in the previous edition of .NET you worked with a Toolbar control that had a Buttons collection. In 2005, the Toolbar control is replaced with a ToolStrip control that has an Items collection. The List View control has an Items collection, as does the Tree View control. Seeing a pattern? After you learn how to work with the Items collection of one control, it's an easy transition to work with the Items collection of another.

Follow these steps to make your toolbar functional:

1. Double-click the Open button on the toolbar to access its `Click` event. Be sure to click the button and not the toolbar. Double-clicking the toolbar accesses a different event altogether. Enter the following code:

```
// Show the open file dialog box.
if (ofdSelectPicture.ShowDialog() == DialogResult.OK)
{
    // Load the picture into the picture box.
    picShowPicture.Image = Image.FromFile(ofdSelectPicture.FileName);
    // Show the name of the file in the form's caption.
    this.Text = string.Concat("Picture Viewer(" + ofdSelectPicture.FileName
+ ")");
}
```

2. Click the frmViewer.cs [Design] tab to return to the form designer.

3. Double-click the Draw Border button and add the following code to its `Click` event:

```
Graphics objGraphics = null;
objGraphics = this.CreateGraphics();
objGraphics.Clear(SystemColors.Control);
objGraphics.DrawRectangle(Pens.Blue,
     picShowPicture.Left - 1, picShowPicture.Top - 1,
     picShowPicture.Width + 1, picShowPicture.Height + 1);
objGraphics.Dispose();
```

4. Click the frmViewer.cs [Design] tab to return to the form designer.

5. Double-click the Options button and add the following code to its Click event:

```
frmOptions frmOptionsDialog = new frmOptions();
frmOptionsDialog.ShowDialog();
```

Go ahead and save your work and then press F5 to run the project. Clicking the toolbar buttons should now perform the same actions as clicking the menu items. In Hour 10, I'll show you how the two controls can share code.

Creating Drop-Down Menus for Toolbar Buttons

Although you're not going to use one in this project, be aware that you can create drop-down menus on toolbars. Visual Studio 2005 uses these in a number of places (see Figure 9.14). To create a menu like this, instead of adding a regular button to the toolbar you add a DropDownButton. Doing so creates a submenu just like when you defined regular menus earlier in this hour.

FIGURE 9.14
You can create drop-down menus like these.

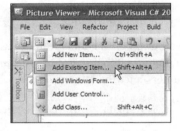

Creating a Status Bar

The last control I'm going to show you in this hour is the Status Bar control. The Status Bar isn't nearly as fancy, or even as useful, as other controls such as the ToolStrip or the MenuStrip (but it's also not as difficult to work with either). A status bar adds value to an application in that it makes available information in a standard location, and users have come to expect it. In its simplest form, a status bar displays a caption and *sizing grip*—the dots to the right of the control that the user can drag with the mouse to change the size of the form.

Add a new status bar to the form now by double-clicking the StatusStrip item in the toolbox (located in the Menus & Toolbars category). You'll need to use the vertical scroll bar to the left in the designer to scroll down and see the status bar at the bottom of your form. Change the name of the StatusStrip to **sbrMyStatusStrip**. Because of the way you have anchored your other controls, the status strip overlays a few controls at the bottom of the form. Fix this now by following these steps:

1. Click the PictureBox on the form and change its Size property to **282,264**.

2. Change the Location.Y property of the Shrink and Enlarge buttons to **293**. Your form should now look like Figure 9.15.

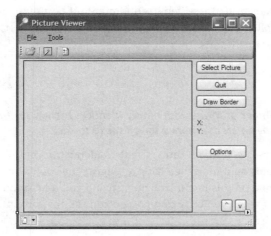

FIGURE 9.15
Status bars always appear at the bottom of a form.

Take a look at the left edge of the StatusStrip. Does it look familiar? It's similar to the interface you have for adding menu items to MenuStrips and buttons to ToolStrips. Click the drop-down arrow now and choose Status Label. A new status label appears. If it does not have the focus, click the label to give it the focus (it has the text ToolStripStatusLabel1), and then change its properties as follows:

Property	Value
Name	**pnlStatus**
Text	**no image loaded**

You probably noticed when you opened the drop-down to create the status label that you can place items of other types on the status strip as well. For now, the label will due. In Hour 10, you'll write code to display the opened picture file name in the label.

Summary

Menus, toolbars, and status bars add tremendous value to an application by greatly enhancing its usability. In this hour, you learned how to use the MenuStrip and ContextMenuStrip controls to build comprehensive menus for your applications. You learned how to add, move, and delete menu items and how to define accelerator and shortcut keys to facilitate better navigation via the keyboard. You also saw how toolbars provide shortcuts for accessing common menu items. You learned how to use the ToolStrip control to create functional toolbars complete with bitmaps and logical groupings. Finally, you discovered how to use a status strip to dress up the application. Implementing these items is an important part of the interface design process for an application, and you now have the skills necessary to start putting them into your own programs.

Q&A

Q. *I have a number of forms with nearly identical menus. Do I really need to take the time to create menus for all these forms?*

A. Not as much as you might think. Create a MenuStrip control that has the common items on it, and then copy and paste the control to other forms. You can then build on this menu structure, saving you a lot of time. Be aware though, that when you copy and paste a control, the corresponding code does not get copied.

Q. *I've seen applications that allow the end user to customize the menus and toolbars. Can I do that with the Visual C# menus and toolbars?*

A. Yes and no. There is no built-in functionality to do this, so you would have to write LOTS of complicated code to allow users to customize your toolbars. A better approach is to purchase a third-party component that provides this functionality. Personally, I think buying a component that supports this is a much better option than attempting to write the code yourself.

Workshop

Quiz

1. True or False: Form menu bars are created using the Context Menu control.

2. To create an accelerator, or hotkey, preface the character with a(n) _____.

3. To place a check mark next to a menu item, you set what property of the item?

4. How do you add code to a menu item?

5. Toolbar items are part of what collection?

6. True or False: Every button on a toolbar has its own `Click` event.

7. What control displays information to the user at the bottom of a form?

Answers

1. False. They are created using the MenuStrip control.

2. Ampersand (&)

3. The `Checked` property

4. Double-click the menu item.

5. The Items collection.

6. True

7. The StatusStrip control

Exercises

1. Create a new project and build a ToolStrip that has a drop-down button.

2. Using the ToolStrip control, figure out how to display status text in place of a button. (Hint: There is a special type of item in the Items collection that does this.)

PART III

Making Things Happen— Programming

HOUR 10

Creating and Calling Methods

What You'll Learn in This Hour:

▶ Creating methods
▶ Calling methods
▶ Exiting methods
▶ Passing parameters
▶ Avoiding recursive methods
▶ Working with tasks

You've now spent about nine hours building the basic skills necessary to navigate Visual C# 2005 and to create an application interface. Creating a good interface is important, but it's only one of many steps toward creating a Windows program. After you've created the basic interface of an application, you need to enable the program to do something. The program might perform an action all on its own, or it might perform actions based on a user interacting with the interface—either way, you write Visual C# code to make your application perform tasks. In this hour, you'll learn how to create sets of code, how to create isolated code routines that can be executed (called *methods*), and how to invoke the methods you create.

Understanding Class Members

A *class* is a place to store the code you write. Before you can begin writing Visual C# code, you must start with a class. As mentioned in previous hours, a class is used as a template to create an object (which may have properties and/or methods). Properties and methods of classes can be either instance members or static members. *Instance members* are associated with an instance of a class—an object created from a class using the keyword new. On the other hand, *static members* belong to the class as a whole, not to a specific instance of a class. You've already worked with one class using instance members to create a form (refer to Hour 5, "Building Forms: The Basics," for more information). When you double-click an object on a form, you access events that reside in the form's class module.

Other languages, such as Visual Basic, differentiate between class methods and public methods that are globally available outside of a class. Visual C# requires all methods to exist in the context of a class, but a globally available method can be achieved by defining *static* methods in your class. Static methods are always available regardless of whether an instance of the class exists. In fact, you can't access a static member through an instance of a class, and attempting to do so results in an exception (error).

Although you could place all of your program's code into a single class module, it's best to create different modules to group related sets of code. In addition, it's best not to place code that isn't specifically related to a form within a form's class module; place such code in the logical class or, preferably, in a specialized class module.

The current development trend centers on object-oriented programming, which revolves around class modules. I'll give you a primer on object-oriented programming in Hour 16, but this is a very advanced topic so I won't be covering it in detail. I highly recommend that you read a book dedicated to the topic of object-oriented programming, such as *Sams Teach Yourself Object-Oriented Programming in 21 Days*, after you are comfortable with the material in this book.

One general rule for creating methods is that you should build classes to group related sets of code. This is not to say you should create dozens of classes. Rather, group related methods into a reasonably sized set of classes. For instance, you might want to create one class that contains all your printing routines and another that holds your data-access routines. In addition, I like to create a general-purpose class in which to place all the various routines that don't necessarily fit into a more specialized class.

You're going to be building on the Picture Viewer application from the Hour 9, "Adding Menus and Toolbars to Forms," so open that now.

If you wanted to create an entirely new class, you would choose Add Class from the Project menu. However, for this example, you're going to create methods in your form class.

Start by clicking frmViewer.cs in the Solution Explorer, and then clicking the View Code button that appears at the top of the Solution Explorer. You are now viewing the code of the frmViewer.cs class (see Figure 10.1). The arrow in the figure shows the opening brace below the class definition. This brace denotes the start of the class code; there's a closing brace at the bottom as well. Notice that all of the event procedures that you've created exist between the opening and closing brace of the class. The methods you create will also be placed between these braces.

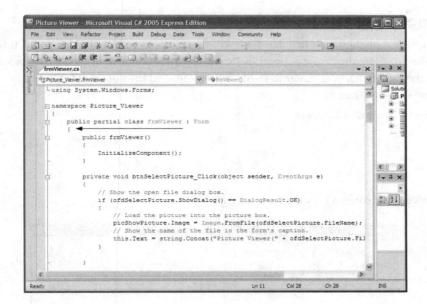

FIGURE 10.1
You create your
methods within
a class.

Defining and Writing Methods

After you've created the classes in which to store your code (in this case, we're using an existing class), you can begin writing methods. A *method* is a discrete set of code that can be called from other code. Methods are much like events, but rather than being executed by a user interacting with a form or control, methods are executed when called by a code statement.

There are two types of procedures in Visual C#:

▶ Methods that return a value

▶ Methods that do not return a value

There are many reasons to create a method that returns a value. For example, a method can return true or false depending on whether it was successful in completing its task. You could also write a method that accepts certain parameters (data passed *to* the method, in contrast to data *returned by* the method) and returns a value based on those parameters. For instance, you could write a method that enables you to pass it a sentence, and in return it passes back the number of spaces within the sentence. The possibilities are limited only by your imagination. Just keep in mind that a method doesn't *have* to return a value.

Declaring Methods That Don't Return Values

To create a method, you first declare it within a class. In your new class, position the cursor to where the arrow appears in Figure 10.1 (position it right next to the brace, on the right side), press Enter to create a new line, and then enter the following three code statements:

```
private void OpenPicture()

{

}
```

You've just created a new method (see Figure 10.2).

FIGURE 10.2
The curly braces denote the beginning and ending of the method's code.

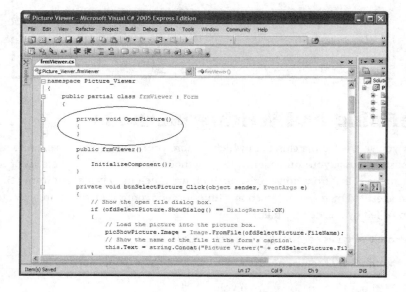

The declaration of a method (the statement used to define a method) has a number of parts. The first word, `private`, is a keyword (that is, a word with a special meaning in Visual C#). The keyword `private` defines the scope of this method (scope is discussed in detail in Hour 11, "Using Constants, Data Types, Variables, and Arrays"), designating that the method can be called from code contained in the current class only. You can use the keyword `public` in place of `private` to allow access to the method by code that resides in other classes. Because we're going to be calling this code from the Picture Viewer form only, we make the procedure `private`.

The word `void` is another Visual C# keyword. The `void` keyword is used to declare a method that doesn't return a value. Later in this hour, you will learn how to create methods that return values.

The third word, OpenPicture, is the name of the method and can be just about any string of text you want it to be. Note, however, that you can't assign a name that's a keyword, nor can you use spaces within a name. In the example you're building, the procedure performs the same function as the Open Picture menu item *and* the Open Picture Toolstrip button, hence the name. You should always give procedures strong names that reflect their purpose. You can have two procedures with the same name only if they have different scope (again, scope is discussed in Hour 11).

Some programmers prefer the readability of spaces in names, but in many instances, such as when naming methods, spaces can't be used. A common technique is to use an underscore (_) in place of a space, such as in Open_Picture, but I recommend that you just use mixed case, as you have in this example.

Immediately following the name of the method is a set of parentheses. Within these parentheses you can define *parameters*—data to be passed to the method by the calling program. In this example, there is no need to pass any data to the method, so you've left the parenthesis empty. As you will see later on, you can create methods that accept data passed to them, in addition to being able to return a result.

You have to supply parentheses, regardless of whether or not a method accepts any parameters.

Add the following code to your OpenPicture() method:

```
// Show the open file dialog box.
if (ofdSelectPicture.ShowDialog() == DialogResult.OK)
{
    // Load the picture into the picture box.
    picShowPicture.Image = Image.FromFile(ofdSelectPicture.FileName);
    // Show the name of the file in the form's caption.
    this.Text = string.Concat("Picture Viewer(" +
        ofdSelectPicture.FileName + ")");
    // Show the name of the file in the status bar.
    sbrMyStatusStrip.Items[0].Text = ofdSelectPicture.FileName;
}
```

Notice that this code is identical to the code you entered in the Open Picture button, menu item, and Toolstrip button from previous hours. You've already entered this code (or a variation of it) in three places, why another? Earlier, I alluded to the idea that having duplicate code isn't optimal and that we'd be addressing it. Whenever you find yourself duplicating code, you should immediately realize that the duplicated code should be placed in a procedure. Then, rather than have the code duplicated, you can just call the procedure as needed. This has a number of advantages, including

▶ Reduction of errors   Each time you enter code, you run the risk of doing something wrong. By entering code only once, you've reduced the likelihood of introducing errors.

▶ Consistency and maintainability   When you duplicate code, you often forget all the places where that code is used. You might fix a bug in one location but not in another, or add a feature to one copy of the code but not another. By using a single procedure, you only have to worry about maintaining one instance of the code.

If you are paying close attention, you might have noticed that I snuck an additional statement in the OpenPicture() method (the last statement in the listing). As promised in Hour 9, this statement displays the file name of the opened picture in the status bar.

You're now going to create a procedure to draw the border around the picture box. Position your cursor after the ending curly brace for the OpenPicture() method (see Figure 10.3), press Enter, and then enter the following code:

```
private void DrawBorder(PictureBox objPicturebox)
{
    Graphics objGraphics = null;
    objGraphics = this.CreateGraphics();
    objGraphics.Clear(SystemColors.Control);
    objGraphics.DrawRectangle(Pens.Blue,
        objPicturebox.Left - 1, objPicturebox.Top - 1,
        objPicturebox.Width + 1, objPicturebox.Height + 1);
    objGraphics.Dispose();
}
```

A few things introduced in this procedure may look new to you. The first is that there is text within the parentheses of the procedure declaration. I mentioned earlier that this is where you can define parameters. Parameters are data passed into the procedure, as opposed to a value returned by the procedure. Parameters are defined much like variables (I'll cover the specifics in Hour 11), but for now I just want you to get the following concept: Code that calls this method will pass into it a reference to a picture box object. The method will then be able to work with the referenced picture box just as though it were manipulating the picture box directly.

Since this method exists in the form, it's not really necessary to pass a reference to the picture box, but I want you to see how this works. The objPicturebox parameter is used throughout the procedure in place of a hard-coded reference to the picture box object on your form. Because this new procedure accepts a reference to a picture box by way of a parameter, the procedure can work with any picture box on the form—the calling code simply has to pass a reference to the picture box in question, and the border will be drawn around it. Your form class should now look like Figure 10.4.

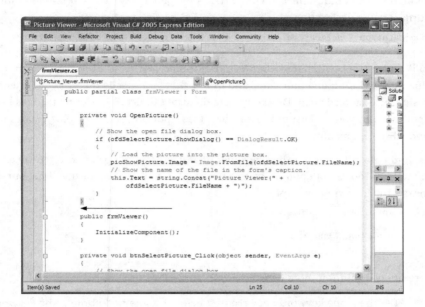

FIGURE 10.3
Start your new procedure where the arrow is pointing.

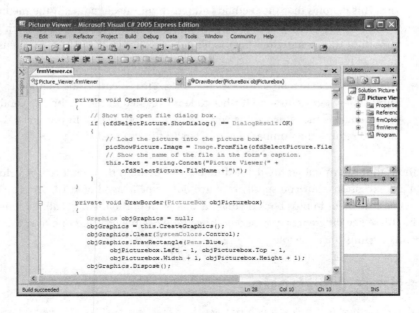

FIGURE 10.4
Each method exists as a single entity, just like event procedures.

Declaring Procedures That Return Values

The procedure you've just created doesn't return a value. You're now going to declare a method that returns a value. Here's the general syntax of a method that returns a value declaration:

```
scope datatype functionname(parameters)
```

You'll notice one key difference between declaring a method that doesn't return a value and declaring one that does, and that is that you specify a data type instead of using the keyword void. Data types are discussed in detail in Hour 11, so it's not important that you understand them now. It is important, however, that you understand what's happening.

The data type entered after the scope identifier denotes the type of data returned by the method. You're not going to create a method in your project at this time, but consider the following example:

```
private int ComputeLength(string strText)
{
    return strText.Length;
}
```

There are two things to note here:

▶ After the scope keyword private and before the method name is the keyword int. This denotes that the method will return an integer value. If the method were to return a string of text, the keyword string would be used instead. It's important that you declare the proper data type for your methods as discussed in Hour 11.

▶ The keyword return accomplishes two tasks. First, it causes the method to immediately terminate—no further code is executed in the method. Second, it passes back as the return value whatever value you specify. In this code, the method returns the number of characters in the supplied string.

Methods that return values are defined much like methods that don't return values, with the exceptions that you specify a return data type instead of void, and you use a return statement to pass back a value as the result of the method call. By remembering these key differences, you should have little trouble creating one over the other as circumstances dictate.

Calling Methods

Calling a method is simple—much simpler than creating one! So far, I've had you create two methods. Each of these methods contains code like that used in no less than three places in your form! You're now going to remove all of that duplicate code, replacing it with calls to the common methods you've just written. Follow these steps to make this happen:

1. Double-click frmViewer.cs in the Solution Explorer to view the form in the Form Designer.

2. The first code you're going to replace is the Open Picture code you've entered for the Open Picture button on the toolbar. Double-click the Open Picture button to access its Click event. Delete all the code between the opening and closing braces of the procedure (see Figure 10.5).

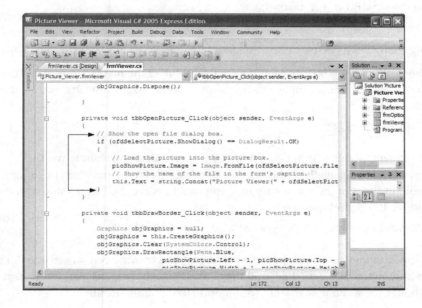

FIGURE 10.5
Delete this code and replace it with the procedure call.

3. With the old code deleted, enter the following statement:

```
this.OpenPicture();
```

That's it! To call a custom method, you simply call it like you would a built-in Visual C# method. If the method expected one or more parameters, you would enter them between the parentheses (you'll do this shortly).

4. We still have two other places in which we used the Open Picture code. Double-click frmViewer.cs in the Solution Explorer to return to design view of the form, click the File menu to open up your menu, and then double-click the Open Picture menu item.

5. Delete the code in the Click event, and replace it with the following:

```
this.OpenPicture();
```

Return to the form designer once more.

So far, you've only created methods that don't return values. As you now know, calling a method is as easy as referencing the class name, then a period, and then the method name and parenthesis. For methods that return values, calling them is a little different. Consider this little method:

```
private long AddTwoNumbers(int intFirst, int intSecond)
{
    return intFirst + intSecond;
}
```

This method accepts two parameters, adds them together, and returns their sum.

When calling a method that returns a value, think of the method in terms of the value it returns. For example, when you set a form's Height property, you set it with code like this:

```
MyForm.Height = 200;
```

This statement sets a form's height to 200. Suppose that you want to use the AddTwoNumbers() method to determine the Height of the form. Thinking of the procedure in terms of the value it returns, you could replace the literal value with the method, like the following:

```
MyForm.Height = this.AddTwoNumbers(1, 5);
```

In this example, the form's height would be set to 6 because you passed 1 and 5 to the parameters of the method, and the method added them together. In the next section, I show you how to work with parameters in more detail.

> When calling methods that return values, you must treat the method call as you would treat the literal value returned by the method. This often means placing a method call on the right side of an equal sign or embedding it in an expression.

At this time, you've created a procedure and called it from two locations—your application is really taking shape! Now that you've got a toolbar *and* a menu, you no longer need the buttons that you first created in Hour 1, "Jumping In with Both Feet: A Visual C# 2005 Programming Tour."

Follow these steps to get rid of the buttons:

1. Double-click the Select Picture button on the right side of the form (you'll need to return to the form designer first). Remove the entire event procedure, including the procedure declaration that begins with `private` and the closing parenthesis (see Figure 10.6).

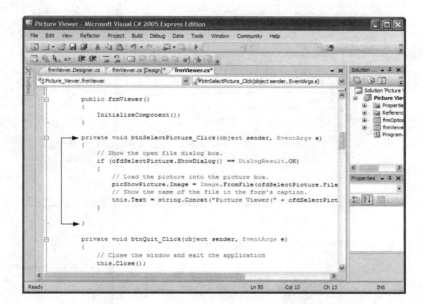

FIGURE 10.6
When deleting a procedure, you must delete the declaration and the closing brace as well.

2. Go back to the Form Designer by clicking the frmViewer.cs[Design]* tab at the top of the work area. You've deleted the actual event procedure, but Visual C# still has an internal reference to the event, and if you try to run your code now you will get a compile error. In fact, run the project now to see the build error. Click No when asked if you want to run the latest build.

3. You will then return to the designer and the Error List at the bottom will contain a single error. Double-click the error to go to it in code.

4. You'll notice that there is still a code reference to the procedure you just deleted (see Figure 10.7). This is the statement that connects the clicking of the button to the event procedure you deleted. When you delete an event procedure, Visual C# doesn't delete this reference automatically. To fix this, delete the entire statement that references the deleted procedure. Your code will now run.

5. Return to the form designer and click the Select Picture button on the form to give it the focus. Next, press Delete to delete the button.

6. Repeat steps 1 through 4 for the Quit button, the Draw Border button, and the Options button. Be sure to delete the procedures for each of them!

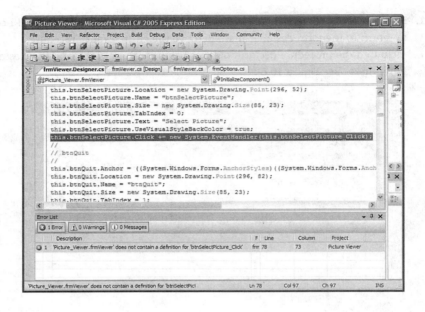

Your screen should now look like Figure 10.8.

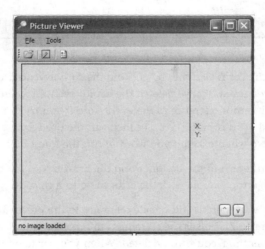

7. Go ahead and clean up the form further. Set the Location property of the X
   label to **334,264**, and set the Location property of the Y label to **334,277**.
   Finally, set the Size the of the Picture box to **320,264**. Now your form should
   look like Figure 10.9.

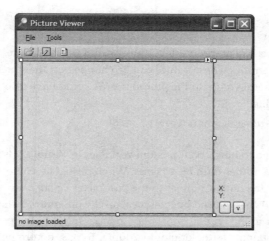

FIGURE 10.9
Much better!

Passing Parameters

Parameters are used within a procedure to allow the calling code to pass data into the procedure. You've already seen how parameters are defined—within the parentheses of a method declaration. A parameter definition consists of the data type and a name for the parameter, as shown here in bold (parameters always appear in parenthesis):

```
private MyProcedure(string strMyStringParameter)
```

> **By the Way**
>
> After you've read about variables in Hour 11, this structure will make much more sense. Here, I just want you to get the general idea of how to define and use parameters.

You can define multiple parameters for a procedure by separating them with a comma, like this:

```
private MyProcedure(string strMyStringParameter,
                    string intMyIntegerParameter)
```

A calling procedure passes data to the parameters by way of *arguments*. This is mostly a semantic issue; when defined in the declaration of a method or event procedure, the item is called a *parameter*. When the item is part of the statement that calls the procedure, it's called an *argument*. Arguments are passed within parentheses—the same as how parameters are defined. If a procedure has multiple arguments, you separate them with commas. For example, you could pass values to the procedure just defined using a statement such as this:

```
MyProcedure("This is a string", 11);
```

The parameter acts like an ordinary variable within the procedure. Remember, variables are storage entities whose values can be changed. In the statement shown previously, we sent literal values to the procedure. We could have also sent the values of variables like this:

```
MyProcedure(strAString, intAnInteger);
```

An important thing to note about passing variables in Visual C# is that parameters are passed *by value* rather than *by reference*. When passed by value, the procedure receives a copy of the data. Changes to the parameter *do not affect* the value of the original variable. When passed by reference, on the other hand, the parameter is actually a pointer to the original variable. Changes made to the parameter within the procedure propagate to the original variable. To pass a parameter by reference, you preface the parameter definition with the keyword ref as shown here:

```
public void MyMethod(ref string strMyStringParameter,
                        int intMyIntegerParameter)
```

Parameters defined without ref are passed by value; this is the default behavior of parameters in Visual C#. Therefore, in the declaration above, the first parameter is passed by reference, whereas the second parameter is passed by value.

You already created a procedure that accepts a parameter. Let's take another look:

```
private void DrawBorder(PictureBox objPicturebox)
{
    Graphics objGraphics = null;
    objGraphics = this.CreateGraphics();
    objGraphics.Clear(SystemColors.Control);
    objGraphics.DrawRectangle(Pens.Blue,
            objPicturebox.Left - 1, objPicturebox.Top - 1,
            objPicturebox.Width + 1, objPicturebox.Height + 1);
    objGraphics.Dispose();
}
```

Follow these steps to hook up the procedure:

1. Display the frmViewer form in the Form Designer.

2. Double-click the Draw Border button on the toolbar and delete the contents of the procedure.

3. Enter the following statement in the Click event:

   ```
   this.DrawBorder(picShowPicture);
   ```

4. Return to the Form Designer once more (you should know how by now), click the Tools menu on your form, and then double-click the Draw Border item.

5. Replace all the code within the procedure with this statement:

```
this.DrawBorder(picShowPicture);
```

You've now hooked up your menus and toolstrip. Press F5 to run your program and try the various menu items and tool buttons (see Figure 10.10). The Confirm on Exit button still doesn't work, but you'll hook that up in the next chapter.

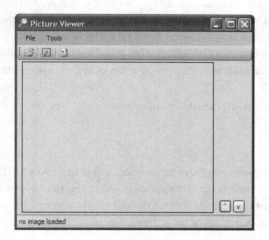

FIGURE 10.10
Professional applications demand good procedure design in addition to good interface design.

Go ahead and stop the running project and save your work.

Exiting Methods

Ordinarily, code within a method executes from beginning to end—literally. However, when a return statement is reached, execution immediately returns to the statement that made the method call; you can force execution to leave the method at any time by using a return statement. If Visual C# encounters a return statement, the method terminates immediately, and code returns to the statement that called the method.

Creating Static Methods

I mentioned earlier in this hour that there are two types of methods you can create. *Instance methods* are methods that belong to objects derived from a class. For example, the OpenPicture() method you wrote earlier is an instance member; it's a method that belongs to an instance of a class; in this case, the form that is derived from the form class. This is why you had to use this. in order call the member—as in this.OpenPicture();. In addition to instance members, you can also create *static methods*. Static methods are methods that belong to the class as a whole, not to any given object derived from the class. A good use of static methods are basic utility methods that really don't apply to a specific object. For example, say you created a method that performs a complicated mathematical function. If you had a number of different math functions, you might create a clsMath.cs class and put all of the methods in that class. But, this would require that you have to create an object based on the class before you could call the method. As I've mentioned before, creating objects takes resources and time. A better solution might be to create a general class and call it something like clsUtility.cs. Then, create the method as a static method. To create a static method, you use the static keyword after the scope designator like this:

```
public static int ComputeLength(string strText)
{
    return strText.Length;
}
```

With instance members, you have to have an object in order to call the member. For example, if the previous method declaration didn't use the keyword static, you'd have to first instantiate an object from the class and then call the method using code similar to this (the mechanics of this is discussed in Hour 16):

```
clsUtility objUtility = new clsUtility();
int intResult;
intResult = objUtility.ComputeLength("Sams Publishing");
```

If you declare the method as a static member, there is no need to instantiate an object—you can just call the method by prefacing it with the class name, like this:

```
int intResult;
intResult = clsUtility.ComputeLength("Sams Publishing");
```

Static members are a great way to expose generic functions that don't require an object instance of a class, and you will create them often.

Avoiding Infinite Recursion

It's possible to call procedures in such a way that a continuous loop occurs. Consider the following two procedures:

```
public static void DoSomething()
{
    DoSomethingElse();
}
public static void DoSomethingElse()
{
```

```
    DoSomething();
}
```

Calling either of these procedures produces an infinite loop of procedure calls and results in the error shown in Figure 10.11.

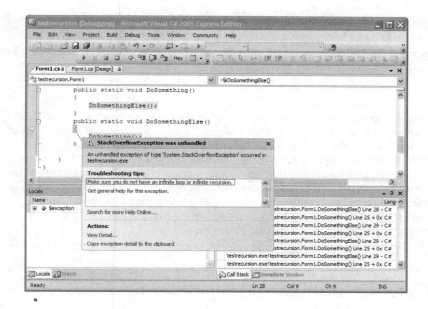

This endless loop is known as a *recursive* loop. Without getting too technical, Visual C# allocates some memory for each procedure call in an area known as the *stack*. Only a finite amount of space is available on the stack, so infinite recursion eventually uses all the available stack space, and an exception occurs. This is a serious error, and steps should be taken to avoid such recursion.

Legitimate uses exist for recursion, most notably in the use of algorithms such as those used in calculus or those used to iterate through all of the folders on a hard drive. Deliberate recursion techniques don't create infinite recursion, however; there is always a point at which the recursion stops (hopefully, before the stack is consumed). If you have an interest in such algorithms, consider reading a book dedicated to the subject.

Summary

In this hour, you learned how a method is a discrete set of code designed to perform a task or related set of tasks. Methods are where you write Visual C# code. Some methods might be as short as a single line of code, whereas others will be pages in length. You learned how to define procedures and how to call them; creating and calling procedures is critical to your success in programming with Visual C#. Be sure to avoid creating recursive procedures! Because you use procedures so often, they'll become second nature to you in no time.

Classes are used to group related procedures. In this hour, I focused on the using the form class you've been working with all along. In Hour 16, you'll build on your experience with classes and work with classes to create new objects, which demands good segregation of discrete methods.

Did you Know?

Keep in mind that every method should perform a specific function; avoid creating methods that perform many different tasks. For example, suppose that you want to create a set of code that draws an ellipse on a form. Consider that you also want to clear the form. If you placed both sets of code in the same method, the ellipse would be drawn and then immediately erased. By placing each set of code in its own method, you can draw the ellipse by calling one method and then erase it at any time by calling the other method. By placing these routines in a new class rather than attaching them to a specific form class, you also make the methods available to any form that needs them.

Q&A

Q. *Do I need to pay much attention to scope when defining my procedures?*

A. It might be tempting to create all your methods as public, but this is bad coding practice for a number of reasons. For one thing, you'll find that in larger projects, you have methods with the same name that do slightly different things. Usually, these routines are relevant only within a limited scope. However, if you create all public methods, you'll run into conflicts when you create a method with the same name in the same scope. If the method isn't needed at the public level, don't define it for public access.

Q. *What is a "reasonable" number of classes?*

A. This is hard to say. There really is no right answer. Instead of worrying about an exact count, you should strive to make sure that your classes are logical and that they contain only appropriate methods and properties.

Workshop

Quiz

1. What are the entities called that are used to house methods?

2. True or False: To access methods in a class module, you must first create an object.

3. Data that has been passed into a method by a calling statement is called a _____?

4. To pass multiple arguments to a method, separate them with a _____?

5. The situation in which a method or set of methods continue to call each other in a looping fashion is called?

Answers

1. Classes

2. False. If the method is declared as a static member, you do not need to instantiate an object to call the member.

3. Parameter.

4. Comma.

5. Recursion.

Exercises

1. Create a method as part of a form that accepts one string and outputs a different string. Add code to the TextChanged() event of a text box to call the procedure, passing the contents of the text box as the argument.

2. Create a single method that calls itself. Call this method from the Click() event of a button and observe the resulting error.

HOUR 11

Using Constants, Data Types, Variables, and Arrays

What You'll Learn in This Hour:

▶ Understanding data types

▶ Determining data type

▶ Converting data to different data types

▶ Defining and using constants

▶ Declaring and referencing variables

▶ Working with arrays

▶ Determining scope

▶ Declaring static variables

▶ Using a naming convention

As you write your Visual C# methods, you'll regularly need to store and retrieve various pieces of information. In fact, I can't think of a single application I've written that didn't need to store and retrieve data in code. For example, you might want to keep track of how many times a method has been called, or you may want to store a property value and use it at a later time. Such data can be stored as *constants*, *variables*, or *arrays*. Constants are named values that you define once at design time and cannot be changed after that, but can be referenced as often as needed. Variables, on the other hand, are like storage bins; you can retrieve or replace the data in a variable as often as you need to. Arrays act like grouped variables, enabling you to store many values in a single array variable.

Whenever you define one of these storage entities, you have to decide the type of data it will contain. For example, is a new variable going to hold a string value (text) or perhaps a number? If it will hold a number, is the number a whole number, an integer, or something else entirely? After you determine the type of data to store, you must choose the level of visibility that the data has to other methods within the project (this visibility is known as *scope*). In this hour, you'll learn the ins and outs of Visual C# data types, how to create and use these "storage" mechanisms, and how to minimize problems in your code by reducing scope.

> In this hour you'll build on the Picture Viewer project from Hour 10, "Creating and Calling Methods." Here, you'll start the process for hooking up the features you created controls for on your Options form.

Understanding Data Types

In every programming language there is a *compiler*. The compiler is the part of the Visual Studio .NET Framework that interprets the code you write into a language the computer can understand. The compiler must understand the type of data you're manipulating in code. For example, if you asked the compiler to add the following values, it would get confused:

```
659 + "Fender"
```

When the compiler gets confused, it either refuses to compile the code (which is the preferred situation because you can address the problem before your users run the application), or it halts execution and displays an exception (error) when it reaches the confusing line of code. (These two types of errors are discussed in detail in Hour 15, "Debugging Your Code.") Obviously, you can't add the word *Fender* to the number 659 because these two values are different types of data. In Visual C#, these two values are said to have two different *data types*. In Visual C#, constants, variables, and arrays must always be defined to hold a specific type of information.

Determining Data Type

Data typing—the act of defining a constant, variable, or array's data type—can be confusing. To Visual C#, a number is not simply a number. A number that contains a decimal value is different from a number that doesn't. Visual C# can perform arithmetic on numbers of different data types, but you can't store data of one type in a variable with an incompatible type. Visual C# supports two categories of data types: value types and reference types. The main difference between these two types is how their values are stored in memory. As you continue to create more complex applications, this difference may have an impact on your programming. For this book, however, this distinction is minimal. Because of this limitation, you must give careful consideration to the type of data you plan to store in a constant, variable, or array at the time you define it. Table 11.1 lists the Visual C# data types and the range of values each one can contain.

TABLE 11.1 The Visual C# Data Types

Data Type—Value	Value Range
bool	True or False
byte	0 to 255 (unsigned)
char	A Unicode character
DateTime	0:00:00 (midnight) on January 1, 0001 through 11:59:59 PM on December 31, 9999
decimal	+/−7.9228162514264337593543950335 with 28 places to the right of the decimal; use this data type for currency values
double	−1.79769313486231570E+308 through 1.79769313486231570E+308
int	−2, 147,483,648 to 2,147,483,647 (signed). This is the same as the data type Int32.
long	−9, 223,372,036,854,775,808 to 9,223,372,036,854,775,807 (signed). This is the same as data type Int64.
sbyte	−128 through 127 (signed)
short	−32,768 to 32,767 (signed). This is the same as data type Int16.
float	−3.4028235e38 through 3.4028235e+8
uint	0 through 4,294,967,295 (unsigned).
ulong	0 through 18,446,744,073,709,551,615 (1.8...E+19) (unsigned)
ushort	0 through 65,535 (unsigned)
Data Type—Reference	**Value Range**
string	0 to approximately 2 billion Unicode characters
Object	Any type can be stored in a variable

Visual C# supports unsigned data types for short, int, and long (the types prefaced with u, such as uint). Because negative numbers are excluded (there is no sign), this has the effect of doubling the positive values for a short, an int, or a long. Signed data types are preferable and should be used unless you have a very good reason for doing otherwise (such as declaring a variable that will never hold a negative value).

Tips for Determining Data Type

The list of data types might seem daunting at first, but you can follow some general guidelines for choosing among them. As you become more familiar with the different types, you'll be able to fine-tune your data type selection.

Following are some helpful guidelines for using data types:

▶ If you want to store text, use the `string` data type. The `string` data type can be used to store any valid keyboard character, including numbers and nonalphabetic characters.

▶ To store only the value True or False, use the `bool` data type.

▶ If you want to store a number that contains no decimal places and is greater than –32,768 and smaller than 32,767, use the `short` data type.

▶ To store numbers with no decimal places, but with values larger or smaller than `short` allows, use the `int` or `long` (an abbreviation for *integer* and *long*) data types.

▶ If you need to store numbers that contain decimal places, use the `float` data type. The `float` data type should work for almost all your values containing decimals, unless you're writing incredibly complex mathematical applications or need to store very large numbers; in that case, use a `double`.

▶ To store currency amounts, use the `decimal` data type.

▶ To store a single character, use the `char` data type.

▶ If you need to store a date and/or a time value, use the `DateTime` data type. When you use the `DateTime` data type, Visual C# recognizes common date and time formats. For example, if you store the value 7/22/2001, Visual C# doesn't treat it as a simple text string; it knows that the text represents July 22, 2001.

▶ Different data types use different amounts of memory. To preserve system resources, it's best to use the data type that consumes the least amount of memory and still provides the ability to store the full range of possible values. For example, if only storing numbers from 1 to 10, use a `short` instead of a `long`.

The Object data type requires special attention. If you define a variable or array as an Object data type, you can store just about any value you care to in it; Visual C# determines what data type to use when you set the variable's value.

Several drawbacks exist to using Object data types. First, Object data types take up more memory than the other data types. In addition, Visual C# takes a little longer to perform calculations on Object data types. Unless you have a specific reason to do so—and there are valid reasons, such as when you don't know the type of data to be stored ahead of time—don't use the Object data type. Instead, become familiar with the explicit data types and use them appropriately.

Casting Data from One Data Type to Another

Under most circumstances, Visual C# won't allow you to move data of one type into a variable of another type. The process of changing a value's data type is known as *casting*. Visual C# supports two types of casting: implicit and explicit. *Implicit* conversions are done automatically by the compiler. These conversions guarantee that no data is lost in the conversion. For instance, you can set the value of a variable declared as double to the value of a variable declared as float without an explicit cast because there is no risk of losing data; the double data type holds a more precise value than does a float, and this type of cast is called a *widening cast*.

Explicit casting is required when a potential exists for data loss or when converting a larger data type into a smaller data type (a narrowing cast). If you tried to place a value in a variable when the value was higher than the variable's supported data type, some data would be lost. Therefore, Visual C# requires that these types of conversions be explicitly written using the cast operator.

Table 11.2 lists some of the type conversions that can be done implicitly with no loss of information.

TABLE 11.2 Safe Conversions

Type	Can Be Safely Converted To
byte	short, int, long, float, double, or decimal
short	int, long, float, double, or decimal
int	long, float, double, or decimal
long	float, double, or decimal
float	double
double	decimal

To explicitly convert data from one type to another, you use one of the methods of the Convert class. Table 11.3 lists these methods. The use of these methods is pretty straightforward: Pass the data to be cast as the parameter, and the method returns the value with the return type. For example, to place the value of a variable declared as `double` into a variable declared as `single`, you could use a statement such as the following:

```
sngVariable = Convert.ToSingle(dblVariable);
```

TABLE 11.3   Some Common Type Conversion Methods of the Convert Class

Function	Converts To
ToBoolean(*expression*)	bool
ToByte(*expression*)	byte
ToChar(*expression*)	char
ToDateTime(*expression*)	DateTime
ToDecimal(*expression*)	decimal
ToDouble(*expression*)	double
ToInt16(*expression*)	16-bit signed integer
ToInt32(*expression*)	integer
ToInt64(*expression*)	long
ToSByte(*expression*)	sbyte
ToSingle(*expression*)	Single
ToString(*expression*)	string
ToUInt16(*expression*)	16-bit unsigned integer
ToUInt32(*expression*)	32-bit unsigned integer
ToUInt64(*expression*)	64-bit unsigned integer

Defining and Using Constants

When you hard-code numbers in your procedures (such as in `intVotingAge = 18`), a myriad of things can go wrong. Hard-coded numbers are generally referred to as *magic numbers* because they're often shrouded in mystery; the meaning of such a number is obscure because the digits themselves give no indication of what the number represents. Constants are used to eliminate the problems of magic numbers.

You define a constant as having a specific value at design time, and that value never changes throughout the life of your program. Constants offer the following benefits:

▶ **Elimination or reduction of data entry problems**   It's much easier to remember to use a constant named c_pi than it is to enter 3.14159265358979 everywhere that pi is needed. The compiler catches misspelled or undeclared constants, but it doesn't care one bit what you enter as a literal value. (Incidentally, you can retrieve the value of pi using System.Math.PI, so you don't have to worry about creating your own constant!)

▶ **Code is easier to update**   If you hard-coded a mortgage interest rate at 6.785, and rate changed to 7.00, you'd have to change every occurrence of 6.785 in code. In addition to the possibility of data entry problems, you'd run the risk of changing a value of 6.785 that had nothing to do with the interest rate—perhaps a value that represented a savings bond yield (OK, a *very* high savings bond yield). With a constant, you change the value once at the constant declaration, and all code that references the constant uses the new value right away.

▶ **Code is easier to read**   Magic numbers are often anything but intuitive. Well-named constants, on the other hand, add clarity to code. For example, which of the following statements makes the most sense to you?

```
decInterestAmount = ((decLoanAmount * 0.075) * 12);
```

or

```
decInterestAmount = ((decLoanAmount * c_fltInterestRate) *
                      c_intMonthsInTerm);
```

Constant definitions have the following syntax:

```
const datatype name = value;
```

To define a constant to hold the value of pi, for example, you could use a statement such as this:

```
const double c_pi = 3.14159265358979;
```

Note how I prefix the constant name with c_. I do this so that it's easier to determine what's a variable and what's a constant when reading code. See the "Naming Conventions" section later in this hour for more information.

After a constant is defined, you can use the constant's name in code in place of the constant's value. For example, to output the result of two times the value of pi, you could use a statement like this (the * character is used for multiplication and is covered in the next hour):

```
Console.WriteLine(c_pi * 2);
```

Using the constant is much easier and less prone to error than typing this:

```
Console.WriteLine(3.14159265358979 * 2);
```

Constants can be referenced only in the scope in which they are defined. I discuss scope in the section "Determining Scope" later in this hour.

You're going to use what you learn in this chapter to enable the options controls that you added in Hour 7, "Working with Traditional Controls." The first thing you'll do is use constants to create default values for the options. Recall from Hour 7 that you created an option form that allowed the user to manipulate the following three options:

▶ The user's name   This is displayed in the Picture Viewer's main form title bar.

▶ Prompt to confirm on exit   This is used to determine whether the user is asked to if they really want to shut down the Picture Viewer application.

▶ The default background color of the picture box   This can be set to Gray (the default) or white.

In the following steps, you'll create a constant for the default value of the Prompt on Exit option. Start by opening the Picture Viewer project from Hour 10 and then follow these steps:

1. Click once on frmViewer.cs in the Solutions Explorer to select it.

2. Click the View Code button at the top of the Solution Explorer to view the code behind frmViewer.vs.

3. The constants you are about to create will be class-level constants. That is, they can be used anywhere within the module in which they are declared. This means that they will not be placed in a specific procedure. The place to put module constants is right after the declaration of the class (public *partial* class *classname*). Position the cursor on the line following the opening brace of the class declaration (see Figure 11.1), press Enter to create a new line, and then enter the following constant declaration:

```
const bool c_defPromptOnExit = false;
```

In the next section, you'll learn how to use this constant to set the value of a variable.

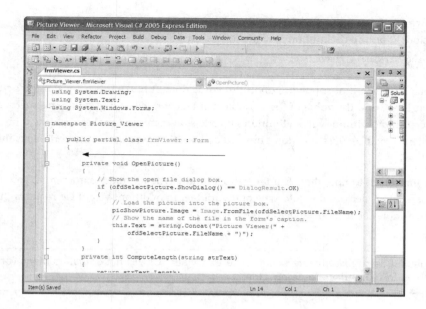

FIGURE 11.1
Create your
class-level con-
stants here.

Declaring and Referencing Variables

Variables are similar to constants in that when you reference a variable's name in code, Visual C# substitutes the variable's value in place of the variable name during code execution. This doesn't happen at compile time, though, as it does with constants. Instead, it happens at runtime—the moment the variable is referenced. This is because variables, unlike constants, can have their values changed at any time.

Declaring Variables

The act of defining a variable is called *declaring*. (Variables with scope other than local are dimensioned in a slightly different way, as discussed in the section on scope.) You've already defined variables in previous hours, so a declaration statement should look familiar to you:

```
datatype variablename = initialvalue;
```

You don't have to specify an initial value for a variable, although being able to do so in the declaration statement is very cool and useful. To create a new string variable and initialize it with a value, for example, you could use two statements, such as the following:

```
string strName;
strName = "Matt Perry";
```

However, if you know the initial value of the variable at design time, you can include it on the declaration statement, like this:

```
string strName = "Matt Perry";
```

Note, however, that supplying an initial value doesn't make this a constant; it's still a variable, and the value of the variable can be changed at any time. This method of creating an initial value eliminates a code statement and makes the code a bit easier to read because you don't have to go looking to see where the variable is initialized.

It's important to note that Visual C# is a strongly typed language; therefore, you must always declare the data type of a variable. In addition, Visual C# requires that all variables be initialized before they're used.

By the Way

Visual Basic programmers should note that Visual C# will *not* default numeric variables to 0 or strings to empty strings.

For example, the following statements would result in a compiler error in Visual C#: Use of unassigned local variable 'fltMyValue'.

```
float fltMyValue;
System.Diagnostics.Debug.WriteLine (fltMyValue + 2);
```

By the Way

You can't use a reserved word to name a constant or a variable. For example, you couldn't use the word private or public as a variable name. There is a master list of reserved words, and you can find it by searching the Help text for **public Keyword**. You'll naturally pick up most of the common ones because you'll use them so often. For others, the compiler will tell you when something is a reserved word. If you use a naming convention for your variables, which consists of giving the variable names a prefix to denote their type, you'll greatly reduce the chance of running into reserved words.

Passing Literal Values to a Variable

The syntax of assigning a *literal* value (a hard-coded value such as 6 or "guitar") to a variable depends on the data type of the variable.

For strings, you must pass the value in quotation marks, like this:

```
strFirstName = "James Tyler";
```

There is one caveat when assigning literal values to strings: Visual C# interprets slashes (\) as being a special type of escape sequence. If you pass a literal string containing one or more slashes to a variable, you'll get an error. What you have to do in such instances is preface the literal with the symbol @, like this:

```
strFilePath = @"c:\Temp";
```

When Visual C# encounters the @ symbol after the equal sign like this, it knows to *not* treat slashes in the string as escape sequences.

To pass a literal value to a char variable, use single quotes instead of double quotes, like this:

```
chrMyCharacter = 'j';
```

For numeric values, you don't enclose the value in anything:

```
intAnswerToEverything = 42;
```

Using Variables in Expressions

Variables can be used anywhere an expression is expected. The arithmetic functions, for example, operate on expressions. You could add two literal numbers and store the result in a variable like this:

```
intMyVariable = 2 + 5;
```

In addition, you could replace either or both literal numbers with numeric variables or constants, as shown next:

```
intMyVariable = intFirstValue + 5;
```

```
intMyVariable = 2 + intSecondValue;
```

```
intMyVariable = intFirstValue + intSecondValue;
```

Variables are a fantastic way to store values during code execution, and you'll use variables all the time—from performing decisions and creating loops to using them as a temporary place to stick a value. Remember to use a constant when you know the value at design time and the value won't change. When you don't know the value ahead of time or the value might change, use a variable with a data type appropriate to the function of the variable.

> In Visual C#, variables are created as objects. Feel free to create a variable and explore the members (that is, the properties and methods) of the variable. You do this by entering the variable name and pressing a period (this works only after you've entered the statement that declares the variable). For example, to determine the length of the text within a string variable, you can use the Length property of a string variable like this:
>
> ```
> strMyVariable.Length
> ```
>
> There are some powerful features dangling off the data type objects.

Working with Arrays

An array is a special type of variable—it's a variable with multiple dimensions. Think of an ordinary variable as a single mail slot. You can retrieve or change the contents of the mail slot by referencing the variable. An array is like having an entire row of mail slots (called *elements*). You can retrieve and set the contents of any of the individual mail slots at any time by referencing the single array variable. You do this by using an index that points to the appropriate slot.

Declaring Arrays

Arrays are declared in much the same way as ordinary variables, with one notable exception. Consider the following statements:

```
string[] strMyArray;
strMyArray = new string[10];
```

The first statement declares strMyArray as an array, and the second statement defines the array as having 10 string elements.

The number in brackets determines how many "mail slots" the array variable will contain, and it can be a literal value, a constant, or the value of another variable.

> It's possible to create arrays that can be resized at runtime. However, this is beyond the scope of this book.

Referencing Array Variables

To place a value in an array index, you specify the index number when referencing the variable. Most computer operations consider 0 to be the first value in a series, not 1, as you might expect. This is how array indexing behaves. For example, for an array dimensioned with 10 elements—declared using [10]—you would reference the elements sequentially using the indexes 0, 1, 2, 3, 4, 5, 6, 7, 8, and 9.

> Notice that the upper index is one less than the number specified when the array was declared. Because 0 is a valid element, you end up with one more than the number you used to declare the array. This can be confusing. To simplify your development, you might just consider ignoring element 0 and using elements 1 through the declared upper value.

By the Way

To place a value in the first element of the array variable, you would use 0 as the index, like this:

```
strMyArray[0] = "This value goes in the first element";
```

To reference the second element, you could use a statement like this:

```
strMyArray[1] = strMyArray[0];
```

> The data type specified for the array variable is used for all the elements in the array. You can use the Object type to hold any type of data in any element, but doing so isn't recommended for all the reasons discussed earlier.

By the Way

Creating Multidimensional Arrays

Array variables require only one declaration, yet they can store numerous pieces of data; this makes them perfect for storing sets of related information. The array example shown previously is a single-dimension array. Arrays can be much more complex than this example and can have multiple dimensions of data. For example, a single array variable could be defined to store personal information for different people. Multidimensional arrays are declared with multiple parameters such as the following:

```
int[,] intMeasurements;
intMeasurements = new int[3,2];
```

These statements create a two-dimensional array. The first dimension (defined as having three elements: 0, 1, 2) serves as an index to the second dimension (defined as having two elements). Suppose that you wanted to store the height and weight of three people in this array. You reference the array as you would a single-dimension array, but you include the extra parameter index. The two indexes together specify an element, much as coordinates in Battleship relate to specific spots on the game board. Figure 11.2 illustrates how the elements are related.

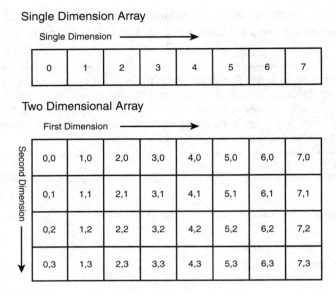

FIGURE 11.2
Two-dimensional
arrays are like a
wall of mail
slots.

Elements are grouped according to the first index specified; think of the first set of indexes as being a single-dimension array. For example, to store the height and weight of a person in the array's first dimension (remember, arrays are zero-based), you could use code such as the following:

```
intMeasurements[0,0] = FirstPersonsHeight;
intMeasurements[0,1] = FirstPersonsWeight;
```

I find it helpful to create constants for the array elements, which makes array references much easier to understand. Consider this:

```
const int c_Height = 0;
const int c_Weight = 1;
intMeasurements[0,c_Height] = FirstPersonsHeight;
intMeasurements[0,c_Weight] = FirstPersonsWeight;
```

You could then store the height and weight of the second and third person like this:

```
intMeasurements[1,c_Height] = SecondPersonsHeight;
intMeasurements[1,c_Weight] = SecondPersonsWeight;
intMeasurements[2,c_Height] = ThirdPersonsHeight;
intMeasurements[2,c_Width] = ThirdPersonsWeight;
```

In this array, I've used the first dimension to differentiate people. I've used the second dimension to store a height and weight for each element in the first dimension. Because I've consistently stored heights in the first slot of the array's second dimension and weights in the second slot of the array's second dimension, it becomes easy to work with these pieces of data. For example, you can retrieve the height and weight of a single person as long as you know the first dimension index used to store the data. You could print out the total weight of all three people using the following code:

```
Console.WriteLine(intMeasurements[0,c_Weight] + intMeasurements[1,c_Weight] +
            intMeasurements[2,c_Weight]);
```

When working with arrays, keep the following points in mind:

► The first element in any dimension of an array has an index of 0.

► Dimension an array to hold only as much data as you intend to put into it.

► Dimension an array with a data type appropriate to the values to be placed in the array's elements.

Arrays are a great way to store and work with related sets of data in Visual C# code. Arrays can make working with larger sets of data much simpler and more efficient than using other methods. To maximize your effectiveness with arrays, study the for loop discussed in Hour 14, "Looping for Efficiency." Using a for loop, you can quickly iterate (loop sequentially) through all the elements in an array.

> This section discussed the rectangular type of a Visual C# multidimensional array. Visual C# also supports another type of multidimensional array called *jagged*. Jagged arrays are an array of one-dimensional arrays, each of which can be of different lengths. However, teaching jagged arrays is beyond the scope of this book.

By the Way

Determining Scope

Constants, variables, and arrays are useful ways to store and retrieve data in Visual C# code. Hardly a program is written that doesn't use at least one of these elements. To properly use them, however, it's critical that you understand scope.

You had your first encounter with scope in Hour 10, with the keywords private and public. You learned that code is written in procedures and that procedures are stored in modules. *Scope* refers to the level that a constant, variable, array, or procedure can be "seen" in code. For a constant or variable, scope can be one of the following:

► Block level

► Method level (local)

► Private

Scope has the same effect on array variables as it does on ordinary variables. For the sake of clarity, I'll reference variables in this discussion on scope, but understand that what I discuss applies equally to arrays (and constants, for that matter).

Understanding Block Scope

Block scope, also called structure scope, is when a variable is declared within a structure, and if so, it gives the variable block scope.

Structures are coding constructs that consist of two statements as opposed to one. For example, the standard do structure is used to create a loop; it looks like this:

```
Do
{
    <statements to execute in the loop
}

while(i <10)
```

Visual C# uses the word *structure* to mean a user-defined type. However, when talking about code, structure is also used to mean a block of code that has a beginning and an end. For the purpose of this discussion, it is this code block that I am referring to.

Another example is the for loop, which looks like this:

```
for (int i = 1;  i<10;i++)
{
    <statements to execute when expression is True>
}
```

If a variable is declared within a structure, the variable's scope is confined to the structure; the variable isn't created until the declaration statement occurs, and it's destroyed when the structure completes. If a variable is needed only within a structure, think about declaring it within the structure to give it block scope. Consider the following example:

```
if (blnCreateLoop)
{
    int intCounter ;

    for (intCounter=1; intCounter<=100; intCounter++)
    {
        // Do something
    }
}
```

By placing the variable declaration statement within the `if` structure, you ensure that the variable is created only if it is needed. In fact, you can create a block simply by enclosing statements in opening and closing braces like this:

```
{
    int intMyVariable = 10;
    Console.WriteLine(intMyVariable);
}
```

The various structures, including looping and decision-making structures, are discussed in later hours.

Understanding Method-Level (Local) Scope

When you declare a constant or variable within a method, that constant or variable has *method-level*, or *local*, scope. Most of the variables you'll create will have method scope. In fact, almost all the variables you've created in previous hours have had method-level scope. You can reference a local constant or variable within the same method, but it isn't visible to other methods. If you try to reference a local constant or variable from a method other than the one in which it's defined, Visual C# .NET returns a compile error to the method making the reference (the variable or constant doesn't exist). It's generally considered best practice to declare all your local variables at the top of a method, but Visual C# .NET doesn't care where you place declaration statements within a method. Note, however, that if you place a declaration statement within a structure, the corresponding variable will have block scope, not local scope.

Understanding Private-Level Scope

When a constant or variable has private-level scope, it can be viewed by all methods within the class containing the declaration. To methods in all other classes, however, the constant or variable doesn't exist. To create a constant or variable with private-level scope, you must place the declaration within a class but not within a method. Class member declarations are generally done at the beginning of the class (right after the opening brace of the class). Use private-level scope when many methods must share the same variable and when passing the value as a parameter is not a workable solution.

For all modules other than those used to generate forms, it's easy to add code to the declarations section; simply add the declaration statements just after the class declaration line and prior to any method definitions, as shown in Figure 11.3.

FIGURE 11.3
The declarations section exists above all declared methods.

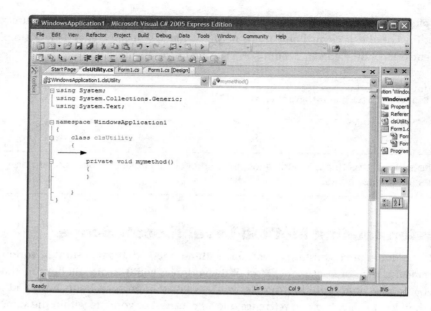

Classes used to generate forms have lots of system-generated code within them, so it might not be so obvious where to place private-level variables. Visual C# inserts many private statements in classes used to build forms, so place your variable declarations after any and all form-type declaration statements in such classes (see Figure 11.4).

Did you Know?

You can hover the pointer over any variable in code and a ToolTip will appear showing you the declaration of the variable.

Did you Know?

In general, the smaller the scope the better. When possible, give a variable block or local scope. If you have to increase scope, attempt to make the variable a private-level variable. You should use public variables only when absolutely necessary (and there are times when it is necessary to do so). The higher the scope, the more possibilities exist for problems and the more difficult it is to debug those problems.

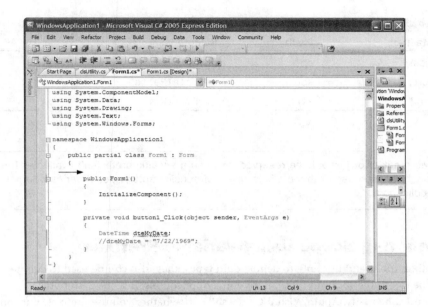

FIGURE 11.4
The declarations section includes the Visual C# generated statements.

Naming Conventions

To make code more self-documenting (always an important goal) and to reduce the chance of programming errors, you need an easy way to determine the exact data type of a variable or the exact type of a referenced control in Visual C# code.

Using Prefixes to Denote Data Type

Table 11.4 lists the prefixes of the common data types. Although you don't have to use prefixes, there are many advantages to be gained by doing so.

TABLE 11.4   Prefixes for Common Data Types

Data Type	Prefix	Sample Value
bool	bln	blnLoggedIn
byte	byt	bytAge
char	chr	chrQuantity
decimal	dec	decSalary
double	dbl	dblCalculatedResult
float	flt	fltInterestRate
int	int	intLoopCounter
long	lng	lngCustomerID

TABLE 11.4   Continued

Data Type	Prefix	Sample Value
object	obj	objWord
short	sho	shoTotalParts
String	str	strFirstName

By the Way

> The prefix of obj should be reserved for when a specific prefix isn't available. The most common use of this prefix is when referencing automation libraries of other applications.

Denoting Scope Using Variable Prefixes

Prefixes are useful not only to denote data types, they also can be used to denote scope (see Table 11.5). In particularly large applications, a scope designator is almost a necessity. Again, Visual C# doesn't care whether you use prefixes, but consistently using prefixes benefits you as well as others who have to review your code.

TABLE 11.5   Prefixes for Variable Scope

Prefix	Description	Example
g	Global	g_strSavePath
m	Private to class	m_blnDataChanged
(no prefix)	Nonstatic variable, local to method	fltInterestRate

Prefixes aren't just for variables. All standard objects (including forms and controls) can use a three-character prefix. There are simply too many controls and objects to list all the prefixes here, although you'll find that I use control prefixes throughout this book.

Using Variables in Your Picture Viewer Project

You've already added a module-level constant to your Picture Viewer project earlier in this hour. In this section, you'll create variables to hold the values for the controls on your Options form. In Hour 16, you will complete hooking up the options for your project.

Creating the Variables for the Options

In past hours, you defined three options for your Picture Viewer project. Let's consider each one now:

▶ User Name   This is where the user can enter their name, which appears in the title bar of the form. Think for a moment about the type of data that will be stored for this option. If you said String (which is text), you're correct.

▶ Prompt to confirm on exit   This option has two possible values, true and false, and therefore we need to use a Boolean value to store this option.

▶ Default picture background color   This is actually a special case. I told you about the common data types, but in addition to those there are dozens of other different data types, one of which is Color. You'll be using a variable of the data type Color to store the user's background color preference.

Follow these steps to create the variables:

1. Display the code for the frmViewer.cs form (not the frmOptions.cs form).

2. Locate the declarations section of the form's module—it's where you created the constant `c_defPromptOnExit`.

3. Enter the following three variable declarations beginning on the line following the constant definition:

```
string m_strUserName = "";
bool m_blnPromptOnExit = c_defPromptOnExit;
Color m_objPictureBackColor;
```

Your code should look like Figure 11.5.

Initializing and Using the Options Variables

Now that the variables have been created, you need to initialize them. Actually, you initialized them when you declared them, but you will need to change their values when your project starts up, so you're going to add code that will allow you to do that now by following these steps:

1. The best place to set up a form is usually in the form's Load event. Start by double-clicking frmViewew.cs in the Solution Explorer to display the form in the form designer, then double-click somewhere on the form (be sure not to double-click a control).

2. Your load event already has two lines of code in it: the two statements you entered to set the value of the X and Y labels. Add the following two statements below the existing code:

```
m_blnPromptOnExit = c_defPromptOnExit;
m_objPictureBackColor = System.Drawing.SystemColors.Control;
```

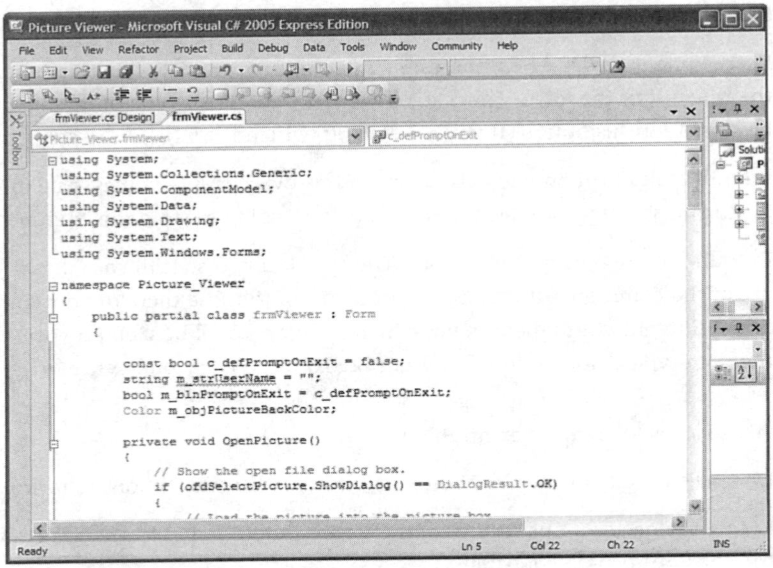

FIGURE 11.5
Class variables go in the declarations section, before code procedures.

The first statement simply sets the module variable that stores the user's prompt on exit setting to the value of the constant you created earlier. I set up the example this way so that you can see how constants and variables work together. If you wanted to change the default behavior of the Close on Exit option, all you would have to do is change the value of the constant in the declarations section.

The second statement sets the default back color to the default system color for controls. I've already explained how this works, so I won't go into detail here. Notice that I did not create an initialization statement for the module-level variable m_strUserName. This is because I already initialized the string when I declared it. I did this so you can see there are multiple approaches to solving a problem.

3. So far, you've created variables for the options and initialized them in code. However, the option values aren't actually used in the project yet. The Prompt on Exit option will be checked when the user closes the form, but the back color of the picture box needs to be set before the form appears. Enter the following statement right below the two you just created:

```
picShowPicture.BackColor = m_objPictureBackColor;
```

OK, all that's left to do in this hour is to hook up the Prompt on Exit function. This takes just a tad more work because you created a menu item that keeps track of whether the Prompt on Exit option is chosen. The first thing you're going to do is make sure that the menu item is in sync with the variable; you don't want the menu item checked if the variable is set to `false` because this would give the opposite response from what the user expects. Continue with these steps to hook up the Prompt on Exit variable:

4. Add this statement to your `Form_Load` event, right below the statement you just entered to set the picture box's back color. This statement ensures that when the form loads, the checked state of the menu item matches the state of the variable. Because you initialized the Boolean variable m_blnPromptOnExit to `false`, the menu item appears *unchecked*.

```
mnuConfirmOnExit.Checked = m_blnPromptOnExit;
```

5. You already created a procedure for the menu item so that it physically changes its `Checked` state when the user clicks it. You can scroll down the code window and locate the procedure mnuConfirmOnExit_Click, or you can switch to design view and double-click the menu item. Remember, there are usually multiple ways to approach a problem in Visual C#! After you've found the procedure, add this statement *below* the existing code:

```
m_blnPromptOnExit = mnuConfirmOnExit.Checked;
```

Did you notice that this statement is the exact opposite of the statement you entered in step 4? You've just told Visual C# to set the value of the variable to the checked state of the menu item, *after* the checked state has been updated in the `Click` event.

6. Now that the variable will stay in sync with the menu item, you need to hook up the actual Prompt on Exit code. Double-click frmViewer.cs in the Solution Explorer to view the form designer and then click the Events button on the Properties Window. Next, locate the `FormClosing` event and double-click it. This will create a new event handler for the `FormClosing` event. Enter the following code exactly as it appears here:

```
if (m_blnPromptOnExit)
{
    if (MessageBox.Show("Close the Picture Viewer program?", "Confirm Exit",
            MessageBoxButtons.YesNo, MessageBoxIcon.Question)
            == DialogResult.No)
    {
        e.Cancel = true;
    }
}
```

I've already mentioned the `MessageBox()` function (and I'll explain it in detail in Hour 17, "Interacting with Users"). All that you need to understand here is that when the user closes the Picture Viewer and the variable m_blnPromptOnExit is true, the `MessageBox.Show()` function asks the user whether he really wants to quit. If the user chooses No, the e.Cancel property is set to `true`, which cancels the form from closing (you can read more about the e object for the FormClosing event in the online help text).

Press F5 to run your project now and give it a try. When you first run the application, the variable is `false`, and the menu item appears unchecked. If you click the Close button in the upper-right corner of the form, the Picture Viewer closes. Run the project again, but this time click the Confirm on Exit menu item to check it before you close the form. This time, when you close the form, you are asked to confirm (see Figure 11.6).

FIGURE 11.6
It's nice to give the user control over their experience!

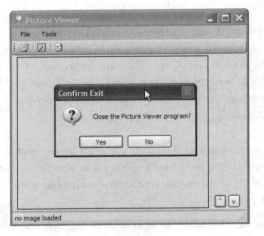

Summary

In this hour, you learned how to eliminate magic numbers by creating constants. By using constants in place of literal values, you increase code readability, reduce the possibilities of coding errors, and make it much easier to change a value in the future.

In addition, you learned how to create variables for data elements in which the initial value isn't known at design time, or for elements whose values will be changed at runtime. You learned how arrays add dimensions to variables and how to declare and reference them in your code.

Visual C# enforces strict data typing, and in this hour you learned about the various data types and how they're used, as well as tips for choosing data types and functions for converting data from one type to another. Finally, you learned about scope—an important programming concept—and how to manage scope within your projects.

Writing code that can be clearly understood by those who didn't write it is a worthwhile goal. Naming prefixes go a long way toward accomplishing this goal. In this hour, you learned the naming prefixes for the common data types, and you learned to use prefixes to denote scope.

In the end, you utilized all these concepts and created a constant and some variables to handle the options of your Picture Viewer program. You even added code to make them work! The Options form is still not "hooked up," but you'll fix that in Hour 16.

Q&A

Q. Are any performance tricks related to the many data types?

A. One trick when using whole numbers (values with no decimal places) is to use the data type that matches your processor. For instance, most current home and office computers have 32-bit processors. The Visual C# Integer data type is made up of 32 bits. Believe it or not, Visual C# can process an int variable faster than it can process a short variable, even though the short variable is smaller. This has to do with the architecture of the CPU, memory, and bus. The explanation is complicated, but the end result is that you should usually use int rather than short, even when working with values that don't require the larger size of the int.

Q. Are arrays limited to two dimensions?

A. Although I showed only two dimensions (that is, intMeasurements[3,1]), arrays can have many dimensions, such as intMeasurements[3,3,3,4]. The technical maximum is 60 dimensions, but you probably won't use more than three.

Workshop

Quiz

1. What data type would you use to hold currency values?

2. Which data type can be used to hold any kind of data and essentially serves as a generic data type?

3. What can you create to eliminate magic numbers by defining a literal value in one place?

4. What type of data element can you create in code that can have its value changed as many times as necessary?

5. What are the first and last indexes of an array dimensioned using `string_strMyArray[5]`?

6. What word is given to describe the visibility of a constant or variable?

7. In general, is it best to limit the scope of a variable or to use the widest scope possible?

Answers

1. The `decimal` data type.

2. The `object` data type.

3. Constants are used to eliminate magic numbers.

4. Variables can have their values changed as often as necessary, within their scope.

5. The first index is 0, and the last index is 4.

6. Scope describes the visibility of a constant, variable, or procedure.

7. It is best to use the narrowest scope possible.

Exercises

1. Create a project with a text box, button, and label control. When the user clicks the button, move the contents of the text box to a variable and then move the contents of the variable to the Text property of the label. (Hint: A `string` variable will do the trick.)

2. Rewrite the following code so that a single array variable is used rather than two standard variables. (Hint: Do not use a multidimensional array.)

```
string strGameTitleOne;
string strGameTitleTwo;
strGameTitleOne = "Quake 4";
strGameTitleTwo = "Call of Duty 2";
```

HOUR 12

Performing Arithmetic, String Manipulation, and Date/Time Adjustments

---

What You'll Learn in This Hour:

▶ Performing arithmetic
▶ Understanding the order of operator precedence
▶ Comparing equalities
▶ Understanding Boolean logic
▶ Manipulating strings
▶ Working with dates and times

Just as arithmetic is a necessary part of everyday life, it's also vital to developing Windows programs. You probably won't write an application that doesn't add, subtract, multiply, or divide some numbers. In this hour, you learn how to perform arithmetic in code. You also learn about order of operator precedence, which determines how Visual C# 2005 evaluates complicated expressions (equations). After you understand operator precedence, you'll learn how to compare equalities—something you'll do all the time.

Boolean logic is the logic Visual C# uses to evaluate expressions in decision-making constructs. If you've never programmed before, Boolean logic might be a new concept to you. In this hour, I explain what you need to know about Boolean logic to create efficient code that performs as expected. Finally, I show you how to manipulate strings and work with dates and times.

Performing Basic Arithmetic Operations with Visual C#

You have to have solid math skills to be a programmer; you'll be performing a lot of basic arithmetic when writing Visual C# applications. To get the results you're looking for in any given calculation, you must

▶ Know the mathematical operator that performs the desired arithmetic function

▶ Understand and correctly use order of precedence

Using the correct mathematical operator is simple. Most are easy to commit to memory, and you can always look up the ones you're not quite sure of. I'm not going to go into great detail on any of the math functions (if you've made it this far, I'm sure that you have a working grasp of basic math), but I will cover them all.

In Hour 15, "Debugging Your Code", you learn about the `System.Diagnostics.Debug.WriteLine()` method. This method prints text to the Output window and is used in the examples throughout this hour. You will not be asked to create a project in this chapter, but you may want to try some of these examples in a test project. Because you will be using several debug statements, it will be helpful to declare the `System.Diagnostics` namespace in the header of your class. This permits you to use the methods of the namespace without having to qualify the entire namespace. The following is the line you need to add at the beginning of your class (put it with the other using statements created automatically by Visual C#):

```
using System.Diagnostics;
```

Performing Addition

Simple addition is performed using the standard addition symbol, the + character. The following line prints the sum of 4, 5, and 6:

```
Debug.WriteLine(4 + 5 + 6);
```

You don't have to use a hard-coded value with arithmetic operators. You can use any of the arithmetic operators on numeric variables and constants. For example:

```
const int c_FirstValue = 4;
const int c_SecondValue = 5;
Debug.WriteLine(c_FirstValue + c_SecondValue);
```

This bit of code prints the sum of the constants c_FirstValue and c_SecondValue, which is 9.

Performing Subtraction and Negation

Like the addition operator, you're probably familiar with the subtraction operator because it's the same one you would use on a calculator or when writing an equation: the – character. The following line of code prints 2 (the total of 6–4):

```
Debug.WriteLine(6 - 4);
```

As with written math, the – character is also used to denote a negative number. For example, to print the value –6, you would use a statement such as the following:

```
Debug.WriteLine(-6);
```

Performing Multiplication

If you work with adding machines, you already know the multiplication operator: the * character. You can enter this character using Shift+8 or by pressing the * key located in the upper row of the keypad section of the keyboard. Although you would ordinarily use a × when writing multiplication equations such as 3 × 2 = 6 on paper, you'll receive an error if you try this in code; you have to use the * character. The following statement prints 20 (5 multiplied by 4):

```
Debug.WriteLine(5 * 4);
```

Performing Division

Division is accomplished using the / operator. This operator is easy to remember if you think of division as fractions. For example, one-eighth is written as 1/8, which literally means one divided by eight. The following statement prints 8 (32 divided by 4):

```
Debug.WriteLine(32 / 4);
```

Visual C# overloads the division operator. This means that based on the input arguments, the results may vary. For example, Visual C# division will return an integer when dividing integers, but it will return a fractional number if a float, a double, or a decimal data type is used. Hence, 32 / 5 will return 6, dropping the remainder (2, in this case). If you wanted to return the actual value of the operation 32 / 5, you would have to specify the numbers with decimal places (that is, 32.0 / 5.0).

Performing Modulus Arithmetic

Modulus arithmetic is the process of performing division on two numbers but keeping only the remainder. Modulus arithmetic is performed using the % operator, rather that the / symbol. The following are examples of modules statements and the values they would print:

```
Debug.WriteLine(10 % 5);      // Prints 0
Debug.WriteLine(10 % 3);      // Prints 1
Debug.WriteLine(12 % 4.3);    // Prints 3.4
Debug.WriteLine(13.6 % 5);    // Prints 3.6
```

The first two statements are relatively easy to understand: 5 goes into 10 twice with no remainder, and 3 goes into 10 three times with a remainder of 1. Visual C# processes the third statement as 4.3 going into 12 two times with a remainder of 3.4. In the last statement, Visual C# performs the modules operation as 5 going into 13.6 twice with a remainder of 3.6.

Determining the Order of Operator Precedence

When several arithmetic operations occur within a single equation (called an *expression*), Visual C# has to resolve the expression in pieces. The order in which these operations are evaluated is known as *operator precedence*. To fully understand operator precedence, you have to brush up a bit on your algebra skills (most of the math you perform in code is algebraic).

Consider the following expression:

```
Debug.WriteLine(6 + 4 * 5);
```

Two arithmetic operations occur in this single expression. To evaluate the expression, Visual C# has to perform both operations: multiplication and addition. Which operation gets done first? Does it matter? Absolutely! If Visual C# performs the addition before the multiplication, you end up with the following:

Step 1: 6 + 4 = 10

Step 2: 10 * 5 = 50

The final result would be that of Visual C# printing 50. Now look at the same equation with the multiplication performed prior to addition:

Step 1: 4 * 5 = 20

Step 2: 20 + 6 = 26

In this case, Visual C# would print 26—a dramatically different number from the one computed when the addition is performed first. To prevent these types of problems, Visual C# consistently performs arithmetic operations in the same order—the order of operator precedence. Table 12.1 lists the order of operator precedence for arithmetic and Boolean operators. (Boolean operators are discussed later in this hour.) If you're familiar with algebra, you'll note that the order of precedence used by Visual C# is the same as that used in algebraic formulas.

TABLE 12.1   Visual C# 2005's Order of Operator Precedence

Category	Operators
Multiplicative	* / %
Additive	+ -
Equality	== (equal), != (not equal)
Logical AND	&
Logical XOR	^
Logical OR	¦
Conditional AND	&&
Conditional OR	¦¦
Conditional	?:

Notice that two equal signs are used to denote equality, not one as you might expect.

By the Way

All *comparison operators* such as >, <, and >= (discussed in the next section) have an equal precedence. When operators have an equal precedence, Visual C# evaluates them from left to right. Notice that multiplication and division operators have an equal precedence, so in an expression that has both, the operators would be evaluated from left to right. The same holds true for addition and subtraction. When expressions contain operators from more than one category (arithmetic, comparison, or logical), arithmetic operators are evaluated first, comparison operators are evaluated next, and *logical operators* are evaluated last.

Just as when writing an equation on paper, you can use parentheses to override the order of operator precedence. Operations placed within parentheses are always evaluated first. Consider the previous example:

```
Debug.WriteLine(6 * 5 + 4);
```

Using the order of operator precedence, Visual C# evaluates the equation like this:

```
Debug.WriteLine((6 * 5) + 4);
```

The multiplication is performed first, and then the addition. If you want the addition performed prior to the multiplication, you could write the statement like this:

```
Debug.WriteLine(6 * (5 + 4));
```

When writing complex expressions, you have to be conscious of the order of operator precedence and use parentheses to override the default precedence when necessary. Personally, I try to always use parentheses so that I'm sure of what's happening and my code is easier to read.

Comparing Equalities

Comparing values, particularly variables, is even more common than performing arithmetic (but you need to know how Visual C# arithmetic works before you can understand the evaluation of equalities).

Comparison operators are most often used in decision-making structures, as explained in the next hour. Indeed, these operators are best understood using a simple `if` decision structure. In an `if` construct, Visual C# considers the expression in the `if` statement, and if the expression equates to `true`, the code statement(s) are executed. For example, the following is an `if` operation (a silly one at that) expressed in English, not in Visual C# code:

IF DOGS BARK, THEN SMILE.

If this were in Visual C# code format, Visual C# would evaluate the `if` condition, which in this case is *dogs bark*. If the condition is found to be `true`, the code following the expression is performed. Because dogs bark, you'd smile. Notice how these two things (dogs barking and you smiling) are relatively unrelated. This doesn't matter; the point is that if the condition evaluates to `true`, certain actions (statements) occur.

You'll often compare the value of one variable to that of another variable or to a specific value when making decisions. The following are some basic comparisons and how Visual C# evaluates them:

```
Debug.WriteLine(6 > 3);      // Evaluates to true
Debug.WriteLine(3 == 4);     // Evaluates to false
Debug.WriteLine(3 >= 3);     // Evaluates to true
Debug.WriteLine(5 <= 4);     // Evaluates to false
```

Performing comparisons is pretty straightforward. If you get stuck writing a particular comparison, attempt to write it in English before creating it in code.

Understanding Boolean Logic

Boolean logic is a special type of arithmetic/comparison. Boolean logic is used to evaluate expressions to either True or False. This might be a new concept to you, but don't worry—it's not difficult to understand. Boolean logic is performed using a logical operator. Consider the following sentence:

If black is a color and wood comes from trees then print "ice cream".

At first glance, it might seem that this is nonsensical. However, Visual C# could make sense of this statement using Boolean logic. First, notice that three expressions are actually being evaluated within this single sentence. I've added parentheses in the following sentence to clarify the two most obvious expressions.

If (black is a color) and (wood comes from trees) then print "ice cream".

Boolean logic evaluates every expression to either True or False. Therefore, substituting True or False for each of these expressions yields the following:

If (True) and (True) then print "ice cream".

Now, for the sake of clarity, here's the same sentence with parentheses placed around the final expression to be evaluated:

If (True And True) then print "ice cream".

This is the point where the logical operators come into play. The And (&) operator returns `true` if the expressions on each side of the And (&) operator are `true` (see Table 12.2 for a complete list of logical operators). In the sentence we're considering, the expressions on both sides of the And (&) operator are `true`, so the expression evaluates to `true`. Replacing the expression with `true` yields:

If True then print "ice cream".

This would result in the word "ice cream" being printed. If the expression had evaluated to False, nothing would print. As you'll see in Hour 13, the decision constructs always evaluate their expressions to either True or False, executing statements according to the results.

TABLE 12.2 Logical (Boolean) Operators

Operator	Description
And (&&)	Evaluates to `true` when the expressions on both sides are `true`.
Not (!)	Evaluates to `true` when its expression evaluates to `false`; otherwise, it returns `false` (the `true`/`false` value of the expression is negated, or reversed).
Or (||)	Evaluates to `true` if an expression on either side evaluates to `true`.
Xor (^)	Evaluates to `true` if one, and only one, expression on either side evaluates to `true`.

Using the And (&) Operator

The And (&) operator is used to perform a logical conjunction. If the expressions on both sides of the And (&) operator evaluate to `true`, the And (&) operation evaluates to `true`. If either expression is `false`, the And (&) operation evaluates to `false`, as illustrated in the following examples:

```
Debug.WriteLine(true & true);              // Prints true
Debug.WriteLine(true & false);             // Prints false
Debug.WriteLine(false & true);             // Prints false
Debug.WriteLine(false & false);            // Prints false
Debug.WriteLine((32 > 4) & (6 == 6));      // Prints true
```

Using the Not (!) Operator

The Not(!) operator performs a logical negation. That is, it returns the opposite of the expression. Consider the following examples:

```
Debug.WriteLine(! (true));       // Prints false
Debug.WriteLine(! (false));      // Prints true
Debug.WriteLine(! (5 == 5));     // Prints false
Debug.WriteLine(!(4 < 2));       // Prints true
```

The first two statements are easy enough; the opposite of `true` is `false` and vice versa. For the third statement, remember that Visual C#'s operator precedence dictates that arithmetic operators are evaluated first (even if no parentheses are used), so the first step of the evaluation would look like this:

```
Debug.WriteLine( ! (true));
```

The opposite of `true` is `false`, of course, so Visual C# prints false.

The fourth statement would evaluate to

```
Debug.WriteLine( !(false));
```

This happens because 4 is *not* less than 2, which is the expression Visual C# .NET evaluates first. Because the opposite of `false` is `true`, this statement would print `true`.

Using the Or (|) Operator

The Or (|) operator is used to perform a logical disjunction. If the expression to the left *or* right of the Or (|) operator evaluates to `true`, the Or (|) operation evaluates to `true`. The following are examples using Or (|) operations, and their results:

```
Debug.WriteLine(true | true);        // Prints true
Debug.WriteLine(true | false);       // Prints true
Debug.WriteLine(false | true);       // Prints true
```

```
Debug.WriteLine(false ¦ false);        // Prints false
Debug.WriteLine((32 < 4) ¦ (6 == 6));  // Prints true
```

Using the Xor (^) Operator

The Xor (^) operator performs a nifty little function. I personally haven't had to use it much, but it's great for those times when its functionality is required. If one—and only one—of the expressions on either side of the Xor (^) operator is true, the Xor (^) operation evaluates to true. Take a close look at the following statement examples to see how this works:

```
Debug.WriteLine(true ^ true);         // Prints false
Debug.WriteLine(true ^ false);        // Prints true
Debug.WriteLine(false ^ true);        // Prints true
Debug.WriteLine(false ^ false);       // Prints false
Debug.WriteLine((32 < 4) ^ (6 == 6)); // Prints true
```

Manipulating Strings

Recall from Hour 11 that a string is text. Visual C# provides many functions for working with strings. Although string manipulation isn't technically arithmetic, the things that you do with strings are similar to things you do with numbers, such as adding two strings together; string manipulation is much like creating equations. Chances are you'll be working with strings a lot in your applications. Visual C# includes a number of functions that enable you to do things with strings, such as retrieve a portion of string or find one string within another. In the following sections, you'll learn the basics of string manipulation.

Concatenating Strings of Text

Visual C# makes it possible to "add" two strings of text together to form one string. Although purists will say it's not truly a form of arithmetic, it's very much like performing arithmetic on strings, so this hour is the logical place in which to present this material. The process of adding two strings together is called *concatenation*. Concatenation is very common. For example, you may want to concatenate variables with hard-coded strings to display meaningful messages to the user, such as Are you sure you want to delete the user XXX?, where XXX is the contents of a variable.

To concatenate two strings, you use the + operator as shown in this line of code:

```
Debug.WriteLine("This is" + "a test.");
```

This statement would print:

```
This isa test.
```

Notice that there is no space between the words *is* and *a*. You could easily add a space by including one after the word *is* in the first string or before the *a* in the second string, or you could concatenate the space as a separate string, like this:

```
Debug.WriteLine("This is" + " " + "a test.");
```

Text placed directly within quotes is called a *literal*. Variables are concatenated in the same way as literals and can even be concatenated with literals. The following code creates two variables, sets the value of the first variable to "Mike," and sets the value of the second variable to the result of concatenating the variable with a space and the literal "Saklar":

```
string strFullName;
string strFirstName = "Mike";
strFullName = strFirstName + " " + "Saklar";
```

The final result is that the variable strFullName contains the string Mike Saklar. Get comfortable with concatenating strings of text—you'll do this often.

Using the Basic String Methods and Properties

Visual C# includes a number of functions that make working with strings of text considerably easier than it might be otherwise. These functions enable you to easily retrieve a piece of text from a string, compute the number of characters in a string, and even determine whether one string contains another. The following is a summary of the basic string functions.

Determining the Number of Characters Using Length

The Length property of the string object returns the variable's length. The following statement prints 26, the total number of characters in the literal string "Pink Floyd reigns supreme." Remember, the quotes surrounding the string tell Visual C# .NET that the text within them is a literal; they are not part of the string.

```
Debug.WriteLine(("Pink Floyd reigns supreme.").Length);    // Prints 26
```

Retrieving Text from a String Using the Substring() Method

The Substring() method retrieves a part of a string and can be used with the following parameters:

```
public string Substring(startposition,numberofcharacters);
```

For example, the following statement prints Queen, the first five characters of the string:

```
Debug.WriteLine(("Queen to Queen's Level Three.").Substring(0,5));
```

The arguments used in this Substring() example are 0 and 5. The 0 indicates starting at the 0 position of the string (beginning). The 5 indicates the specified length to return (characters to retrieve).

The Substring() method is commonly used with the IndexOf() method (discussed shortly) to retrieve the path portion of a variable containing a filename and path combination, such as c:\Myfile.txt. If you know where the \ character is, you can use Substring() to get the path.

If the number of characters requested is greater than the number of characters in the string, an exception (error) occurs. If you're unsure about the number of characters in the string, use the Length property of the string to find out. (Exception handling is reviewed in Hour 15.)

Determining Whether One String Contains Another Using IndexOf() Method

At times you'll need to determine whether one string exists within another. For example, suppose you let users enter their full names into a text box, and you want to separate the first and last names before saving them into individual fields in a database. The easiest way to do this is to look for the space in the string that separates the first name from the last. You could use a loop to examine each character in the string until you find the space, but Visual C# includes a string method that does this for you, faster and easier than you could do it yourself: the IndexOf() method. The basic IndexOf() method has the following syntax:

```
MyString.IndexOf(searchstring);
```

The IndexOf() method of a string searches the string for the occurrence of a string passed as an argument. If the string is found, the location of the start of the string is returned (with 0 being the first character, 1 being the second, etc.). If the search string is not found within the other string, -1 is returned. The IndexOf() method can be used with the following arguments (actually, there are additional ways and these are listed in the online help text):

- ▶ `public int IndexOf(searchstring);`
- ▶ `public int IndexOf(searchstring, startinglocation);`
- ▶ `public int IndexOf(searchstring, startinglocation, numberofcharacterstosearch);`

The following code searches a variable containing the text "Monte Sothman", locates the space, and uses the Substring() method and Length property to place the first and last names in separate variables.

```
string strFullName = "Monte Sothman";
string strFirstName, strLastName;
int intLocation, intLength;

intLength = strFullName.Length;
intLocation = strFullName.IndexOf(" ");

strFirstName = strFullName.Substring(0, intLocation);
strLastName = strFullName.Substring(intLocation + 1);
```

Did you Know?

> This code assumes that a space will be found and that it won't be the first or last character in the string. In your applications, your code may need to be more robust, including checking to ensure that IndexOf() returned a value other than -1, which would indicate that no space was found.

When this code runs, IndexOf() returns 5, the ordinal position of the first space found (remember, 0 is the first character, not 1). Notice how I subtracted an additional character when using SubString() to initialize the strLastName variable; this was to take the space into account.

Trimming Beginning and Trailing Spaces from a String

As you work with strings, you'll often encounter situations in which spaces exist at the beginning or ending of strings. The .NET Framework includes the following four methods for automatically removing spaces from the beginning or end of a string:

Method	Description
String.Trim()	Removes spaces from the beginning and end of a string
String.TrimEnd()	Removes spaces from the end of a string
String.TrimStart()	Removes spaces from the beginning of a string
String.Remove ()	Removes a specified number of characters from a specified index position in a string

Replacing Text Within a String

It's not uncommon to have to replace a piece of text within a string with some other text. For example, some people still put two spaces at the end of a sentence, even though this is no longer necessary because of proportional fonts. You could replace all double-spaces with a single space using a loop and the string manipulation functions discussed so far, but there is an easier way: the `Replace()` method of the `String` class. A basic `Replace()` method call has the following syntax:

```
Stringobject.Replace(findtext, replacetext);
```

The *findtext* argument is used to specify the text to look for within *expression*, and the *replacetext* argument is used to specify the text used to replace the *findtext*. Consider the following code:

```
string strText = "Give a man a fish";
strText = strText.Replace("fish", "sandwich");
```

When this code completes, `strText` contains the string 'Give a man a sandwich'. Replace is a powerful function that can save many lines of code, and you should use it in place of a "home-grown" replace function whenever possible.

Working with Dates and Times

Dates are a unique beast. In some ways, they act like strings, where you can concatenate and parse pieces. In other ways, dates seem more like numbers in that you can add to or subtract from them. You'll often perform math-type functions on dates (such as adding a number of days to a date or determining the number of months between two dates), but you won't use the typical arithmetic operations. Instead, you use functions specifically designed for working with dates.

Understanding the `DateTime` Data Type

Working with dates is very common. No matter the application, you'll probably need to create a variable to hold a date using the `DateTime` data type. You can get a date into a `DateTime` variable in several ways. Recall that when setting a string variable to a literal value, the literal is enclosed in quotes. When setting a numeric variable to a literal number, the number is not closed in quotes:

```
string strMyString = "This is a string literal";
int intMyInteger = 69;
```

The more common way to set a `DateTime` variable to a literal date is to instantiate the variable passing in the date, like this (year, month, day):

```
DateTime dteMyBirthday = new DateTime(1969,7,22);
```

You cannot pass a string directly to a `DateTime` variable. For instance, if you let the user enter a date into a text box and you want to move the entry to a `DateTime` variable, you'll have to parse out the string to be able to adhere to one of the allowable `DateTime` constructors. The `DateTime` data type is one of the more complicated data types. This chapter will expose you to enough information to get started, but this is only the tip of the iceberg. I suggest reviewing the Microsoft Developers Network (MSDN) documentation of this curious data type for more information.

It's important to note that `DateTime` variables store a date and a time—always. Take a look at the example in the following code:

```
DateTime dteMyBirthday = new DateTime(1969,7,22);
Debug.WriteLine(dteMyBirthday.ToString());
```

It produces this output:

```
7/22/1969 12:00:00 AM
```

Notice that this example printed the time `12:00:00` AM, even though no time was specified for the variable. This is the default time placed in a `DateTime` variable when only a date is specified. Although a `DateTime` variable always holds a date and a time, on occasion, you'll be concerned only with either the date or the time. Later, I'll show you how to use the `GetDateTimeFormats()` method to retrieve just a date or a time.

Adding to or Subtracting from a Date or Time

To add a specific amount of time (such as one day or three months) to a specific date or time, you use methods of the `DateTime` class. Table 12.3 lists the methods as described in MSDN. These methods do not change the value of the current `DataTime` variable; instead, they return a new `DateTime` instance whose value is the result of the operation.

TABLE 12.3 Common Available Data Adding Methods (Source MSDN)

Method	Description
AddDays	Adds the specified number of days to the value of this instance
AddHours	Adds the specified number of hours to the value of this instance
AddMilliseconds	Adds the specified number of milliseconds to the value of this instance
AddMinutes	Adds the specified number of minutes to the value of this instance
AddMonths	Adds the specified number of months to the value of this instance

TABLE 12.3   Continued

Method	Description
AddSeconds	Adds the specified number of seconds to the value of this instance
AddYears	Adds the specified number of years to the value of this instance

For instance, to add six months to the date 7/22/69, you could use the following statements:

```
DateTime dteMyBirthday = new DateTime(1969,7,22);
DateTime dteNewDate = dteMyBirthday.AddMonths(6);
```

After this second statement executes, dteNewDate contains the date 1/22/1970 12:00:00 AM.

The following code shows sample addition methods and the date they would return:

```
dteNewDate = dteMyBirthday.AddYears(2);      // Returns 7/22/1971   12:00:00 AM
dteNewDate = dteMyBirthday.AddMonths(5);     // Returns 12/22/1969  12:00:00 AM
dteNewDate = dteMyBirthday.AddMonths(-1);    // Returns 6/22/1971   12:00:00 AM
dteNewDate = dteMyBirthday.AddHours(7);      // Returns 7/22/1969   7:00:00 AM
```

Retrieving Parts of a Date

Sometimes, it can be extremely useful to know just a part of a date. For example, you may have let a user enter his or her birth date, and you want to perform an action based on the month in which they were born. To retrieve part of a date, the DateTime class exposes properties such as Month, Day, Year, Hour, Minute, Second, and so on.

The following should illustrate the retrieval of some properties of the DateTime class (the instance date is 7/22/1969):

```
dteMyBirthday.Month       // Returns 7
dteMyBirthday.Day         // Returns 22
dteMyBirthday.DayOfWeek   // Returns Tuesday
```

The Hour property will return the hour in military format. Also, note that DayOfWeek() returns an enumerated value.

By the Way

Formatting Dates and Times

As I stated earlier, at times you'll want to work with only the date or a time within a DateTime variable. In addition, you'll probably want to control the format in which a date or time is displayed. All this and more can be accomplished via the DateTime class by way of the following:

▶ Using the DateTime methods to retrieve formatted strings

▶ Using standard-format strings

▶ Using custom-format strings

It's impossible to show everything regarding formatting a DateTime value here, but it is important to see how to use formatting to output either the date portion or the time portion of a DateTime variable.

The following illustrates some basic formatting methods available with the DateTime class. (Note that the instance date is still 7/22/1969 12:00:00 AM.)

```
dteMyBirthday.ToLongDateString();     // Returns Tuesday, July 22, 1969
dteMyBirthday.ToShortDateString();    // Returns 7/22/1969
dteMyBirthday.ToLongTimeString();     // Returns 12:00:00 AM
dteMyBirthday.ToShortTimeString();    // Returns 12:00 AM
```

Retrieving the Current System Date and Time

Visual C# gives you the capability to retrieve the current system date and time. Again, this is accomplished by way of the DateTime class. For example, the Today property returns the current system date. To place the current system date into a new DateTime variable, for example, you could use a statement such as this:

```
DateTime dteToday = DateTime.Today;
```

To retrieve the current system date *and* time, use the Now property of DateTime, like this:

```
DateTime dteToday = DateTime.Now;
```

Commit DateTime.Today and DateTime.Now to memory. You'll need to retrieve the system date and/or time in an application, and this is by far the easiest way to get that information.

Summary

Being able to work with all sorts of data is crucial to your success as a Visual C# developer. Just as you need to understand basic math to function in society, you need to be able to perform basic math in code to write even the simplest of applications. Knowing the arithmetic operators, as well as understanding the order of operator precedence, will take you a long way in performing math using Visual C# code.

Boolean logic is a special form of evaluation used by Visual C# to evaluate simple and complex expressions down to a value of true or false. In the following hours, you'll learn how to create loops and how to perform decisions in code. What you learned here about Boolean logic is critical to your success with loops and decision structures; you'll use Boolean logic perhaps even more often than you'll perform arithmetic.

Manipulating strings and dates each takes special considerations. In this hour, you learned how to work with both types of data to extract portions of values and to add pieces of data together to form a new whole. String manipulation is straightforward, and you'll get the hang of it soon enough as you start to use some of the string functions. Date manipulation, on the other hand, can be a bit tricky. Even experienced developers need to refer to the online help at times. You learned the basics in this hour, but don't be afraid to experiment on your own.

Q&A

Q. *Should I always specify parentheses to ensure that operators are evaluated as I expect them to be?*

A. Visual C# never fails to evaluate expressions according to the order of operator precedence, so using parentheses isn't necessary when the order of precedence is correct for an expression. However, using parentheses assures *you* that the expression is being evaluated the way you want it to, and might make the expression easier to read by other people. This really is your choice.

Q. *I would like to learn more about the properties and methods available in the* DateTime *structure; where can I find all the members listed?*

A. I would look at the DateTime members documentation found within the .NET Framework documentation. This is available on the MSDN site and as an installable option when installing Visual C#.

Workshop

Quiz

1. To get only the remainder of a division operation, you use which operator?

2. Which operation is performed first in the following expression—the addition or the multiplication? x = 6 + 5 * 4

3. Which Boolean operator performs a logical negation?

4. The process of appending one string to another is called?

5. What property can be used to return the month of a given date?

Answers

1. The (%) operator.

2. 5 * 4 is performed first.

3. The Not operator (!).

4. Concatenation

5. Month

Exercises

1. Create a project that has a single text box on a form. Assume that the user enters a first name, a middle initial, and a last name into the text box. Parse the contents into three variables—one for each part of the name.

2. Create a project that has a single text box on a form. Assume that the user enters a valid birthday into the text box. Use the date functions to tell the user exactly how many days old he or she is.

HOUR 13

Making Decisions in Visual C# Code

What You'll Learn in This Hour:

▶ Making decisions using `if` statements
▶ Expanding the capability of `if` statements using `else`
▶ Evaluating an expression for multiple values using the `switch` statement

In Hour 10, "Creating and Calling Methods," you learned to separate code into multiple procedures so that they can be called in any order required. This goes a long way in organizing code, but you still need a way to selectively execute code procedures or groups of statements within a procedure. You can use decision-making techniques to accomplish this. Decision-making constructs are coding structures that enable you to execute or omit code based on a condition, such as the value of a variable. Visual C# includes two constructs that enable you to make any type of branching decision you can think of: `if...else` and `switch`.

In this hour, you'll learn how to use the decision constructs provided by Visual C# to perform robust yet efficient decisions in Visual C# code. You'll probably create decision constructs in every application you build, so the faster you master these skills, the easier it will be to create robust applications.

Making Decisions Using `if...else`

By far the most common decision-making construct used in programming is the `if` construct. A simple `if` construct looks like this:

```
if (expression)
    ... statement to execute when expression is true;
```

The `if` construct uses Boolean logic, as discussed in Hour 12, "Performing Arithmetic, String Manipulation, and Date/Time Adjustments," to evaluate an expression to either `true` or `false`. The expression may be simple (if `(x == 6)`) or complicated (if `(x==6 && y>10)`). If the expression evaluates to `true`, the statement or block of statements (if enclosed in braces) gets executed. If the expression evaluates to `false`, Visual C# doesn't execute the statement or statement block for the `if` construct.

By the Way

Remember that compound statements, also frequently called *block* statements, can be used anywhere a statement is expected. A compound statement consists of zero or more statements enclosed in braces (`{}`). Following is an example of the `if` construct using a block statement:

```
if (expression)
    {
    statement 1 to execute when expression is true;
    statement 2 to execute when expression is true;
    ... statement n to execute when expression is true;
    }
```

You're going to create a simple `if` construct in a Visual C# project. Create a new Windows Application named **Decisions** and follow these steps:

1. Right click Form1.vs in the Solution Explorer, choose Rename, and change the name of the default form to **frmDecisions.cs**. Next, set the Text property of the form to **Decisions Example**.

2. Add a new text box to the form by double-clicking the Textbox icon in the toolbox. Set the properties of the text box as follows:

Property	Value
Name	**txtInput**
Location	**44,44**

3. Add a new button to the form by double-clicking the Button icon in the toolbox. Set the button's properties as follows:

Property	Value
Name	**btnIsLessThanHundred**
Location	**156,42**
Size	**100,23**
Text	**Is text < 100?**

Your form should now look like the one in Figure 13.1.

FIGURE 13.1
You'll use the
if statement to
determine
whether the
value of the text
entered into the
text box is less
than 100.

You're now going to add code to the button's Click() event. This code will use a simple if construct and the int.Parse() method. The int.Parse() method is used to convert text into its numeric equivalent, and you'll use it to convert the text in txtInput into an integer. The if statement will then determine whether the number entered into the text box is less than 100. Double-click the button now to access its Click event, and enter the following code:

```
if (int.Parse(txtInput.Text)< 100 )
    MessageBox.Show("The text entered is less than 100.");
```

This code is simple when examined one statement at a time. Look closely at the first statement and recall that a simple if statement looks like this:

```
if (expression)
    statement;
```

In the code you entered, *expression* is

```
int.Parse(txtInput.Text)< 100
```

What you are doing is asking Visual C# to evaluate whether the parsed integer is less than 100. In this case, Parse is a method of the int (integer) class. Int.Parse() converts a supplied string to an integer data type—which can be used for numerical computations and evaluations. So, the value in the text box is cast to an integer and then compared to see if it is less than 100. If it is, the evaluation returns true. If the value is greater than or equal to 100, the expression returns false. If the evaluation returns true, execution proceeds with the line immediately following the if statement and a message is displayed. If the evaluation returns false, the line statement (or block of statements) following the if statement doesn't execute, and no message is displayed.

> If the user leaves the text box empty or enters anything other than an integer, an exception will be thrown. Therefore, you'd normally implement exception handling around this type of code or better yet add code that prevents the user from entering anything other than a number to begin with. You'll learn about exception handling in Hour 15, "Debugging Your Code."

Executing Code When *Expression* Is False

If you want to execute some code when *expression* evaluates to false, include the optional else keyword, like this:

```
if (expression)
    statement to execute when expression is true;
else
    statement to execute when expression is false;
```

> If you want to execute code only when *expression* equates to false, not when true, use the not-equal operator (!=) in the expression. Refer to Hour 12 for more information on Boolean logic.

By including an else clause, you can have one or more statements execute when *expression* is true and other statements execute when the *expression* is false. In the example you've built, if a user enters a number less than 100, the user will get a message. However, if the number is greater than or equal to 100, the user receives no feedback. Modify your code to look like the following, which ensures that the user always gets a message:

```
if (int.Parse(txtInput.Text)< 100 )
   MessageBox.Show("The text entered is less than 100.");
else
   MessageBox.Show("The text entered is greater than or equal to 100.");
```

Now, if the user enters a whole number less than 100, the message The text entered is less than 100 is displayed, but nothing more. When Visual C# encounters the else statement, it ignores the statement(s) associated with the else statement. The statements for the else condition execute only when *expression* is false. Likewise, if the user enters text that is greater than or equal to 100, the message The text entered is greater than or equal to 100 is displayed, but nothing more; when *expression* evaluates to false, execution immediately jumps to the else statement.

Follow these steps:

1. Click Save All on the toolbar to save your work.

2. Press F5 to run the project.

3. Enter a whole number into the text box and click the button.

A message box appears, telling you whether the number you entered is less than or greater than 100 (see Figure 13.2).

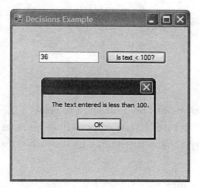

FIGURE 13.2
As implied with this message box, the if statement gives you great flexibility in making decisions.

Feel free to enter other whole numbers and click the button as often as you like. When you're satisfied that the code is working, choose Stop Debugging from the Debug menu.

Get comfortable with if; chances are good that you'll include at least one in every project you create.

Did you Know?

Nesting if...else **Constructs**

As mentioned earlier, you can nest if statements to further refine your decision making. The format you use can be something like the following:

```
if ( expression1 )
   if ( expression2 )
   ...
   else
      ...
else
   ...
```

Evaluating an Expression for Multiple Values Using switch

At times, the if construct isn't capable of handling a decision situation without a lot of extra work. One such situation is when you need to perform different actions based on numerous possible values of an expression, not just true or false. For instance, suppose that you wanted to perform actions based on a user's profession. The following shows what you might create using if:

```
if (strProfession =="programmer")
    ...
else if (strProfession =="teacher")
    ...
else if (strProfession =="accountant")
    ...
else
    ...
```

As you can see, this structure can be a bit hard to read. If the number of supported professions increases, this type of construction will get harder to read and debug. In addition, executing many if statements like this is rather inefficient from a processing standpoint.

The important thing to realize here is that each else...if is really evaluating the same expression (strProfession) but considering different values for the expression. Visual C# includes a much better decision construct for evaluating a single expression for multiple possible values: switch.

A basic switch construct looks like the following:

```
switch (expression)
{
    case  value1:
            ...
        jump-statement

    default:
            ...
        jump-statement

}
```

---

default is used to define code that executes only when *expression* doesn't evaluate to any of the values in the case statements. Use of default is optional.

Here's the Profession example shown previously, but this time switch is used:

```
switch (strProfession)
{
case "teacher":
        MessageBox.Show("You educate our young");
        break;
    case "programmer":
        MessageBox.Show("You are most likely a geek");
        break;
    case "accountant":
        MessageBox.Show("You are a bean counter");
        break;
    default:
        MessageBox.Show("Profession not found in switch statement");
        break;
}
```

The flow of the switch statement is as follows: When the case expression is matched, the code statement or statements within the case are executed. This must be followed by a jump statement, such as break, to transfer control out of the case body.

If you create a case construct but fail to put code statements or a jump-statement within the case, execution will fall through to the next case statement, even if the expression doesn't match.

By the Way

The switch makes decisions much easier to follow. Again, the key with switch is that it's used to evaluate a single expression for more than one possible value.

Building a switch Example

You're now going to build a project that uses advanced expression evaluation in a switch structure. This simple application displays a list of animals to the user in a combo box. When the user clicks a button, the application displays the number of legs of the animal chosen in the list (if an animal is selected). Start by creating a new Windows Application named **Switch Example** and then follow these steps:

1. Right-click Form1.cs in the Solution Explorer, choose Rename, and then change the name of the form to **frmSwitchExample.cs**. Next, set the form's Text property to **Switch Example** (you'll have to click the form once to view its design properties).

2. Add a new combo box to the form by double-clicking the ComboBox item on the toolbox. Set the combo box's properties as follows:

Property	Value
Name	**cboAnimals**
Location	**80,100**

3. Next, add some items to the list. Click the Items property of the combo box, and then click the Build button that appears in the property to access the String Collection Editor for the combo box. Enter the text as shown in Figure 13.3; be sure to press Enter at the end of each list item to make the next item appear on its own line.

FIGURE 13.3
Each line you
enter here
becomes an
item in the
combo box at
runtime.

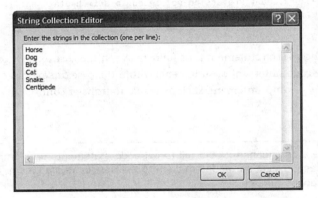

4. Add a Button control. When the button is clicked, a switch construct is used to determine which animal the user selected and to tell the user how many legs the selected animal has. Add a new button to the form by double-clicking the Button tool in the toolbox. Set the button's properties as follows:

Property	Value
Name	**btnShowLegs**
Location	**102,130**
Text	**Show Legs**

Your form should now look like the one in Figure 13.4. Click Save All on the toolbar to save your work before continuing.

All that's left to do is add the code. Double-click the Button control to access its Click event and then enter the following code:

```
switch (cboAnimals.Text)
{
    case "Bird":
```

```
    MessageBox.Show("The animal has 2 legs.");
    break;
case "Dog":
    // Notice there is no code here to execute.
case "Horse":
    // Notice there is no code here to execute.
case "Cat":
    MessageBox.Show("The animal has 4 legs.");
    break;
case "Snake":
    MessageBox.Show("The animal has no legs.");
    break;
case "Centipede":
    MessageBox.Show("The animal has 100 legs.");
    break;
default:
    MessageBox.Show("You did not select from the list!");
    break;
}
```

FIGURE 13.4
This example uses only a combo box and a Button control.

Here's what's happening:

▶ The switch construct compares the content of the cboAnimals combo box to a set of predetermined values. Each case statement is evaluated in the order in which it appears in the list. Therefore, the expression is first compared to "Bird." If the content of the combo box is Bird, the MessageBox.Show() method immediately following the case statement is called, followed by the break statement, which transfers control outside of the switch construct.

▶ If the combo box doesn't contain Bird, Visual C# looks to see if the content is "Dog," and so on. Notice that the Dog case contains no code. When a case statement has no code, the execution of the code in the following case is executed. In this situation, that would be (Horse), which also has no code. Visual C# continues down the list of case statements until it finds one with code and uses that. In this example, that would be the code for (Cat). This is known as *execution falling through*, and it's used to allow you to create one set of code that can be used for multiple case situations. In this example, you end up with the correct output. However, what happens if you move the Snake case in front of Cat? You'd end up telling the user that the dog has no legs! When using this technique, you must be careful that all situations will produce the desired behavior.

▶ Each successive case statement is evaluated in the same way. If no matches are found for any of the case statements, the MessageBox.Show() method in the default statement is called. If there were no matches and no default statement, no code would execute.

As you can see, adding a new animal to the list can be as simple as adding a case statement.

Try it now by pressing F5 to run the project and then follow these steps:

1. Select an animal from the list and click the button.

2. Try clearing the contents of the combo box and clicking the button.

3. When you're finished, choose Debug, Stop Debugging to stop the project, and click Save All on the toolbar.

Summary

In this hour you learned how to use Visual C#'s decision constructs to make decisions in Visual C# code. You learned how to use if statements to execute code when an expression evaluates to true and to use else to run code when the expression evaluates to false. For more complicated decisions, you learned how to use else...if to add further comparisons to the decision construct and nest if structures for more flexibility.

In addition to if, you learned how to use switch to create powerful decision constructs to evaluate a single expression for many possible values. Finally, you learned how you can check for multiple possible values using a fall-through case statement.

Decision-making constructs are often the backbone of applications. Without the capability to run specific sets of code based on changing situations, your code would be very linear and hence very limited. Become comfortable with the decision constructs and make a conscious effort to use the best construct for any given situation. The better you are at writing decision constructs, the faster you'll be able to produce solid and understandable code.

Q&A

Q. *What if I want to execute code only when an expression in an `if` statement is false, not true? Do I need to place the code in an `else` clause, and no code after the `if`?*

A. This is where Boolean logic helps. What you need to do is make the expression evaluate to `true` for the code you want to run. This is accomplished using the not operator (!) in the expression, like this:

```
if (!expression)
. . .
```

Q. *How important is the order in which `case` statements are created?*

A. This all depends on the situation. In the earlier example in which the selected animal was considered and the number of legs it has was displayed, the order of the Dog and Horse case was important. If all `case` statements contained code, the order has no effect.

Workshop

Quiz

1. Which decision construct should you use to evaluate a single expression to either `true` or `false`?

2. Evaluating expressions to `true` or `false` for both types of decision constructs is accomplished using _____ logic.

3. If you want code to execute when the expression of an `if` statement evaluates to `false`, include an _____ clause.

4. Which decision construct should you use when evaluating the result of an expression that may equate to one of many possible values?

5. Is it possible that more than one `case` statement may have its code execute?

Answers

1. The `if` construct

2. Boolean

3. `else`

4. switch

5. No, never.

Exercises

1. Create a project that enables the user to enter text into a text box. Use an if construct to determine whether the text entered is a Circle, Triangle, Square, or Pentagon, and display the number of sides the entered shape has. If the text doesn't match one of these shapes, let the users know that they must enter a shape.

2. Rewrite the the project you created in Exercise 1 so that it uses a switch construct instead of an if construct.

HOUR 14

Looping for Efficiency

What You'll Learn in This Hour:

▶ Looping a specific number of times using `for` statements
▶ Looping based on a condition using `do...while` and `while` statements

You will often encounter situations in which you need to execute the same code statement or group of statements repeatedly. You will need to execute some of these statements a specific number of times, whereas others might need to be executed as long as a certain condition persists (an expression is `true`) or until a condition occurs (an expression *becomes* `true`). Visual C# includes constructs that enable you to easily define and execute these repetitive code routines: *loops*. This hour shows you how to use the two major looping constructs to make your code smaller, faster, and more efficient.

Looping a Specific Number of Times Using `for`

The simplest type of loop to create is the `for` loop, which has been around since the earliest forms of the BASIC language. With a `for` loop, you instruct Visual C# to begin a loop by starting a counter at a specific value. Visual C# then executes the code within the loop, increments the counter by a defined incremental value, and repeats the loop until the counter reaches an upper limit you've set. The following is the syntax for the basic `for` loop:

```
for ([initializers]; [expression]; [iterator]) statement
```

Initiating the Loop Using `for`

The `for` statement both sets up and starts the loop. The `for` statement has the components shown in Table 14.1.

TABLE 14.1   Components of the for Statement

Part	Description
initializers	An expression that defines and initializes the loop variable.
expression	An expression that can be evaluated using Boolean logic. This expression is used to determine when to keep looping and when to terminate the loop.
operator	Expression statement that specifies how much to increment or decrement the loop variable.
statement	The embedded statement(s) to execute.

The *operator* is used to specify the amount to increment or decrement the loop. Visual C# includes a number of operators, and they may seem foreign to you at first. An operator is like a shortcut for a math function. The following lists the most commonly used Visual C# operators and their effects:

▶ ++   Increments the variable by one.

▶ --   Decrements the variable by one.

▶ +=   Adds the value on the right of the operator to the value on the left. For example, x += Y has the same result as X = X + Y.

▶ -+   Subtracts the value on the right of the operator from the value on the left. For example, X -= Y has the same result as X = X - Y.

The most common *iterator* used is loopvariable++, which increments the variable *loopvariable* by one. To decrement the counter variable by 1, you would use loopvariable--. To use a value other than 1 for the amount to change the *loopvariable*, you would use += (or -= for decrementing), followed by the value to increment (or decrement) the variable by, like this: loopvariable += 0.05.

The following is a simple example of a for loop, followed by an explanation of what it's doing:

```
for (int intCounter = 1; intCounter <= 100; intCounter++)
    Debug.WriteLine(intCounter);
```

This for statement initializes an Integer named intCounter at 1; the condition intCounter <= 100 is tested and returns true; therefore, the statement debug.WriteLine(lngCounter) is executed. After the statement(s) are executed, the variable intCounter is incremented by one (intCounter++). This loop would execute 100 times, printing the numbers 1 through 100 to the Output debug window.

> To use the Debug object, you need to use the System.Diagnostics namespace.

By the Way

To execute multiple statements within a for loop, braces ({}) are used; a single-line for statement does not require braces. Here is the preceding for loop written to execute multiple statements:

```
for (int intCounter = 1; intCounter <= 100; intCounter++)
{
   Debug.WriteLine(intCounter);
   Debug.WriteLine(intCounter-1);
}
```

> There may be times when you want to terminate a for loop before the expression evaluates to true. To exit a for loop at any time, use the break statement.

By the Way

Creating a for **Example**

You're now going to create a procedure containing a for loop that counts backward from 100 to 0 and sets opacity of a form to the value of the loop variable (the form will fade out).

Create a new Windows Application named **Fading Form** and then follow these steps:

1. Right-click Form1.cs in the Solution Explorer, choose Rename, and change the name of the default form to **frmFadingForm.cs**. Next, set the form's Text property to **Fading Form** (you'll need to click the form once to access its design properties).

2. Add a button to the form by double-clicking the Button item in the toolbox. Set the button's properties as follows:

Property	Value
Name	**btnFadeForm**
Location	**105,113**
Size	**75,23**
Text	**Fade Form**

Your form should look like the one shown in Figure 14.1.

FIGURE 14.1
This simple proj-
ect does some-
thing pretty
cool...

All that's left to do is to write the code. Double-click the button to access its `Click()`
event and enter the following:

```
for (double dblOpacity = 1; dblOpacity > 0; dblOpacity += -0.05)
{
    this.Opacity = dblOpacity;
    // Let the form repaint itself.
    this.Refresh();
    // Create a delay.
    System.Threading.Thread.Sleep(200);
}
// Show the form again.
this.Opacity = 1;
```

By the Way

The code `dblOpacity += -0.05` could also be written as `dblOpacity -= 0.05`.

Much of this code should make sense to you by now. Here's what's happening:

▶ The first statement initializes the loop. It creates a variable of type double
called `dblOpacity`. You have to use double because Opacity works with values of 0 to 1 and Integers don't support decimal places. The variable
`dblOpacity` is initialed to 1, and the loop expression is defined as `dblOpacity
> 0`. This means the loop will continue to execute as long as `dblOpacity` is
greater than 0. Finally, the last section dictates that each time the loop completes, the variable `dblOpacity` is decremented by 0.05 (notice the negative
sign in front of the value in code). All of this means that the loop will start at
1, and decrement the counter variable by .05 until the variable reaches 0, at
which time the loop will no longer execute and code execution will jump to
the first statement following the closing brace of the loop.

▶ The second statement (after the opening brace for the loop code) sets the Opacity of the form to the value of the loop variable. The next line (after the comment) calls the `Refresh()` method of the form, which forces it to repaint itself. If you don't do this, Windows might not get around to repainting the form between iterations. Feel free to comment out the `Refresh()` statement (put a comment character in front of the statement so Visual C# treats it as a comment and doesn't execute it) to see what happens once you've successfully completed this example.

▶ The next statement (the `Sleep()` statement) tells Visual C# to pause. The number in parentheses is the number of milliseconds to wait. In this case, 200. This is a nifty function! We could have used another `for` loop to create a pause, but then the duration of the pause would be dependent on the speed of the user's computer. By using `Sleep()`, we've guaranteed the pause to be the same on every machine that executes this code.

▶ The closing brace sends execution back to the `for` statement, where the variable is decremented and tested to make sure that we haven't reached the stop value.

▶ When the loop is finished, the form will be invisible. The last statement simply sets the Opacity property of the form back to 1, in effect showing the form.

Click Save All on the toolbar and press F5 to run the project. When the form first appears, it looks normal. Click the button, though, and watch the form fade out (see Figure 14.2)!

If you were to forgo a loop and write each line of code necessary to change the opacity, you would have to duplicate the statements 20 times each! Using a simple `for` loop, you performed the same task in just a few lines of code.

Use a `for` loop when you know the number of times you want the loop to execute. This doesn't mean that you have to actually know the number of times you want the loop to execute at design time; it simply means that you must know the number of times you want the loop to execute when you first start the loop. You can use a variable to define any of the parameters for the `for` loop, as illustrated in the following code:

```
int intUpperLimit=100;
for (int intCounter=1; intCounter<=intUpperLimit;intCounter++)
    Debug.WriteLine(intCounter);
```

FIGURE 14.2
This would take
a lot of code
without a loop!

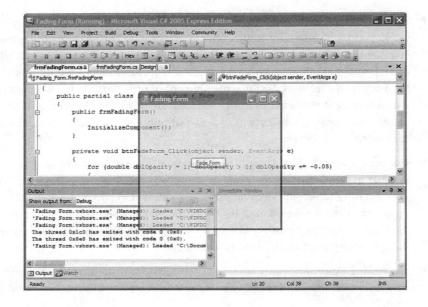

> One of the keys to writing efficient code is to eliminate redundancy. If you find
> yourself typing the same (or a similar) line of code repeatedly, chances are it's a
> good candidate for a loop.

Using while **and** do...while **to Loop an Indeterminate Number of Times**

In some situations, you won't know the exact number of times a loop must be performed—not even when the loop begins. You could start a for loop specifying an upper limit that you know is larger than the number of loops needed, check for a terminating condition within the loop, and exit the loop using a break statement when the condition is met. However, this approach is inefficient and usually impractical. When you need to create such a loop, using do...while is the answer.

Creating a do...while

The most basic form of a do...while has the following syntax:

```
do statement while (expression);
```

By the Way

The following syntax is used to execute multiple statements:

```
do
{
    [Statements]
} while (expression);
```

Ending a do...while Loop

A do...while loop without some sort of exit mechanism or defined condition is an endless loop. In its most basic form, nothing is present to tell the loop when to stop looping. At times you may need an endless loop (game programming is an example), but more often, you'll need to exit the loop when a certain condition is met. As with the for loop, you can use the break statement to exit a do...while loop at any time. For example, you could expand the do...while loop to include a break statement like the following:

```
do
{
    Statements
    if (expression)
        break;
} while (x==x);
```

In this code, the loop would execute until *expression* evaluates to true. Generally, the expression is based on a variable that's modified somewhere within the loop. Obviously, if the expression never changes, the loop never ends.

Another flavor of the while loop is the while...do loop. The following is a simple while...do loop:

```
while (expression) statement
```

or

```
while (expression)
{
    Statements
}
```

As long as *expression* evaluates to true, the loop continues to occur. If *expression* evaluates to false when the loop first starts, the code between the statement(s) doesn't execute—not even once.

The difference between the do...while and the while loops is that the code statements within the do...while loop *always* execute at least once; *expression* isn't evaluated until the loop has completed its first cycle. Therefore, such a loop always executes at least once, regardless of the value of expression. The while loop evaluates the expression first; therefore, the statements associated with it may not execute at all.

Creating a do...while **Example**

You're now going to create an example using a do...while. In this project, you are going to find the first 10 numbers that are evenly divisible by 3. Although you know you want to find 10 numbers, you don't know how many numbers you will have to evaluate—therefore the do...while is the best choice.

Create a new Windows application named **No Remainders** and then follow these steps:

1. Right-click Form1.cs in the Solution Explorer, choose Rename, and then change the name of the default form to **frmNoRemainders.cs**. Next, set the Text property of the form to **No Remainders**.

2. Add a button to the form and set the new button's properties as follows:

Property	Value
Name	**btnFindNumbers**
Location	**99,39**
Size	**94,23**
Text	**Find Numbers**

3. Add a ListBox control to the form and set its properties as follows:

Property	Value
Name	**lstResults**
Location	**86,86**
Size	**120,160**

Your form should now look like the one shown in Figure 14.3.

Double-click the new button to access its Click() event and then enter the following code:

```
int intSeek = 1;
int intFound = 0;

do
{
    if ((intSeek % 3) == 0)
    {
        lstResults.Items.Add( intSeek.ToString());
        intFound++;
```

```
     }
     intSeek++;
} while (intFound < 10);
```

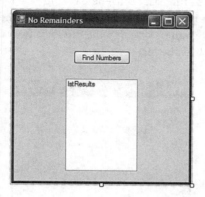

FIGURE 14.3
What better con-
trol to show a
list of results
than a list box?

Again, this code is more easily understood when broken down:

▶ The first two statements simply create a couple of integer variables. The variable intSeek will be the number we'll test to see whether it's evenly divisible by three (meaning it has no remainder). The variable intFound will be our counter; we'll increment this by one each time we find a number evenly divisible by three.

▶ The do statement starts the loop. There is no condition at the start of the loop because we want the loop to execute at least once – we test the condition at the end of the loop using while.

▶ In Hour 12, "Performing Arithmetic, String Manipulation, and Date/Time Adjustments," I mentioned how the % operator can be used to determine a remainder. Here we're using % to determine if intSeek is evenly divisible by three by seeing if there is a remainder when intSeek is divided by 3.

▶ If the number in question is evenly divisible by 3 (there is no remainder), the number in intSeek is added to the results list box and intFound is incremented by 1.

▶ The next statement is the closing curly brace for the if construct. After this, intSeek is incremented by 1. Notice that intSeek is incremented during each pass of the loop, since the statement is placed outside of the if block.

▶ The last statement closes the loop. It also tests intFound and, and if less than 10 numbers have been found, the loop code gets executed again.

Click Save All on the toolbar to save the project and then press F5 to run it. Click the Find Numbers button and watch the results fill up—fast (see Figure 14.4)!

The do...while loop was the best choice here because we really didn't know how many numbers we were going to have to evaluate (that is, how many times to iterate the loop). If we only wanted to search the numbers from 1 to 100, for example, a for loop would have been better.

FIGURE 14.4
Visual C# performs math functions very fast.

Summary

Looping is a powerful technique that enables you to write tighter code. Tighter code is smaller, more efficient, and usually—but not always—more readable. In this hour, you learned to write for loops for situations in which you know the precise number of times you want a loop executed. Remember, it's not necessary to know the number of iterations at design time, but you must know the number at runtime to use a for loop. You learned how to use iterators to increment the counter of a for loop, and even how to exit a loop prematurely using break.

In this hour, you also learned how to use the very powerful do...while loop. The do...while loop enables you to create very flexible loops that can handle almost any looping scenario. You learned how evaluating *expression* in a do...while loop makes the loop behave differently than when evaluating the expression in a while loop. If a for loop can't do the job, some form of the do...while or while loop will.

In addition to learning the specifics about loops, you've seen firsthand how multiple solutions to a problem can exist. Often, one approach is clearly superior to all other approaches, although you may not always find it. Other times, one approach may be only marginally superior or multiple approaches may all be equally applicable. Expert programmers are able to consistently find the best approaches to any given problem. With time, you'll be able to do the same.

Q&A

Q. *Is there ever a situation where you would want a loop to run indefinitely?*

A. Game programmers often create a single loop that runs indefinitely, and all logic and user input takes place in this main loop. Other than such a very specific situation, all loops should terminate at some point.

Q. *Should I be concerned about the performance differences between the two types of loops?*

A. With today's fast processors, chances are good that the performance difference between the two loop types in any given situation will be overshadowed by the readability and functionality of the best choice of loop. If you have a situation in which performance is critical, write the loop using all the ways you can think of, benchmark the results, and choose the fastest loop.

Workshop

Quiz

1. True or False: You have to know the start and end values of a for loop at design time to use this type of loop.

2. Is it possible to nest loops?

3. What type of loop would you most likely need to create if you didn't have any idea how many times the loop would need to occur?

4. If you evaluate the expression in a do...while on the while statement, is it possible that the code within the loop may never execute?

5. What statement do you use to terminate a do...while without evaluating the expression on the do or while statements?

Answers

1. False, you can use a variable to define the start or end values of a for loop.

2. Yes, you can nest loops—even loops of different types.

3. A do...while loop.

4. No, the code will always execute at least once.

5. You use a break statement.

Exercises

1. Create a text box in your No Remainders project and let the user enter a number. Find the first 10 numbers that are evenly divisible by the number entered by the user.

2. Use two for loops nested within each other to size a label in two dimensions. Have the outer loop change the Width property of the label from 1 to 100, and have the inner loop change the Height property from 1 to 100. Don't be surprised by the end result—it's rather odd.

HOUR 15

Debugging Your Code

What You'll Learn in This Hour:

▶ Adding comments to your code
▶ Identifying the two basic types of errors
▶ Using the Command window
▶ Using the Output window
▶ Creating a structured error handler

No one writes perfect code. You're most certainly familiar with those problems that prevent code from executing properly—they're called *bugs*. Being new to Visual C#, your code will probably contain a fair number of bugs. As you gain proficiency, the number of bugs in your code will decrease but bugs will *never* disappear entirely. This book can't teach you how to debug every possible build or runtime error you might encounter; debugging is a skill *and* an art. In this hour, however, you will learn the basic skills necessary to trace and correct most bugs in your code.

Before proceeding, create a new Windows Application project named **Debugging Example**. Next, follow these steps to build the project:

1. Right-click Form1.cs in the Solution Explorer, choose Rename, and then change the name of the form to **frmDebuggingExample.cs**. Next, set the form's Text property to **Debugging Example** (you will need to click the form once to access its design properties).

2. Add a new text box to the form by double-clicking the TextBox item in the toolbox. Set the text box's properties as follows:

Property	Value
Name	**txtInput**
Location	**88,112**
Size	**120,20**

3. Add a new button to the form by double-clicking the Button item in the toolbox and set its properties as follows:

Property	Value
Name	**btnPerformDivision**
Location	**96,144**
Size	**104,23**
Text	**Perform Division**

Your form should now look like the one shown in Figure 15.1.

FIGURE 15.1
This simple interface will help you learn debugging techniques.

This little project is going to divide 100 by whatever is entered into the text box. As you write the code to accomplish this, various bugs will be introduced on purpose, and you'll learn to correct them. Save your project now by clicking the Save All button on the toolbar.

Adding Comments to Your Code

One of the simplest things you can do to reduce bugs from the beginning—and make tracking down existing bugs easier—is to add comments to your code. A code *comment* is simply a line of text that Visual C# knows isn't actual code and therefore ignores. Comment lines are stripped from the code when the project is compiled to create a distributable component, so comments don't affect performance. Visual C#'s code window shows comments as green text. This makes it easier to read and understand procedures. Consider adding comments to the top of each procedure stating the procedure's purpose. In addition, you should add liberal comments throughout all procedures, detailing what's occurring in the code.

To create a comment, precede the comment text with the two forward slash characters (//). A simple comment might look like this, for example:

```
// This is a comment because it is preceded by double forward slashes.
```

Comments can also be placed at the end of a line of code, like this:

```
int intAge;        // Used to store the user's age in years.
```

Everything to the right of and including the double-slashes in this statement is a comment.

Visual C# also supports a second type of comment, one that allows for comments to span multiple lines without forcing you to add // characters to each line. Such a comment begins with an open comment mark of a forward slash, followed by an asterisk (/*), and the comment closes with a close mark of an asterisk followed by a forward slash (*/). For example, a comment can look like this:

```
/*     Chapter 15 in Sams TY Visual C# 2005
focuses on debugging code; something most developers
spend a lot of time on.   */
```

By adding comments to your code procedures, you don't have to rely on memory to decipher a procedure's purpose or mechanics. If you've ever had to go back and work with code you haven't looked at in a while, or had to work with someone else's code, you probably already have a great appreciation for comments.

Double-click the button now to access its `Click` event and add the following two lines of code (comments, actually):

```
// This procedure divides 100 by the value entered in
// the text box txtInput.
```

Notice that after you type the second forward slash, both slashes turn green.

When creating code comments, do your best to do the following:

▶ Document the purpose of the code (the *why*, not the *how*).

▶ Clearly indicate the thinking and logic behind the code.

▶ Call attention to important turning points in code.

▶ Reduce the need for readers to run a simulation of code execution in their heads.

▶ Comment your code as you are typing it. If you wait until the code is complete, you probably won't go back and add comments.

> Visual C# also supports an additional type of comment denoted with three slashes (///). When the Visual C# compiler encounters these comments, it processes them into an XML file. These types of comments are often used to create documentation for code. Creating XML files from comments is a bit advanced for this book, but if these features intrigue you, I highly recommend that you look into it.

Identifying the Two Basic Types of Errors

There are basically two types of errors that can occur in code: *compile errors* and *runtime errors*. A compile error (commonly called a *build error*) is code that prevents Visual C#'s compiler from being able to process the code; Visual C# won't compile a project that has a build error in it. A statement that calls a procedure with incorrect parameters, for example, generates a build error. Runtime errors are those that don't occur at compile time but are encountered when the project is being run. Runtime errors are usually a result of trying to perform an invalid operation on a variable.

To illustrate, consider this next statement which *won't* generate a compile error:

```
intResult = 10 / intDenominator;
```

Under most circumstances, this code won't even generate a runtime error. However, what happens if the value of intDenominator is 0? Ten divided by zero is undefined, which won't fit into intResult (intResult is an int variable). Attempting to run the code with the intDenominator variable having a value of 0 causes Visual C# to return a runtime error. A runtime error is called an **exception**, and when an exception occurs, it's said to be **thrown** (that is, Visual C# throws an exception when a runtime error occurs). When an exception is thrown, code execution stops at the offending statement and Visual C# displays an error message. You can prevent Visual C# from stopping execution when an exception is thrown by writing special code to handle the exception, which you'll learn about later in this hour.

Add the following statements to your Click() event now, right below the two comment lines:

```
long lngAnswer;
lngAnswer = 100 / Convert.ToInt64(txtInput.Text);
MessageBox.Show("100/" + txtInput.Text + " is " + lngAnswer)
```

The missing semicolon in the MessageBox.Show() line is intentional; type in the preceding line of code exactly as it appears. Although you've missed the ending semicolon, Visual C# doesn't return an immediate error. However, notice how Visual C# displays a wavy red line at the end of the statement. Note that you may have to press Enter to move to a different line to get it to show up. Choose Error List from the View menu now, and notice that Visual C# displays an information tip explaining the nature of the error (see Figure 15.2). All build errors in the current project appear in the Error List. To view a particular offending line of code, double-click an item in the Error List.

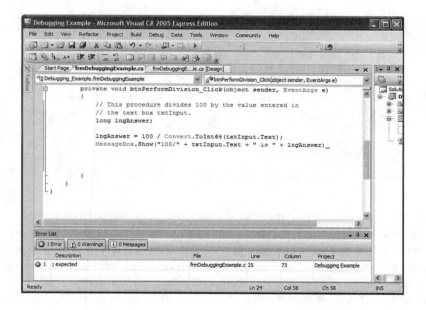

FIGURE 15.2
Visual C# highlights build errors in the code window by using wavy lines.

Press F5 to run the project. When you do, Visual C# displays a message that a build error was found and asks whether you want to continue by running the last successful build. Because the code won't run as is, there's no point in continuing, so click No to return to the code editor.

Build errors are very serious in that they prevent code from being compiled and therefore they completely prevent execution; build errors must be corrected before you can run the project. Double-click the build error in the Error List to go directly to the error now.

Correct the problem by adding a semicolon to the end of the `MessageBox.Show()` statement. After you've made this change, press F5 to run the project. Visual C# no longer returns a build error; you've just successfully debugged a problem!

Click the Perform Division button now, and you'll receive another error (see Figure 15.3).

FIGURE 15.3
A runtime
exception halts
code execution
at the offending
line.

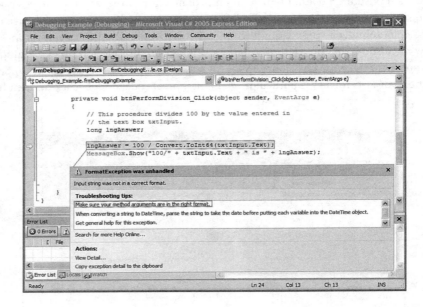

This time, the error is a runtime error, or exception. If an exception occurs, you know that the code compiled without a problem because build errors prevent code from compiling and executing. This particular exception is a Format exception. Format exceptions generally occur when you attempt to perform a method using a variable, and the variable is of an incompatible data type for the specified operation. Visual C# denotes the offending statement with a yellow arrow (the arrow indicates the current statement).

At this point, you know that the statement has a "bug," and you know it is related to data typing. Choose Stop Debugging from the Debug menu to stop the running project and return to the code editor.

Using Visual C# Debugging Tools

Visual C# includes a number of debugging tools to help you track down and eliminate bugs. In this section, you'll learn to use the primary tools of break points, the

Immediate window, and the Error List window—three tools that form the foundation of any debugging arsenal. There are more tools, such as the Watch window and Locals window, and as you progress into more detailed development, you should explore these tools.

Working with Break Points

Just as an exception halts the execution of a procedure, you can deliberately stop execution at any statement of code by creating a **break point**. When Visual C# encounters a break point while executing code, execution is halted at the break statement *before* it is executed. Break points enable you to query or change the value of variables at a specific instance in time, and they let you step through code execution one line at a time.

You're going to create a break point to help troubleshoot the exception in your `lngAnswer` = statement.

Adding a break point is simple. Just click in the gray area to the left of the statement at which you want to break code execution (you could have also placed the cursor on the statement and pressed F9 to toggle the breakpoint on and off). When you do so, Visual C# displays a red circle, denoting a break point at that statement (see Figure 15.4). To clear the break point, you would click the red circle (but don't do this now).

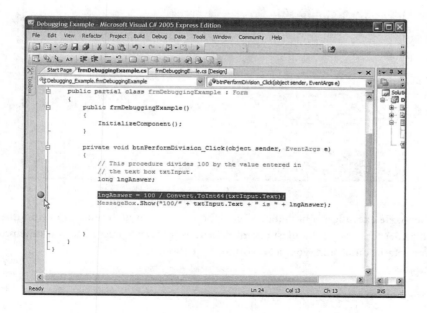

FIGURE 15.4
Break points give you control over code execution.

By the Way

> Break points are saved with the project. You don't have to reset all your break points each time you open the project.

Click the gray area to the left of the lnAnswer = statement to create a break point as shown in Figure 15.4. After you've set the break point, press F5 to run the program. Click the Perform Division button again. When Visual C# encounters the break point, code execution is halted—right before the statement with the break point executes, and the procedure with the break point is shown. In addition, the cursor is conveniently placed at the statement with the current break point. Notice the yellow arrow overlaying the red circle of the break point (see Figure 15.5). This yellow arrow marks the next statement to be executed. It just so happens that the statement has a break point, so the yellow arrow appears over the red circle (the yellow arrow won't always be over a red circle, but it will always appear in the gray area aligned with the next statement that will execute).

FIGURE 15.5
A yellow arrow denotes the next statement to be executed.

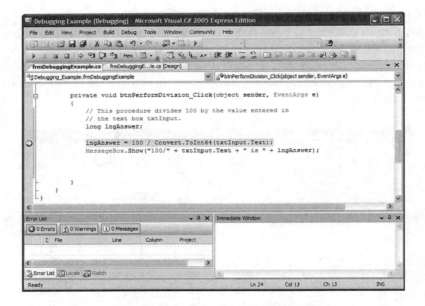

When code execution is halted at a break point, you can do a number of things. See Table 15.1 for a list of the most common actions. For now, press F5 to continue program execution. Again, you get a Format Exception.

TABLE 15.1 Actions That Can Be Taken at a Break Point

Action	Keystroke	Description
Continue Code Execution	F5	Continues execution at the current break statement.
Step Into	F11	Executes the statement at the break point and then stops at the next statement. If the current statement is a function call, F11 enters the function and stops at the first statement in the function.
Step Over	F10	Executes the statement at the break point and then stops at the next statement. If the current statement is a function call, the function is run in its entirety; execution stops at the statement following the function call.
Step Out	Shift+F11	Runs all the statements in the current procedure and halts execution at the statement following the one that called the current procedure.
Stop Debugging	Shift+F5	Stops debugging the project and returns to design mode.

Using the Immediate Window

Break points themselves aren't usually sufficient to debug a procedure. In addition to break points, you'll often use the Immediate window to debug code. The Immediate window is a Visual Studio IDE window that generally appears only when your project is in Run mode. If the Immediate window isn't displayed, you can show it by opening the Debug menu, then choosing Windows > Immediate. Using the Immediate window, you can type in code statements that Visual C# executes immediately (hence the name). You'll use the Immediate window now to debug our problem statement example.

Type the following statement into the Immediate window and press Enter:

```
? txtInput.Text
```

Although it isn't intuitive, the ? character has been used in programming for many years as a shortcut for the word *print*. The statement you entered simply prints the contents of the Text property of the text box to the Immediate window.

Notice how the Immediate window displays the text `" "`. This indicates that the text box is empty. The statement throwing the exception is attempting to use `Convert.ToInt64()` to convert the contents of the text box to a long (which is a 64 bit integer). The `Convert.ToInt64()` method expects data to be passed to it, yet the text box has no data (the `Text` property contains an empty string). Consequently, a Format exception occurs because `Convert.ToInt64()` doesn't know how to convert an empty string to a number.

You can do a number of things to prevent this error. The most obvious is to ensure that the text box contains a value before attempting to use `Convert.ToInt64()`. You're going to do this now.

Visual C# now supports on-the-fly code editing—something that was sorely lacking in earlier versions of .NET. This means you can now modify code while debugging it, so that you no longer have to stop the project to make changes and then run it once more to test your changes.

Close the exception window and put the cursor between the declaration statement (long lngAnswer;) and the statement with the error and press Enter. Next, enter the following code statements:

```
if (txtInput.Text.Length == 0) return;
```

Now, remember the yellow arrow used to indicate the next statement that will execute? It indicates that if you continue code execution now, the statement that throws the exception will run once more. We want our new statements to execute. Follow these steps to designate the new code as the next code to be executed:

1. Click on the yellow arrow and hold down the mouse button.

2. Drag the yellow arrow to the new `if` statement.

3. Release the mouse button.

Now, the yellow arrow should indicate that the next statement to execute will be the if statement (see Figure 15.6).

Now, press F5 to continue running the project. This time, Visual C# won't throw an exception, and it won't halt execution at your break point because the test you just created caused code execution to leave the procedure before the statement with the break point was reached.

Next, follow these steps:

1. Type your name into the text box and click the Perform Division button again. Now that the text box is no longer empty, execution passes the statement with the exit test and stops at the break point.

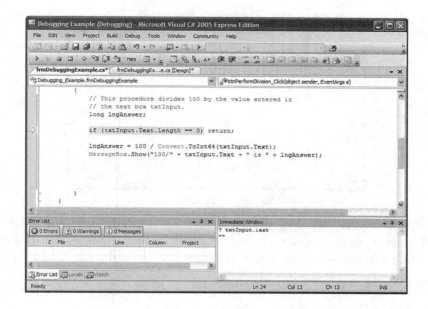

FIGURE 15.6
You can drag the yellow arrow to change which statement gets executed next.

2. Press F5 to continue executing the code, and again you'll receive an exception. This exception is once again a Format exception; the statement still doesn't like the format of the data being dealt with.

3. Close the exception window (click the little x in the upper-right corner), and type the following into the Immediate window (be sure to press Enter when you're finished):

```
? txtInput.Text
```

The Immediate window prints your name.

Well, you eliminated the problem of not supplying any data to the `Convert.ToInt64()` method, but something else is wrong.

Press F5 to continue executing the code and take a closer look at the description of the exception. Toward the bottom of the Exception window is the text View Detail Click this link now, and Visual C# displays a View Detail window with more information about the exception (see Figure 15.7).

The text on the View Detail window says {"Input string was not in a correct format."}. It apparently still doesn't like what's being passed to the `Convert.ToInt64()`.

FIGURE 15.7
The View Detail window gives you important information for fixing exception problems.

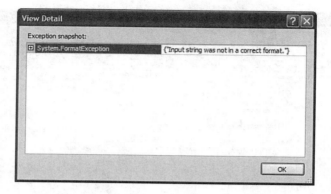

By now, it might have occurred to you that no logical way exists to convert alphanumeric text to a number; Convert.ToInt64() needs a number to work with. You can easily test this by following these steps:

1. Click OK to close the View Detail window.

2. Choose Stop Debugging from the Debug menu.

3. Press F5 to run the project.

4. Enter a number into the text box and click the button. Code execution again stops at the break point.

5. Press F11 to execute the statement only. No errors this time! Press F5 to continue execution, and Visual C# displays the message box (finally). Click OK to dismiss the message box and then close the form to stop the project.

You can use the Immediate window to change the value of a variable.

Because the Convert.ToInt64() expects a number, but the text box contains no intrinsic way to force numeric input, you have to accommodate for this situation in your code. You will learn how to deal with exceptions later on in this chapter using a catch statement.

Using the Output Window

The Output window (see Figure 15.8) is used by Visual C# to display various status messages and build errors. The most useful feature of the Output window, for general use, is the capability to send data to it from a running application. This is especially handy when debugging applications.

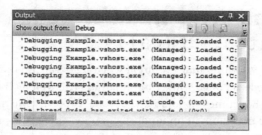

FIGURE 15.8
The Output window displays a lot of useful information—if you know what you're looking for.

You've already used the Output window in previous hours, but you might not have seriously considered its application as related to debugging. As you can see from Figure 15.8, some data sent to the Output window by Visual C# isn't that intuitive—in fact, you can ignore much of what is automatically sent to the Output window. What you'll want to use the Output window for is printing data for debugging (as you have done and will do throughout this book). Therefore, it's no coincidence that printing to the Output window is accomplished via the Debug object.

To print data to the Output window, use the WriteLine() method of the Debug object, like this:

```
System.Diagnostics.Debug.WriteLine("Results = " + lngResults);
```

Whatever you place within the parentheses of the WriteLine() method is what is printed to the Output window. Note that you can print literal text and numbers, variables, or expressions. WriteLine() is most useful in cases where you want to know the value of a variable, but you don't want to halt code execution using a break point. For instance, suppose you have a number of statements that manipulate a variable. You can sprinkle WriteLine() statements into the code to print the variable's contents at strategic points. When you do this, you'll want to print some text along with the variable's value so that the output makes sense to you. For example:

```
System.Diagnostics.Debug.WriteLine
        ("Results of area calculation = " + sngArea);
```

You can also use WriteLine() to create checkpoints in your code, like this:

```
System.Diagnostics.Debug.WriteLine("Passed Checkpoint 1");
// Execute statement here
System.Diagnostics.Debug.WriteLine("Passed Checkpoint 2");
// Execute another statement here
System.Diagnostics.Debug.WriteLine("Passed Checkpoint 3");
```

Many creative uses exist for the Output window. Just remember that the Output window isn't available to a compiled component; calls to the Debug object are ignored by the compiler when creating distributable components.

Writing an Error Handler Using
`Try...Catch...Finally`

It's useful to have Visual C# halt execution when an exception occurs when debugging. When the code is halted while running in the IDE, you receive an error message, and you're shown the offending line of code. However, when your project is run as a compiled program, an unhandled exception causes the program to terminate (aka crash to the desktop). This is one of the most *undesirable* things an application can do. Fortunately, you can prevent exceptions from stopping code execution (and terminating compiled programs) by writing code specifically designed to deal with exceptions. Exception-handling code instructs Visual C# on how to deal with an exception instead of relying on Visual C#'s default behavior of aborting the application.

Visual C# supports *structured exception handling* (a formal way of dealing with errors) in the form of the `try` block. Creating structured error-handling code can be a bit confusing at first, and like most coding principles, it's best understood by doing it.

Create a new Windows Application called **Structured Exception Handling** and follow these steps to build the project:

1. Right-click Form1.cs in the Solution Explorer, choose Rename, and change the name of the default form to **frmExceptionHandlingExample.cs**. Next, set the form's Text property to **Structured Exception Handling**.

2. Add a new button to the form and set its properties as follows:

Property	Value
Name	**btnCatchException**
Location	**104,128**
Size	**96,23**
Text	**Catch Exception**

3. Double-click the button and add the following code to its `Click()` event:

   ```
   try
   {
      Debug.WriteLine("Try");
   }
   catch (Exception ex)
   {
      Debug.WriteLine("Catch");
   }
   finally
   ```

```
{
    Debug.WriteLine("Finally");
}
Debug.WriteLine("Done Trying");
```

4. The code won't work at this time because you didn't specify the full name-space reference to the Debug object. As I mentioned in an earlier chapter, you can add a using statement at the top of the class so that you don't have to provide the full qualifier each time you use the Debug object. Scroll up to the top of the class and locate the section with existing using statements, and then add the following using statement below the existing ones:

```
using System.Diagnostics;
```

As you can see, the try, catch, and finally statements use the braces ({}) to enclose statements. The try, catch, and finally structure is used to wrap code that may cause an exception; it provides the means of dealing with thrown exceptions. Table 15.2 explains the sections of this structure.

TABLE 15.2   Sections of the `Try...Catch-Finally` **Structure**

Section	Description
try	The try section is where you place code that might cause an exception. You can place all of a procedure's code within the try section, or just a few lines.
catch	Code within the catch section executes only when an exception occurs; it's the code you write to catch the exception.
finally	Code within the finally section occurs when the code within the try and/or code within the catch sections completes. This section is where you place your *cleanup code*—code that you want always executed regardless of whether an exception occurs.

There are three forms of try statements:
- ▶ A try block followed by one or more catch blocks.
- ▶ A try block followed by a finally block.
- ▶ A try block followed by one or more catch blocks, followed by a finally block.

By the Way

Press F5 to run the project and then click the button. Next, take a look at the contents of the Output window. The Output window should contain the following lines of text (among others):

```
Try
Finally
Done Trying
```

Here's what happened:

1. The `try` block begins, and code within the `try` section executes.

2. Catch sections are used to trap exceptions. Because no exception occurs, code within the `catch` section is ignored.

3. When all statements within the `try` section finish executing, the code within the `finally` section executes.

4. When all statements within the `finally` section finish executing, execution jumps to the statement immediately following the `try`, `catch`, and `finally` statements.

Stop the project now by choosing Debug, Stop Debugging from the menu.

Now that you understand the basic mechanics of the `try`, `catch`, and `finally` structure, you're going to add statements within the structure so that an exception occurs and gets handled.

Change the contents of the procedure to match this code:

```
long lngNumerator = 10;
long lngDenominator = 0;
long lngResult;

try
{
    Debug.WriteLine("Try");
    lngResult = lngNumerator / lngDenominator;
}
catch
{
    Debug.WriteLine("Catch");
}
finally
{
    Debug.WriteLine("Finally");
}

Debug.WriteLine("Done Trying");
```

Again, press F5 to run the project. Click the button and take a look at the Output window. This time, the text in the Output window should read

```
Try
A first chance exception of type 'System.DivideByZeroException' occurred
in Structured Exception Handling.exe
Catch
```

```
Finally
Done Trying
```

Notice that this time the code within the `catch` section executes. That's because the statement that sets `lngResult` causes a DivideByZero exception. Had this statement not been placed within a `try` block, Visual C# would have raised the exception, and an error dialog box would've appeared. However, because the statement is placed within the `try` block, the exception is *caught*. Caught means that when the exception occurred, Visual C# directed execution to the `catch` section. (You do not have to use a `catch` section. If you omit a `catch` section, caught exceptions are simply ignored.) Notice also how the code within the `finally` section executes after the code within the `catch` section. Remember that code within the `finally` section *always* executes, regardless of whether an exception occurs.

Dealing with an Exception

Catching exceptions so that they don't crash your application is a noble thing to do, but it's only part of the error-handling process. You'll usually want to tell the user (in a friendly way) that an exception has occurred. You'll probably also want to tell the user what type of exception occurred. To do this, you must have a way of knowing what exception was thrown. This is also important if you intend to write code to deal with specific exceptions. The `catch` statement enables you to specify a variable to hold a reference to an `Exception` object. Using an `Exception` object, you can get information about the exception. The following is the syntax used to place the exception in an `exception` object:

```
catch ( Exception variablename)
```

Modify your `catch` section to match the following:

```
catch (Exception objException)
{
    Debug.WriteLine("Catch");
    MessageBox.Show("An error has occurred: " + objException.Message);
}
```

The `Message` property of the `Exception` object contains the text that describes the specific exception that occurred. Run the project and click the button, and Visual C# displays your custom error message (see Figure 15.9).

FIGURE 15.9
Structured exception handling enables you to decide what to do when an exception occurs.

Handling an Anticipated Exception

At times, you'll anticipate a specific exception being thrown. For example, you might write code that attempts to open a file when the file does not exist. In such an instance, you'll probably want the program to perform certain actions when this exception is thrown. When you anticipate a specific exception, you can create a catch section designed specifically to deal with that one exception.

Recall from the previous section that you can retrieve information about the current exception using a catch statement, such as

```
catch (Exception objException)
```

By creating a generic Exception variable, this catch statement catches any and all exceptions thrown by statements within the try section. To catch a specific exception, change the data type of the exception variable to a specific exception type. Remember the code you wrote earlier that caused a format exception when an attempt was made to pass an empty string to the Convert.ToInt64() method? You could have used a try structure to deal with the exception, using code such as this:

```
long lngAnswer;

try
{
    lngAnswer = 100 / long.Parse(txtInput.Text);
    MessageBox.Show("100/" + txtInput.Text + " is " + lngAnswer);
}
catch (System.FormatException)
{
MessageBox.Show("You must enter a number in the text box.");
}
catch
{
    MessageBox.Show("Caught an exception that wasn't a format exception.");
}
```

Notice that there are two catch statements in this structure. The first catch statement is designed to catch only a format exception; it won't catch exceptions of any other type. The second catch statement doesn't care what type of exception is thrown; it catches all of them. The second catch statement acts as a catch-all for any exceptions that aren't overflow exceptions because catch sections are evaluated from top to bottom, much like case statements in the switch structure. You could add more catch sections to catch other specific exceptions if the situation calls for it.

This next example, you're going to build on the Picture Viewer project last edited in Hour 11, "Using Constants, Data Types, Variables, and Arrays," so go ahead and open that project now. First, I want you to see the exception that you are going to catch. Follow these steps to cause an exception to occur:

1. Press F5 to run the project.

2. Click the Open Picture button on the toolbar to display the Select Picture dialog box.

3. In the File Name: box, enter ***.*** and press Enter. This changes your filter so that you can now select files that aren't images. Locate a file on your hard drive that you know is not an image. Files with the extension .txt, .ini, or .pdf are perfect.

4. After you've located a file that isn't an image file, click it to select it and then Click Open.

You have now caused an Out of Memory Exception (see Figure 15.10). This is the exception thrown by the picture box when you attempt to load a file that isn't a picture. Your first reaction might be something along the lines of "why do I have to worry about that; no one would do that." Well, welcome to programming my friend! A lot of your time will be spent writing code to protect users from themselves. It's not fair and usually not fun, but it is a reality.

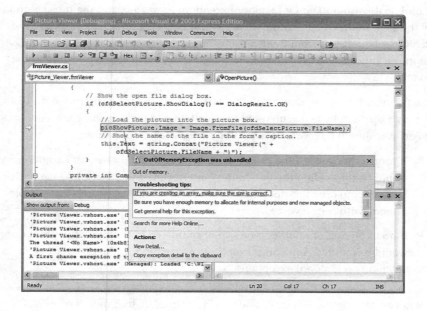

FIGURE 15.10
You never want an unhandled exception to occur—ever.

Go ahead and choose Stop Debugging on the toolbar to stop the running project. Rather than take you step by step through the changes, it will be easier to just show you the code for the new `OpenPicture()` procedure. Change your code to the code shown here:

```
try
{
    // Show the open file dialog box.
    if (ofdSelectPicture.ShowDialog() == DialogResult.OK)
    {
        // Load the picture into the picture box.
        picShowPicture.Image = Image.FromFile(ofdSelectPicture.FileName);
        // Show the name of the file in the form's caption.
        this.Text = string.Concat("Picture Viewer(" +
            ofdSelectPicture.FileName + ")");
    }
}
catch (System.OutOfMemoryException)
{
    MessageBox.Show("The file you have chosen is not an image file.",
        "Invalid File", MessageBoxButtons.OK);
}
```

What you've just done is wrapped the procedure in an error-handler that watches for and deals with an Out Of Memory Exception. Press F5 to run the project, and follow the steps outlined earlier to load a file that isn't an image. Now, rather than receiving an exception from the IDE, your application displays a custom message box that is much more user friendly, and that won't crash the application to the desktop!

Although you have now eliminated the possibility of the user generating an Out Of Memory exception by choosing a file that isn't a valid picture, there are some caveats you should be aware of regarding the code changes you made:

▶ If some other code in the procedure caused an Out Of Memory Exception, you would be misleading the user with your error message. You could address this by wrapping only the statement that loads the selected picture into the picturebox within its own try/catch structure.

▶ If an exception of another type was encountered in the procedure, that error would be ignored. You can prevent this by creating a generic catch block to catch any additional exceptions.

As you can see, the mechanics of adding a try structure to handle exceptions is relatively easy, whereas knowing what specifically to catch and how to handle the situation when an exception is caught can prove to be challenging.

Summary

In this hour, you learned the basics for debugging applications. You learned how adding useful and plentiful comments to your procedures makes debugging easier. However, no matter how good your comments are, you'll still have bugs.

You learned about the two basic types of errors: build errors and runtime errors (exceptions). Build errors are easier to troubleshoot because the compiler tells you exactly what line contains a build error and generally provides useful information about how to correct it. Exceptions, on the other hand, can crash your application if not handled properly. You learned how to track down exceptions using break points and the Immediate window, and you learned how to send text to the Output window at runtime. Finally, you learned to how to make your applications more robust by creating structured error handlers using the try structure.

No book can teach you everything you need to know to write bug-free code. However, this hour taught you the basic skills you need to track down and eliminate many types of errors in your programs. As your skills as a programmer improve, so will your debugging abilities.

Q&A

Q. Should I alert the user that an exception has occurred or just let the code keep running?

A. If you've written code to handle the specific exception, there's probably no need to tell the user about it. However, if an exception occurs that the code doesn't know how to address, you should provide the user with the exception information so that they can report the problem accurately so that you can fix it.

Q. Should I comment every statement in my application?

A. Probably not. However, consider commenting every decision-making and looping construct in your program. Such sections of code are usually pivotal to the success of the procedure, and what they do isn't always obvious.

Workshop

Quiz

1. What type of error prevents Visual C# from compiling and running code?

2. What is another name for a runtime error?

3. What characters are used to denote a single comment line?

4. To halt execution at a specific statement in code, you set a _____.

5. Explain the yellow arrow and red circles that can appear in the gray area in the code editor.

6. What IDE window would you use to poll the contents of a variable in break mode?

7. True or False: You must always specify a catch section in a try structure.

Answers

1. A Build error.

2. An exception.

3. Two forward slash characters (//).

4. Breakpoint

5. The yellow arrow denotes the next statement to be executed during debugging. The red circles denote break points—statements where code execution halts when reached.

6. The Immediate window.

7. False. If you omit a catch section, the exception will be ignored.

Exercises

1. In the code example that sets lngAnswer to the result of a division expression, change lngAnswer from a long to a single (call it sngAnswer). Next, remove the if statements that test the contents of the text box before performing the division. Do you get the same exception(s) that you did when the variable was a long? Why or why not?

2. Rewrite the code that sets lngAnswer to the result of a division expression so that the code is wrapped in a try structure. Remove the if statement that performs data validation, and create catch sections for the exception that might be thrown.

Designing Objects Using Classes

What You'll Learn in This Hour:

▶ Encapsulating data and code using classes
▶ Comparing classes to standard modules
▶ Creating an object interface
▶ Exposing object attributes as properties
▶ Instantiating objects from classes
▶ Binding an object reference to a variable
▶ Understanding object lifetime
▶ Releasing object references

You learned about what makes an object an object in Hour 3, "Understanding Objects and Collections." Since that hour, you've learned how to manipulate objects such as forms and controls. The real power of leveraging objects comes from being able to design and implement custom objects of your own. In this hour, you'll learn how to create your own objects by using classes. You'll learn how to define the template for an object and how to create your own custom properties and methods.

There is simply no way to become an expert on programming classes in a single hour. However, when you've finished with this hour, you'll have a working knowledge of creating classes and deriving custom objects from those classes; consider this hour a primer on object-oriented programming. I strongly encourage you to seek other texts that focus on object-oriented programming after you feel comfortable with the material presented throughout this book.

Understanding Classes

Classes enable you to develop applications using object-oriented programming (OOP) techniques (recall that I discussed OOP briefly in Hour 3). Classes are templates that define objects. Although you might not have known it, you've been programming with classes throughout this book. When you create a new form in a Visual C# project, you're actually creating a class that defines a form; forms instantiated at runtime are derived from the class. Using objects derived from predefined classes (such as a Visual C# Form class), is just the start of enjoying the benefits of object-oriented programming—to truly realize the benefits of OOP, you must create your own classes.

The philosophy of programming with classes is considerably different from that of traditional programming. Proper class-programming techniques can make your programs better, both in structure and in reliability. Class programming forces you to consider the logistics of your code and data more thoroughly, causing you to create more reusable and extendable object-based code.

Encapsulating Data and Code Using Classes

An object derived from a class is an encapsulation of data and code; that is, the object comprises its code *and* all the data it uses. For example, suppose that you need to keep track of employees in an organization and that you must store many pieces of information for each employee, such as name, date hired, and title. In addition, suppose that you need methods for adding and removing employees, and you want all this information *and* functionality available to many functions within your application. You could use standard modules to manipulate the data, but doing so would most likely require many variable arrays as well as code to manage those arrays.

A better approach is to *encapsulate* all the employee data and functionality (adding and deleting routines and so forth) into a single, reusable object. Encapsulation is the process of integrating data and code into one entity: an object. Your application, as well as external applications, could then work with the employee data through a consistent interface—the Employee object's interface. (An *interface* is a set of exposed functionality—essentially, code routines that define methods, properties, and events.)

Creating objects for use outside your application is beyond the scope of this book. The techniques you'll learn in this hour, however, are directly applicable to creating externally creatable objects.

The encapsulation of data and code is the key idea of classes. By encapsulating the data *and* the routines to manipulate the data into a single object by way of a class, you free up application code that needs to manipulate the data from the intricacies of data maintenance. For example, suppose that company policy has changed so that when a new employee is added to the system, a special tax record must be generated, and a form must be printed. If the data and code routines weren't encapsulated in a common object but instead were written in various places throughout your code, you would have to modify each and every module that contained code to create a new employee record. By using a class to create an object, you need to change the code in only one location: within the object. As long as you don't modify the interface of the object (discussed shortly), all the routines that use the object to create a new employee will instantly have the policy change in effect.

Comparing Instance Members with Static Members

You learned in Hour 10, "Creating and Calling Methods," that Visual C# does not support global methods, but supports only class methods. By creating static methods, you create methods that can be accessed from anywhere in the project through the class itself—without needing to instantiate an object from the class.

Instance methods are similar to static methods in how they appear in the Visual C# design environment and in the way in which you write code within them. However, the behavior of classes at runtime differs greatly from that of static members. With static members, all static data is shared by all members of the class. In addition, there are never multiple instances of the static class data. With instance member classes, objects are instantiated from a class and each object receives its own set of data. Static methods are accessed through the class, whereas nonstatic methods (also called instance methods) are accessed through instances of the class.

Instance methods differ from static methods in more ways than just how their data behaves. When you define a static method, it is instantly available to other classes within your application. However, instant member classes aren't immediately available in code. Classes are templates for objects. At runtime, your code doesn't interact with the code in the class per se, but it instantiates objects derived from the class. Each object acts as its own class "module" and thus it has its own set of data. When classes are exposed externally to other applications, the application containing the class's code is called the *server*. Applications that create and use instances of objects are called *clients*. When you use instances of classes in the application that contains those classes, the application itself acts as both a client and a server. In this hour, I'll refer to the code instantiating an object derived from a class as *client code*.

Begin by creating a new Windows Application titled **Class Programming Example**, and then follow these steps to create your project:

1. Right-click Form1.cs in the Solution Explorer, choose Rename, and change the name of the form to **frmClassExample.cs**. Next, set the form's Text property to **Class Programming Example**.

2. Add a new class to the project by choosing Project, Add Class from the menu. Save the class with the name **clsMyClass.cs** (see Figure 16.1).

FIGURE 16.1
Classes are
added to a proj-
ect just as other
object files are
added.

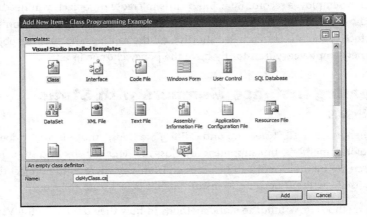

Understanding Constructors and Destructors

As you open your new class file, you'll notice that Visual C# added the public class declaration class clsMyClass. All code, including methods, variables, and property procedures goes between the opening and closing braces of the class declaration.

> Objects consume system resources. The .NET Framework (discussed in Hour 24, "The 10,000-Foot View") has a built-in mechanism to free resources used by objects. This mechanism is called the *garbage collector* (and it is discussed in Hour 24 as well). Essentially, the garbage collector determines when an object is no longer being used and then destroys the object. When the garbage collector destroys an object, it calls the object's destructor method. If you aren't careful about how you implement a destructor method, you can cause problems.

Creating an Object Interface

For an object to be created from a class, the class must expose an interface. As I mentioned earlier, an interface is a set of exposed functionality (properties, methods, and events). An interface is the means by which client code communicates with the object derived from the class. Some classes expose a limited interface, whereas some expose complex interfaces. The content and quantity of your class's interface is entirely up to you.

The interface of a class consists of one or more of the following members:

- ▶ Properties
- ▶ Methods
- ▶ Events

For example, assume that you're creating an Employee object (that is, a class used to derive employee objects). You must first decide how you want client code to interact with your object. You'll want to consider both the data contained within the object and the functions that the object can perform. You might want client code to be able to retrieve the name of an employee and other information such as sex, age, and the date of hire. For client code to get these values from the object, the object must expose an interface member for each of these items. You'll recall from Hour 3 that values exposed by an object are called *properties*. Therefore, each piece of data discussed here would have to be exposed as a property of the Employee object.

In addition to properties, you can expose functions—such as a `Delete()` or `AddNew()` function. These functions may be simple in nature or complex. The `Delete` function of the `Employee` object, for example, might be quite complex. It would need to perform all the actions necessary to delete an employee, including such things as removing the employee from an assigned department, notifying the accounting department to remove the employee from the payroll, notifying the security area to revoke the employee's security access, and so on. Publicly exposed functions of an object, as you should again remember from Hour 3, are called *methods*.

Properties and methods are the most commonly used interface members. Although designing properties and methods might be new to you, by now using them isn't— you've been using properties and methods in almost every hour so far. Here, you're going to learn the techniques for creating properties and methods for your own objects.

For even more interaction between the client and the object, you can expose custom events. Custom object events are similar to the events of a form or a text box. However, with custom events you have complete control over the following:

- ▶ The name of the event
- ▶ The parameters passed to the event
- ▶ When the event occurs

Creating custom events is complicated, and I'll cover only custom properties and methods in this hour.

Properties, methods, and events together make up an object's interface. This interface acts as a contract between the client application and the object. Any and all communication between the client and the object must transpire through this interface (see Figure 16.2).

FIGURE 16.2
Clients interact with an object via the object's interface.

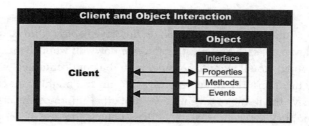

The technical details of the interaction between the client and the object by way of the interface are, mercifully, handled for you by Visual C#. Your responsibility is to define the properties, methods, and events of an object so that its interface is logical, consistent, and exposes all the functionality a client must have available to use the object productively.

Exposing Object Attributes as Properties

Properties are the attributes of objects. Properties can be read-only, or they can allow both reading and writing of their values. For example, you might want to let a client retrieve the value of a property containing the path of the component but not let the client change it because the path of a running component can't be changed.

You can add properties to a class in two ways. The first is to declare public variables. Any variable declared as public instantly becomes a property of the class (actually, it acts like a property but it isn't technically a property). For example, suppose that you have the following statement in the Declarations section of a class:

```
public int Quantity;
```

Clients could read from and write to the "property" (actually, public variables act like a property but they are called *fields*) using code like the following

```
objMyObject.Quantity = 139;
```

This works, but significant limitations exist that make this approach less than desirable:

▶ You can't execute code when a property value changes. For example, what if you wanted to write the quantity change to a database? Because the client application can access the variable directly, you have no way of knowing when the value of the variable changes.

▶ You can't prevent client code from changing a property because the client code accesses the variable directly.

▶ Perhaps the biggest problem is this: How do you control data validation? For instance, how could you ensure that Quantity was never set to a negative value?

It's simply not possible to work around these issues using a public variable (field). Instead of exposing public variables, you should create class properties using property procedures.

Property procedures enable you to execute code when a property is changed, to validate property values, and to dictate whether a property is read-only, write-only, or both readable and writable. Declaring a property procedure is similar to declaring a standard method procedure but with some important differences. The basic structure of a property procedure looks like this:

```
private int privatevalue;

public int  propertyname
{
    get
    {
      return privatevalue;    // Code to return the property's value.
    }
    set
    {
      privatevalue = value;   // Code that accepts a new value.
    }
}
```

The first word in the property declaration simply designates the scope of the property (usually public or private). Properties declared with public are available to code outside the class (they can be accessed by client code). If the application exposes its objects to other applications, public procedures will be visible outside of the application. Properties declared as private are available only to code within the class. Immediately following the scope identifier is the data type of property value. Next comes the property name.

Type the following two statements into your class (between the two braces that define class clsMyClass:

```
private int m_intHeight;

public int Height
{
    get
    {
    }
    set
    {
    }
}
```

After entering the statements, press Enter to commit them (see Figure 16.3).

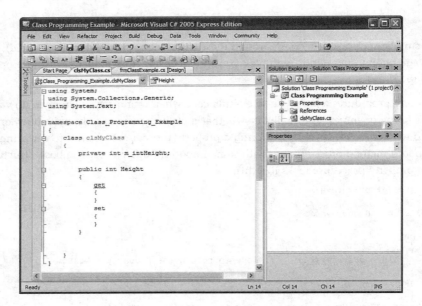

You might be wondering why you just created a module-level variable along with the property procedure. After all, I just finished preaching about the problems of using a module-level variable as a property. The reason is that a property has to get its value from *somewhere*, and a module-level variable is usually the best place to store it. The property procedure will act as a wrapper for this variable. Notice that the variable is declared as private rather than as public. This means that no code outside the class can view or modify the contents of this variable; as far as client code is concerned, this variable doesn't exist.

Between the property declaration's opening and ending braces are two constructs: the get construct and a set construct. Each of these constructs is discussed in its own section.

Creating Readable Properties Using the get Construct

Think of the get construct as a function (a method that returns a value); whatever you return as the result of the function becomes the property value. Add the following statement between the get brackets:

```
return m_intHeight;
```

All this statement does is return the value of the variable m_intHeight when client code requests the value of the Height property.

Creating Writable Properties Using the set Construct

The set construct is where you place code that accepts a new property value from client code.

Add the following statement between the braces of the set portion of the property:

```
m_intHeight = value;
```

The set clause uses a special variable called *value*, which is provided automatically by Visual C# and always contains the value being passed to the property by the client code. The statement you just entered assigns the new value to the module-level variable.

As you can see, the property procedure is a wrapper around the module-level variable. When the client code sets the property, the set construct stores the new value in the variable. When the client retrieves the value of the property, the get construct returns the value in the module-level variable.

So far, the property procedure, with its get and set constructs, doesn't do anything differently from what it would do if you were to simply declare a public variable (only the property procedure requires more code). However, look at this variation of the same set construct:

```
set
{
if (value >=10)
   m_intHeight = value;
}
```

This set construct restricts the client to setting the Height property to a value greater than or equal to 10. If a value less than 10 is passed to the property, the property procedure terminates without setting m_intHeight. You're not limited to just performing data validation; you can pretty much add whatever code you want and even call other procedures. Go ahead and add the verification statement to your procedure so that the set construct looks like this one. Your code should now look like the procedure shown in Figure 16.4.

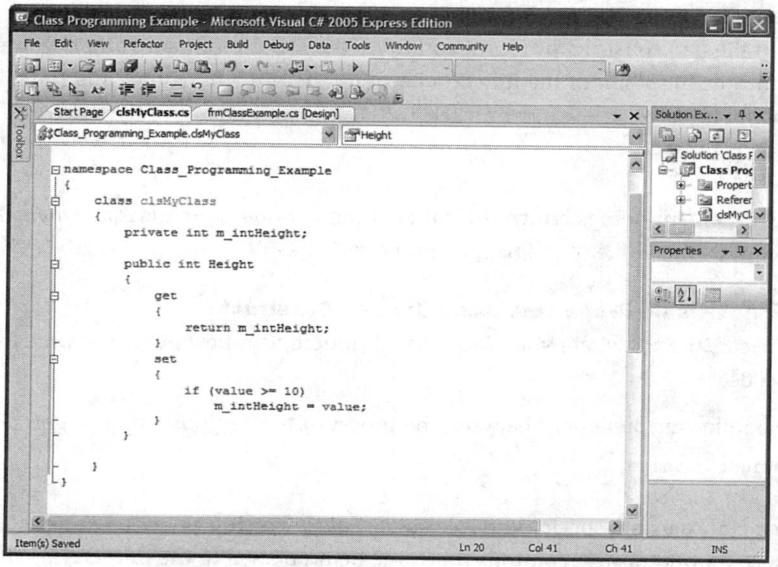

FIGURE 16.4
This is a property procedure, complete with data validation.

Creating Read-Only or Write-Only Properties

There will be times that you will want to create properties that can be read but not changed. Such properties are called *read only* properties. In the fictitious Dog object from Hour 3, I talked about creating a property called NumberOfLegs. With such an object, you might want to expose the property as read only—code can get the number of legs, but cannot change it. To create a read only property, you simply leave out the set construct (the set statement and its braces) For example, if you wanted the property procedure you just created to define a read only procedure, you might declare it like this:

```
public int Height
{
   get
   {
      return m_intHeight;
   }
}
```

> Although far more rare, it is possible to create a write only property—where the property can be set, but not read. To do so, you would specify a set construct but omit a get construct.

Exposing Functions as Methods

Unlike a property that acts as an object attribute, a method is a function exposed by an object (you learned how to create methods in Hour 10). Create the following method in your class now. Enter this code on the line right below the class the variable declaration for m_intHeight:

```
public long AddTwoNumbers(int intNumber1, int intNumber2)
{
    return intNumber1 + intNumber2;
}
```

Recall that methods defined with a data type return values, whereas methods defined with void don't. To make a method private to the class and therefore invisible to client code, declare the method as private rather than public.

Instantiating Objects from Classes

After you obtain a reference to an object and assign it to a variable, you can manipulate the object using an object variable. Let's do so now.

Click the frmClassExample.cs Design tab to view the Form Designer and add a button to the form by double-clicking the Button item in the toolbox. Set the button's properties as follows:

Property	Value
Name	**btnCreateObject**
Location	**104,120**
Size	**88,23**
Text	**Create Object**

Next, double-click the button to access its Click event and enter the following code:

```
clsMyClass objMyObject = new clsMyClass();
MessageBox.Show(objMyObject.AddTwoNumbers(1,2).ToString());
```

The first statement creates a variable of type clsMyClass. (Declaring variables was discussed in Hour 11, "Using Constants, Data Types, Variables, and Arrays.") The new keyword tells Visual C# to create a new object, and the text following new is the name of the class to use to derive the object (remember, classes are object templates). So, this first step creates a variable holding a reference to a new object based on clsMyClass. The last statement calls the AddTwoNumbers() method of your class and displays the result in a message box after converting the return value to a string.

Go ahead and run the project by pressing F5 and then click the button to make sure that everything is working correctly. When finished, stop the project and save your work.

Binding an Object Reference to a Variable

An object can contain any number of properties, methods, and events; every object is different. When you write code to manipulate an object, Visual C# has to understand the interface of the object, or your code won't work. Resolving the interface members (the properties, methods, and events of the object) occurs when an object variable is bound to an object. There are two forms of binding: *early binding* (which occurs at compile time) and *late binding* (which occurs at runtime). It's important that you have at least a working understanding of binding if you're to create code based on classes. Although I can't explain the intricacies and technical details of early binding versus late binding in this hour, I'll teach you what you need to know to perform each type of binding.

Benefits exist to both types of binding, but early binding is generally superior to late binding because code that uses late-bound objects requires more work by Visual C# than code that uses early-bound objects.

Late Binding an Object Variable

When you dimension a variable as data type Object, as shown in the following code sample, you're late binding to the object:

```
object obj;
obj = new clsMyClass();
MessageBox.Show(obj.AddTwoNumbers(1, 2).ToString());
```

When you late bind an object, the binding occurs at runtime when the variable is set to reference an object. For a member of the object to be referenced, Visual C# must determine and use an internal ID of the specified member. Fortunately, because Visual C# handles all the details, you don't need to know the ID of a member. Just be aware that Visual C# *does* need to know the ID of a member to use it. When you late bind an object variable (dimension the variable As Object), the following occurs behind the scenes:

1. Visual C# obtains a special ID (the Dispatch ID) of the property, method, or event that you want to call. This takes time and resources.

2. An internal array containing the parameters of the member, if any, is created.

3. The member is invoked using the ID obtained in step 1.

The preceding steps require a great deal of overhead and adversely affect the performance of an application. Therefore, late binding isn't the preferred method of binding. Late binding does have some attractive uses, but most of them are related to using objects outside your application, not to using objects derived from classes within the project.

One of the main drawbacks of late binding is the inability of the compiler to check the syntax of the code manipulating an object. Because the ID of a member and the parameters it uses aren't determined until runtime, the compiler has no way of knowing whether you're using a member correctly—or even if the member you're referencing exists. This can result in a runtime exception or some other unexpected behavior.

Early Binding an Object Variable

If Visual C# can determine a Dispatch ID for a member at compile time, there's no need to look up the ID when the member is referenced at runtime. This results in considerably faster calls to object members. Not only that, but Visual C# can also validate the member call at compile time, reducing the chance of errors in your code.

Early binding occurs when you dimension a variable as a specific type of object, rather than just as object. When a variable is early bound, Visual C# looks up the Dispatch IDs of the object's members at compile time, rather than at runtime.

The following are important reasons to use early binding:

▶ Speed.

▶ More speed.

▶ Objects, their properties, and their methods appear in IntelliSense drop-down lists.

▶ The compiler can check for syntax and reference errors in your code so that many problems are found at compile time, rather than at runtime.

For early binding to take place, an object variable must be declared as a specific object type (that is, not as object).

Creating a New Object When Dimensioning a Variable

You can instantiate a new object on the declaration statement by including the keyword new, as you did in this example. This approach alleviates the need for a second statement to create a new instance of the object. However, if you do this, the variable will always contain a reference to an object. If a chance exists that you might not need the object, you should probably avoid using the new keyword on the declaration statement. Consider the following:

```
clsMyClass obj;

if (condition)
{
    obj = new clsMyClass();
    /// Code to use the custom object would go here.
}
```

Remember that instantiating an object takes resources. In this code, no object is created when *condition* is False. If you were to place the word new on the declarations statement, a new object would be instantiated whenever this code was executed, regardless of the value of *condition*.

Releasing Object References

When an object is no longer needed, it should be destroyed so that all the resources used by the object can be reclaimed. Objects are destroyed automatically when the last reference to the object is released. Although two primary ways exist to release an object reference, one is clearly better than the other.

One way to release a reference to an object is simply to let the object variable holding the reference go out of scope. As you might recall from Hour 11, variables are destroyed when they go out of scope. This is no less true for object variables. However, you can't necessarily be assured that an object is fully released and that all the memory being used by an object is freed by letting an object's variable go out of scope. Therefore, relying on scope to release objects isn't a good idea.

To explicitly release an object, set the object variable equal to null, like this:

```
objMyObject = null;
```

When you set an object variable equal to null, you're assured that the object reference is fully released. Again, just because the reference is released does not mean the object is destroyed! The garbage collector will periodically check for unused objects and reclaim the resources they consume, but this may occur a considerable length of time after the object is no longer used. Therefore, you should add a Dispose() method to all your classes. You should place cleanup code within your

Dispose() method and always call Dispose() when you are finished with an object. One thing to keep in mind is that it's technically possible to have more than one variable referencing an object. When this occurs, calling Dispose() may cause cleanup code to execute and therefore cause problems for the code using the second object variable. As you can see, you need to consider many things when programming objects.

If you don't correctly release object references, your application might experience resource leaks, become sluggish, and consume more resources than it should.

Understanding the Lifetime of an Object

An object created from a class exists as long as a variable holds a reference to it. Fortunately, Visual C# (or more specifically, the .NET Framework as discussed in Hour 24) handles the details of keeping track of the references to a given object; you don't have to worry about this when creating or using objects. When all the references to an object are released, the object is flagged and eventually destroyed by the garbage collector.

The following are key points to remember about an object's lifetime, and what they mean to your application:

▶ An object is created (and hence referenced) when an object variable is *declared* using the keyword new. For example:

```
clsMyClass objMyObject = new clsMyClass();
```

▶ An object is created (and hence referenced) when an object variable is *assigned* an object using the keyword new. For example:

```
objMyObject = new clsMyClass();
```

▶ An object is referenced when an object variable is assigned an existing object. For example:

```
objThisObject = objThatObject;
```

▶ An object reference is released when an object variable is set to null (see the section "Releasing Object References" earlier in this hour).

▶ An object becomes eligible for garbage collection after the last reference to it is released. Many factors, including available system resources, determine when the garbage collector executes next and destroys unused objects (please see Hour 24 for more information on the garbage collector).

Understanding the lifetime of objects is important. You've now seen how and when object references are created, but you also need to know how to explicitly release an object reference. Only when all references to an object are released is the object flagged for destruction and the resources it uses reclaimed.

Summary

Object-oriented programming is an advanced methodology that enables you to create more robust applications, and programming classes is the foundation of OOP. In this hour, you learned how to create classes, which are the templates used to instantiate objects. You also learned how to create a custom interface consisting of properties and methods, and how to use the classes you've defined to instantiate and manipulate objects by way of object variables.

You've also learned how you should implement a `Dispose()` method for classes that consume resources and how it is important to call `Dispose()` on objects that implement it to ensure that the object frees up its resources as soon as possible. Finally, you learned how objects aren't destroyed as soon as they are no longer needed; rather, they become eligible for garbage collection and are destroyed when the garbage collector next cleans up.

In this hour, you learned the basic mechanics of programming objects with classes. Object-oriented programming takes considerable skill, and you'll need to master the concepts in this book before you can really begin to take advantage of what OOP has to offer. Nevertheless, what you learned in this hour will take you further than you might think. Using an OOP methodology is as much a way of thinking as it is a way of programming; consider how things in your projects might work as objects, and before you know it, you'll be creating robust classes.

Q&A

Q. *Should I always try to place code into instance classes rather than static classes?*

A. Not necessarily. As with most things, there are no hard and fast rules. Correctly programming instance classes takes some skill and experience, and programming static is easier for the beginner. If you want to experiment with instance classes, I encourage you to do so. However, don't feel as though you have to place everything into instantiated classes.

Q. *I want to create a general class with a lot of miscellaneous methods—sort of a "catchall" class. What's the best way to do this?*

A. If you want to create some sort of utility class, I recommend calling the class something like `clsUtility`. Then you can use this class throughout your application to access the utility functions.

Workshop

Quiz

1. To create objects, you must first create a template. This template is called a _____.

2. One of the primary benefits of object-oriented programming is that objects contain both their data and their code. This is called _____.

3. With static classes, public variables and routines are always available to code via the static class in other modules. Is this true with public variables and routines in classes?

4. True or False: Each object derived from a class has its own set of module-level data.

5. What must you do to create a property that can be read but not changed by client code?

6. What's the best way to store the internal value of a property within a class?

7. Which is generally superior, early binding or late binding?

8. If an object variable is declared as `object`, is it early bound or late bound?

9. What's the best way to destroy an object reference?

Answers

1. Class

2. Encapsulation

3. No, an object would first have to be instantiated before the variables and methods would be available.

4. True

5. Omit the set construct in the property procedure.

6. Store the internal value in a private class-level variable.

7. Early binding is almost always superior to late binding.

8. The object is late bound.

9. Set the object variable equal to null.

Exercises

1. Add a new property to your class called DropsInABucket. Make this property a long, and set it up so that client code can read the property value but not set it. Finally, add a button to the form that, when clicked, prints the value of the property to the Output window. When this is working, modify the code so that the property always returns 1,000,000.

2. Add a button to your form that creates two object variables of type clsMyClass(). Use the new keyword to instantiate a new instance of the class in one of the variables. Then set the second variable to reference the same object and print the contents of the Height property to the Output window.

HOUR 17

Interacting with Users

What You'll Learn in This Hour:

▶ Displaying messages using the `MessageBox.Show()` function
▶ Creating custom dialog boxes
▶ Interacting with the keyboard
▶ Using the common mouse events

Forms and controls are the primary means by which users interact with an application and vice versa. However, program interaction can and often does go deeper than that. For example, a program can display customized messages to a user, and it can be finely tuned to deal with certain keystrokes or mouse clicks. In this hour, you'll learn how to create functional and cohesive interaction between your application and the user. In addition, you'll learn how to program the keyboard and the mouse so that you can expand the interactivity of your program beyond what's natively supported by a form and its controls.

Displaying Messages Using the `MessageBox.Show()` Method

A *message box* is a small dialog box that displays a message to the user (just in case that wasn't obvious enough). Message boxes are often used to tell the user the result of some action, such as "The file has been copied." or "The file could not be found." A message box is dismissed when the user clicks one of the message box's available buttons. Most applications have *many* message boxes, but developers don't often display messages correctly. It's important to remember that when you display a message to a user, you're communicating with the user. In this section, I'm going to teach you not only how to use the `MessageBox.Show()` function to display messages, but how to use the statement effectively.

The `MessageBox.Show()` function can be used to tell a user something or ask the user a question. In addition to text, which is its primary function, you can also use this function to display an icon or display one or more buttons that the user can click. Although you're free to display whatever text you want, you must choose from a predefined list of icons and buttons.

The `MessageBox.Show()` method is an overloaded method. This means that the method was written with numerous constructs supporting various options. While coding in Visual C#, IntelliSense displays a drop-down scrolling list displaying any of the 21 overloaded `MessageBox.Show()` method calls to aid in coding. Following are a few ways to call `MessageBox.Show()`:

To display a message box with specified text, a caption in the title bar, and an OK button, use this syntax:

```
MessageBox.Show(MessageText, Caption);
```

To display a message box with specified text, caption, and one or more specific buttons, use this syntax:

```
MessageBox.Show(MessageText, Caption, Buttons);
```

To display a message box with specified text, caption, buttons, and icon, use this syntax:

```
MessageBox.Show(MessageText, Caption, Buttons, Icon);
```

In all these statements, *MessageText* is the text to display in the message box, *Caption* determines what appears in the title bar of the message box, *Buttons* determines which buttons the user sees, and *Icon* determines what icon (if any) appears in the message box. Consider the following statement, which produces the message box shown in Figure 17.1.

```
MessageBox.Show("This is a message.", "Hello There");
```

FIGURE 17.1
A very simple message box.

As you can see, if you omit *Buttons*, Visual C# displays only an OK button. You should always ensure that the buttons displayed are appropriate for the message.

Specifying Buttons and an Icon

Using the *Buttons* parameter, you can display one or more buttons in the message box. The *Buttons* parameter type is *MessageBoxButtons*, and Table 17.1 shows the allowable values.

TABLE 17.1 Allowable Enumerators for `MessageBoxButtons`

Member	Description
AbortRetryIgnore	Displays Abort, Retry, and Ignore buttons
OK	Displays OK button only
OKCancel	Displays OK and Cancel buttons
YesNoCancel	Displays Yes, No, and Cancel buttons
YesNo	Displays Yes and No buttons
RetryCancel	Displays Retry and Cancel buttons

Because the *Buttons* parameter is an enumerated type, Visual C# gives you an IntelliSense drop-down list when specifying a value for this parameter. Therefore, committing these values to memory isn't all that important; you'll commit the ones you use most often to memory fairly quickly.

The *Icon* parameter determines the symbol displayed in the message box. The *Icon* parameter is an enumeration from the `MessageBoxIcon` type. Table 17.2 shows the most commonly used values of `MessageBoxIcon`.

TABLE 17.2 Common Enumerators for `MessageBoxIcon`

Member	Description
Exclamation	Displays a symbol consisting of an exclamation point in a triangle with a yellow background
Information	Displays a symbol consisting of a lowercase letter i in a circle
None	Displays no symbol
Question	Displays a symbol consisting of a question mark in a circle
Stop	Displays a symbol consisting of a white X in a circle with a red background
Warning	Displays a symbol consisting of an exclamation point in a triangle with a yellow background

The *Icon* parameter is also an enumerated type; therefore, Visual C# gives you an IntelliSense drop-down list when specifying a value for this parameter.

The message box in Figure 17.2 was created with the following statement:

```
MessageBox.Show("I'm about to do something...","MessageBox sample",
    MessageBoxButtons.OKCancel,MessageBoxIcon.Information);
```

FIGURE 17.2
Assign the
Information icon
to general mes-
sages.

The message box in Figure 17.3 was created with a statement almost identical to the previous one, except that the second button is designated as the default button. If a user presses the Enter key with a message box displayed, the message box acts as though the user clicked the default button. You'll want to give careful consideration to the default button in each message box. For example, if the application is about to do something that the user probably doesn't want to do, it's best to make the Cancel button the default button—in case the user is a bit quick when pressing the Enter key. Following is the statement used to generate the message box in Figure 17.3:

```
MessageBox.Show("I'm about to do something irreversible...",
    "MessageBox sample",
    MessageBoxButtons.OKCancel,MessageBoxIcon.Information,
    MessageBoxDefaultButton.Button2);
```

FIGURE 17.3
The default but-
ton has a dark
border.

The Error icon is shown in Figure 17.4. The Error icon is best used in rare circumstances, such as when an exception has occurred. Overusing the Error icon is like crying wolf—when a real problem emerges, the user might not take notice. Notice here how I've only displayed the OK button. If something has already happened and there's nothing the user can do about it, don't bother giving the user a Cancel button. The following statement generates the message box shown in Figure 17.4:

```
MessageBox.Show("Something bad has happened!","MessageBox sample",
    MessageBoxButtons.OK, MessageBoxIcon.Error);
```

In Figure 17.5, a question has been posed to the user, so the message displays the Question icon. Also note how the message box assumes that the user would probably choose No, so the second button is set as the default. In the next section, you'll learn how to determine which button the user clicks. Here's the statement used to generate the message box shown in Figure 17.5:

```
MessageBox.Show("Would you like to format your hard drive now?",
    "MessageBox sample",MessageBoxButtons.YesNo,MessageBoxIcon.Question,
    MessageBoxDefaultButton.Button2);
```

FIGURE 17.4
If users have no control over what has occurred, don't give them a Cancel button.

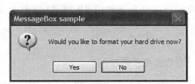

FIGURE 17.5
A message box can be used to ask a question.

As you can see, designating buttons and icons isn't all that difficult. The real effort comes in determining which buttons and icons are appropriate for a given situation.

Determining Which Button Is Clicked

You'll probably find that many of your message boxes are simple, containing only an OK button. For other message boxes, however, you must determine which button a user clicks. Why give the user a choice if you're not going to act on it?

The `MessageBox.Show()` method returns the button clicked as a `DialogResult` enumeration. The `DialogResult` has the values shown in Table 17.3.

TABLE 17.3   Enumerators for `DialogResult`

Member	Description
Abort	Return value Abort; usually sent from a button labeled Abort.
Cancel	Return value Cancel; usually sent from a button labeled Cancel.
Ignore	Return value Ignore; usually sent from a button labeled Ignore.
No	Return value No; usually sent from a button labeled No.
None	Nothing is returned from the dialog box. The model dialog continues running.
OK	Return value OK; usually sent from a button labeled OK.
Retry	Return value Retry; usually sent from a button labeled Retry.
Yes	Return value Yes; usually sent from a button labeled Yes.

Note the text "usually sent from" in the descriptions of the `DialogResult` values. When you create custom dialog boxes (as shown later in this hour), you can assign a `DialogResult` to any button of your choosing.

Performing actions based on the button clicked is a matter of using one of the decision constructs. For example:

```
if (MessageBox.Show("Would you like to do X?", "MessageBox sample",
    MessageBoxButtons.YesNo, MessageBoxIcon.Question) == DialogResult.Yes)
{
    // Code to do X would go here.
}
```

As you can see, `MessageBox.Show()` is a method that gives you a lot of bang for your buck; it offers considerable flexibility.

Creating Good Messages

The `MessageBox.Show()` method is surprisingly simple to use, considering all the different forms of messages it enables you to create. The real trick is in providing appropriate messages to users at appropriate times. In addition to considering the icon and buttons to display in a message, you should follow these guidelines for crafting message text:

▶ Use a formal tone. Don't use large words, and avoid using contractions. Strive to make the text immediately understandable and not overly fancy; a message box is not a place to show off your literary skills.

▶ Limit messages to two or three lines. Lengthy messages are not only more difficult for users to read, but they can also be intimidating. When a message box is used to ask a question, make the question as succinct as possible.

▶ Never make users feel as though they've done something wrong. Users will, and do, make mistakes, but you should craft messages that take the sting out of the situation.

▶ Spell check all message text. The Visual C# code editor doesn't spell check for you, so you should type your messages in a program such as Word and spell check the text before pasting it into your code. Spelling errors have an adverse effect on a user's perception of a program.

▶ Avoid technical jargon. Just because someone uses software doesn't mean that they are a technical person; explain things in plain English (or whatever the native language of the GUI happens to be).

▶ Be sure that the buttons match the text! For example, don't show the Yes/No buttons if the text doesn't present a question to the user.

Creating Custom Dialog Boxes

Most of the time, the `MessageBox.Show()` method should be a sufficient means to display messages to a user. At times, however, the `MessageBox.Show()` method is too limited for a given purpose. Suppose that you want to display a lot of text to a user, such as a log file of some sort, for example, and therefore want a message box that is sizable by the user.

Custom dialog boxes are nothing more than standard modal forms with one notable exception: One or more buttons are designated to return a dialog result, just as the buttons on a message box shown with the `MessageBox.Show()` method return a dialog result.

You're now going to create a custom dialog box. Begin by creating a new Windows Application titled **Custom Dialog Example** and then follow these steps to build the project:

1. Right-click Form1.cs in the Solution Explorer, choose Rename, and change the name of the default form to **frmMain.cs**. Next, set the form's Text property to **Custom Dialog Box Example**.

2. Add a new button to the form and set its properties as follows:

Property	Value
Name	**btnShowCustomDialogBox**
Location	**72,180**
Size	**152,23**
Text	**Show Custom Dialog Box**

3. Next, you're going to create the custom dialog box. Add a new form to the project by choosing Project, Add Windows Form from the menu. Save the new form with the name **fclsCustomDialogBox.cs**.

4. Change the Text property of the new form to **This is a custom dialog box**, and set its FormBorderStyle to FixedDialog.

5. Add a new text box to the form and set its properties as follows:

Property	Value
Name	**txtCustomMessage**
Location	**8,8**
Multiline	**True**
ReadOnly	**True**
Size	**275,220**
Text	**Custom message goes here**

For a custom dialog box to return a result like a standard message box does, it must have buttons that are designated to return a dialog result. This is accomplished by setting the DialogResult property of a button (see Figure 17.6).

6. Add a new button to the form and set its properties as shown in the following table. This button will act as the custom dialog box's Cancel button.

Property	Value
Name	**btnCancel**
DialogResult	**Cancel**
Location	**216,240**
Size	**75,23**
Text	**Cancel**

FIGURE 17.6
The DialogResult property determines the return value of the button.

7. You need to create an OK button for the custom dialog box. Create another button and set its properties as follows:

Property	Value
Name	**btnOK**
DialogResult	**OK**
Location	**135,240**
Size	**75,23**
Text	**OK**

Specifying a dialog result for one or more buttons is the first step in making a form a custom dialog box. The second part of the process is in how the form is shown. As you learned in Hour 5, "Building Forms—The Basics," forms are displayed by calling the Show() method of a form variable. However, to show a form as a custom dialog box, you call the ShowDialog() method instead. When a form is displayed using ShowDialog(), the following occurs:

▶ The form is shown modally.

▶ If the user clicks a button that has its DialogResult property set to return a value, the form is immediately closed, and that value is returned as the result of the ShowDialog() method call.

Notice how you don't have to write code to close the form; clicking a button with a dialog result closes the form automatically. This simplifies the process of creating custom dialog boxes.

8. Return to the first form in the Form Designer by double-clicking frmMain.cs in the Solution Explorer.

9. Double-click the button you created and add the following code:

```
fclsCustomDialogBox frmCustomDialogBox = new fclsCustomDialogBox();

if (frmCustomDialogBox.ShowDialog() == DialogResult.OK)
   MessageBox.Show("You clicked OK.");
else
   MessageBox.Show("You clicked Cancel.");

frmCustomDialogBox = null;
```

When you typed the equal sign and then a space after the word ShowDialog(), did you notice that Visual C# gave you an IntelliSense drop-down list with the possible dialog results? These results correspond directly with the values you can assign a button using the DialogResult property. Press F5 to run the project, click the button to display your custom dialog box (see Figure 17.7), and then click one of the available dialog box buttons. When you're satisfied that the project is working correctly, stop the project and save your work.

**By the**
Way

If you click the Close (X) button in the upper-right corner of the form, the form is closed, and the code behaves as if you've clicked Cancel because the `else` code occurs.

FIGURE 17.7
The `ShowDialog()` method enables you to create custom message boxes.

The ability to create custom dialog boxes is a powerful feature. A call to `MessageBox.Show()` is usually sufficient, but when you need more control over the appearance and contents of a message box, creating a custom dialog box is the way to go.

Interacting with the Keyboard

Although most every control on a form handles its own keyboard input, on occasion you'll want to handle keyboard input directly. For example, you might want to perform an action when the user presses a specific key or releases a specific key. Most controls support three events that you can use to work directly with keyboard input. These are listed in Table 17.4.

TABLE 17.4   Events That Handle Keyboard Input

Event Name	Description
KeyDown	Occurs when a key is pressed down while the control has the focus.
KeyPress	Occurs when a key is pressed while the control has the focus. If the user holds the key down, this event will fire multiple times.
KeyUp	Occurs when a key is released while the control has the focus.

These events fire in the same order in which they appear in Table 17.4. Suppose, for example, that the user presses a key while a text box has the focus. The following list shows how the events would fire for the text box:

1. When the user presses a key, the KeyDown event fires.

2. Once the key is down, the KeyPress event fires. This event will repeat as long as the key is held down.

3. When the user releases a key, the KeyUp event fires, completing the cycle of keystroke events.

You're now going to create a project that illustrates handling keystrokes. This project has a text box that will refuse to accept the letter "k." Start by creating a new Windows Application titled **Keyboard Example** and then follow these steps to build the project:

1. Right-click Form1.cs in the Solution Explorer, choose Rename, and change the name of the default form to **frmKeyboardExample.cs**. Next, set the form's Text property to **Keyboard Example**.

2. Add a new text box to the form and set its properties as shown in the following table:

Property	Value
Name	**txtInput**
Location	**24,80**
Multiline	**True**
Size	**240,120**

3. You're going to add code to the KeyPress event of the text box to "eat" keystrokes made with the letter "k." Select the text box on the form and click the Events button on the Properties window to view the text box's events.

4. Locate and double-click KeyPress in the event list to create a new KeyPress event procedure. Your code editor should look now look like Figure 17.8.

As you learned in Hour 4, "Understanding Events," the e parameter contains information specific to the occurrence of this event. In the keyboard-related events, the e parameter contains information about the key being pressed; it's what you'll be using to work with the keystroke made by the user.

The key being pressed is available as the KeyChar property of the e parameter. You're going to write code that handles the keystroke when the pressed key is the letter "k."

FIGURE 17.8
The KeyPress
event is a good
place to handle
keyboard entry.

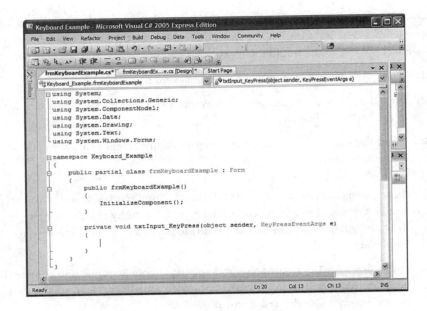

Add the following code to the KeyPress event:

```
if (e.KeyChar == 'k')
        e.Handled = true;
```

By the
Way Be sure to surround the 'k' with single quotes, not double quotes, because you're dealing with a single character (char), not a string.

I imagine that you're curious about the Handled property of the e object. When you set this property to True, you're telling Visual C# that *you* handled the keystroke, and that Visual C# should ignore it (that is, not add it to the text box). To see the effect this has, press F5 to run the project and enter the following text into the text box:

Heard any good jokes lately?

What you'll end up with is the text shown in Figure 17.9. Notice how the letter "k" was "eaten" by your code.

Go ahead, try to enter another "k"—you can't. Next, try to enter an uppercase "K"; Visual C# allows you to do this because uppercase and lowercase characters are considered different characters. Want to catch all K's regardless of case? You could do so by adding the OR (¦¦) operand to your decision construct, like this:

```
if (e.KeyChar == 'k'|| e.KeyChar == 'K')
    e.Handled = true;
```

FIGURE 17.9
The keyboard events enable you to handle keystrokes as you see fit.

When you paste data from the clipboard, the KeyPress event isn't fired for each keystroke. It's therefore possible that a "k" could appear in the text box. If you absolutely needed to keep the letter "k" out of the text box, you'd need to make use of the TextChanged event.

It's not often that I need to catch a keypress, but every now and then I do. The three keystroke events listed in Table 17.4 have always made it easy to do what I need to do, but if there's one caveat I've discovered, it's that you need to give careful consideration to which event you choose (such as KeyPress or KeyUp, for example). Different events work best in different situations, and the best thing to do is to start with what seems like the most logical event, test the code, and change the event if necessary.

Using the Common Mouse Events

As with keyboard input, most controls support mouse input natively; you don't have to write code to deal with mouse input. At times, you might need more control than that offered by the native functionality of a control, however. Visual C# supports eight events that enable you to deal with mouse input directly. These events are listed in Table 17.5 in the order in which they occur.

TABLE 17.5   Events Used to Handle Mouse Input

Event Name	Description
MouseEnter	Occurs when the pointer enters a control
MouseMove	Occurs when the pointer moves over a control
MouseHover	Occurs when the pointer hovers over a control
MouseDown	Occurs when the pointer is over a control and a button is pressed
MouseUp	Occurs when the pointer is over a control and a button is released
MouseLeave	Occurs when the pointer leaves a control
Click	Occurs between the MouseDown and MouseUp events
DoubleClick	Occurs when the user presses the mouse button twice in rapid succession

You're now going to build a project that illustrates interacting with the mouse using the MouseMove event. This project will enable a user to draw on a form, much like you can draw in a paint program. Begin by creating a new Windows Application titled **Mouse Paint**, and then follow these steps to create the project:

1. Right-click Form1.cs in the Solution Explorer, choose Rename, and then change the name of the default form to **frmMousePaint.cs**. Next, set the form's Text property to **Paint with the Mouse**.

2. Double-click the form to access its default event, the Load event. Enter the following statement into the Load event:

   ```
   m_objGraphics = this.CreateGraphics();
   ```

   You've already used a graphics object a few times. What you're doing here is setting a graphics object to the client area of the form; any drawing performed on the object appears on the form. Because you're going to draw to this graphics object each time the mouse moves over the form, there's no point in creating a new graphics object each time you need to draw to it. Therefore, you're going to make m_objGraphics a module-level variable, which is instantiated only once—in the Load event of the form.

3. Enter this statement below the opening curly brace after the public partial class frmMousePaint : Form class declaration:

   ```
   private Graphics m_objGraphics;
   ```

As mentioned previously, always destroy objects when you're done with them. In this case, you want the object to remain in existence for the life of the form. Therefore, you'll destroy it in the FormClosed event of the form, which occurs when the form is unloaded.

4. Return to the frmMousePaint.cs[Design] tab, open the events list in the Property window, and double-click the FormClosed event to create and open the code window to the FormClosed event. Enter the following statement in the FormClosed event:

```
m_objGraphics.Dispose();
```

Your class should now look like the one shown in Figure 17.10.

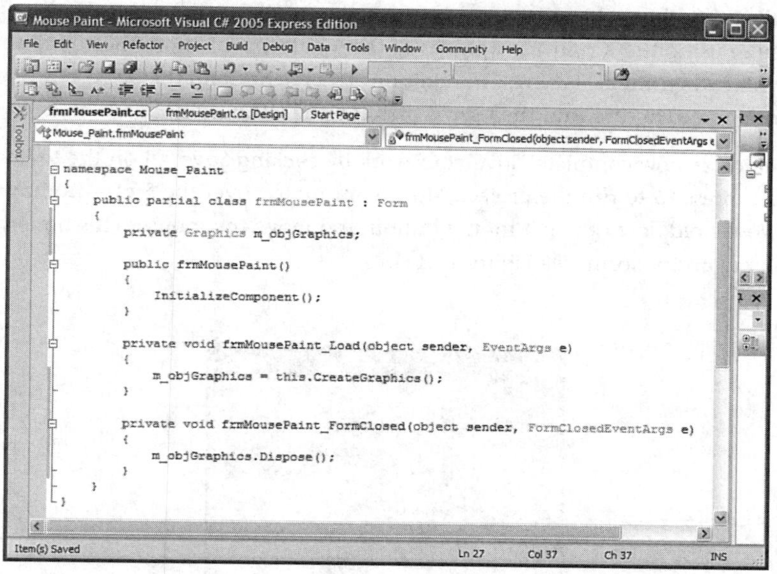

FIGURE 17.10
Code in many places often works together to achieve one goal.

The last bit of code you need to add is the code that will draw on the form. You're going to place code in the MouseMove event of the form to do this. First, the code will make sure that the left mouse button is held down. If it isn't, no drawing takes place; the user must hold down the mouse button to draw. Next, a rectangle will be created. The coordinates of the mouse pointer will be used to create a small rectangle that will be passed to the DrawEllipse() method of the graphics object. This has the effect of drawing a tiny circle where the mouse pointer is positioned.

5. Again, return to the frmMousePaint.cs[Design] tab, open the events list in the Property window (if it's not currently displayed), and double-click the MouseMove event to create a new MouseMove event procedure. Add the following code to the MouseMove event:

```
Rectangle rectEllipse = new Rectangle() ;

if (e.Button != MouseButtons.Left) return;

rectEllipse.X = e.X - 1;
rectEllipse.Y = e.Y - 1;
rectEllipse.Width = 2;
rectEllipse.Height = 2;

m_objGraphics.DrawEllipse(System.Drawing.Pens.Blue, rectEllipse);
```

Like all events, the e object contains information related to the event. In this example, you're using the X and Y properties of the e object, which are the coordinates of the pointer when the event fires. In addition, you're checking the Button property of the object to make sure that the user is pressing the left button.

Your project is now complete! Save your work by clicking Save All on the toolbar, and then press F5 to run the project. Move your mouse over the form—nothing happens. Now, hold down the left mouse button and move the mouse. This time, you'll be drawing on the form (see Figure 17.11).

FIGURE 17.11
Capturing mouse events opens many exciting possibilities.

Notice that the faster you move the mouse, the more space appears between circles. This shows you that the user can move the mouse faster than the MouseMove event can fire, so you can't get every single movement of the mouse. This is important to remember.

Summary

Forms and controls allow for a lot of flexibility in the way a user interacts with an application. However, solid interactivity goes beyond just what is placed on a form. In this hour, you learned how to use the `MessageBox.Show()` function to create informational dialog boxes. You learned how to specify an icon, buttons, and even how to designate a specific button as the default button. You also learned some valuable tips to help you create the best messages possible. You'll create message boxes frequently, so mastering this skill is important.

Finally, you learned how to interact with the keyboard and the mouse directly through numerous events. The mouse or keyboard capabilities of a control some-times fall short of what you want to accomplish. By understanding the concepts pre-sented in this hour, you can go beyond the native capabilities of controls to create a rich, interactive experience for your users.

Q&A

Q. *Is it possible to capture keystrokes at the form level, rather than capturing them in control events?*

A. Yes. For the form's keyboard-related events to fire when a control has the focus, however, you must set the form's `KeyPreview` property to `true`. The control's keyboard events will still fire, unless you set `KeyPressEventArgs.Handled` to `true` in the control's `KeyPress` event.

Q. *You don't seem to always specify a button in your* `MessageBox.Show()` *statements throughout this book. Why?*

A. If you don't explicitly designate a button or buttons, Visual C# displays the OK button. Therefore, if all you want is an OK button, you don't need to pass a value to the *Buttons* argument.

Workshop

Quiz

1. What arguments must you always supply a value for when calling `MessageBox.Show()`?

2. If you don't supply a value for the *caption* parameter of `MessageBox.Show()`, what is displayed in the title bar of the message?

3. How many icons can you show in a message box at once?

4. Which event fires first, the KeyUp or KeyPress event?

5. How do you determine which button is being pressed in a mouse-related event?

Answers

1. The prompt and the dialog title (*caption*). Actually, the caption is technically optional, but it's such a bad idea to leave it off that I consider it required.

2. Nothing gets displayed—the title bar is empty.

3. Only one icon can be shown at once.

4. The KeyPress event fires before the KeyUp event.

5. By using the e.Button property in the event.

Exercises

1. Modify your custom dialog box project so that the OK button is the Accept button of the form. That way, the user must only press Enter to dismiss the dialog box. Next, make the Cancel button the Cancel button of the form so that the user can also press the Escape key to dismiss the form.

2. Modify your mouse paint project so that the form clears each time the user starts drawing. Hint: Clear the graphics object in the MouseDown event.

HOUR 18

Working with Graphics

What You'll Learn in This Hour:

▶ Understanding the Graphics object
▶ Working with pens
▶ Using system colors
▶ Working with rectangles
▶ Drawing shapes
▶ Drawing text
▶ Persisting graphics on a form

Visual C# provides an amazingly powerful array of drawing capabilities. However, this power comes at the price of a steeper learning curve. Drawing isn't intuitive; you can't sit down for a few minutes with the online Help text and start drawing graphics. However, after you learn the basic principles involved, you'll find that drawing isn't that complicated. In this hour, you'll learn the basic skills for drawing shapes and text to a form or other graphical surface. You'll learn about pens, colors, and brushes (objects that help define graphics that you draw). In addition, you'll learn how to persist graphics on a form—and even how to create bitmaps that exist solely in memory.

Understanding the Graphics Object

At first, you might not come up with many reasons to draw to the screen, preferring to use the many advanced controls found within Visual C# to build your interfaces. However, as your applications grow in size and complexity, you'll find more and more occasion to draw your own interfaces directly to the screen; when you need this functionality, you *really* need this functionality. You might even choose to design your own controls (which you can do with Visual C#). In this hour, you'll learn the basics of drawing and printing to the screen. Using the skills you acquire in this hour, you'll be able to build incredibly detailed interfaces that look exactly the way you want them to look.

The code within the Windows operating system that handles drawing everything to the screen, including text, lines, and shapes, is called the *Graphics Device Interface* (*GDI*). The GDI processes all drawing instructions from applications as well as from Windows itself and generates the output for the current display. Because the GDI generates what you see onscreen, it has the responsibility of dealing with the particular display driver installed on the computer and the settings of the driver, such as resolution and color depth. That means applications (and their developers) don't have to worry about these details; you write code that tells the GDI what to output, and the GDI does whatever is necessary to produce that output. This behavior is called *device independence* because applications can instruct the GDI to display text and graphics using code that's independent of the particular display device.

Visual C# code communicates with the GDI primarily via the Graphics object. The basic process is as follows:

▶ An object variable is created to hold a reference to a Graphics object.

▶ The object variable is set to a valid Graphics object (new or existing).

▶ To draw or print, you call methods of the Graphics object.

Creating a Graphics Object for a Form or Control

If you want to draw directly to a form or control, you can easily get a reference to the drawing surface by calling the `CreateGraphics()` method of the object in question. For example, to create a Graphics object that draws to a text box, you could use code such as this:

```
System.Drawing.Graphics objGraphics;
objGraphics = this.textBox1.CreateGraphics();
```

When you call `CreateGraphics()`, you're setting the object variable to hold a reference to the Graphics object of the form or control's client area. The client area of a form is the gray area within the borders and title bar of the form, whereas the client area of a control is usually the entire control. All drawing and printing done using the Graphics object is sent to the client area. In the code shown previously, the Graphics object references the client area of a text box, so all drawing methods executed on the Graphics object would draw directly to the text box.

When you draw directly to a form or control, the object in question doesn't persist what's drawn on it. If the form is obscured in any way, such as by a window covering it or by minimizing the form, the next time the form is painted, it won't contain anything that was drawn on it. Later in this hour, I'll teach you how to persist graphics on a form.

By the
Way

Creating a Graphics Object for a New Bitmap

You don't have to set a Graphics object to the client area of a form or control; you can also set a Graphics object to a bitmap that exists only in memory. For performance reasons, you might want to use a memory bitmap to store temporary images or as a place to build complex graphics before sending them to a visible element (such as a form or control). To do this, you first have to create a new bitmap.

To create a new bitmap, you dimension a variable to hold a reference to the new bitmap using the following syntax:

```
Bitmapvariable = new Bitmap(width, height, pixelformat);
```

The *width* and *height* arguments are exactly what they appear to be: the width and height of the new bitmap. The *pixelformat* argument, however, is less intuitive. This argument determines the color depth of the bitmap and might also specify whether the bitmap has an alpha layer (used for transparent portions of bitmaps). Table 18.1 lists a few of the common values for *pixelformat* (see Visual C#'s online Help for the complete list of values and their meanings).

Table 18.1 Common Values for *pixelformat*

Value	Description
Format16bppGrayScale	The pixel format is 16 bits per pixel. The color information specifies 65,536 shades of gray.
Format16bppRgb555	The pixel format is 16 bits per pixel. The color information specifies 32,768 shades of color, of which 5 bits are red, 5 bits are green, and 5 bits are blue.
Format24bppRgb	The pixel format is 24 bits per pixel. The color information specifies 16,777,216 shades of color, of which 8 bits are red, 8 bits are green, and 8 bits are blue.

To create a new bitmap that's 640 pixels wide by 480 pixels tall and has a pixel depth of 24 bits, for example, you could use this statement (assuming you had a variable named objMyBitMap declared):

```
objMyBitMap =  new Bitmap(640, 480,
        System.Drawing.Imaging.PixelFormat.Format24bppRgb);
```

After the bitmap is created, you can create a Graphics object that references the
bitmap using the FromImage() method, like this:

```
objGraphics = Graphics.FromImage(objMyBitMap);
```

Now any drawing or printing done using objGraphics would be performed on the
memory bitmap. For the user to see the bitmap, you'd have to send the bitmap to a
form or control. You'll do this later in this hour in the section "Persisting Graphics
on a Form."

Disposing of an Object When It Is No Longer Needed

When you're finished with a Graphics object, you should call its Dispose() method
to ensure that all resources used by the Graphics object are freed. Simply letting an
object variable go out of scope doesn't ensure that the resources used by the object
are freed. Graphics objects can use considerable resources, so you should always call
Dispose() when you're finished with any graphics object (including Pens and other
types of objects).

Visual C# also supports a way of automatically disposing object resources. This can
be accomplished utilizing Visual C# using statement. The using statement wraps a
declared object or objects in a block and disposes of those objects after the block is
done. As a result, after the code is executed in a block, the block is exited and the
resources are disposed of on exit. Following is the syntax for the using statement
and a small sample:

```
using (expression ¦ type identifier = initializer)
{
    // Statements to execute
}
```

Example:

```
using (MyClass objClass = new MyClass())
{
    objClass.Method1();
    objClass.Method2();
}
```

One thing to keep in mind is that the using statement acts as a wrapper for an
object within a specified block of code; therefore, it is only useful for declaring
objects that are used and scoped within a method (scope is discussed in Hour 11,
"Using Constants, Data Types, Variables, and Arrays").

Earlier in the book you learned how to use a using statement to include a name-space, such as System.Diagnostics. Note that the use of using in this case is dif-ferent; the same keyword is used for multiple purposes.

Working with Pens

A *pen* is an object that defines characteristics of a line. Pens are used to define color, line width, and line style (solid, dashed, and so on). Pens are used with almost all the drawing methods you'll learn about in this hour.

Visual C# supplies a number of predefined pens, and you can also create your own. To create your own pen, use the following syntax:

```
penvariable = new Pen(color, width);
```

After a pen is created, you can set its properties to adjust its appearance. For exam-ple, all Pen objects have a DashStyle property that determines the appearance of lines drawn with the pen. Table 18.2 lists the possible values for DashStyle.

Table 18.2   Possible Values for DashStyle

Value	Description
Dash	Specifies a line consisting of dashes.
DashDot	Specifies a line consisting of a pattern of dashes and dots.
DashDotDot	Specifies a line consisting of alternating dashes and double dots.
Dot	Specified a line consisting of dots.
Solid	Specifies a solid line.
Custom	Specifies a custom dash style. The Pen object contains properties that can be used to define the custom line.

The enumeration for DashStyle is part of the Drawing.Drawing2D namespace. Therefore, to create a new, dark blue pen that draws a dotted line, you would use code like the following:

```
Pen objMyPen = new Pen(System.Drawing.Color.DarkBlue, 3);
objMyPen.DashStyle = System.Drawing.Drawing2D.DashStyle.Dot;
```

If System.Drawing was declared with a using statement, you would not need to use the fully qualified names here.

The 3 passed as the second argument to create the new Pen defines the width of the pen in pixels.

Visual C# includes many standard pens, which are available via the `System.Drawing.Pens` class, as in

```
objPen = System.Drawing.Pens.DarkBlue;
```

When drawing using the techniques discussed shortly, you can use custom pens or system-defined pens—it's your choice.

Using System Colors

At some point, you might have changed your Windows theme, or perhaps you changed the image or color of your desktop. What you might not be aware of is that Windows enables you to customize the colors of almost all Windows interface elements. The colors that Windows allows you to change are called *system colors*. To change your system colors, right-click the desktop, choose Properties from the shortcut menu to display the Display Properties dialog box, and then click the Appearance tab (see Figure 18.1). To change the color for a specific item, you click the Advanced button, select the color attribute to change, and then choose a new color (if you're running a version of Windows other than Windows XP, your dialog box might be slightly different).

When you change a system color using the Display Properties dialog box, all loaded applications should change their appearance to match your selection. In addition, when you start any new application, it should also match its appearance to your selection. If you had to write code to manage this behavior, you'd have to write a *lot* of code, and you'd be justified in avoiding the whole mess. However, making an application adjust its appearance to match the user's system color selections is actually trivial, so there's no reason not to do it. For the most part, it's automatic with controls that you add to a form.

To designate that an interface color should stay in sync with a user's system colors, you assign a system color to a color property of the item in question (see Figure 18.2). If you wanted to ensure that the color of a button matches the user's system color, for example, you would assign the System Color `Control` to the `BackColor` property of the Button control. Table 18.3 lists the most common system colors you can use. For a complete list, consult the online Help.

When a user changes a system color using the Display Properties dialog box, Visual C# automatically updates the appearance of objects that use system colors; you don't have to write a single line of code to do this. Fortunately, when you create new forms and when you add controls to forms, Visual C# automatically assigns the proper system color to the appropriate properties, so you don't usually have to muck with them.

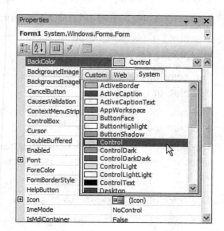

FIGURE 18.2
System colors are assigned using the System palette tab.

Be aware that you aren't limited to assigning system colors to their logically associated properties. You can assign system colors to any color property you want, and you can also use system colors when drawing. This enables you to draw custom interface elements that match the user's system colors, for example. Be aware, however, that if you do draw with system colors, Visual C# won't update the colors automatically when the user changes system colors; you would have to redraw the elements with the new system color. In addition, if you apply system colors to properties that aren't usually assigned system colors, you run the risk of displaying odd color combinations, such as black on black, depending on the user's color settings.

By the Way

> Users don't just change their system colors for aesthetic purposes. I work with a programmer who is color-blind. He's modified his system colors so that he can see things better on the screen. If you don't allow your applications to adjust to the color preferences of the user, you might make using your program unnecessarily difficult, or even impossible, for someone with color-blindness or visual acuity issues.

Table 18.3   System Colors

Enumeration	Description
ActiveCaption	The color of the background of an active caption bar (title bar).
ActiveCaptionText	The color of the text of the active caption bar (title bar).
Control	The color of the background of push buttons and other 3D elements.
ControlDark	The color of shadows on a 3D element.
ControlLight	The color of highlights on a 3D element.
ControlText	The color of the text on buttons and other 3D elements.
Desktop	The color of the Windows desktop.
GrayText	The color of the text on a user interface element when it's disabled or dimmed.
Highlight	The color of the background of highlighted text. This includes selected menu items as well as selected text.
HighlightText	The color of the foreground of highlighted text. This includes selected menu items as well as selected text.
InactiveBorder	The color of an inactive window border.
InactiveCaption	The color of the background of an inactive caption bar.
InactiveCaptionText	The color of the text of an inactive caption bar.
Menu	The color of the menu background.
MenuText	The color of the menu text.
Window	The color of the background in the client area of a window.

Working with Rectangles

Before learning how to draw shapes, you need to understand the concept of a rectangle as it relates to Visual C# programming. A rectangle is a structure used to hold bounding coordinates used to draw a shape. A rectangle isn't necessarily used to draw a rectangle (although it can be). Obviously, a square can fit within a rectangle. However, so can circles and ellipses. Figure 18.3 illustrates how most shapes can be bound by a rectangle.

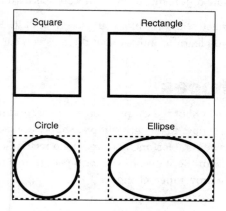

FIGURE 18.3
Rectangles are used to define the bounds of most shapes.

To draw most shapes, you must have a rectangle. The rectangle you pass to a drawing method is used as a bounding rectangle; the proper shape (circle, ellipse, and so on) is always drawn within the confines of the bounding rectangle. Creating a rectangle is easy. First, you dimension a variable as Rectangle, and then you set the X, Y, Width, and Height properties of the object variable. The X, Y value is the coordinate of the upper-left corner of the rectangle—the Height and Width properties are self-explanatory.

The following code creates a rectangle that has its upper-left corner at coordinate 0,0, has a width of 100, and height of 50. Note, this code simply defines a rectangle in code, it doesn't draw a rectangle to the screen:

```
Rectangle rectBounding = new Rectangle();
rectBounding.X = 0;
rectBounding.Y = 0;
rectBounding.Width = 100;
rectBounding.Height = 50;
```

The Rectangle object enables you to send the X, Y, Height, and Width values as part of its initialize construct. Using this technique, you could create the same rectangle with only a single line of code:

```
Rectangle rectBounding = new Rectangle(0,0,100,50);
```

You can do a number of things with a rectangle after it's defined. Perhaps the most useful is the ability to enlarge or shrink the rectangle with a single statement. You enlarge or shrink a rectangle using the Inflate() method. The most common syntax of Inflate() is the following:

```
object.Inflate(changeinwidth, changeinheight);
```

When called this way, the rectangle width and the height are enlarged (the center of the rectangle stays in place). To leave the size of the height or width unchanged, pass 0 as the appropriate argument. To shrink a side, specify a negative number.

If you're going to do much with drawing, you'll use a lot of Rectangle objects, and I strongly suggest that you learn as much about them as you can.

Drawing Shapes

Now that you've learned about the Graphics object, pens, and rectangles, you'll probably find drawing shapes to be fairly simple. Shapes are drawn by calling methods of a Graphics object. Most methods require a rectangle, which is used as the bounding rectangle for the shape, as well as a pen. In this section, you'll learn what you need to do to draw different shapes.

I've chosen to discuss only the most commonly drawn shapes. The Graphics object contains many methods for drawing additional shapes.

Drawing Lines

Drawing lines is accomplished with the DrawLine() method of the Graphics object. DrawLine() is one of the few drawing methods that doesn't require a rectangle. The basic syntax for DrawLine() is

```
object.DrawLine(pen, x1, y1, x2, y2);
```

Object refers to a Graphics object and pen refers to a Pen object, both of which have already been discussed. X1, Y1 is the coordinate of the starting point of the line, whereas X2, Y2 is the coordinate of the ending point; Visual C# draws a line between the two points using the specified pen.

Drawing Rectangles

Drawing rectangles (and squares, for that matter) is accomplished using the DrawRectangle() method of a Graphics object. As you might expect,

DrawRectangle() accepts a pen and a rectangle. Here's the syntax for calling DrawRectangle() in this way:

```
object.DrawRectangle(pen, rectangle);
```

If you don't have a Rectangle object (and you don't want to create one), you can call DrawRectangle() using the following format:

```
object.DrawRectangle(pen, X, Y, width, height);
```

Drawing Circles and Ellipses

Drawing circles and ellipses is accomplished by calling the DrawEllipse() method. If you're familiar with geometry, you'll know that a circle is simply an ellipse that has the same height as it does width. This is why no specific method exists for drawing circles: DrawEllipse() works perfectly. Like the DrawRectangle() method, DrawEllipse() accepts a pen and a rectangle. The rectangle is used as a bounding rectangle—the width of the rectangle is the width of the ellipse, whereas the height of the rectangle is the height of the ellipse. DrawEllipse() has the following syntax:

```
object.DrawEllipse(pen, rectangle);
```

In the event that you don't have a Rectangle object defined (and you don't want to create one), you can call DrawEllipse() with this syntax:

```
object.DrawEllipse(pen, X, Y, Width, Height);
```

Clearing a Drawing Surface

To clear the surface of a Graphics object, call the Clear() method, passing it the color to paint the surface like this:

```
objGraphics.Clear(Drawing.SystemColors.Control);
```

When using the graphics object of a form, you could use the following code to clear the form using the BackColor of the form:

```
objGraphics.Clear(this.BackColor);
```

Drawing Text

Drawing text on a Graphics object is similar to drawing a shape, and the method name even contains the word *Draw*, in contrast to *Print*. To draw text on a Graphics object, call the `DrawString()` method. The basic format for `DrawString()` looks like this:

```
object.DrawString(stringoftext, font, brush, topX, leftY);
```

A few of these items are probably new to you. The argument *stringoftext* is self-explanatory: It's the string you want to draw on the Graphics object. The *topX* and *leftY* arguments represent the coordinate at which drawing will take place; they represent the upper-left corner of the string, as illustrated in Figure 18.4.

FIGURE 18.4
The coordinate specified in `DrawString()` represents the upper-left corner of the printed text.

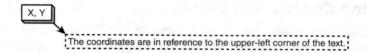

The arguments *brush* and *font* aren't so obvious. Both arguments accept objects. A brush is similar to a pen, but whereas a pen describes the characteristics of a line, a brush describes the characteristics of a fill. For example, both pens and brushes have a color, but where pens have an attribute for defining a line style such as dashed or solid, a brush has an attribute for a fill pattern such as solid, hatched, weave, or trellis. When drawing text, a solid brush is usually sufficient. You can create brushes in much the same way as you create pens, or you can use one of the standard brushes available from the `System.Drawing.Brushes` class.

A Font object defines characteristics used to format text, including the character set (Times New Roman, Courier, and so on), size (point size), and style (bold, italic, normal, underlined, and so on). To create a new Font object, you could use code such as the following:

```
Font objFont;
objFont = new System.Drawing.Font("Arial", 30);
```

The text Arial in this code is the name of a font installed on my computer. In fact, Arial is one of the few fonts installed on *all* Windows computers. If you supply the name of a font that doesn't exist on the machine at runtime, Visual C# will use a default font. The second parameter is the point size of the text. If you want to use a style other than normal, you can provide a style value as a third parameter, like this (note the logical Or, as discussed in Hour 12, "Performing Arithmetic, String Manipulation, and Date/Time Adjustments"):

```
objFont = new System.Drawing.Font("Arial Black", 30, FontStyle.Bold |
FontSytle.Italic);
```

In addition to creating a Font object, you can also use the font of an existing object, such as a form. For example, the following statement prints text to a Graphics object using the font of the current form:

```
objGraphics.DrawString("This is the text that prints!",
                        this.Font, System.Drawing.Brushes.Blue, 0, 0);
```

Persisting Graphics on a Form

You will find it necessary at times to use the techniques discussed in this hour to draw to a form. However, you might recall from earlier hours that when you draw to a form (actually, you draw to a Graphics object that references a form), the things that you draw aren't persisted; the next time the form paints itself, the drawn elements will disappear. If the user minimizes the form or obscures the form with another window, for example, the next time the form is painted it will be missing all drawn elements that were obscured. You can use a couple of approaches to deal with this behavior:

- Place all code that draws to the form in the form's Paint event.

- Draw to a memory bitmap and copy the contents of the memory bitmap to the form in the form's Paint event.

If you're drawing only a few items, placing the drawing code in the Paint event might be a good approach. However, consider a situation in which you have a lot of drawing code. Perhaps the graphics are drawn in response to user input, so you can't re-create them all at once. In these situations, the second approach is clearly better.

Building a Graphics Project Example

You're now going to build a project that uses the skills you've learned to draw to a form. In this project, you'll use the technique of drawing to a memory bitmap to persist the graphics each time the form paints itself.

> The project you're about to build is perhaps the most difficult yet. I'll explain each step of the process of creating this project, but I won't spend any time explaining the objects and methods that I've already discussed.

By the Way

To make things interesting, I've used random numbers to determine font size as well as the X, Y coordinate of the text you're going to draw to the form. The Random class and its `Next()` method will be used to generate pseudo-random numbers. To generate a random number within a specific range (such as a random number between 1 and 10), you use the following:

```
randomGenerator.Next(1,10);
```

Start by creating a new Windows Application titled **Persisting Graphics** and then follow these steps to build the project:

1. Right-click Form1.cs in the Solution Explorer, choose Rename, and then change the name of the default form to **frmMain.cs**. Next, set the form's Text property to **Persisting Graphics Example**.

2. The interface of your form will consist of a text box and a button. When the user clicks the button, the contents of the text box will be drawn on the form in a random location and with a random font size. Add a new text box to your form and set its properties as follows:

Property	Value
Name	**txtInput**
Location	**56,184**
Size	**100,20**

3. Add a new button to the form and set its properties as follows:

Property	Value
Name	**btnDrawText**
Location	**160,184**
Text	**Draw Text**

Time for the code to fly!

As mentioned earlier, all drawing will be performed using a memory bitmap, which will then be copied to the form. You'll reference this bitmap in multiple places, so you're going to make it a module-level variable.

4. Double-click the form to access its Load event.

5. Locate the statement public partial class frmMain : Form and position your cursor immediately *after* the left bracket ({) on the next line.

6. Enter the following statement:

```
private Bitmap m_objDrawingSurface;
```

7. For the bitmap variable to be used, it must reference a Bitmap object. A good place to initialize things is in the form's Load event, so put your cursor back in the Load event now and enter the following code:

```
// Create a drawing surface with the same dimensions as the client
// area of the form.
m_objDrawingSurface = new Bitmap(this.ClientRectangle.Width,
    this.ClientRectangle.Height,
    System.Drawing.Imaging.PixelFormat.Format24bppRgb);
InitializeSurface();
```

Your procedure should now look like the one shown in Figure 18.5.

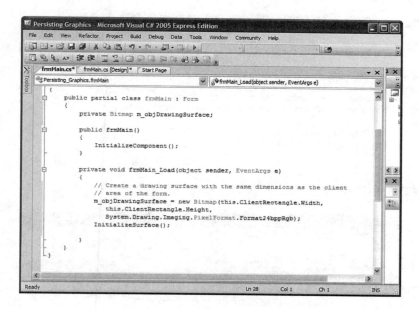

FIGURE 18.5
Make sure that your code appears exactly as it does here.

The first statement creates a new bitmap in memory. Because the contents of the bitmap are to be sent to the form, it makes sense to use the dimensions of the client area of the form as the size of the new bitmap—which is exactly what you've done. The final statement calls a procedure that you haven't yet created.

8. Position the cursor after the closing bracket (}) of the frmMain_Load event, and press Enter to create a new line. You're now going to write code to initialize the bitmap. The code will clear the bitmap to the system color named Control and then draw an ellipse that has the dimensions of the bitmap. (I've added comments to the code so that you can follow along with what's happening; all the concepts in this code have been discussed already.) Enter the following in its entirety:

```csharp
private void InitializeSurface()
{
    Graphics objGraphics;
    Rectangle rectBounds;

    // Create a Graphics object that references the bitmap and clear it.
    objGraphics = Graphics.FromImage(m_objDrawingSurface);

    objGraphics.Clear(SystemColors.Control);

    //Create a rectangle the same size as the bitmap.
    rectBounds = new Rectangle(0, 0,
                m_objDrawingSurface.Width,m_objDrawingSurface.Height);
    //Reduce the rectangle slightly so the ellipse won't appear on the
border.
    rectBounds.Inflate(-1, -1);

    // Draw an ellipse that fills the form.
    objGraphics.DrawEllipse(Pens.Orange, rectBounds);

    // Free up resources.
    objGraphics.Dispose();
}
```

Your procedure should now look like the one shown in Figure 18.6.

FIGURE 18.6
Verify that your code is entered correctly.

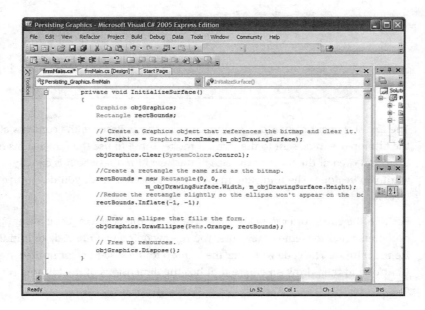

If you run your project now, you'll find that nothing is drawn to the form. This is because the drawing is being done to a bitmap in memory, and you haven't yet added the code to copy the bitmap to the form. The place to do this is in the form's Paint event so that the contents of the bitmap are sent to the form every time the form paints itself. This ensures that the items you draw always appear on the form.

9. Create an event handler for the form's Paint event by first returning to the form designer and selecting the form. Click the Event icon in the Properties window and then double-click Paint to create a new Paint event procedure. Add the following code to the Paint event:

```
// Draw the contents of the bitmap on the form.
e.Graphics.DrawImage(m_objDrawingSurface, 0, 0,
    m_objDrawingSurface.Width,
    m_objDrawingSurface.Height);
e.Graphics.Dispose();
```

The e parameter of the Paint event has a property that references the Graphics object of the form. The method DrawImage() draws the image in a bitmap to the surface of a Graphics object, so the last statement is simply sending the contents of the bitmap that exists in memory to the form.

If you run the project now, you'll find that the ellipse appears on the form. Furthermore, you can cover the form with another window, or even minimize it, and the ellipse will always appear on the form when it's displayed again—the graphics persist.

10. The last thing you're going to do is write code that draws the contents entered into the text box on the form. The text will be drawn with a random size and location. Return to the Form Designer and double-click the button to access its Click event. Add the following code:

```
Graphics objGraphics;
Font objFont;
int intFontSize, intTextX, intTextY;

Random randomGenerator = new Random();

// If no text has been entered, get out.
if (txtInput.Text == "") return;

// Create a graphics object using the memory bitmap.
objGraphics = Graphics.FromImage(m_objDrawingSurface);

// Create a random number for the font size. Keep it between 8 and 48.
intFontSize = randomGenerator.Next(8,48);
// Create a random number for the X coordinate of the text.
```

```
intTextX = randomGenerator.Next(0,this.ClientRectangle.Width);
// Create a random number for the Y coordinate of the text.
intTextY = randomGenerator.Next(0,this.ClientRectangle.Height);

// Create a new font object.
objFont = new System.Drawing.Font("Arial", intFontSize, FontStyle.Bold);
// Draw the user's text.
objGraphics.DrawString(txtInput.Text, objFont,
System.Drawing.Brushes.Red, intTextX, intTextY);
// Clean up.
objGraphics.Dispose();
// Force the form to paint itself. This triggers the Paint event.
this.Invalidate();
```

The comments I've included should make the code self-explanatory. However, the last statement bears discussing. The `Invalidate()` method of a form invalidates the client rectangle. This operation tells Windows that the appearance of the form is no longer accurate and that the form needs to be repainted. This, in turn, triggers the `Paint` event of the form. Because the `Paint` event contains the code that copies the contents of the memory bitmap to the form, invalidating the form causes the text to appear. If you don't call `Invalidate()` here, the text won't appear on the form (but it is still drawn on the memory bitmap).

By the Way

> If you draw elements that are based on the size of the form, you'll need to call `Invalidate()` in the `Resize` event of the form; resizing a form doesn't trigger the form's `Paint` event.

The last thing you need to do is make sure you free up the resources used by your module-level `Graphics` object. Using the Properties window, add an event handler for the `FormClosed` event of the form now, and enter the following statement:

```
m_objDrawingSurface.Dispose();
```

Your project is now complete! Click Save All on the toolbar to save your work, and then press F5 to run the project. You'll notice immediately that the ellipse is drawn on the form. Type something into the text box and click the button. Click it again. Each time you click the button, the text is drawn on the form using the same brush, but with a different size and location (see Figure 18.7).

FIGURE 18.7
Text is drawn on a form, much like ordinary shapes.

Summary

You won't need to add drawing capabilities to every project you create. However, when you need the capabilities, *you need the capabilities*. In this hour, you learned the basic skills for drawing to a graphics surface, which can be a form, control, memory bitmap, or one of many other types of surfaces. You learned that all drawing is done using a Graphics object, and you now know how to create a Graphics object for a form or control, and even how to create a Graphics object for a bitmap that exists in memory.

Most drawing methods require a pen and a rectangle, and you can now create rectangles and pens using the techniques you learned in this hour. After learning about pens and rectangles, you've found that the drawing methods themselves are pretty easy to use. Even drawing text is simple when you have a Graphics object to work with.

Persisting graphics on a form can be a bit complicated, and I suspect this will confuse many new Visual C# programmers who try to figure it out on their own. However, you've now built an example that persists graphics on a form, and you'll be able to leverage the techniques involved when you have to do this in your own projects.

I don't expect you to be able to sit down for an hour and create an Adobe Photoshop knock-off. However, you now have a solid foundation on which to build. If you're going to attempt a project that performs a lot of drawing, you'll want to dig deeper into the Graphics object.

Q&A

Q. *What if I need to draw a lot of lines, one starting where another ends? Do I need to call* `DrawLine()` *for each line?*

A. The Graphics object has a method called `DrawLines()`, which accepts a series of points. The method draws lines connecting the sequence of points.

Q. *Is there a way to fill a shape?*

A. The Graphics object includes methods that draw filled shapes, such as `FillEllipse()` and `FillRectangle()`.

Workshop

Quiz

1. What object is used to draw to a surface?

2. To set a Graphics object to draw to a form directly, you call what method of the form?

3. What object defines the characteristics of a line? A fill pattern?

4. How do you make a color property adjust with the user's Windows settings?

5. What object is used to define the bounds of a shape to be drawn?

6. What method do you call to draw an irregular ellipse? A circle?

7. What method do you call to print text on a Graphics surface?

8. To ensure that graphics persist on a form, the graphics must be drawn on the form in what event?

Answers

1. The Graphics object

2. The `CreateGraphics()` method

3. Lines are defined by Pen objects; fill characteristics are defined by Brush objects.

4. Use System Colors.

5. A Rectangle object

6. Both shapes are drawn with the `DrawEllipse()` method.

7. The `DrawString()` method

8. The form's `Paint` event

Exercises

1. Modify the example in this hour to use a font other than Arial. If you're not sure what fonts are installed on your computer, open the Start menu and choose Settings, Control Panel. You'll have an option on the Control Panel for viewing your system fonts.

2. Create a project that draws an ellipse that fills the form, much like the one you created in this hour. However, draw the ellipse directly to the form in the `Paint` event. Make sure that the ellipse is redrawn when the form is sized. (Hint: Invalidate the form in the form's `Resize()` event.)

PART IV

Working with Data

HOUR 19

Performing File Operations

What You'll Learn in This Hour:

▶ Using the Open File Dialog and Save File Dialog controls
▶ Manipulating files with `System.IO.File`
▶ Manipulating directories with `System.IO.Directory`

It's difficult to imagine any application other than a tiny utility program that doesn't use the file system. In this hour, you'll learn how to use controls to make it easy for a user to browse and select files. In addition, you'll learn how to use the `System.IO.File` and `System.IO.Directory` objects to manipulate the file system more easily than you might think (IO stands for Input/Output). Using these objects, you can delete files and directories, move them, rename them, and more. These objects are powerful, but remember: Play nice!

Using the Open File Dialog and Save File Dialog Controls

In Hour 1, "Jumping In with Both Feet: A Visual C# 2005 Programming Tour," you used the Open File Dialog control to enable a user to browse for pictures to display in your Picture Viewer program. In this section, you'll move beyond those basics to learn important details about working with the Open File Dialog, as well as its sister control, the Save File Dialog.

You're going to build a project to illustrate most of the file-manipulation concepts discussed in this hour. Begin by creating a new Windows application called **Manipulating Files**, and then follow these steps:

1. Right-click Form1.cs in the Solution Explorer, choose Rename, and then change the name of the default form to **frmManipulatingFiles.cs**. Next, set the form's Text property to **Manipulating Files**.

2. Add a new text box to the form and set its properties as shown in the following table:

Property	Value
Name	**txtSource**
Location	**95,8**
Size	**184,20**

Using the Open File Dialog Control

The Open File Dialog control is used to display a dialog box that enables the user to browse and select a file (see Figure 19.1). It's important to note that usually the Open File Dialog doesn't actually open a file, but it allows a user to select a file so that it can then be opened by code within the application.

FIGURE 19.1
The Open File Dialog control is used to browse for a file.

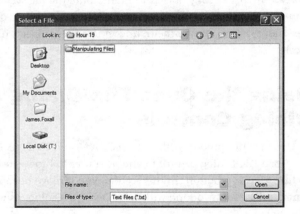

Add a new Open File Dialog control to your project now by double-clicking the OpenFileDialog item in the toolbox. The Open File Dialog doesn't have an interface per se, so it appears in the area below the form rather than on it (see Figure 19.2). For the user to browse for files, you have to manipulate the Open File Dialog using its properties and methods.

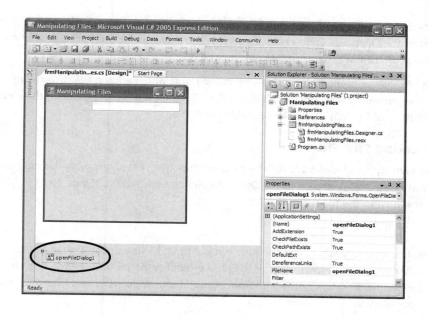

FIGURE 19.2
The Open File dialog box is hosted below the form, not on it.

You're going to add a button to the form that, when clicked, enables a user to locate and select a file. If a user selects a file, the filename is placed in the text box you've created.

1. Add a button to the form now, and set its properties as follows:

Property	Value
Name	**btnOpenFile**
Location	**8,8**
Size	**80,23**
Text	**Source:**

2. Next, double-click the button and add the following code to its Click event:

```
openFileDialog1.InitialDirectory = @"C:\";
openFileDialog1.Title = "Select a File";
openFileDialog1.FileName = "";
```

The first statement specifies the directory to display when the dialog box is first shown. If you don't specify a directory for the InitialDirectory property, the active system directory is used (for example, the last directory browsed to with a different Open File dialog box).

The `Title` property of the Open File Dialog determines the text displayed in the title bar of the Open File dialog box. If you don't specify text for the `Title` property, Visual C# displays the word `Open` in the title bar.

The `FileName` property is used to return the name of the chosen file. If you don't set this to an empty string before showing the File Open dialog, the name of the control will be used by default—not a desirable result.

Creating File Filters

Different types of files have different extensions. The `Filter` property determines what types of files appear in the Open File dialog box (refer to Figure 19.1). A filter is specified in the following format:

```
Description|*.extension
```

The text that appears before the pipe symbol (|) is the descriptive text of the file type to filter on, whereas the text after the pipe symbol is the pattern used to filter files. For example, to display only Windows bitmap files, you could use a filter such as the following:

```
control.Filter = "Windows Bitmaps (*.bmp)|*.bmp";
```

You can specify more than one filter type. To do so, add a pipe symbol between the filters, like this:

```
control.Filter = "Windows Bitmaps (*.bmp)|*.bmp|JPEG Files (*.jpg)|*.jpg";
```

You're going to restrict your Open File dialog box to show only text files, so enter this statement in your procedure:

```
openFileDialog1.Filter = "Text Files (*.txt)|*.txt";
```

When you have more than one filter, you can specify which filter appears selected by default using the `FilterIndex` property. Although you've specified only one filter type in this example, it's still a good idea to designate the default filter, so add this statement to your procedure:

```
openFileDialog1.FilterIndex = 1;
```

Unlike most other collections, the `FilterIndex` property is 1-based, not 0-based, so 1 is the first filter listed.

Showing the File Open Dialog Box

Finally, you need to show the Open File dialog box and take action based on whether the user selects a file. The ShowDialog() method of the Open File Dialog control acts much like the method of forms by the same name, returning a result that indicates the user's selection on the dialog box.

Enter the following statements into your procedure:

```
if (openFileDialog1.ShowDialog() != DialogResult.Cancel)
    txtSource.Text = openFileDialog1.FileName;
else
    txtSource.Text = "";
```

This code just places the selected filename into the text box txtSource. If the user clicks Cancel, the contents of the text box are cleared.

Press F5 to run the project and click the button. You'll get the same dialog box shown in Figure 19.1 (with different files and directories, of course). Select a text file and click Open, and Visual C# places the name of the file into the text box.

The Open File Dialog control makes allowing a user to browse and select a file almost trivial. Without this component, you would have to write an astounding amount of difficult code and probably still wouldn't come up with all the functionality supported by this control.

Using the Save File Dialog Control

The Save File Dialog control is similar to the Open File Dialog control, but it's used to allow a user to browse directories and specify a file to save, rather than open. Again, it's important to note that the Save File Dialog control doesn't actually save a file; it's used to allow a user to specify a filename to save. You'll have to write code to do something with the filename returned by the control.

You're going to use the Save File Dialog control to let the user specify a filename. This filename will be the target of various file operations that you'll learn about later in this hour. Follow these steps to create the File Save dialog:

1. Create a new text box on your form and set its properties as follows:

Property	Value
Name	**txtDestination**
Location	**95,40**
Size	**184,20**

2. You're now going to create a button that, when clicked, enables the user to specify a filename to save a file. Add a new button to the form and set its properties as shown in the following table:

Property	Value
Name	**btnSaveFile**
Location	**8,40**
Size	**80,23**
Text	**Destination:**

3. Of course, none of this will work without adding a Save File dialog box. Double-click the `SaveFileDialog` item in the toolbox to add a new control to the project.

4. Next, double-click the new button you just created (btnSaveFile) and add the following code to its `Click` event:

```
saveFileDialog1.Title = "Specify Destination File Name";
saveFileDialog1.Filter = "Text Files (*.txt)|*.txt";
saveFileDialog1.FilterIndex = 1;

saveFileDialog1.OverwritePrompt = true;
```

The first three statements set properties identical to those of the Open File Dialog. The `OverwritePrompt` property, however, is unique to the Save File Dialog. When this property is set to `true`, Visual C# asks users to confirm their selections when they choose a file that already exists, as shown in Figure 19.3. I highly recommend that you prompt the user about replacing files by ensuring that the `OverwritePrompt` property is set to True.

FIGURE 19.3
It's a good idea to get confirmation before replacing an existing file.

If you want the Save File dialog box to prompt users when the file they specify *doesn't* exist, set the `CreatePrompt` property of the Save File Dialog control to True.

By the Way

5. The last bit of code you need to add places the selected filename in the txtDestination text box. Enter the code as shown here:

```
if (saveFileDialog1.ShowDialog() != DialogResult.Cancel)
   txtDestination.Text = saveFileDialog1.FileName;
```

Press F5 to run the project and then click each of the buttons and select a file. When you're satisfied that your selections are being sent to the appropriate text box, stop the project and save your work. If your selected filenames aren't being sent to the proper text box, compare your code against the code I've provided.

The Open File Dialog and Save File Dialog controls are similar in design and appearance, but each serves a specific purpose. You'll be using the interface you've just created throughout the rest of this hour.

Manipulating Files with the File Object

Visual C# includes a powerful namespace called `System.IO` (the IO object acts like an object property of the `System` namespace). Using various properties, methods, and object properties of `System.IO`, you can do just about anything you can imagine with the file system. In particular, the `System.IO.File` and `System.IO.Directory` objects provide you with extensive file and directory (folder) manipulation.

In the following sections, you'll continue to expand the project that you've created. You'll write code that manipulates the selected filenames by using the Open File Dialog and Save File Dialog controls.

> The code you're about to write in the following sections is "the real thing." For example, the code for deleting a file really does delete a file. Don't forget this as you test your project; the files selected as the source and as the destination *will* be affected by your actions. I provide the cannon, and it's up to you not to shoot yourself in the foot.

Determining Whether a File Exists

Before attempting any operation on a file, such as copying or deleting it, it's a good idea to make certain the file exists. For example, if the user doesn't click the Source button to select a file but instead types the name and path of a file into the text box, the user could type an invalid or nonexistent filename. Attempting to manipulate a nonexistent file could result in an exception—which you don't want to happen. Because you're going to work with the source file selected by the user in many routines, you're going to create a central function that can be called to determine whether the source file exists. The function uses the `Exists()` method of the `System.IO.File` object to determine whether the file exists.

Add the following method to your form class:

```
bool SourceFileExists()
{
if (!System.IO.File.Exists(txtSource.Text))
    {
        MessageBox.Show("The source file does not exist!");
        return false;
    }
    else
        return true;
}
```

The `SourceFileExists()` method uses the value in the text box txtSource. If the filename specified in the text box exists, `SourceFileExists()` returns `true`; otherwise, it returns `false`.

Copying a File

Copying files is a common task. For example, you might want to create an application that backs up important data files by copying them to another location. For the most part, copying is pretty safe—as long as you use a destination filename that doesn't already exist. Copying files is accomplished using the `Copy()` method of the `System.IO.File` class.

You're now going to add a button to your form. When the user clicks this button, the file specified in the source text box will be copied to a new file with the name given in the destination text box. Follow these steps to create the Copy functionality:

1. Add a button to your form now and set its properties as shown in the following table:

Property	Value
Name	**btnCopyFile**
Location	**96,80**
Size	**75,23**
Text	**Copy**

2. Double-click the Copy button and add the following code:

```
if (!SourceFileExists()) return;
System.IO.File.Copy(txtSource.Text, txtDestination.Text);
MessageBox.Show("The file has been successfully copied.");
```

The Copy() method has two arguments. The first is the file that you want to copy, and the second is the name and path of the new copy of the file. In this example, you're using the filenames selected in the two text boxes.

Press F5 to run the project and test your copy code now by following these steps:

1. Click the Source button and select a text file.

2. Click the Destination button to display the Save File dialog box. Don't select an existing file. Instead, type a new filename into the File Name text box and click Save. If you're asked whether you want to replace a file, click No and change your filename; don't use the name of an existing file.

3. Click Copy to copy the file.

After you get the message box telling you the file was copied, you can use Explorer to locate the new file and open it. Stop the project and save your work before continuing.

Moving a File

When you move a file, it's taken out of its current directory and placed in a new one. You can specify a new name for the file or use its original name. Moving a file is accomplished with the Move() method of the System.IO.File object. Follow these steps to create a button on your form that moves the file selected as the source to the path and the filename selected as the destination:

> I recommend that you use Notepad to create a text file, and use this temporary text file when testing from this point forward. This code, as well as the rest of the examples presented in this hour, can permanently alter or destroy a file.

1. Add a new button to the form and set its properties as follows:

Property	Value
Name	**btnMove**
Location	**96,112**
Size	**75,23**
Text	**Move**

2. Double-click the Move button and add the following code to its `Click` event:

```
if (!SourceFileExists()) return;
System.IO.File.Move(txtSource.Text, txtDestination.Text);
MessageBox.Show("The file has been successfully moved.");
```

Go ahead and press F5 to test your project. Select a file to move (again, I recommend you create a dummy file in Notepad) and supply a destination filename. When you click Move, the file will be moved to the new location and given the new name. Remember, if you specify a name for the destination that isn't the same as that of the source, the file will be given the new name when it's moved.

Renaming a File

When you rename a file, it remains in the same directory, and nothing materially happens to the contents of the file—the name is just changed to something else. Because the original file isn't altered, renaming a file isn't as risky as performing an action such as deleting the file. Nevertheless, it's frustrating trying to determine what happened to a file when it was mistakenly renamed. To rename a file, use the `Move()` method of `System.IO.File`, specifying a new filename but keeping the same path.

Deleting a File

Deleting a file can be a risky proposition. The `Delete()` method of `System.IO.File` deletes a file permanently—it doesn't send the file to the Recycle Bin. For this reason, take great care when deleting files. First and foremost, this means testing your code. When you write a routine to delete a file, be sure to test it under many conditions. For example, if you reference the wrong text box in this code, you would inadvertently delete the wrong file! Users aren't forgiving of such mistakes.

Follow these steps to add a button to your project that deletes the source file when clicked. Remember: Be careful when testing this code.

1. Add a button to the form now and set its properties as follows:

Property	Value
Name	**btnDelete**
Location	**96,144**
Size	**75,23**
Text	**Delete**

2. Next, double-click the button and add the following code to its Click event:

```
if (!SourceFileExists()) return;

if (MessageBox.Show("Are you sure you want to delete the source file?",
    "Delete Verification",MessageBoxButtons.YesNo,
    MessageBoxIcon.Question) == DialogResult.Yes)
{
    System.IO.File.Delete(txtSource.Text);
    MessageBox.Show("The file has been successfully deleted.");
}
```

Notice that you've included a message box to confirm the user's intentions. It's a good idea to do this *whenever* you're about to perform a serious action that can't be undone. In fact, the more information you can give the user, the better. For example, I suggest that if this was production code (code meant for end users), you should include the name of the file in the message box so that the user would know *without a doubt* what the program intends to do. If you're feeling brave, press F5 to run the project and then select a file and delete it.

Retrieving a File's Properties

Although many people don't realize it, files have a number of properties—such as the date the file was last modified. The easiest way to see these properties is to use Explorer. View the attributes of a file now by starting Explorer, right-clicking any file displayed in Explorer, and choosing Properties. Explorer shows the File Properties window with information about the file (see Figure 19.4).

The System.IO.File object provides ways to get at most of the data displayed on the General tab of the File Properties dialog box shown in Figure 19.4. Some of this data is available directly from the File object, whereas other data is accessed using a FileAttributes object.

FIGURE 19.4
Visual C# provides a means to easily obtain most file properties.

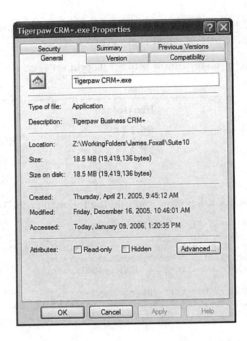

Getting Date and Time Information About a File

Getting the date created, the last date accessed, and the last date modified of a file is easy; the System.IO.File object supports a method for each of these dates. Table 19.1 lists the applicable properties and what they return.

Table 19.1   File Object Properties to Retrieve Data Information

Property	Description
GetCreationTime	Returns the date and time the file was created
GetLastAccessTime	Returns the date and time the file was last accessed
GetLastWriteTime	Returns the date and time the file was last modified

Getting the Attributes of a File

The attributes of a file (refer to the bottom of the dialog box shown in Figure 19.4) aren't available as properties of the System.IO.File object. How you determine an attribute is complicated. The GetAttributes() method of System.IO.File returns a FileAttributes enumeration. This enumeration acts as a set of flags for the various attributes. The first step in determining the attributes is to get the FileAttributes containing the flags for the attributes of the file. To do this, you would create a FileAttributes variable and call GetAttributes(), like this:

```
System.IO.FileAttributes  objfileAttributes ;
objFileAttributes = System.IO.File.GetAttributes(txtSource.Text);
```

Once you retrieve the file attributes into the variable `objFileAttributes`, you can use one of the members of the `FileAttributes` enumeration shown in Table 19.2 to determine whether a particular attribute is set.

Table 19.2   Common `FileAttribute` Enumeration Members

Attribute	Meaning
Archive	The file's archive status. Applications use this attribute to mark files for backup and removal.
Directory	The file is a directory.
Hidden	The file is hidden and therefore isn't included in an ordinary directory listing.
Normal	The file is normal and has no other attributes set.
ReadOnly	The file is a read-only file.
System	The file is part of the operating system or is used exclusively by the operating system.
Temporary	The file is a temporary file.

Writing Code to Retrieve a File's Properties

Now that you know how to retrieve the properties of an object, you're going to modify your Picture Viewer project so that the user can view file properties of a picture file they have displayed. Start by opening the Picture Viewer project you last modified in Hour 15, "Debugging Your Code," and then follow these steps to add the file attributes functionality:

1. Begin by adding a new tool button to the Toolstrip (the toolbar) and set its name to **tbbGetFileAttributes**.

2. If you have downloaded the sample code, set the image to Properties.ico. Next, set the `ToolTipText` property to **Get File Attributes**.

   The code you enter into the `Click` event of this button will be a bit longer than most of the code you've entered so far. Therefore, I'll show the code in its entirety and then I'll explain what the code does.

3. Double-click the new button and add the following code to the button's `Click` event:

```
// Make sure a file is open.
if ((ofdSelectPicture.FileName) == "")
{
```

```
        MessageBox.Show("There is no file open");
        return;
}

// Create the string builder object to concatenate strings.
System.Text.StringBuilder stbProperties = new
System.Text.StringBuilder("");
System.IO.FileAttributes fileAttributes;

// Get the dates.
stbProperties.Append("Created: ");
stbProperties.Append(System.IO.File.GetCreationTime(ofdSelectPicture.FileNa
me));
stbProperties.Append("\r\n");

stbProperties.Append("Accessed: ");
stbProperties.Append(System.IO.File.GetLastAccessTime(ofdSelectPicture.File
Name));
stbProperties.Append("\r\n");

stbProperties.Append("Modified: ");
stbProperties.Append(System.IO.File.GetLastWriteTime(ofdSelectPicture.FileN
ame));

// Get File Attributes
fileAttributes = System.IO.File.GetAttributes(ofdSelectPicture.FileName);
stbProperties.Append("\r\n");

// Use a binary AND to extract the specific attributes.
stbProperties.Append("Normal: ");
stbProperties.Append(
        Convert.ToBoolean((fileAttributes & System.IO.FileAttributes.Normal)
            == System.IO.FileAttributes.Normal));
stbProperties.Append("\r\n");

stbProperties.Append("Hidden: ");
stbProperties.Append(
        Convert.ToBoolean((fileAttributes & System.IO.FileAttributes.Hidden)
            == System.IO.FileAttributes.Hidden));
stbProperties.Append("\r\n");

stbProperties.Append("ReadOnly: ");
stbProperties.Append(
        Convert.ToBoolean((fileAttributes &
System.IO.FileAttributes.ReadOnly)
            == System.IO.FileAttributes.ReadOnly));
stbProperties.Append("\r\n");

stbProperties.Append("System: ");
stbProperties.Append(
        Convert.ToBoolean((fileAttributes & System.IO.FileAttributes.System)
            == System.IO.FileAttributes.System));
stbProperties.Append("\r\n");

stbProperties.Append("Temporary File: ");
stbProperties.Append(
        Convert.ToBoolean((fileAttributes &
System.IO.FileAttributes.Temporary)
            == System.IO.FileAttributes.Temporary));
```

```
stbProperties.Append("\r\n");

stbProperties.Append("Archive: ");
stbProperties.Append(
    Convert.ToBoolean((fileAttributes & System.IO.FileAttributes.Archive)
        == System.IO.FileAttributes.Archive));
MessageBox.Show(stbProperties.ToString());
```

The first thing this procedure does is see whether the user is viewing a file. We look at the File Open Dialog control for this—because that is where we got the filename from the user. If the Open File Dialog control has no filename, the user hasn't viewed a file yet.

All the various properties of the file are appended to the `StringBuilder` variable `stbProperties`. The `"\r\n"` denotes a carriage return and a linefeed, and appending this into the string ensures that each property appears on its own line.

The first statement declares an empty `StringBuilder` variable called `stbProperties`. The `StringBuilder` object was designed for optimizing string concatenation and essentially just used to add strings together. You're using the append method of the `StringBuilder` class to create the file properties text (each append adds new text to the existing string). The second set of statements call the `GetCreateTime()`, `GetLastAccessTime()`, and `GetLastWriteTime()` methods to get the values of the date-related properties. These methods are self-explanatory. Next, the attributes are retrieved using the `GetAttributes()` method and the FileAttributes enumeration. The `Convert.ToBoolean()` method is used when concatenating each attribute in the final result string so that the words True and False appear.

Press F5 to run the project, open a picture file to display it, and then click the Get File Attributes button on the toolbar. If you entered the code exactly as shown, the attributes of the image file should appear in the text box as they do in Figure 19.5.

Manipulating Directories with the Directory Object

Manipulating directories (folders) is similar to manipulating files. However, instead of using `System.IO.File`, you use `System.IO.Directory`. If any of these method calls confuse you, refer to the previous section on `System.IO.File` for more detailed information. The following are the method calls:

▶ To create a directory, call the `CreateDirectory()` method of `System.IO.Directory` and pass the name of the new folder, like this:

```
System.IO.Directory.CreateDirectory(@"c:\my new directory");
```

FIGURE 19.5
The System.IO.File object enables you to look at the properties of a file.

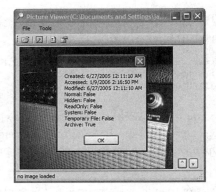

▶ To determine whether a directory exists, call the Exists() method of System.IO.Directory and pass it the directory name in question, like this:

```
MessageBox.Show(Convert.ToString(System.IO.Directory.Exists(@"c:\temp")));
```

▶ To move a directory, call the Move() method of System.IO.Directory. The Move() method takes two arguments. The first is the current name of the directory, and the second is the new name and path of the directory. When you move a directory, the contents of it are moved as well. Note that the current directory and new directory must have identical roots—that is they must be on the same drive. The following illustrates a call to Move():

```
System.IO.Directory.Move(@"c:\current directory name",
    @"d:\new directory name");
```

▶ Deleting directories is even more perilous than deleting files because when you delete a directory, you also delete all files and subdirectories within the directory. To delete a directory, call the Delete() method of System.IO.Directory and pass it the directory to delete as well as true for the second parameter, which indicates a recursive delete. *I can't overstate that you have to be careful when calling this method*; it can you get you in a lot of trouble. The following statement illustrates deleting a directory:

```
System.IO.Directory.Delete(@"c:\temp", true);
```

Summary

The Open File Dialog and Save File Dialog controls, coupled with System.IO, enable you to do many powerful things with a user's file system. In this hour, you learned how to let a user browse and select a file for opening and how to let a user browse and select a file for saving. Determining a user's file selection is only the first part of the process, however. You also learned how to manipulate files and directories, including renaming, moving, and deleting, by using System.IO. Finally, you learned how to retrieve the properties and attributes of a file.

With the techniques shown in this hour, you should be able to do most of what you'll need to do with files and directories. None of this material is difficult, but don't be fooled by the simplicity; use care whenever manipulating a user's file system.

Q&A

Q. *What if I want to perform an operation on a file, but something is preventing the operation, such as the file might be open or I don't have rights to the file?*

A. All the method calls have one or more exceptions that can be thrown in the event that the method fails. These method calls are listed in the online help. You can use the techniques discussed in Hour 15 to trap the exceptions.

Q. *What if a user types a filename into one of the file dialog boxes, but the user doesn't include the extension?*

A. By default, both file dialog controls have their AddExtension properties set to true. When this property is set to true, Visual C# automatically appends the extension of the currently selected filter.

Workshop

Quiz

1. True or False: The Open File dialog box automatically opens a file.

2. What symbol is used to separate a filter description from its extension?

3. What Namespace is used to manipulate files?

4. What arguments are expected by System.IO.File.Copy()?

5. How would you rename a file?

6. True or False: Files deleted with System.IO.File.Delete() are sent to the Recycle Bin.

7. What object is used to manipulate folders?

Answers

1. False

2. The Pipe symbol (|)

3. System.IO

4. The name and path of the source file and a name and path for the copy.

5. Use the Move() method while retaining the path.

6. False. The files are permanently deleted.

7. System.IO.Directory

Exercises

1. Create a project that enables a user to select a file with the Open Dialog control. Store the filename in a text box. Provide another button that, when clicked, creates a backup of the file by making a copy of it with the extension .bak.

2. Create a project with a text box on a form in which the user can type in a three-digit file extension. Include a button that shows an Open File dialog box when clicked, with the filter set to the extension entered by the user.

HOUR 20

Working with Text Files and the Registry

What You'll Learn in This Hour:

▶ Using the `Registry` object to create and delete Registry keys and values
▶ Using a `StreamWriter` object to open, read, and edit text files
▶ Modifying your Picture Viewer program to use a text file and the Registry

Text files have been around since the early days of computing, and even today they are a useful method of storing data. For robust applications, a database is the way to go, but for storing simple sets of data, it doesn't get much easier than using a text file.

In the first edition of this book, I neglected to cover working with text files thinking that most users were moving to databases. After many emails from readers, I got the point: Text files are still used regularly, and they aren't going anywhere. This chapter teaches you the basics of creating, opening, reading, and editing text files.

 By the Way

Another common method of storing data—particularly user settings and program configuration options, is the Windows Registry. The Registry is a database-like storage entity in Windows that resembles a tree with nodes. Accessing the Registry is fast, handled through a consistent interface, and is often preferred over the old method of using INI text files. In this chapter, you'll learn how to store data in and get data from the Windows Registry.

Working with the Registry

The Windows Registry is a repository used to store application, user, and machine-specific information. It's the perfect place to store configuration data such as user preferences, database connection strings, file locations, and more. Before you start mucking with the Registry, however, you must first be aware that changes to the Registry can cripple an application or even cause Windows to crash! Be sure to know what you are changing and the ramifications of the change before modifying the Windows Registry.

Don't pollute the Registry! I'm constantly amazed by the amount of junk that a program will store in the Registry. Keep in mind that the Registry is not your personal database. In fact, if your application uses a database, it's often a better idea to store information in the database itself.

Understanding the Structure of the Windows Registry

The Registry is organized in a hierarchical structure—like a tree. The top nodes in the tree (called *hives*) are predefined—you can't add to, modify, or delete them. Table 20.1 lists the hives (top levels) of the Registry.

Table 20.1 Top Nodes of the Windows Registry

Node	Description
HKEY_CURRENT_USER	Contains configuration information for the user currently logged on to Windows.
HKEY_USERS	Contains all user profiles on the computer. When a user logs in, HKEY_CURRENT_USER is set as an alias to a specific user in HKEY_USERS.
HKEY_LOCAL_MACHINE	Contains configuration information specific to the computer, regardless of the user logged in.
HKEY_CLASSES_ROOT	Contains information that associates file types with programs and configuration data for COM components.
HKEY_CURRENT_CONFIG	Contains information about the hardware profile used by the local computer during startup.

Under each hive listed in Table 20.1 are a number of keys. Figure 20.1 shows what the Registry looks like on my computer. Notice how Printers is a key that belongs to the HKEY_CURRENT_USER hive.

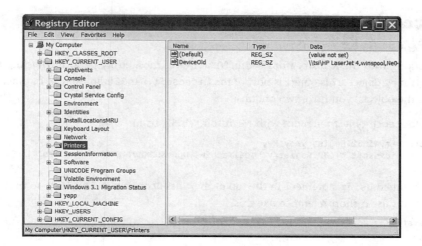

FIGURE 20.1
The Registry is
a hierarchical
structure of
hives, keys, and
values.

Keys can contain one or more values. In Figure 20.1, notice that the Printers key
has two values (they appear in the list view on the right). Keys are used to provide a
framework for storing data; values actually hold the data in question. Value items
have specific data types, though they are different from the data types in Visual C#.
Table 20.2 lists the possible data types for Registry values.

Table 20.2   Common Registry Value Data Types

Data Type	Used For
REG_SZ	This is the primary type of string data. It is used to store fixed-length string data or other short text values.
REG_EXPAND_SZ	This is an expandable string value that can hold system variables whose values get resolved at runtime.
REG_MULTI_SZ	This holds multiple text strings formatted as an array. Each "element" string is terminated by a null character.
REG_BINARY	Used to store binary data.

By far, the most commonly used data type is the REG_SZ string data type. You can
store all sorts of things in a REG_SZ value, such as text (obviously), "True", "False",
"0", "1", and more. In fact, this is usually the only data type I use for my applications. When saving Boolean values, I just format them as either "1" or "0".

Accessing the Registry with `Registry` and `RegistryKey`

Working with the Registry from within Visual C# is most easily performed using the `Registry` object. This object is part of the `Microsoft.Win32` namespace. In order to use the objects, you have two options:

Preface each object reference with Microsoft.Win32, as in:

```
Microsoft.Win32.RegistryKey key =
    Microsoft.Win32.Registry.LocalMachine.OpenSubKey("Software", true);
```

Or create a using statement in the top of the class accessing the Registry, so that you can use a short reference like this:

```
RegistryKey key = Registry.LocalMachine.OpenSubKey("Software", true);
```

You have created a using statement in the past. To do so, you find the existing using statements at the top of the class, and add the following using statement below them:

```
using Microsoft.Win32;
```

You will be doing this in the example that you build in this hour.

Creating Registry Keys

The `Registry` object has a number of properties. Among these are object properties that relate to the hives of the Registry shown in Table 20.1. Table 20.3 lists the properties that reference the Registry's hives.

Table 20.3   Common Top Node Properties of the `Registry` Object

Property	Used To Access
ClassesRoot	HKEY_CLASSES_ROOT
CurrentConfig	HKEY_CURRENT_CONFIG
CurrentUser	HKEY_CURRENT_USER
LocalMachine	HKEY_LOCAL_MACHINE
Users	HKEY_USERS

Creating Registry keys using `Registry` is a snap. First, you have to identify the hive under which you want to create the key. When you know the hive, you just call the `CreateSubKey()` method of the corresponding hive object property, passing it the name of the key to create. For example, consider this statement:

```
Registry.CurrentUser.CreateSubKey("UserSettings");
```

This statement would create the Key UserSettings under HKEY_CURRENT_USER. Now, you have to realize that an application rarely creates a key directly under a hive. There are many subkeys you can use for each hive, but perhaps the most common is the \Software key. Most applications create a corporate-named key under \Software and then create product keys below the corporate subkey. For example, suppose that your company name is CleverSoftware, you're going to ship the Picture Viewer program, and you want to store some application settings in the Registry (in fact, you will modify your Picture Viewer to do this later in this hour). You want to end up with a key structure that looks like this:

```
HKEY_CURRENT_USER\Software\CleverSoftware\PictureViewer
```

Fortunately, the CreateSubKey() method allows you to specify multiple levels of keys in one method call. To create this structure, you would use the following statement:

```
Registry.CurrentUser.CreateSubKey(@"Software\CleverSoftware\PictureViewer");
```

By the Way

> Remember, Visual C# treats the slash character \ in a string as an escape character. By prefacing the string with the @ symbol, you tell Visual C# to use the string as a literal value.

Visual C# would parse out this statement by first locating the hive HKEY_CURRENT_USER and then looking for a \Software key. It would find one, because all Windows machines have this key, but it would not overwrite this key. It would then look for CleverSoftware. Assuming that it did not find this key, it would create it and the subkey that you specified. Note that if Visual C# finds an existing subkey that you defined in your statement (all subkeys are separated by a slash \), it will not overwrite it.

By the Way

> Why HKEY_CURRENT_USER instead of HKEY_LOCAL_MACHINE? In general, it's best to save application settings in HKEY_CURRENT_USER so that each user who uses of your application can have his or her own settings. If you store your settings in HKEY_LOCAL_MACHINE, the settings will be global to all users who run the application from the computer in question. Also, some administrators restrict access to HKEY_LOCAL_MACHINE, and your application will fail if it attempts to access restricted keys.

Deleting Registry Keys

You can use two methods to delete a Registry key: DeleteSubKey() and DeleteSubKeyTree(). DeleteSubKey(),deletes a key and all its values *as long as the key contains no subkeys.* DeleteSubKeyTree(),deletes a key, its values, and all subkeys and values found below it. Use this one with care!

Here's a statement that could be used to delete the subkey created with the previous sample:

```
Registry.CurrentUser.DeleteSubKey(@"Software\CleverSoftware\PictureViewer");
```

> DeleteSubKey()throws an exception if the key you specify does not exist. Whenever writing code to work with the Registry, try to account for the unexpected.

Getting and Setting Key Values

Creating and deleting keys is useful, but only in the sense that keys provide the structure for the important items: the value items. You've already learned that keys can have one or more value items and that value items are defined as a specific data type. All that's left is to learn the code used to manipulate Registry values.

Unfortunately, getting and setting key values isn't as easy as defining keys. When defining keys, the Registry object makes it easy to work with hives by giving you an object property for each hive. To create a new value item, or to set the value of an existing value item, you use Registry.SetValue(). The SetValue() method has the following basic syntax:

```
SetValue(keypath, itemname, value)
```

Unfortunately, you have to specify the hive name in *keypath*, as you will see. Notice that you do not specify the data type; Visual C# sets the data type according to the *value* that is passed to the method. For example, to create a RegistrationName value item for the Registry key discussed in the previous section, you would use a statement like this:

```
Registry.SetValue(@"HKEY_CURRENT_USER\Software\CleverSoftware\PictureViewer\",
                  "RegistrationName", "James");
```

This statement would produce a value item as shown in Figure 20.2.

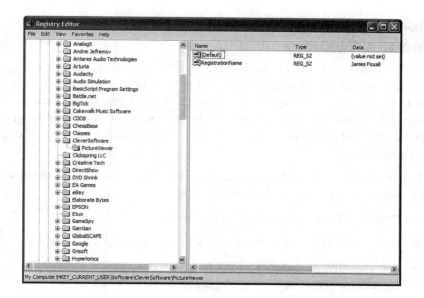

FIGURE 20.2
Values appear
attached to
keys.

To change the value, you would call SetValue() again, passing it the same key and item name, but a different value—nice and easy!

To retrieve a value from the Registry, you use the GetValue() method. This method also requires a full hive/key path. The basic format of GetValue() is this:

```
GetValue(keypath, itemname, defaultvalue)
```

The parameters *keypath* and *itemname* are the same as used with SetValue(). Sometimes, when you go to retrieve a value from the Registry, the value and perhaps even the key won't exist. There are a number of reasons for this—another application might have deleted the value, the user might have manually deleted the value, or the user might have restored a backup of her Registry from before the value was created. The *defaultvalue* parameter is used to define what GetValue() returns if it is unable to find the value item. This eliminates the need to catch an exception in the event that the value item is missing. The following statements display the value in the RegistrationName as created in the previous example:

```
string strRegName;
strRegName = Convert.ToString(

Registry.GetValue(@"HKEY_CURRENT_USER\Software\CleverSoftware\PictureViewer\",
    "RegistrationName", ""));
MessageBox.Show(strRegName);
```

Modifying Your Picture Viewer Project to Use the Registry

In this section, you're going to modify your Picture Viewer project so that the user's settings on the Options dialog box are saved to the Registry. When the user first starts the Picture Viewer program, the settings are loaded from the Registry. Start by opening the Picture Viewer project you last worked on in Hour 19, "Performing File Operations," and then double-click frmOptions.cs in the Solution Explorer to display the Options form.

Follow these steps to create the using statement so that you don't have to preface every Registry instance with Microsoft.Win32:

1. Double-click the form to access its Load event.

2. Scroll to the top of the class and locate the existing using statements.

3. Add the following statement below the existing using statements:

   ```
   using Microsoft.Win32;
   ```

Displaying Options from the Registry

The first thing you need to do is show the current user's settings when the Options form displays. Follow these steps to display the options stored in the Registry:

1. Scroll down and locate the frmOptions_Load procedure.

2. Add the following code statements to the Load event:

   ```
   txtUserName.Text = Convert.ToString(Registry.GetValue(
       @"HKEY_CURRENT_USER\Software\CleverSoftware\PictureViewer\",
       "UserName", ""));

   chkPromptOnExit.Checked = Convert.ToBoolean(Registry.GetValue(
       @"HKEY_CURRENT_USER\Software\CleverSoftware\PictureViewer\",
       "PromptOnExit", "false"));

   if (Convert.ToString(Registry.GetValue(
       @"HKEY_CURRENT_USER\Software\CleverSoftware\PictureViewer\",
       "BackColor", "Gray")) == "Gray")
       optBackgroundDefault.Checked = true;
   else
       optBackgroundWhite.Checked = true;
   ```

All this code should be familiar to you by now. The first statement is used to set the value of the txtUserName text box to the user name stored in the Registry. The first time the Options form loads, there is no entry in the Registry, so an empty string is used. Notice that we wrapped the Registry call in Convert.ToString(), so that whatever value we pull from the Registry will be converted to a string, which is what a text box accepts.

The second statement sets the checked state of the Prompt on Exit check box to the value stored in the Registry. If no value is found, as is the case the first time the Options form is loaded, the `Checked` property is set to `false`. Once again, you had to wrap the result of `GetValue()` with a conversion function—in this case, `Convert.ToBoolean()`—to convert the value to a boolean.

The next statement starts an `if...else` construct that looks for a color name in the Registry and sets the appropriate option button's `Checked` property to `true`. Because we're comparing the Registry result to text, we wrap the result in `Convert.ToString()` to cast the result as a string.

Saving Options to the Registry

Now that the Options form displays the current values stored in the Registry, you can add the code to save the changes the user makes to these values. Follow these steps:

1. Use the scroll bar to locate the `btnOK_Click` procedure.

2. Enter the following code into the `btnOK_Click` event. Be sure to put the code *in front of* the existing statement `this.Close()`:

```
Registry.SetValue(
        @"HKEY_CURRENT_USER\Software\CleverSoftware\PictureViewer\",
        "UserName", txtUserName.Text);

Registry.SetValue(
        @"HKEY_CURRENT_USER\Software\CleverSoftware\PictureViewer\",
        "PromptOnExit", chkPromptOnExit.Checked);

if (optBackgroundDefault.Checked)
    Registry.SetValue(
            @"HKEY_CURRENT_USER\Software\CleverSoftware\PictureViewer\",
            "BackColor", "Gray");
else
    Registry.SetValue(
            @"HKEY_CURRENT_USER\Software\CleverSoftware\PictureViewer\",
            "BackColor", "White");
```

This code is essentially the opposite of the code you entered in the Load event; it stores the values from the controls into the Registry. You should be able to follow this code on your own.

Using the Options Stored in the Registry

You're now allowing the user to view and change the settings stored in the Registry, but you're not actually using the user's preferences. Follow these steps to use the values stored in the Registry:

1. Double-click frmViewer.cs in the Solution Explorer window to display the main Picture Viewer form in the designer.

2. Double-click the form to access its Load event.

3. Scroll to the top of the procedure and add the following statement to the end of the using block:

```
using Microsoft.Win32;
```

4. Scroll down to the frmViewer.Load event. This event currently contains six lines of code. The first statements we are interested in are the following:

```
m_blnPromptOnExit = c_defPromptOnExit;
mnuConfirmOnExit.Checked = m_blnPromptOnExit;
```

Recall that we keep track of the Prompt On Exit flag as a module variable. The first statement sets this flag to the constant you defined as the default value. The second statement sets the checked state of the menu item to the variable.

5. Delete the statement m_blnPromptOnExit = c_defPromptOnExit; and replace it with this:

```
m_blnPromptOnExit = Convert.ToBoolean(Registry.GetValue(
    @"HKEY_CURRENT_USER\Software\CleverSoftware\PictureViewer\",
    "PromptOnExit", "false"));
```

This is almost identical to the statement you created on the Load event of the Options form. It retrieves the Prompt on Exit flag from the Registry, but this time it sets the module variable instead of a check box on the form.

6. The next statement you're going to replace is this:

```
m_objPictureBackColor = System.Drawing.SystemColors.Control;
```

This sets the default back color of the picture box to the system color Control, which by default is a shade of gray. Replace this statement with the following code:

```
if (Convert.ToString(Registry.GetValue(
    @"HKEY_CURRENT_USER\Software\CleverSoftware\PictureViewer\",
    "BackColor", "Gray")) == "Gray")
  m_objPictureBackColor = System.Drawing.SystemColors.Control;
else
    m_objPictureBackColor = System.Drawing.Color.White;
```

Testing and Debugging Your Picture Viewer Project

Press F5 to run the project. Next, click the Options button on the toolbar to display the Options form. Nothing looks different yet. Follow these steps to see the effect of your new code:

1. In the User Name text box, enter your name.

2. Click the Prompt to Confirm Exit check box to check it.

3. Click the Appearance tab and then click the White option button to select it.

4. Click OK to close the Options dialog box.

5. Click the Options button on the toolbar again to display the Options dialog box. Click the Appearance tab if it's not the current tab and notice that White is now chosen as the Default Picture Background color.

6. Click the General tab and notice that your name is in the User Name text box and that the Prompt to Confirm on Exit check box is selected.

7. Click OK to close the Options dialog box.

8. Close the Picture Viewer.

Notice that you weren't prompted to confirm exiting. This occurs because the main Picture Viewer form is not being updated to reflect the changes made to the Registry. You're now going to use the skills you learned for creating procedures to make your code work properly. Follow these steps:

1. Double-click frmViewer.cs in the Solution Explorer window to show the form in the designer.

2. Double-click the form to show its Load event.

3. Highlight all the code except the first two statements (see Figure 20.3), and press Ctrl+XC to cut the code.

4. Enter the following statement:

   `LoadDefaults();`

5. Position the cursor at the end of the closing brace that completes the definition of the `frmViewer_Load` event and press Enter to create a new line.

6. Type the following statements and press Enter:

   ```
   private void LoadDefaults()
   {
   ```

FIGURE 20.3
Cut the high-
lighted code.

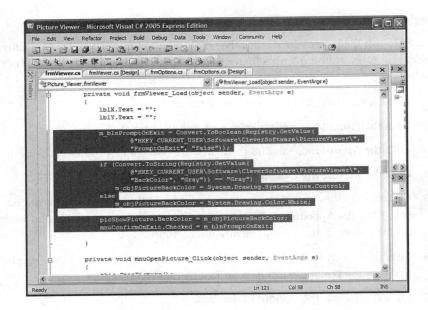

FIGURE 20.3
Cut the high-
lighted code.

7. Press Ctrl+V to paste the code you deleted from the Form_Load event.

8. Enter the following and press Enter:

   }

9. Your code window should look like that in Figure 20.4.

   You now have a procedure that you can call when the user saves new settings to the Registry.

10. Scroll to the procedure mnuOptions_Click() and enter the following statement *after* the current two statements:

    LoadDefaults();

11. Scroll to the procedure tbbOptions_Click() and enter the following statement *after* the current two statements:

    LoadDefaults();

12. Press F5 once again to run the project.

13. Click the Options button on the toolbar to display the Options form and change the default background color to White on the Appearance tab. When you click OK to save the settings and close the Options form, the background of the picture box changes to white immediately.

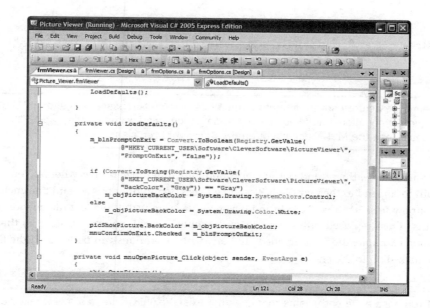

FIGURE 20.4
Procedures are
all about group-
ing related sets
of code.

The Registry is a powerful tool to have at your disposal—if used properly! In this section, you learned all the necessary techniques to implement Registry functionality in
your applications.

Reading and Writing Text Files

The Registry is a handy place to store user options and program configuration settings. It's not a good place, however, to store a lot of data such as a text document.
If you have a lot of text data to store and retrieve, a good old-fashioned text file is
probably the best place to put it (assuming that a real database such as Microsoft
SQL is not an option). Visual C# includes classes that makes it relatively easy to
manipulate text files: StreamWriter and StreamReader. Notice that reading and
writing text files are performed by two different objects, only one of which can
access a file at any given time. If you want to simultaneously read and write to a
single file, you're probably best off to use a real database.

Writing to a Text File

Writing to text files is done using the StreamWriter class. The first step to using this
class is to declare an object of type StreamWriter, like this:

```
System.IO.StreamWriter objFile = new System.IO.StreamWriter(@"C:\test.txt");
```

Or like this:

```
System.IO.StreamWriter objFile = new System.IO.StreamWriter(@"C:\test.txt",
true);
```

> There are actually seven different forms of StreamWriter usage. I'm showing you the most common, but if you're going to do serious work with text files, you should read the MSDN document on the StreamWriter class.

As you can see, the second parameter is optional, and it determines whether you want to append to the text file if it already exists. If you omit this second parameter, or supply false as its value, a brand-new text file is created. If the text file already exists, it gets replaced with a new file of the same name. If you pass true, as in the second example, the file is opened, and any write operations you perform on the file are tacked on to the end of the file.

> If you pass a file path/name that does not exist, Visual C# creates a new text file for you when you write data to the StreamWriter object.

After you have an object that points to a StreamWriter object, you can store data in the text file using one of the following two methods:

- ▶ WriteLine()   Sends a single line of text to the file and automatically appends a carriage return to the end of the line. Each call to WriteLine() creates a new line.

- ▶ Write()   Sends data to the file but does not automatically append a carriage return to create a new line.

These two methods are best understood by example. Consider the following code snippet:

```
System.IO.StreamWriter objFile = new System.IO.StreamWriter(@"C:\test.txt");
objFile.WriteLine("text1");
objFile.WriteLine("text2");
objFile.WriteLine("text3");
objFile.Close();
objFile.Dispose();
```

This snippet would produce the following data in the text file:

```
text1
text2
text3
```

> Notice the last statement: objFile.Close(). It's absolutely vital that you close a text file when you're finished with it, and the Close() method does this. In addition, you should also call objFile.Dispose() to make sure the file is fully released.

By the
Way

Now, consider the same code snippet that uses Write() instead of WriteLine():

```
System.IO.StreamWriter objFile = new System.IO.StreamWriter(@"C:\test.txt");
objFile.Write("text1");
objFile.Write("text2");
objFile.Write("text3");
objFile.Close();
objFile.Dispose();
```

This snippet produces a text file that contains the following:

```
text1text2text3
```

See how WriteLine() creates lines of data, while Write() simply streams the data into the file? This is an incredibly important distinction, and understanding the difference is crucial to your success writing text files. Which method you choose depends entirely on what you are trying to accomplish. I think perhaps that WriteLine() is the most common way. The following code illustrates how you could use WriteLine() to store a list of albums (assuming that you have the list in a list box titled lstAlbums):

```
System.IO.StreamWriter objFile = new System.IO.StreamWriter(@"C:\albums.txt");

for (int intCounter = 0; intCounter <= lstAlbums.Items.Count -1; intCounter++)
{
    objFile.WriteLine(Convert.ToString(lstAlbums.Items[intCounter]));
}

objFile.Close();
objFile.Dispose();
```

Reading a Text File

Reading a text file is handled by the StreamReader class, which behaves similarly to the StreamWriter class. First, you need to define an object of type StreamWriter, like this:

```
System.IO.StreamReader objFile = new System.IO.StreamReader(@"C:\test.txt");
```

A key difference in declaring a StreamReader object versus a StreamWriter object is how the code behaves if the file is not found. The StreamWriter object is happy to create a new text file for you if the specified file isn't found. If the StreamReader can't find the specified file, it will throw an exception—something you need to account for in your code.

Just as `StreamWriter` lets you write the data to the file in one of seven ways, `StreamReader` also has multiple ways to read the data. The first of the most common two ways is using the `ReadToEnd()` method, which reads the entire file and is used to place the contents of the file into a variable. You would use `ReadToEnd()` like this:

```
System.IO.StreamReader objFile = new System.IO.StreamReader(@"C:\test.txt");
string strContents;
strContents = objFile.ReadToEnd();
objFile.Close();
objFile.Dispose();
MessageBox.Show(strContents);
```

The `ReadtoEnd()` method can be handy, but sometimes you just want to get a single line of text at a time. For example, consider the text file created by the previous example, the one with a list of albums. Say that you wanted to read the text file and place all the albums found in the text file into a list box named lstAlbums. The `ReadToEnd()` method would allow you to get the data, but then you would have to find a way to parse each album name. The proper solution for reading one line at a time is to use the `ReadLine()` method. The following code shows how you could load the Albums.txt text file, one line at a time, and place each album name in a list box:

```
System.IO.StreamReader objFile = new System.IO.StreamReader(@"C:\albums.txt");
string strAlbumName;

strAlbumName = objFile.ReadLine();

while (strAlbumName != null)
{
    lstAlbums.Items.Add(strAlbumName);
    strAlbumName = objFile.ReadLine();
}
objFile.Close();
objFile.Dispose();
```

A couple of important concepts in this example need discussing. The first is how do you know when you've reached the end of a text file? The answer is that the return result will be `null`. So, the first thing this code does (after creating the `StreamReader` object and the `string` variable) is get the first line from the text file. It's possible that the text file could be empty, so the `while` loop tests for this. If the string is `null`, the file is empty, so the loop doesn't execute. If the string is not `null`, the loop begins. The first statement in the loop adds the string to the list box. The next statement gets the next line from the file. This sends execution back to the `while` statement, which again tests to see whether we're at the end of the file. One thing this code doesn't test for is a zero-length string (""). If there is a blank line in the text file, the string variable will hold a zero-length string. You might want to test for a situation like this when working with text files in your code.

That's it! Text files are not database files; you'll never get the power and flexibility from a text file that you would from a real database. With that said, text files are easy to work with and provide amazing and quick results within the context of their design.

Modifying Your Picture Viewer Project to Use a Text File

In this section, you're going to modify your Picture Viewer project to use a text file. What you'll be doing is have the Picture Viewer update a log (a text file) every time the user views a picture. You'll then create a simple dialog box that the user can open to view the log file. If you no longer have the Picture Viewer project open from earlier, open it now.

Creating the Picture Viewer Log File

In this section, you'll modify the Picture Viewer project to create the log file. Follow these steps to implement the log functionality:

1. Double-click frmViewer.cs in the Solution Explorer window to display the form in the designer.

2. Recall that you created a single procedure that is called from both the menu and the toolbar to open a picture. This makes it easier because you only have to add the log code in one place. Double-click the Open Picture button on the toolbar to access its Click event.

3. You now need to go to the OpenPicture() function. Here's an easy way to do this: Right-click the code this.OpenPicture(); and choose Go To Definition from the shortcut menu (see Figure 20.5). Whenever you do this to a procedure call, Visual C# displays the code of procedure being referenced.

4. Now, take a look at the OpenPicture() procedure. Where would you place the code to create a log file? Would you enter all of the log file code right into this procedure? First, the log file should be updated only when a picture is successfully loaded, which would be in the try block, right after the statement that updates the sbrMyStatusStrip control. Second, the log code should be isolated from this procedure, so all you are going to add is a single function call. Add this statement at the end of but still in the try block:

```
UpdateLog(ofdSelectPicture.FileName);
```

Your code should now look like Figure 20.6.

FIGURE 20.5
Go To Definition
is a quick way
to view a proce-
dure being
called in code.

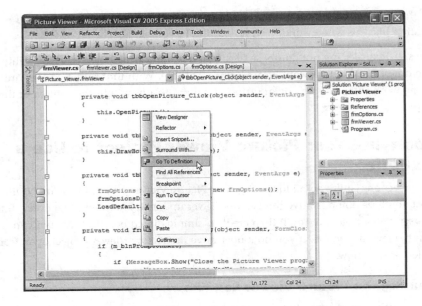

FIGURE 20.6
It's always a
good idea to
isolate code
into cohesive
procedures.

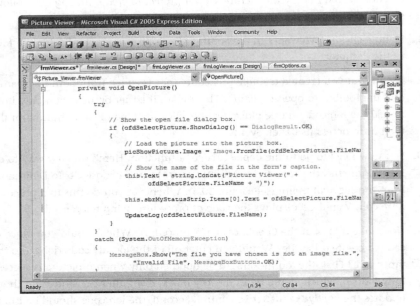

5. Now, position the cursor between the closing brace of OpenPicture() procedure and press Enter to create a new line and then enter the following procedure code:

```
private void UpdateLog(string strFileName)
{
    System.IO.StreamWriter objFile = new System.IO.StreamWriter(
        System.AppDomain.CurrentDomain.BaseDirectory +
        @"\PictureLog.txt", true);

    objFile.WriteLine(DateTime.Now + " " + strFileName);
    objFile.Close();
    objFile.Dispose();
}
```

Most of this code should be recognizable, but consider this snippet:

```
System.AppDomain.CurrentDomain.BaseDirectory + @"\PictureLog.txt"
```

The method `BaseDirectory()` returns the path of the running program. This is a great trick to know! What you've done here is append the filename PictureLog.txt to the application path, so that the log file is always created in the application path. This makes it easy for the user to find it. In a robust application, you might let the user specify a path, perhaps storing it in the Registry. For our purposes, the application path works just fine.

> When debugging an application in the Visual C# IDE, the application path might not be exactly what you expect. When you compile and test your application, Visual C# creates a `bin\Debug` folder under the folder containing your project. This is where it places the temporary .exe it creates for debugging, and this is your application path. If you go looking for the log file in your project folder, you won't find it. You need to drill down into the `\bin\Debug` folder to get it.

Displaying the Picture Viewer Log File

In this section, you'll modify the Picture Viewer project to include a dialog box that the user can display to view the log file. Follow these steps to implement the log viewer functionality:

1. Choose Project, Add Windows Form from the menu to display the Add New Item dialog box. Enter **frmLogViewer.cs** for the new form name and click Add to create the form.

2. Set the properties of the new form as follows:

Property	Value
Size	**520,344**
MaximizeBox	**False**
MinimizeBox	**False**
Text	**Picture Viewer History Log**

3. Add a new button to the form and set its properties as follows:

Property	Value
Name	**btnOK**
Anchor	**Bottom, Right**
Location	**425,275**
Text	**OK**

4. Add a new text box to the form and set its properties as follows:

Property	Value
Name	**txtLog**
Anchor	**Top, Bottom, Left, Right**
Multiline	**True**
Location	**12,12**
ReadOnly	**True**
Size	**488,257**

5. Double-click the OK button to access its Click event, and enter the following statement:

```
this.Close();
```

6. Add the code that actually displays the log. Double-click frmViewer.cs in the Solution Explorer and then double-click the form to access its Load event.

7. Enter the following code into the Form_Load event:

```
try
{
    System.IO.StreamReader objFile = new System.IO.StreamReader(
        System.AppDomain.CurrentDomain.BaseDirectory +
        @"\PictureLog.txt");
    txtLog.Text = objFile.ReadToEnd();
    objFile.Close();
    objFile.Dispose();
}
catch
    {
        txtLog.Text = "The log file could not be found.";
    }
```

This code is just like the code discussed earlier on reading text files. It uses ReadToEnd() to load the entire log into the text box. The whole thing is wrapped in a try block to handle the situation of there being no log file.

8. All that's left is to add a button to the toolbar of the Picture Viewer to display the log. Double-click frmViewer.cs in the Solution Explorer to display the form in the designer.

9. Click the toolstrip to select it, and then click the Items property in the Properties window.

10. Click the build button in the Items property in the Property window to access the Items Collection Editor and then create a new button on the toolbar. Set the new button's properties as follows:

Property	Value
Name	**tbbShowLog**
Image	**Log.ico** (found on my website)
Text	**View Picture Log**
ToolTipText	**View Picture Log**

11. Click OK to save the new button, and then double-click the new button on the toolbar and add the following code:

```
frmLogViewer objLog = new frmLogViewer();
objLog.ShowDialog();
```

Testing Your Picture Viewer Log

Save your project now and press F5 to run it. Follow these steps to test the project:

1. Click the View Picture Log button on the toolbar to display the Picture Viewer History Log. Notice that the text box displays *The log file could not be found.* This means the try block worked!

2. Click OK to close the Log Viewer form.

3. Click the Open Picture button on the toolbar, browse to a picture file, and display it.

4. Now, click the View Picture Log button again and notice that the log now displays a log entry (see Figure 20.7).

FIGURE 20.7
Text files make
creating logs
easy.

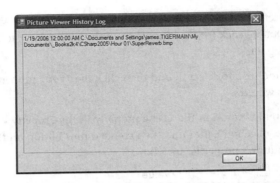

Summary

In this hour, you learned how to use the Registry to store and retrieve user settings.
You learned about the structure of the Registry and how to use hives, keys, and values. The Registry is a powerful tool, and you should use it when applicable.
Remember that the Registry isn't your personal repository; respect the Registry!
*Windows relies on certain data in the Registry, and if you mess up the Registry, you can
actually prevent a computer from booting to Windows.* As you were able to see first hand
with the Picture Viewer project, saving data to and retrieving data from the Registry
is relatively easy, but how you handle the data is the real trick.

Next, you learned about the power (and limitations) of working with text files. You
can read and write text files, but you can't do both to a single text file at the same
time. If you need that functionality, a database is the way to go. However, you
learned that it's relatively easy to store and retrieve sequential information in a text
file—a log file, for example. Finally, you were able to utilize what you learned to .
implement log functionality for the Picture Viewer project.

Q&A

Q. Can I use a text file to save configuration information?

A. Yes, you could do that. You would need some way to denote the data element.
For example, how would you know that the first line was the BackColor setting, as opposed to a default file path, for example? One method would be to
append the data element to a caption, as in `BackColor=White`. You would then
have to parse the data as you read it from the text file. The Registry is probably a better solution for something like this, but a text file could be useful if
you wanted to transfer settings to a different computer.

Q. *Can I store binary data instead of text to a file?*

A. Visual C# 2005 includes classes designed to work with binary files: `BinaryWriter` and `BinaryReader`. You would need to use objects based on these classes, instead of using `StreamWriter` and `StreamReader` objects.

Workshop

Quiz

1. Under what hive should you store a user's confirmation information in the Registry?

2. What is the full object/method used to create a key in the CURRENTUSER hive of the Registry?

3. What are the two methods used to delete a key from the Registry, and what is the difference between the two?

4. What classes do you use to write and read text files?

5. What method of the `StreamReader` class do you use to read the entire contents of a text file at once?

6. What happens if you attempt to open a file that doesn't exist with the `StreamReader` class?

Answers

1. You should store user configuration in the HKEY_CURRENT_USER hive.

2. `Microsoft.Win32.Registry.CurrentUser.CreateSubKey()`.

3. The method `DeleteSubKey()` deletes a key, but only if there are no subkeys for the specified key. The method `DeleteSubKeyTree()` deletes a key and any subkeys of the specified key.

4. The `StreamWriter` class is used to write to a text file, whereas the `StreamReader` class is used to read data from a text file.

5. The `ReadToEnd()` method.

6. An exception is thrown.

Exercises

1. Every toolbar item should have a corresponding menu item. Create a menu item on the Tools menu for displaying the log. While you're at it, create one for viewing the file properties to match the toolbar item you created in the previous hour.

2. Create a button on the Log Viewer form called btnClearLog. Change the text of the button to **Clear**. When the user clicks the button, delete the log file from the hard drive and close the Log Viewer form.

HOUR 21

Working with a Database

What You'll Learn in This Hour:

- ▶ Introduction to ADO.NET
- ▶ Connecting to a database
- ▶ Understanding DataTables
- ▶ Creating a DataAdapter
- ▶ Referencing fields in a DataRow
- ▶ Navigating records
- ▶ Adding, editing, and deleting records
- ▶ Building an ADO.NET example

You've heard it so many times that it's almost a cliché: This is the Information Age. Information is data, and managing information means working with databases. Database design is a skill unto itself, and entire books are devoted to database design and management. In this hour, you'll learn the basics of working with a database using ADO.NET, Microsoft's newest database technology. Although high-end solutions are built around advanced database technologies such as Microsoft's SQL Server, the Microsoft Jet database used by Microsoft Access is more readily available and easier to learn, so you'll build working examples that use a Jet database. Be aware, however, that 99% of what you learn here is directly applicable to working with SQL Server as well.

> You'll learn a lot in this hour, but realize that this material is really the tip of the iceberg. Database programming can be, and often is, complex. This hour is intended to get you writing database code as quickly as possible, but if you plan to do a lot of database programming, you'll want to consult a dedicated book (or two) on the subject.

By the Way

Begin by creating a new Windows Application named **Database Example**. Next right-click Form1.cs in the Solution Explorer window, choose Rename, and then change the name of the default form to **frmMain.cs**. Next, set the form's Text property to **Database Example**.

Now that the project has been created, follow the steps in the following sections to build your database project.

Introducing ADO.NET

ADO.NET is the .NET platform's new database technology, and it builds on ADO (Active Data Objects). ADO.NET provides DataSet and DataTable objects that are optimized for moving disconnected sets of data across the Internet and intranets, including through firewalls. At the same time, ADO.NET includes the traditional connection and command objects, as well as an object called a DataReader, (which resembles a forward-only, read-only ADO RecordSet, in case you're familiar with ADO). Together, these objects provide the best performance and throughput for retrieving data from a database.

In short, you'll learn about the following objects as you progress through this hour:

▶ OleDBConnection   Used to establish a connection to an OLEDB data source.

▶ SqlConnection   Used to establish a connection to a SQL Server data source.

▶ DataSet   A memory-resident representation of data. There are many ways of working with a DataSet, such as through DataTables.

▶ DataTable   Holds a resultset of data for manipulation and navigation.

▶ DataAdapter   Used to populate a DataReader.

Connecting to a Database

To access data in a database, you must first establish a connection using an ADO.NET connection object. There are multiple connection objects included in the .NET Framework, such as the OleDbConnection object (for working with the same OLE DB data providers you would access through traditional ADO) and the SqlConnection object (for optimized access to Microsoft SQL Server). Because these examples connect to the Microsoft Jet Database, you'll be using the OleDbConnection object. To create an object variable of type OleDbConnection and initialize the variable to a new connection, you could use a statement like this:

```
OleDbConnection cnADONetConnection = new OleDbConnection();
```

To use ADO.NET, the first step that you need to take is to add the proper Namespace to your project. Double-click the form now to access its events. Scroll to the top of the class and add the following using statement on the line below the other using statements:

```
using System.Data.OleDb;
```

You're going to create a module-level variable to hold the connection, so place the cursor below the left bracket ({) that follows the statement public partial class frmMain : Form and press Enter to create a new line. Enter the following statement:

```
OleDbConnection m_cnADONetConnection = new OleDbConnection();
```

Before using this connection, you must specify the data source to which you want to connect. This is done through the ConnectionString property of the ADO.NET connection object. The ConnectionString contains connection information such as the name of the provider, username, and password. The ConnectionString might contain many connection parameters; the set of parameters available varies depending on the source of data that you're connecting to. Table 21.1 lists some of the parameters used in the OLE DB ConnectionString. If you specify multiple parameters, separate them with a semicolon.

Table 21.1 Common Parameters for ConnectionString

Parameter	Description
Provider	The name of the data provider (Jet, SQL, and so on) to use.
Data Source	The name of the data source (database) to connect to. The type of data is determined by the provider.
User ID	A valid username to use when connecting to the data source.
Password	A password to use when connecting to the data source.
DRIVER	The name of the database driver to use. This isn't required if a DSN is specified.
SERVER	The network name of the data source server.

The Provider= parameter is one of the most important at this point and is governed by the type of database you're accessing. For example, when accessing a SQL Server database, you specify the provider information for SQL Server, and when accessing a Jet database, you specify the provider for Jet. In this example, you'll be accessing a Jet (Microsoft Access) database, so you'll use the provider information for Jet.

In addition to specifying the provider, you're also going to specify the database. I've provided a sample database at the Web site for this book. This code assumes that you've placed the database in a folder called C:\Temp. If you're using a different folder, you'll need to change the code accordingly. Follow these steps:

1. Specify the ConnectionString property of your ADO.NET connection now by placing the following statement in the Load event of your form:

   ```
   m_cnADONetConnection.ConnectionString =
       @"Provider=Microsoft.Jet.OLEDB.4.0;Data Source=C:\temp\contacts.mdb";
   ```

2. After the connection string is defined, a connection to a data source is established by using the Open() method of the connection object. Add the following statement to the Load event, right after the statement that sets the connection string:

   ```
   m_cnADONetConnection.Open();
   ```

> Refer to the online documentation for information on the connection strings for providers other than Jet.

When you attach to an unsecured Jet database it isn't necessary to provide a username and password. When attaching to a secured Jet database, however, you must to provide a username and a password. This is done by passing the username and password as parameters in the ConnectionString property. The sample database I've provided isn't secured, so it isn't necessary to provide a username and password.

Closing a Connection to a Data Source

You should always *explicitly* close a connection to a data source. That means you shouldn't rely on a variable going out of scope to close a connection. Instead, you should force an explicit disconnect via code. This is accomplished by calling the Close() method of the connection object.

You're now going to write code to explicitly close the connection when the form is closed. Follow these steps:

1. Start by clicking the frmMain.cs [Design] tab to return to the form designer.

2. Click the Events button on the Properties window (the lightning bolt) to access the list of events for the form.

3. Double-click the FormClosing event to create a new event handler. Enter the following statements in the event:

   ```
   m_cnADONetConnection.Close();
   m_cnADONetConnection.Dispose();
   ```

Manipulating Data

The easiest way to manipulate data using ADO.NET is to create a `DataTable` object containing the resultset of a table, query, or stored procedure. Using a `DataTable` object, you can add, edit, delete, find, and navigate records. The following sections explain how to use `DataTables`.

Understanding `DataTables`

`DataTables` contain a snapshot of data in the data source. You generally start by filling a `DataTable`, manipulating its results, and finally sending the changes back to the data source. The `DataTable` is populated using the `Fill()` method of a `DataAdapter` object, and changes are sent back to the database using the `Update()` method of a `DataAdapter`. *Any changes made to the `DataTable` appear only in the local copy of the data until you call the Update method.* Having a local copy of the data reduces contention by preventing users from blocking others from reading the data while it's being viewed. If you're familiar with ADO, you'll note that this is similar to the Optimistic Batch Client Cursor in ADO.

Creating a `DataAdapter`

To populate a `DataTable`, you must create a `DataAdapter`. The `DataAdapter` you're going to create uses the connection you've already defined to connect to the data source and then executes a query you'll provide. The results of that query will be pushed into a `DataTable`.

As I mentioned earlier, there are multiple connection objects in the .NET Framework. There are multiple ADO.NET `DataAdapter` objects as well. You'll be using the `OleDbDataAdapter` because you will be connecting to Microsoft Access database.

The constructor for a `DataAdapter` optionally takes the command to execute when filling a `DataTable` or `DataSet`, as well as a connection specifying the data source (you could have multiple connections open in a single project). This constructor has the following syntax:

```
OleDbDataAdapter cnADONetAdapter = new
    OleDbDataAdapter([CommandText],[Connection]);
```

To add a `DataAdapter` to your project, follow these steps:

1. Add the following statement immediately below the statement you entered to declare the m_cnADONewConnection object (in the class header, not in the Load event) to create a module-level variable:

   ```
   OleDbDataAdapter m_daDataAdapter;
   ```

2. Add the following statement at the bottom of the Load event of the form (immediately following the statement that opens the connection):

```
m_daDataAdapter =
new OleDbDataAdapter("Select * From Contacts",m_cnADONetConnection);
```

Because you're going to use the DataAdapter to update the original data source, you must specify the insert, update, and delete statements to use to submit changes from the DataTable to the data source. ADO.NET lets you customize how updates are submitted by enabling you to manually specify these statements as database commands or stored procedures. In this case, you're going to have ADO.NET automatically generate these statements for you by creating a CommandBuilder object.

3. Enter this statement in the class header (with the other two variable declarations) to create the CommandBuilder module-level variable:

```
OleDbCommandBuilder m_cbCommandBuilder;
```

The CommandBuilder is an interesting object in that after you initialize it, you no longer work with it directly: It works behind the scenes to handle the updating, inserting, and deleting of data. To make this work, you have to attach the CommandBuilder to a DataAdapter. You do so by passing a DataAdapter to the CommandBuilder. The CommandBuilder then registers for update events on the DataAdapter and provides the insert, update, and delete commands as needed.

4. Add the following statement to the end of the Load event to initialize the CommandBuilder object:

```
OleDbCommandBuilder m_cbCommandBuilder =
        new OleDbCommandBuilder(m_daDataAdapter);
```

When using a Jet database, the CommandBuilder object can create the dynamic SQL code only if the table in question has a primary key defined.

Your code should now look like Figure 21.1 (notice that I collapsed the public frmMain procedure to make more code visible in the figure).

Creating and Populating DataTables

You're going to create a module-level DataTable in your project. Follow these steps:

1. Create the DataTable variable by adding the following statement on the class header to create another module-level variable:

```
DataTable m_dtContacts = new DataTable();
```

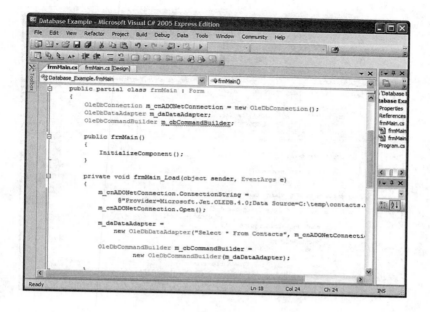

FIGURE 21.1
You will be
jumping around
a lot in this
example. Be
sure to follow
the steps
exactly!

2. You're going to use an integer variable to keep track of the user's current position (row) within the DataTable. To do this, add the following statement immediately below the statement you just entered to declare the new DataTable object:

```
int m_rowPosition = 0;
```

3. You now have a DataAdapter that allows access to a data source via the connection. You've declared a DataTable that will hold a reference to data. Next, add the following statement to the Load event of the form, after the existing code, to fill the DataTable with data:

```
m_daDataAdapter.Fill(m_dtContacts);
```

Because the DataTable doesn't hold a connection to the data source, it isn't necessary to close it when you're finished. Your class should now look like the one in Figure 21.2.

Referencing Fields in a DataRow

DataTables contain a collection of DataRows. To access a row within the DataTable, you specify the ordinal (index) of that DataRow. For example, you could access the first row of your DataTable like this:

```
DataRow m_rwContact = m_dtContacts.Rows[0];
```

FIGURE 21.2
This code accesses a database and creates a DataTable that can be used anywhere in the class.

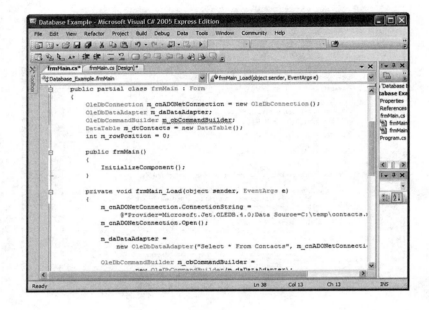

Data elements in a DataRow are called *columns*. In the Contacts table I've created, for example, there are two columns: ContactName and State. To reference the value of a column, you can pass the column name to the DataRow like this:

```
// Change the value of the column.
m_rwContact["ContactName"] = "Bob Brown";
```

or

```
// Get the value of the column.
strContactName = m_rwContact("ContactName");
```

By the Way

> If you spell a column name incorrectly, an exception occurs when the statement executes at runtime; no errors are raised at compile time.

You're now going to create a procedure that's used to display the current record in the data table. Follow these steps:

1. Position the cursor *after* the right bracket that ends the frmMain_FormClosing event and press Enter a few times to create some blank lines.

2. Enter the following procedure in its entirety:
   ```
   private void ShowCurrentRecord()
   {
       if (m_dtContacts.Rows.Count==0)
   ```

```
    {
        txtContactName.Text = "";
        txtState.Text = "";
        return;
    }
    txtContactName.Text =
        m_dtContacts.Rows[m_rowPosition]["ContactName"].ToString();
    txtState.Text = m_dtContacts.Rows[m_rowPosition]["State"].ToString();
}
```

3. Make sure that the first record is shown when the form loads by adding this statement to the Load event, *after* the existing statements:

```
this.ShowCurrentRecord();
```

You've now ensured that the first record in the DataTable is shown when the form first loads. To display the data, you must add a few controls to the form.

4. Switch to the form designer, create a new text box, and set its properties as follows (you may have to switch back to view the properties if the events are still visible):

Property	Value
Name	**txtContactName**
Location	**48,112**
Size	**112,20**

5. Add a second text box to the form and set its properties according to the following table:

Property	Value
Name	**txtState**
Location	**168,112**
Size	**80,20**

6. Press F5 to run the project, and you'll see the first contact in the Contacts table displayed in the text box (see Figure 21.3).

Navigating Records

The ADO.NET DataTable object supports a number of methods that can be used to access its DataRows. The simplest of these is the ordinal accessor that you used in your ShowCurrentRecord() method. Because the DataTable has no dependency on the source of the data, this same functionality is available regardless of where the data comes from.

FIGURE 21.3
It takes quite a
bit of prep work
to display data.

You're now going to create buttons that the user can click to navigate the DataTable. The first button will be used to move to the first record in the DataTable. Follow these steps:

1. Stop the running project and display the Form Designer for frmMain.

2. Add a new button to the form and set its properties as follows:

Property	Value
Name	**btnMoveFirst**
Location	**16,152**
Size	**32,23**
Text	**<<**

3. Double-click the button and add the following code to its Click event:

```
// Move to the first row and show the data.
m_rowPosition = 0;
this.ShowCurrentRecord();
```

4. A second button will be used to move to the previous record in the DataTable. Add another button to the form and set its properties as shown in the following table:

Property	Value
Name	**btnMovePrevious**
Location	**56,152**
Size	**32,23**
Text	**<**

5. Double-click the button and add the following code to its Click event:

```
// If not at the first row, go back one row and show the record.
if  (m_rowPosition != 0)
{
    mm_rowPosition—;
    this.ShowCurrentRecord();
}
```

6. A third button will be used to move to the next record in the DataTable. Add a third button to the form and set its properties as shown in the following table:

Property	Value
Name	**btnMoveNext**
Location	**96,152**
Size	**32,23**
Text	>

7. Double-click the button and add the following code to its Click event:

```
// If not on the last row, advance one row and show the record.
if  (m_rowPosition < m_dtContacts.Rows.Count-1)
{
    m_rowPosition++;
    this.ShowCurrentRecord();
}
```

8. A fourth button will be used to move to the last record in the DataTable. Add yet another button to the form and set its properties as shown in the following table:

Property	Value
Name	**btnMoveLast**
Location	**136,152**
Size	**32,23**
Text	>>

9. Double-click the button and add the following code to its Click event:

```
// If there are any rows in the data table,
// move to the last and show the record.
if (m_dtContacts.Rows.Count != 0)
{
    m_rowPosition = m_dtContacts.Rows.Count-1;
    this.ShowCurrentRecord();
}
```

Editing Records

To edit records in a `DataTable`, you change the value of a particular column in the desired `DataRow`. Remember, though, that changes aren't made to the original data source until you call `Update()` on the `DataAdapter`, passing in the `DataTable` containing the changes.

You're now going to add a button that the user can click to update the current record. Follow these steps:

1. Add a new button to the form now and set its properties as follows:

Property	Value
Name	**btnSave**
Location	**176,152**
Size	**40,23**
Text	**Save**

2. Double-click the Save button and add the following code to its `Click` event:

   ```
   // If there is existing data, update it.
   if (m_dtContacts.Rows.Count !=0)
   {
       m_dtContacts.Rows[m_rowPosition]["ContactName"]= txtContactName.Text;
       m_dtContacts.Rows[m_rowPosition]["State"] = txtState.Text;
       m_daDataAdapter.Update(m_dtContacts);
   }
   ```

Creating New Records

Adding records to a `DataTable` is performed much like editing records. However, to create a new row in the `DataTable`, you must first call the `NewRow()` method. After creating the new row, you can set its column values. The row isn't actually added to the `DataTable`, however, until you call the `Add()` method on the `DataTable`'s RowCollection.

You're now going to modify your interface so that the user can add new records. You'll use one text box for the contact name and a second text box for the state. When the user clicks the button you'll provide, the values in these text boxes will be written to the Contacts table as a new record. Follow these steps:

1. Start by adding a group box to the form and setting its properties as shown in the following table:

Property	Value
Name	**grpNewRecord**
Location	**16,192**
Size	**264,64**
Text	**New Contact**

2. Next, add a new text box *to the group box* and set its properties as follows:

Property	Value
Name	**txtNewContactName**
Location	**8,24**
Size	**112,20**

3. Add a second text box to the group box and set its properties as shown:

Property	Value
Name	**txtNewState**
Location	**126,24**
Size	**80,20**

4. Finally, add a button to the group box and set its properties as follows:

Property	Value
Name	**btnAddNew**
Location	**212,24**
Size	**40,20**
Text	**Add**

5. Double-click the Add button and add the following code to its `Click` event:

```
DataRow drNewRow = m_dtContacts.NewRow();
drNewRow["ContactName"] = txtNewContactName.Text;
drNewRow["State"] = txtNewState.Text;
m_dtContacts.Rows.Add(drNewRow);
m_daDataAdapter.Update(m_dtContacts);
m_rowPosition = m_dtContacts.Rows.Count-1;
this.ShowCurrentRecord();
```

Notice that after the new record is added, the position is set to the last row, and the `ShowCurrentRecord()` procedure is called. This causes the new record to appear in the display text boxes you created earlier.

Deleting Records

To delete a record from a `DataTable`, you call the `Delete()` method on the `DataRow` to be deleted. Follow these steps:

1. Add a new button to your form (*not to the group box*) and set its properties as shown in the following table:

Property	Value
Name	**btnDelete**
Location	**224,152**
Size	**56,23**
Text	**Delete**

2. Double-click the Delete button and add the following code to its `Click` event:

```
// If there is data, delete the current row.
if  (m_dtContacts.Rows.Count !=0)
{
    m_dtContacts.Rows[m_rowPosition].Delete();
    m_daDataAdapter.Update(m_dtContacts);
    m_rowPosition=0;
    this.ShowCurrentRecord();
}
```

Your form should now look like that in Figure 21.4.

FIGURE 21.4
A basic data-entry form.

Running the Database Example

Press F5 to run the project. If you entered all the code correctly and you placed the Contacts database into the C:\Temp folder (or modified the path used in code), the form should display without errors, and the first record in the database will appear. Click the navigation buttons to move forward and backward. Feel free to change the information of a contact; click the Save button, and your changes will be made to the underlying database. Next, enter your name and state into the New Contact section of the form and click Add. Your name will be added to the database and displayed in the appropriate text boxes. Note, there is no provision in the code to deal with duplicate records, so attempting to add a duplicate name will generate an error.

Summary

Most commercial applications use some sort of database. Becoming a good database programmer requires extending your skills beyond just being a good programmer. There's so much to know about optimizing databases and database code, creating usable database interfaces, creating a database schema—the list goes on and on. Writing any database application, however, begins with the basic skills you learned in this hour. You learned how to connect to a database, create and populate a DataTable, and navigate the records in the DataTable. In addition, you learned how to edit records and how to add and delete records. Although this just scratches the surface of database programming, it is all you need to begin writing your own small database application.

Q&A

Q. *If I want to connect to a data source other than Jet, how do I know what connection string to use?*

A. Not only is different connection information available for different types of data sources but also for different versions of different data sources. The best way of determining the connection string is to consult the documentation for the data source to which you want to attach.

Q. *What if I don't know where the database will be at runtime?*

A. For file-based data sources such as Jet, you can add an Open File Dialog control to the form and let the user browse and select the database. Then concatenate the filename with the rest of the connection information (such as the provider string).

Workshop

Quiz

1. What is the name of the data access namespace used in the .NET Framework?

2. What is the name given to a collection of `DataRows`?

3. How do I get data into and out of a `DataTable`?

4. What object is used to connect to a data source?

5. What argument of a connection string contains information about the type of data being connected to?

6. What object provides update, delete, and insert capabilities to a `DataAdapter`?

7. What method of a `DataTable` object do you call to create a new row?

Answers

1. `System.Data`.

2. A `DataSet`.

3. You use a `DataAdapter`.

4. There are multiple connection objects. You have to use the connection object appropriate for the type of data you are accessing.

5. The `Provider` argument.

6. A `CommandBuilder` object.

7. The `Add()` method is used to create the row. The `Update()` method saves your changes to the new row.

Exercises

1. Create a new project that connects to the same database used in this example. Rather than displaying a single record in two text boxes, put a list box on the form and fill the list box with the names of the people in the database.

2. Right now, your code will save an empty name to the database. Add code to the `Click` event of the Add button so that it first tests to see if the user entered a contact name. If not, tell the user a name is required and then exit the procedure.

HOUR 22

Controlling Other Applications Using Automation

What You'll Learn in This Hour:

▶ Creating a reference to an automation library
▶ Creating an instance of an automation server
▶ Manipulating the objects of an automation server

In Hour 16, "Designing Objects Using Classes," you learned how to use classes to create objects. In that hour, I mentioned that objects could be exposed to outside applications. Excel, for example, exposes most of its functionality as a set of objects. The process of using objects from another application is called *automation*. The externally accessible objects of an application compose its *object model*. Using automation to manipulate a program's object model enables you to reuse components. You can use automation with Excel, for instance, to perform complex mathematical functions using the code that's been written and tested within Excel instead of writing and debugging the complex code yourself.

Programs that expose objects are called *servers*, and the programs that consume those objects are called *clients*. Creating automation servers requires advanced skills, including a thorough understanding of programming classes. On the other hand, creating clients to use objects from other applications is relatively simple. In this hour, you'll learn how to create a client application that uses objects of an external server application.

To understand automation, you're going to build two projects. The first will be a Microsoft Excel client—a program that automates Excel via Excel's object model. The second project will automate Microsoft Word.

> These exercises are designed to work with Microsoft Excel 2003 and Microsoft Word 2003. You must have these programs installed in order for the examples to work.

Begin by creating a new Windows Application named **Automate Excel**. Right-click Form1.cs in the Solution Explorer, choose Rename, and then change the name of the default form to **frmMain.cs**. Next, set the form's Text property to **Automate Excel**.

Next, add a button to the form by double-clicking the Button item in the toolbox and set the button's properties as follows:

Property	Value
Name	**btnAutomateExcel**
Location	**96,128**
Size	**104,23**
Text	**Automate Excel**

Creating a Reference to an Automation Library

To use the objects of a program that supports automation (a server), you have to reference the program's *type library*. A program's type library (also called its *object library*) is a file containing a description of the program's object model. After you've referenced the type library of an automation server (also called a *component*), you can access the objects of the server as though they were internal Visual C# objects.

You create the reference to Excel's automation library much like you created a reference to the System.Data namespace in Hour 21, "Working with a Database." To create a reference to the Excel library, follow these steps:

1. Display the Add Reference dialog box by choosing Project, Add Reference.

2. Click the COM tab to display the available COM components (programs that have a type library) on your computer.

3. Scroll the list and locate the Microsoft Excel 11 Object Library (see Figure 22.1). Double-click the Excel item to create a reference to it and close the dialog box.

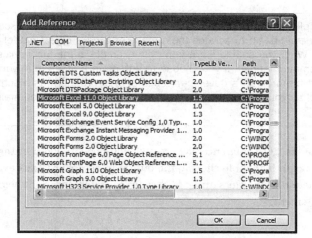

FIGURE 22.1
Visual C# .NET projects can use COM objects created by other tools.

If you don't see Microsoft Excel 11.0 Object Library in your list of available COM references, you probably don't have Excel 2003 installed, and this example will not work.

By the Way

Visual C# doesn't work directly with COM components (as did previous versions of Visual C#). Instead, it interacts through a *wrapper*, a set of code and objects that works as an intermediary between Visual C# and a COM component. When you add the reference to a COM component, .NET automatically creates this wrapper for you.

By the Way

Creating an Instance of an Automation Server

Referencing a type library allows Visual C# to integrate the available objects of the type library with its own internal objects. After this is done, you can create object variables based on object types found in the type library. Excel has an object called `Application`, which acts as the primary object in the Excel object model. In fact, most Office programs have an `Application` object. How do you know what objects an automation server supports? The only sure way is to consult the documentation of the program in question or use the Object Browser discussed in Hour 3, "Understanding Objects and Collections."

In this example, you'll be using about a half-dozen members of an Excel object. This doesn't even begin to scratch the surface of Excel's object model, nor is it intended to. What you should learn from this example is the mechanics of working with an automation server. If you choose to automate a program in your own projects, consult the program's developer documentation to learn as much about its object model as you can—you're sure to be surprised at the functionality available to you.

In order to use the COM reference you created, you need to add a using statement to your class. Begin by double-clicking the button to access its Click event, and then scroll up to the top of the class and add this using statement, right below the existing using statements:

```
using Excel;
```

Next, enter the following code, which creates a new Excel Application object into the btnAutomaticeExcel_Click event:

```
Excel.Application objExcel = new Excel.Application();
```

Notice that Visual C# included Excel in its IntelliSense drop-down list of available objects. It could do this because you referenced Excel's type library and created the using statement. If you neglected to do either of these two things, Excel would not show up and the code would not work. Excel is the reference to the server, and Application is an object supported by the server. This statement creates a new Application object based on the Excel object model.

Manipulating the Server

After you have an instance of an object from an automation server, manipulating the server (creating objects, setting properties, calling methods, and so forth) is accomplished by manipulating the object. In the following sections, you'll manipulate the new Excel object by setting properties and calling methods, and in so doing you will be manipulating Excel itself.

Forcing Excel to Show Itself

When Excel is started using automation, it's loaded but not shown. Remaining hidden enables the developer to use Excel's functionality and then close it without the user knowing what happened. For example, you could create an instance of an Excel object, perform a complicated formula to obtain a result, close Excel, and return the result to the user—all without the user seeing Excel. In this example, you *want* to see Excel so that you can see what your code is doing. Fortunately, showing Excel couldn't be any easier. Add the following statement to make Excel visible:

```
objExcel.Visible = true;
```

Creating an Excel Workbook

In Excel, a workbook is the file in which you work and store your data; you can't manipulate data without a workbook. When you first start Excel from the Start menu, an empty workbook is created for you. When you start Excel via automation, however, Excel doesn't create a workbook; you have to do it yourself. To create a new workbook, you use the Add method of the Workbooks collection. Enter the following statements to create a new workbook and reference the default worksheet (explained in the next section):

```
//start a new workbook and a worksheet.
Excel.Workbook objBook =
                objExcel.Workbooks.Add(System.Reflection.Missing.Value);
Excel.Worksheet objSheet = (Excel.Worksheet)objBook.Worksheets.get_Item(1);
```

Working with Data in an Excel Workbook

Workbooks contain a single worksheet by default. In this section, you're going to manipulate data in the worksheet. The following describes what you'll do:

1. Add data to four cells in the worksheet.

2. Select the four cells.

3. Total the selected cells and place the sum into a fifth cell.

4. Bold all five cells.

To manipulate cells in the worksheet, you manipulate the ActiveCell object, which is an object property of the Application object. Entering data into a cell involves first selecting a cell and then passing data to it. Selecting a cell is accomplished by calling the Select method of the Range object; the Range object is used to select one or more cells. The Select method accepts a starting column and row and an ending column and row. If you want to select only a single cell, as we do here, you can omit the ending column and row. After the range is set, you pass data to the FormulaR1C1 property of the ActiveCell object (which references the cell specified by the Range object). Setting the FormulaR1C1 property has the effect of sending data to the cell. Sound confusing? Well, it is to some extent. Programs that support automation are often vast and complex, and programming them is usually far from intuitive.

The following section of code uses the techniques just described to add data to four cells. Follow these steps now to automate sending the data to Excel:

1. Enter this code into your procedure:

```
Excel.Range objRange;

objRange = objSheet.get_Range("A1", System.Reflection.Missing.Value);
objRange.Value2 = 75;

objRange = objSheet.get_Range("B1", System.Reflection.Missing.Value);
objRange.Value2 = 125;

objRange = objSheet.get_Range("C1", System.Reflection.Missing.Value);
objRange.Value2 = 255;

objRange = objSheet.get_Range("D1", System.Reflection.Missing.Value);
objRange.Value2 = 295;
```

The next step is to have Excel total the four cells. You'll do this by using the Range object to select the cells, activating a new cell in which to place the total, and then using `FormulaR1C1` again to create the total by passing it a formula rather than a literal value.

2. Enter this code into your procedure:

```
objRange = objSheet.get_Range("E1", System.Reflection.Missing.Value);
objRange.set_Value(System.Reflection.Missing.Value, "=SUM(RC[-4]:RC[-1])"
);
```

3. Next, select all five cells and bold them. Enter the following statements to accomplish this:

```
objRange = objSheet.get_Range("A1", "E1");
objRange.Font.Bold=true;
```

The last thing you need to do is destroy the object reference by setting the object variable to Nothing. Excel remains open even though you've destroyed the automation instance (not all servers do this).

4. Add this last statement to your procedure to release the reference to Excel:

```
objExcel=null;
```

To help ensure that everything is entered correctly, Listing 22.1 shows the procedure in its entirety.

Listing 22.1   Code to Automate Excel

```
private void btnAutomateExcel_Click(object sender, EventArgs e)
    {
        Excel.Application objExcel = new Excel.Application();

        objExcel.Visible = true;

        // Start a new workbook and a worksheet.
        Excel.Workbook objBook =
objExcel.Workbooks.Add(System.Reflection.Missing.Value);
        Excel.Worksheet objSheet =
(Excel.Worksheet)objBook.Worksheets.get_Item(1);

        // Use a Range object to select cells and set data.
        Excel.Range objRange;

        objRange = objSheet.get_Range("A1",
System.Reflection.Missing.Value);
        objRange.Value2 = 75;

        objRange = objSheet.get_Range("B1",
System.Reflection.Missing.Value);
        objRange.Value2 = 125;

        objRange = objSheet.get_Range("C1",
System.Reflection.Missing.Value);
        objRange.Value2 = 255;

        objRange = objSheet.get_Range("D1",
System.Reflection.Missing.Value);
        objRange.Value2 = 295;

        // Use a Range object to select cells and sum them.
        objRange = objSheet.get_Range("E1",
System.Reflection.Missing.Value);
        objRange.set_Value(System.Reflection.Missing.Value,
"=SUM(RC[-4]:RC[-1])");

        objRange = objSheet.get_Range("A1", "E1");
        objRange.Font.Bold=true;

        objExcel = null;
    }
```

Testing Your Client Application

Now that your project is complete, press F5 to run it and click the button to automate Excel. If you entered the code correctly, Excel will start, data will be placed into four cells, the total of the four cells will be placed into a fifth cell, and all cells will be made bold (see Figure 22.2).

FIGURE 22.2
You can control almost every aspect of Excel using its object model.

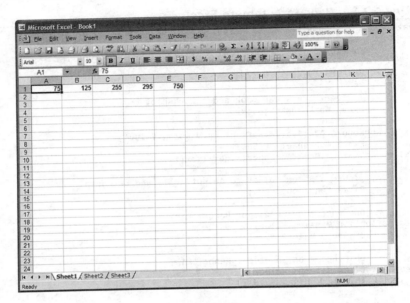

Automating Microsoft Word 2003

You're now going to build another simple application that automates Microsoft Word 2003. Begin by creating a new project titled **Automate Word**. Right-click Form1.cs in the Solution Explorer, choose Rename, and then change the default form's name to **frmMain.cs**. Next, change the form's Text property to **Automate Word**.

Creating a Reference to an Automation Library

To automate Microsoft Word, you have to reference Word's object library—just like you did for Excel. Follow these steps to reference the library:

1. Display the Add Reference dialog box by choosing Project, Add Reference.

2. Click the COM tab to display the available COM components (programs that have a type library) on your computer.

3. Scroll the list and locate the Microsoft Word 11 Object Library (see Figure 22.3). Double-click the Excel item to create a reference to it and close the dialog box.

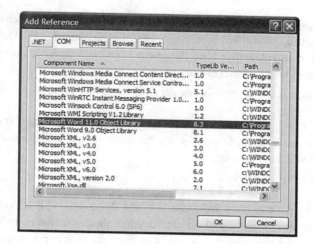

FIGURE 22.3
You have to reference Word's Automation Library to use it in code.

If you don't see Microsoft Word 11.0 Object Library in your list of available COM references, you probably don't have Word 2003 installed, and this example will not work.

By the Way

Creating an Instance of an Automation Server

As with the previous example, all the code for automating Word is placed in the Click event of a button, but first you have to add a using statement. Follow these steps to create the button and associated code:

1. Add a button to the form now by double-clicking the Button item in the toolbox and set the button's properties as follows:

Property	Value
Name	**btnAutomateWord**
Location	**96,128**
Size	**104,23**
Text	**Automate Word**

2. Double-click the button to access its Click event.

3. Scroll to the top of the class and add this statement right below the existing using statements:

```
using Word;
```

4. To work with Word's object model, you have to have an instance of Word's Application object. Put your cursor back in the btnAutomateWord_Click event and enter the following statement to create a variable that contains an instance of Word's Application object:

```
Word.Application objWord = new Word.Application();
```

5. As with Excel, Word starts up hidden, so the user doesn't know it's running. Because you're going to want to see the fruits of your labor, add this statement to force Word to show itself:

```
objWord.Visible = true;
```

6. Next, you need to have Word create a new document. This is accomplished using the Add() method of the Documents collection. This method expects four optional parameters. Since they're optional, you're not going to pass them any data. However, you still have to include the arguments in your call to the method. Rather than use System.Reflection.Missing.Value for each optional parameter, which is essentially like leaving out an argument like you did in the Excel example, you'll create a variable to hold this value and use the variable in the call to Add(). Enter these statements to declare the variables and create the new document:

```
Word.Document objDoc;
object objMissing = System.Reflection.Missing.Value;

objDoc = objWord.Documents.Add(ref objMissing, ref objMissing,
    ref objMissing, ref objMissing);
```

7. There are many ways to send text to Word. Perhaps the easiest is the TypeText() method of the Selection object. The Selection object refers to currently selected text in the Word document. When a new document is created, there is no text, and the selection object simply refers to the edit cursor at the start of the document. Sending text to Word using Select.TypeText() inserts the text at the top of the document. Enter this statement to send text to Word:

```
objWord.Selection.TypeText("This is text from a C# 2005 application.");
```

8. The last statement you need to enter sets the Word object to null to release the reference to it:

```
objWord = null;
```

Now, press F5 to run the program. You should see Word start, and then a new document is created using the text you specified with `TypeText()` (see Figure 22.4).

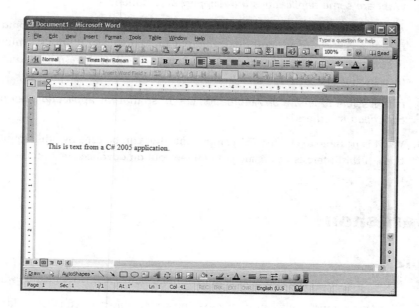

FIGURE 22.4
A simple but effective demonstration of automating Word.

> Automating applications, particularly Office products such as Excel and Word, requires a lot of system resources. If you intend to perform a lot of automation, you should use the fastest machine with the most memory that you can afford. Also, be aware that for automation to work, the server application (Excel or Word in this case) has to be installed on the user's computer in addition to your application.

By the Way

Summary

In this hour, you learned how a program can make available an object model that client applications can use to manipulate the program. You learned that the first step in automating a program (server) is to reference the type library of the server. After the type library is referenced, the objects of the server are available as though they're internal Visual C# objects. As you've seen, the mechanics of automating a program aren't that difficult—they build on the object-programming skills you've already learned in this book. The real challenge comes in learning the object model of a given server and in making the most productive use of the objects available.

Q&A

Q. *What are some applications that support automation?*

A. All the Microsoft Office products, as well as Microsoft Visio, support automation. You can create a robust application by building a client that uses multiple automation servers. For example, you could calculate data in Excel and then format and print the data in Word.

Q. *Is it possible to create an Automation server so that my application can be controlled by others?*

A. Yes, it is possible to create .NET components that can be used by other applications. If this interests you, I suggest you seek out an advanced text on the subject.

Workshop

Quiz

1. Before you can early bind objects in an automation server, you must do what?

2. What is the most likely cause of not seeing a type library listed in the Add References dialog box?

3. For Visual C# to use a COM library, it must create a _____.

4. To manipulate a server via automation, you manipulate:

5. To learn about the object library of a component, you should:

Answers

1. Add a reference to the server's type library.

2. You do not have the application installed.

3. Wrapper around the COM library.

4. An object that holds an instantiated object from the server.

5. Consult the programmer's help file for the component.

Exercises

1. Modify the Excel example to save the workbook. Hint: Consider the `SaveAs()` method of the Workbooks collection.

2. Modify your Excel example so that after summing the four cells, you retrieve the sum from Excel and then send the value to a new Word document.

PART V

Developing Solutions and Beyond

HOUR 23

Deploying Applications

What You'll Learn in This Hour:

▶ Understanding ClickOnce technology
▶ Using the Publish Wizard to create a ClickOnce program
▶ Testing a ClickOnce install program
▶ Setting Advanced Options when creating ClickOnce programs

Now that you've learned how to create a Visual C# 2005 application, you're probably just itching to create a project and send it to the world. Fortunately, Visual C# 2005 includes the tools you need to create a setup program for an application. In this hour, you'll learn how to use these tools to create a setup program that a user can run to install an application you've developed. In fact, you'll be creating a setup program for the Picture Viewer application you've been working on since Hour 1, "Jumping In with Both Feet: A Visual C# 2005 Programming Tour."

Understanding ClickOnce Technology

Microsoft can't seem to settle on a deployment technology. Before .NET, serious developers were forced to use third-party applications to build installation programs. Then Microsoft introduced Windows Installer Technology, where developers created an MSI file that installed an application. With Visual C# 2005, Microsoft has introduced yet another technology: ClickOnce. ClickOnce technology has its drawbacks, mostly in its lack of flexibility, but ClickOnce does have some significant improvements over earlier technologies. Many of the improvements will be appreciated mostly by experienced developers who have been battling install technology for some time; they might not make a lot of sense to you. This hour covers the highlights of ClickOnce technology. After you understand what the ClickOnce technology offers, I'll walk you through creating a ClickOnce program that will install your Picture Viewer program on a user's computer.

The following points are highlights of the new ClickOnce technology:

▶ ClickOnce is designed to bring the ease of deploying a web application to the deployment of desktop applications. Traditionally, to distribute a desktop application you had to touch each and every client computer—running the setup program and installing the appropriate files. Web applications, on the other hand, only need to be updated in one place: on the web server. ClickOnce provides desktop applications with update functionality similar to web applications.

▶ Applications deployed with ClickOnce can update themselves. They can check the Web for a newer version and install the newer version automatically.

▶ ClickOnce programs have the capability to update only necessary files. With previous installation technologies, entire applications had to be reinstalled to be updated.

▶ ClickOnce allows applications to install their components in such a way that they don't interfere with other installed applications. In other words, they are *self-contained* applications. With Windows Installer deployments (that is, the "old way"), applications shared components such as custom controls. If one application mistakenly installed an older version of a component, deleted a component, or installed an incompatible version of a component, it would break other installed applications that used the shared component.

▶ ClickOnce programs do not require the user to have administrative permissions. With Windows Installer deployments, users had to have administrative permissions to install an application. Trust me, this is a serious issue, and I'm glad to see ClickOnce address this.

▶ A ClickOnce application can be installed in one of three ways: from a web page, from a network file share, or from media such as a CD-ROM.

▶ A ClickOnce application can be installed on a user's computer, so it can be run when the user is offline, or it can be run in an online-only mode, where it doesn't permanently install anything on the user's computer.

Using the Publish Wizard to Create a ClickOnce Application

You're now going to create a ClickOnce program that installs the Picture Viewer program you've been building throughout this book. Begin by opening the Picture Viewer project from Hour 20, "Working with Text Files and the Registry," and then follow these steps:

1. Open the Build menu and choose Publish Picture Viewer. This displays the Publish Wizard shown in Figure 23.1. This page is used to specify where you want the ClickOnce file created.

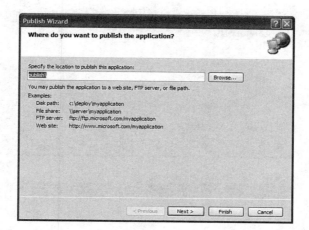

FIGURE 23.1
The Publish Wizard is used to create ClickOnce programs.

2. Specify the location for the ClickOnce install files. Be aware that you must enter a path that already exists; Visual C# does not create a path for you. If you specify an invalid path, you'll get a Build error at the end of the wizard. Notice the examples listed on this page; you can specify a file path, a file share, an ftp server, or a website. After you've supplied a valid path, click Next.

3. On the next page of the Publishing Wizard, specify the method users will employ to install your program (see Figure 23.2). Although you can specify a website or UNC share, choose From a CD-ROM or DVD-ROM for this example and click Next.

4. The next page of the Publishing Wizard asks you whether the application will check for updates (see Figure 23.3). If your application supports this feature, select the appropriate option button and specify a location where the update files will be placed. The Picture Viewer is a simple application and does not need this advanced functionality, so leave The Application Will Not Check for Updates option selected and click Next.

5. The final page of the Publish Wizard is simply a confirmation page (see Figure 23.4). Verify that the information displayed is how you want it. Don't be concerned about the formatting applied to your path. Visual C# will modify it to create a valid UNC path. Click Finish to create the install.

FIGURE 23.2
Users can install your application in one of three ways.

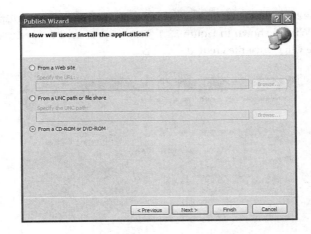

FIGURE 23.3
ClickOnce applications can update themselves if you design them to do so.

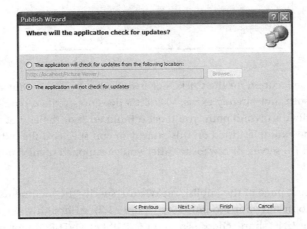

FIGURE 23.4
Make sure that everything is correct before you finish the wizard.

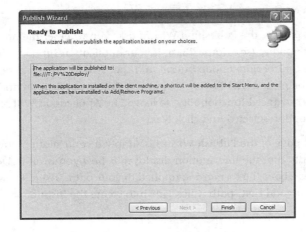

When you click Finish, the Publishing Wizard creates the ClickOnce application and opens the folder containing the install files (see Figure 23.5). Notice how the version number of the application is used when naming files and folders. To distribute this application, you would simply burn the contents of this folder, including the sub-folder and its contents, to a CD-ROM or DVD-ROM and send it to a user.

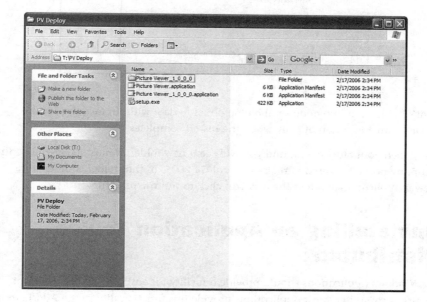

FIGURE 23.5
These files (and the subfolder) make up the ClickOnce program.

Testing Your Picture Viewer ClickOnce Install Program

Run the Setup.exe file in your designated ClickOnce folder to start the install. You might notice a quick window that shows an animated dialog indicating that the computer is checking for a valid Internet connection (you might also get prompted to allow such access if you have a firewall in place). The first dialog you can interact with is a security warning as shown in Figure 23.6. The publisher of the component is listed as unknown because the file isn't digitally signed.

Digitally signing a file is beyond the scope of this book, but if this is important to you, you can learn more at http://www.verisign.com/ (search for Code Signing).

Did you Know?

Click Install to install the Picture Viewer.

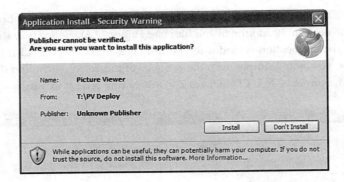

That's it! There are no additional dialog boxes to deal with. In fact, the Picture Viewer launches automatically when the install completes.

Now, open your Start menu, and you will see a new folder. It most likely will be the company name you used to register Visual C# 2005. In that folder is the Picture Viewer application shortcut the user can click to run the program.

Uninstalling an Application You've Distributed

All Windows applications should provide a facility for easily being removed from the user's computer. Most applications provide this functionality in the Add/Remove Programs dialog box, and yours is no exception. In fact, all ClickOnce programs create an entry in the Add/Remove Programs dialog box automatically. Follow these steps to uninstall the Picture Viewer program:

1. Open the Start menu and choose Control Panel.

2. Locate the Add/Remove Programs icon and click it.

3. Scroll down in your Add/Remove programs dialog box until you find the Picture Viewer program (see Figure 23.7).

4. To uninstall the program, click it to select it and then click Change/Remove.

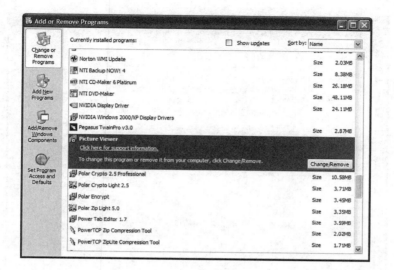

FIGURE 23.7
Your program
can be unin-
stalled using the
Add/Remove
Programs dialog
box.

Setting Advanced Options for Creating ClickOnce Programs

The Publishing Wizard is the easiest way to create a ClickOnce program, but it does-n't give you access to all the features of ClickOnce. To view all the available settings, right-click the project name in the Solution Explorer and choose Properties. If you don't click the correct node in the Solution Explorer, you'll get the wrong properties. Another method to use is to open the Project menu and choose Picture Viewer Properties.

Next, click the Publish tab, and you'll see a page of publishing options (see Figure 23.8). Using this page, you can specify prerequisites, such as whether to install the .NET Framework, which is required to run any .NET application (by default, the Publishing Wizard creates your ClickOnce application such that it will install the .NET Framework from the Web if the user performing the install doesn't have the Framework installed). The Publish Wizard walks you through many of these options, but the most control is gained by setting your options here and clicking the Publish Now button, which appears at the bottom-right of the Publish page.

FIGURE 23.8
Advanced
ClickOnce set-
tings can be set
on the Publish
tab of the
Project
Properties.

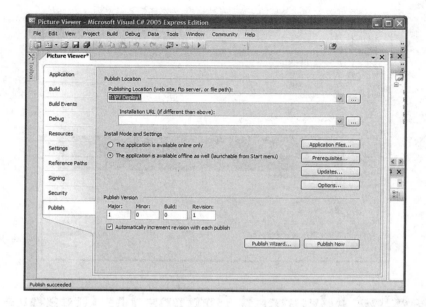

Summary

In this hour, you learned about ClickOnce and why Microsoft is moving to
ClickOnce from Windows Installer technology. You also learned how to use the
Publish Wizard to create a ClickOnce program to distribute an application you've
built using Visual C# 2005. Creating installs for robust applications requires a lot
more effort and in many cases more tools, but the skills you learned in this hour
will allow you to distribute most projects that you'll build as a beginner with Visual
C# 2005.

Q&A

Q. *How can I create the great installation wizards I see other install applications use?*

A. If you want to create robust installations that gather user input in wizards,
make changes to the Registry, allow you to include additional files, create
shortcuts, and so on, you need to use a tool that uses the Windows Installer
technology.

Q. *Should I assume that a user will always have the .NET Framework on her computer?*

A. Generally, no. When distributing updates to your project, it's probably a safe bet that the user has installed the .NET Framework. For an initial installation, you should specify the .NET Framework as a prerequisite (note that this is set by default).

Workshop

Quiz

1. What is the name of the new install technology?

2. True or False: ClickOnce programs can be self-updating.

3. True or False: ClickOnce programs have more flexibility than Windows Installer programs.

4. What are the three ways a user can install a ClickOnce program?

5. What wizard is used to create a ClickOnce program?

Answers

1. The new install technology is called ClickOnce.

2. True.

3. False. Windows Installer technology provides much more flexibility than ClickOnce programs.

4. A user can install a ClickOnce program from a web page, from a network file share, or from media such as a CD-ROM.

5. The Publish Wizard is used to create a ClickOnce program.

Exercises

1. Use the Publish Wizard to create an install for the Automate Excel project in Hour 22, "Controlling Other Applications Using Automation." Try installing the ClickOnce program on a computer that doesn't have Excel and see what happens when you run the program.

2. If you have access to a web server, use the Publish Wizard to deploy the Picture Viewer to the web server and then install the application on a different computer from the web server.

HOUR 24

The 10,000-Foot View

What You'll Learn in This Hour:

▶ Understanding the .NET Framework
▶ Understanding the Common Language Runtime (CLR)
▶ How Visual C# 2005 Uses the Microsoft Intermediate Language
▶ Using Visual Studio .NET Namespaces
▶ Understanding the Common Type System
▶ Understanding Garbage Collection

You know a lot about Visual C# 2005 now. You can create projects, you can use forms and controls to build an interface, and you know how to add menus and toolbars to a form. You've also learned how to create modules and procedures and how to write code to make things happen. You can use variables, make decisions, perform looping, and even debug your code. The question you might be thinking now is, "Where to next?" In fact, this is the number one question I receive from readers via emails.

Throughout this book, I've focused my discussions on Visual C#. When it comes to Microsoft's .NET Framework, however, Visual C# is just part of the picture. This hour provides an overview of Microsoft's .NET Framework so that you can see how Visual C# relates to .NET as a whole. After completing this hour, you'll understand the various pieces of .NET and how they're interrelated. I hope you'll be able to combine this information with your current personal and professional needs to determine the facets of .NET that you want to explore in more detail.

The .NET Framework

The components and technology that make up Microsoft .NET are collectively called the *.NET Framework*. The .NET Framework comprises numerous classes and includes components such as the Common Language Runtime, Microsoft Intermediate Language, and

ADO.NET. The following sections explain the various pieces that make up the .NET Framework.

Common Language Runtime

A *language runtime* allows an application to run on a target computer; it consists of code that's shared among all applications developed using a supported language. A runtime contains the "guts" of language code, such as code that draws forms to the screen, handles user input, and manages data. The runtime of .NET is called the *common language runtime*.

Unlike runtimes for other languages, the Common Language Runtime is designed as a multilanguage runtime. For example, both Visual Basic and Visual C# use the common language runtime. In fact, currently more than 15 language compilers are being developed to use the Common Language Runtime.

Because all .NET languages share the common language runtime, they also share the same IDE, forms engine, exception-handling mechanism, garbage collector (discussed shortly), and much more. One benefit of the multilanguage capability of the common language runtime is that programmers can leverage their knowledge of a given .NET language.

For example, some developers on a team might be comfortable with Visual C#, whereas others are more comfortable with Visual Basic. Because both languages share the same runtime, both can be integrated to deliver a single solution. In addition, a common exception-handling mechanism is built into the Common Language Runtime so that exceptions can be thrown from code written in one .NET language and caught in code written in another.

Code that runs within the common language runtime is called *managed* code because the code and resources used by the code (variables, objects, and so on) are fully managed by the common language runtime. Where Visual Basic is restricted to working only in managed code, other languages such as Visual C# are capable of dropping to *unmanaged* code—code that isn't managed by the common language runtime.

Another advantage of the common language runtime is that all .NET tools share the same debugging and code-profiling tools. In the past, tools like Visual Basic were limited in its debugging tools, whereas applications such as C++ had many third-party debugging tools available. All languages now share the same tools. That means that as advancements are made to the debugging tools of one product, they're made to tools of all products because the tools are shared. This aspect goes beyond debugging tools. Add-ins to the IDE such as code managers, for example, are just as readily available to Visual C# as they are to Visual Basic—or any other .NET language, for that matter.

Although Microsoft hasn't announced any official plans to do so, it's possible that it could produce a version of the common language runtime that runs on other operating systems, such as Macintosh OS or Linux. If this occurs, the applications that you've written for Windows should run on a newly supported operating system with little or no modification.

By the Way

Microsoft Intermediate Language

As you can see in Figure 24.1, all .NET code, regardless of the language syntax used, compiles to Intermediate Language (IL) code. IL code is the only code the Common Language Runtime understands; it doesn't understand Visual C#, Visual Basic, or any other developer syntax. IL gives .NET its multilanguage capabilities; as long as an original source language can be compiled to IL, it can become a .NET program. For example, people have developed a .NET compiler for COBOL—a mainframe language with a long history. This compiler takes existing COBOL code and compiles it to IL so that it will run within the .NET Framework using the Common Language Runtime. COBOL itself isn't a Windows language and doesn't support many of the features found in a true Windows language (such as a Windows Forms engine), so you can imagine the excitement of COBOL programmers when they first learned of being able to leverage their existing code and programming skills to create powerful Windows applications.

A potential drawback of IL is that it can be susceptible to reverse compilation. This has many people questioning the security of .NET code and the security of the .NET Framework in general. If code security is a serious concern for you, I encourage you to research this matter on your own.

By the Way

IL code isn't the final step in the process of compiling and running an application. For a processor (CPU) to execute programmed instructions, those instructions must be in *machine language* format. When you run a .NET application, a just-in-time compiler (called a *JITter*) compiles the IL to machine-language instructions that the processor can understand. IL code is *processor independent*, which again brings up the possibility that JITters could be built to create machine code for computers that

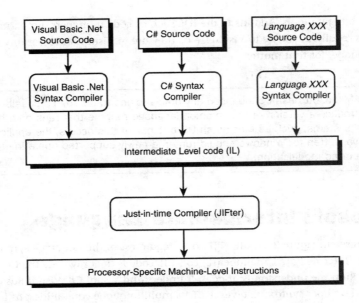

are using something other than Intel-compatible processors. If Microsoft were to
offer a common language runtime for operating systems other than Windows,
many of the differences would lie in the way IL would be compiled by the JITter.

As .NET evolves, changes made to the common language runtime will benefit all
.NET applications. For example, if Microsoft finds a way to further increase the
speed at which forms are drawn to the screen by making improvements to the
Common Language Runtime, all .NET applications will immediately benefit from
the improvement. However, optimizations made to a specific syntax compiler, such
as the one that compiles Visual C# code to IL, are language specific. This means
that even though all .NET languages compile to IL code and use the common language runtime, it's possible for one language to have small advantages over another because of the way in which the language's code is compiled to IL.

Namespaces

As mentioned earlier in this book, the .NET Framework is composed of classes—
many classes. Namespaces are the method used to create a hierarchical structure of
all these classes, and they help prevent naming collisions. A naming collision occurs
when two classes have the same name. Because namespaces provide a hierarchy, it's
possible to have two classes with the same name as long as they exist in different
namespaces. Namespaces, in effect, create scope for classes.

The base namespace in the .NET Framework is the System namespace. The System namespace contains classes for garbage collection (discussed shortly), exception handling, data typing, and so much more. The System namespace is just the tip of the iceberg. There are literally dozens of namespaces. Table 24.1 lists some of the more common namespaces, many of which you've used in this book. All the controls that you've placed on forms and even the forms themselves belong to the System.Windows.Forms namespace. Use Table 24.1 as a guide; if a certain namespace interests you, I suggest that you research it further in the Visual Studio .NET online help.

Table 24.1 Commonly Used Namespaces

Namespace	Description
Microsoft.VisualBasic	Contains classes that support compilation and code generation using the Visual Basic language.
System	Contains fundamental classes and base classes that define commonly used value and reference data types, event handlers, interfaces, attributes, and exceptions. This is the base namespace of .NET.
System.Data	Contains classes that constitute the ADO.NET architecture.
System.Diagnostics	Contains classes that enable you to debug your application and to trace the execution of your code.
System.Drawing	Contains classes that provide access to the Graphical Device Interface (GDI+) basic graphics functionality.
System.IO	Contains classes that allow reading from and writing to data streams and files.
System.Net	Contains classes that provide a simple programming interface to many of the protocols found on the network.
System.Security	Contains classes that provide the underlying structure of the common language runtime security system.
System.Web	Contains classes that provide interfaces that enable browser/server communication.
System.Windows.Forms	Contains classes for creating Windows-based applications that take advantage of the rich user interface features available in the Microsoft Windows operating system.
System.XML	Contains classes that provide standards-based support for processing XML.

Common Type System

The Common Type System in the Common Language Runtime is the component that defines how data types are declared and used. The fact that the common language runtime can support cross-language integration to the level it does is due largely to the Common Type System. In the past, each language used its own data types and managed data in its own way. This made it difficult for applications developed in different languages to communicate because no standard way existed in which to pass data between them.

The Common Type System ensures that all .NET applications use the same data types, provides for self-describing type information (called *metadata*), and controls all the data manipulation mechanisms so that data is handled (stored and processed) in the same way among all .NET applications. This allows data (including objects) to be treated the same way in all .NET languages.

Garbage Collection

Although I've talked a lot about objects (you can't talk about anything .NET related without talking about objects), I've avoided discussing the underlying technical details of how .NET creates, manages, and destroys objects. Although you don't need to know the complex minutiae of how .NET works with objects, you do need to understand a few details of how objects are destroyed.

As discussed in previous hours, setting an object variable to `null` or letting it go out of scope destroys the object. However, as mentioned in Hour 16, "Designing Objects Using Classes," this isn't the whole story. The .NET platform uses a *garbage collector* for destroying objects. The specific type of garbage collection implemented by .NET is called *reference-tracing garbage collection*. Essentially, the garbage collector monitors the resources used by a program, and when consumed resources reach a defined threshold, the garbage collector proceeds to look for unused objects. When the garbage collector finds an unused object, it destroys it, freeing all the memory and resources the object was using.

An important thing to remember about garbage collection is that releasing an object by setting it to `null` or letting an object variable go out of scope doesn't mean that the object will be destroyed immediately. The object won't be destroyed until the garbage collector is triggered to go looking for unused objects.

Further Reading

Readers often ask me what books they should read next. I do not have a specific answer to this question because it depends entirely on the person asking it. Chances are, you're learning .NET for one of the following reasons:

▶ School

▶ Professional requirements

▶ Personal interests or as a hobby

The reasons for you learning .NET have a lot to do with where you should proceed from here. If you're just learning .NET as a hobby, take a route that interests you, such as web development or database development. If you're looking to advance your career, consider the companies you want to work for. What types of things are they doing—security, databases, web development? How can you make yourself more valuable to those companies? Instead of just picking a direction, choose a goal and move in the direction of the goal.

If a subject simply does not jump out to you, my recommendation is that you learn how to program databases. Get a book dedicated to your database of choice (mine is Microsoft SQL Server). Most applications these days use a database, and database skills are *always* a plus! Database programming and database design are really two different subjects, and if you really want to make yourself valuable, you should learn how to properly design, normalize, and optimize databases, in addition to programming them for users to access.

Summary

Now that you've completed this book, you should have a solid working understanding of developing applications with Visual C# 2005. Nevertheless, you've just embarked on your journey. One of the things I love about developing applications for a living is that there's always something more to learn, and there's always a better approach to a development problem. In this hour, you saw the bigger picture of Microsoft's .NET platform by seeing the .NET Framework and its various components. Consider the information you learned in this book a primer; what you do with this information and where you go from here is entirely up to you.

I wish you the best of luck on your programming endeavors!

Index

modifying

databases

accessing rows, 443-445

objects, 441-442

records, 447-450

directories, 409-410

files, 401

copying, 402-403

determining existence
of, 402

moving, 403-405

renaming, 404

retrieving properties,
405-409

forms

borders, 112-114

colors, 107-108

naming, 104

properties, 105-114

List View with code, 193-194

Registry, 414, 420-423

servers (Excel), 456-460

system colors, 376-379

text, 429-433

modules

class, 52

reserved words, 67

modulus (%) character, 273

mouse events, 365-368

MouseDown event, 89-90

MouseEventArgs event, 90

MouseMove event, 366

Move( ) method, 403-404

moving

controls, 134

forms, 117-118

items, 206

**multidimensional arrays, creating,
257-258**

Multiline property, 156

**multiline text boxes, creating,
156-157**

multiple document interfaces.
See MDIs

**multiple values, switch
statements, 294-298**

multiplication (*) character, 273

N

Name property, 13-15, 104

namespaces, 482-483

naming

conventions, 263

forms, 104

objects, 13-15

prefixes

applying, 263

denoting with
variable, 264

projects, 10, 35

navigating

IDE, 36

records, 441, 445-447

nesting if, else statements, 293

.NET

ADO.NET databases, 438

accessing DataTable rows,
443-445

applying DataTable
objects, 441

closing connections, 440

connecting, 438-440

creating DataTable
records, 448-449

deleting DataTable
records, 450

editing DataTable
records, 448

navigating DataTable
records, 445-447

populating DataTable
objects, 441-442

Framework, 479

Common Type System, 484

garbage collection, 484

IL, 481

namespaces, 482-483

new keyword, 349

New Project dialog box, 9-10, 35

**new projects, creating (Start
Page), 34-35**

NewRow( ) method, 448

nodes

library (Objects tree), 79

properties (Registry),
416-417

Tree View

adding, 195-197

clearing, 198

deleting, 198

How can we make this index more useful? Email us at indexes@samspublishing.com

License Agreement Addendum

What's on the CD-ROM

The book companion CD-ROM contains Microsoft® Visual C# 2005 Express Edition and Microsoft® SQL Server 2005 Express Edition x86.

Installation Instructions

1. Insert the disc into your CD-ROM drive.

2. From the desktop, double-click on the My Computer icon.

3. Double-click on the icon representing your CD-ROM drive.

4. Double-click on the icon titled autorun.exe to run the installation program.

5. If you do not have the requirements to install the programs, the setup program will prompt you to satisfy the requirements. Please note that you may need to reboot your machine after this step; simply restart autorun.exe when you have rebooted your machine.

6. When prompted to do so, select either or both Microsoft Visual Basic 2005 Express Edition and Microsoft SQL Server 2005 Express Edition.

7. Follow the on-screen prompts to finish the installation.

> **Note:** If you have the AutoPlay feature enabled, the autorun.exe program starts automatically whenever you insert the disc into your CD-ROM drive.